击剑规则

国家体育总局自剑中心击剑部　审定

北京体育大学出版社

策划编辑：秦德斌
责任编辑：秦德斌
责任校对：吴海燕
版式设计：华泰联合

图书在版编目 (CIP) 数据

击剑规则 / 国家体育总局自剑中心击剑部审定.
-- 北京：北京体育大学出版社，2017.5（2025.9 重印）
978-7-5644-2602-6

Ⅰ.①击… Ⅱ.①国… Ⅲ.①击剑—竞赛规则 Ⅳ.
① G885.04

中国版本图书馆 CIP 数据核字 (2017) 第 217202 号

击剑规则 国家体育总局自剑中心击剑部 审定

出版发行：北京体育大学出版社
地　　址：北京市海淀区农大南路1号院硅谷亮城2B-212
邮　　编：100084
发 行 部：010-62989320
邮 购 部：北京体育大学出版社读者服务部 010-62989432

印　　刷：北京科信印刷有限公司
开　　本：710 mm × 1000 mm 1/16
成品尺寸：170 mm × 240 mm
印　　张：25
字　　数：440千字
版　　次：2017 年 5 月第 1 版
印　　次：2025 年 9 月第 6 次印刷
定　　价：60.00 元

翻译编订说明

本《击剑规则》是根据国际击剑联合会发布的《击剑规则》（2016版）翻译编订。

《击剑规则》的翻译编订力求忠实于原文，由于规则文本体量庞大，翻译和审校工作可能存在疏漏之处，如在执行过程中出现争议，以国际剑联官方语言法文版的解释为准。

王雷、邵静、赵彤、赵传杰、侯志刚、袁向阳、秦建秋、储石生、韩婷等参与了此次翻译与编订工作（按姓氏笔画排序）。

国家体育总局自剑中心击剑部

2017年6月

目录 TABLE OF CONTENTS

BOOK 1. TECHNICAL RULES

Article

PART I. GENERAL RULES AND RULES COMMON TO THE THREE WEAPONS

技术规则

第一部分　三个剑种的技术规则概述和通则

PART 2. FOIL

THE CONVENTIONS OF FENCING

PART 3. EPEE

THE CONVENTIONS OF FENCING

第二部分　花剑　交锋协定

第三部分　重剑　交锋协定

PART 4. SABRE
THE CONVENTIONS OF FENCING

PART 5. DISCIPLINARY RULES
FOR COMPETITIONS

第四部分　佩剑 交锋协定

第五部分　纪律规则

RULES FOR COMPETITIONS

BOOK 2. ORGANISATION RULES

Article

组织规则

RULES FOR COMPETITIONS

BOOK 3. MATERIAL RULES

Article

PART 1. FENCERS' WEAPONS AND EQUIPMENT

器材规则

第一部分　运动员的武器和装备

PART 2. FITTINGS AND MATERIAL PROVIDED BY THE ORGANISERS

第二部分　组织者提供的设备和器材

ANNEXE A TO THE MATERIAL RULES
Manufacturers' Safety Standards for Fencers' Weapons, Equipment and Clothing

Paragraph

附录A　运动员武器、装备及服装生产商安全标准

ANNEXE B TO THE MATERIAL RULES
Characteristics of Scoring Apparatus

ANNEXE C TO THE MATERIAL RULES

附录B 裁判器的特性

附录C 决赛用计分器板

RULES FOR COMPETITIONS

APPENDIX — FENCERS' PUBLICITY CODE

Application 1st Jan 2016 unless otherwise stated

广告规则

技术规则

BOOK 1. TECHNICAL RULES

PART 1. GENERAL RULES AND RULES COMMON TO THE THREE WEAPONS

CHAPTER 1. APPLICATION OF THE RULES

OBLIGATORY USE OF THE RULES

t.1. These Rules are obligatory **without modification** for the 'Official Competitions of the FIE', viz.:

— The World Championships, in all categories
— The fencing events at the Olympic Games
— All World Cup competitions.
— The Zonal Championships.

CHAPTER 2. GLOSSARY

COMPETITIONS

Assaults and bouts

t.2. **A friendly combat** between two fencers is called an ***assault.*** When the score of such an assault is kept to determine a result it is called a ***bout.***

Match

t.3. The aggregate of the bouts fought between the fencers of two different **teams** is called a ***match***.

Competition

t.4.
1. A ***competition*** is the **aggregate** of the bouts (individual competitions) or of the matches (team competitions) required to determine the winner of the event.
2. Competitions **are distinguished** by weapons, by the competitors' sex, by their age and by the fact that they are for individuals or for teams.

Championship

t.5. A ***championship*** is the name given to a competition **held to determine the best fencer or the best team** at each weapon for a federation, for a specific region or for the world and **for a specific period of time**.

第一部分 三个剑种的技术规则概述和通则

第一章 规则的适用

适用规则的义务

t.1. 此规则必须“原封不动”地适用于国际剑联正式比赛，即：

—— 世界锦标赛各组别比赛；

—— 奥运会击剑比赛；

—— 所有的世界杯赛；

—— 洲际锦标赛。

第二章 术语

比 赛

实战与比赛

t.2. 两名击剑运动员之间的友好交锋叫作一次实战。如果为这种实战记录比分并计算成绩，便成为一局比赛。

团体比赛

t.3. 两个不同队的运动员之间进行的若干局比赛的集合称为一场团体比赛。

一站比赛

t.4. 1. 为了确定竞赛的优胜者而进行的个人比赛或团体比赛的集合称为一站比赛。

2. 比赛按照剑种、参赛者性别、年龄以及个人或团体来划分。

锦标赛

t.5. 对于一个协会、一个地区、或全世界，在一个特定的时期，为确定每个剑种的最佳击剑运动员或最优秀团体而进行的一站比赛称作“锦标赛”。

EXPLANATION OF SOME TECHNICAL TERMS COMMONLY USED IN THE JUDGING OF FENCING[1]

Fencing time

t.6. *Fencing time* is the time required to perform one simple fencing action.

Offensive and defensive actions

t.7. **1.** The ***offensive actions*** are the attack, the riposte and the counter-riposte.

— The ***attack*** is the initial offensive action made by extending the arm and continuously threatening the opponent's target, preceding the launching of the lunge or flèche (cf. t.56ss, t.75ss).

— The ***riposte*** is the offensive action made by the fencer who has parried the attack.

— The ***counter-riposte*** is the offensive action made by the fencer who has parried the riposte.

2. The ***defensive actions*** are the parries.

— The ***parry*** is the defensive action made with the weapon to prevent an offensive action arriving.

Explanation

t.8. *Offensive actions*

1. The *attack*

The action is ***simple*** when it is executed in one movement and is

— either ***direct*** (in the same line)

— or ***indirect*** (in another line).

The action is ***compound*** when it is executed in several movements.

2. The *riposte*

The riposte may be ***immediate*** or ***delayed***, depending on what action takes place and the speed at which it is carried out.

Ripostes are:

a) Simple, direct

— ***Direct riposte***: a riposte which hits the opponent without leaving the line in which the parry was made.

— ***Riposte along the blade***: a riposte which hits the opponent by grazing along the blade after the parry.

b) Simple, indirect

— ***Riposte by disengagement***: a riposte which hits the opponent in the opposite line to that in which the parry was formed (by passing under the opponent's blade if the parry was formed in the high line, and over the blade if the parry was formed in the low line).

— ***Riposte with a coupé***: a riposte which hits the opponent in the opposite line to that in which the parry was formed (the blade always passing over the opponent's point).

击剑比赛中常用术语解释

击剑时间

t.6. 击剑时间指完成一个简单击剑动作所用的时间。

攻击与防御动作

t.7. 1. **攻击动作**包括进攻、还击与反还击。

—— **进攻**是一个攻击性动作，首先伸出手臂，在完成弓步或冲刺动作之前，连续威胁对手的有效部位（参见t.56、t.75）；

—— **还击**是对进攻进行防守后的攻击性动作；

—— **反还击**是对还击进行防守后的攻击性动作；

2. **防御动作**包括各种防守行为。

—— 防守是指为阻止对方的进攻性动作击中自己，用武器所做的防御性动作。

说 明

t.8. **攻击动作**

1. 进 攻

当进攻通过单一动作实现时，即为简单进攻，简单进攻可以是：

—— **直接**的（在同一条线上）

—— 或**间接**的（在另一条线上）

当进攻由多个动作组成时即为复杂进攻。

2. 还 击

根据具体的还击动作和该动作的速度，还击有及时与不及时之分。还击分为：

a. 简单，直接

—— **直接还击**：防守后未离开防守线而击中对手的还击；

—— **压剑还击**：防守后在对方剑身上擦过并击中对手的还击。

b. 简单，间接

—— **转移还击**：防守以后，在相反线上击中对手的还击（如果防守是在上线，那么经过对手剑的下方还击；如果防守在下线，那么经过对手剑的上方还击）；

—— **交叉还击**：防守以后，在相反线上击中对手的还击（剑身总是从对手剑尖上方经过）。

c) Compound

— ***Riposte with a doublé***: a riposte which hits the opponent in the opposite line to that in which the parry was formed, but after having described a complete circle round the opponent's blade.

— ***Riposte with a one–two***: a riposte which hits the opponent in the same line as that in which the parry was formed but after the blade has first been into the opposite line, by passing under the opponent's blade.

3. *Counter-attacks*

Counter-attacks are offensive or offensive–defensive actions made during the offensive action of the opponent.

a) The ***stop hit***

A counter-attack made into an attack.

b) The ***stop hit made with opposition***

A counter-attack made while closing the line in which the opponent's attack will be completed (cf. t.56ss, t.64ss and t.76ss).

c) The ***stop hit made within a period of fencing time***, i.e. 'in time' (cf. t.59, t.79).

4. Other offensive actions

a) The ***remise***

A **simple and immediate offensive** action which follows the original attack, **without withdrawing the arm**, after the opponent has parried or retreated, when the latter has either quitted contact with the blade without riposting or has made a riposte which is delayed, indirect or compound.

b) The *redoublement*

A new action, either simple or compound, made against an opponent who has parried without riposting or who has merely avoided the first action by retreating or displacing the target.

c) The *reprise of the attack*

A new attack executed immediately **after a return to the on-guard position**.

d) *Counter-time*

Any action made by the attacker against a stop hit made by his opponent.

Defensive actions

t.9. Parries are ***simple, direct***, when they are made in the same line as the attack.

They are ***circular*** (counter-parries) when they are made in the opposite line to that of the attack.

The point in line position

t.10. The **point in line** position is a specific position in which the fencer's sword arm is kept straight and the point of his weapon continually threatens his opponent's valid target (cf. t.56.3.a/b/c, t.60.4.e, t.60.5.a, t.76, t.80.3.e, t.80.4.a/b).

c. 复杂还击

—— **画圆还击：**防守后，在对方剑的周围画了一个完整圆周，而在相反线上击中对手的还击。

—— **两次转移还击：**防守后首先经过对手剑的下方转移到相反线上，再回到防守线后击中对手的还击。

3. 反攻

反攻是在对手攻击动作进行中，做出的攻击动作或防御性的攻击动作。

a. 一般反攻

对一个攻击动作做出的反攻。

b. 对抗反攻

关闭对方进攻线而中止对方进攻所做的反攻（参见t.56、t.64和t.76）。

c. 及时反攻

对复杂进攻具有击剑时间优势的反攻（参见t.59、t.79）。

4. 其他攻击动作

a. 延续进攻

紧接第一个攻击动作之后，没有收回手臂，在对方防守或后退之后立即做出的简单攻击，而对手表现为放弃还击或者还击迟缓，或者是间接的、复杂的还击。

b. 连续进攻

当对手防守后没有还击，或只是用后退或躲闪的方式避开第一个攻击动作后，针对其做出的新的简单的或复杂的攻击动作。

c. 重新进攻

在恢复实战姿势后立即做出新的进攻。

d. 反反攻

进攻者对于对手的反攻动作所做出的任何动作。

防御动作

t.9. 在进攻线上做出的防守是简单、直接防守，在进攻相反线上实施的防守是画圆防守。

击剑线

t.10. 运动员持剑手臂保持伸直，剑尖连续威胁对手有效部位，称为“击剑线”（参见 t.56.3.a/b/c、t.60.4.e、t.60.5.a、t.76、t.80.3.e、t.80.4.a/b）。

CHAPTER 3. THE FIELD OF PLAY

t.11. The **field of play** should have an even surface. It should give neither advantage nor disadvantage to either of the two fencers concerned, especially as regards light.

t.12. **1.** That portion of the field of play which is used for fencing is called the ***piste.***

2. Competitions **at all three weapons** are fenced on the same pistes.

t.13. **1.** The piste is from 1.50 metres to 2 metres **wide**.

2. The piste is 14 metres **long**, so that each competitor**,** being placed at 2 metres from the centre line**,** has at his disposal for retreating a total distance of 5 metres without it being necessary for him to cross the rear limit of the piste with both feet.

t.14. **Five lines** should be drawn very clearly on the piste at right angles to its length, as follows:

a) **one *centre line*** which must be drawn as a broken line across the whole width of the piste;

b) **two *on-guard lines*** at 2 metres on each side of the centre line. These must be drawn across the whole width of the piste;

c) **two *lines at the rear limits*** of the piste, which must be drawn across the whole width of the piste, at a distance of 7 metres from the centre line.

d) In addition, **the last 2 metres** of the piste before these rear limit lines must be clearly distinguished — if possible by a different colour of piste — to make it easy for the fencers to be aware of their position on the piste (see Figures 1 and 2).

第三章　比赛场地

t.11. **场地**表面必须平坦并成水平状态，不能有利于也不能不利于双方运动员中的任何一方，特别是在光线问题上。

t.12. 1. 比赛场地用于击剑实战的部分叫做剑道。

2. **三个剑种的比赛**均在同样的剑道上进行。

t.13. 1. 剑道的**宽度**为1.5米~ 2米。

2. 剑道的长度为14米。以中心线为界，比赛开始时，双方运动员应各自位于距离中心线两侧2米处，身后5米的剑道为其活动空间。可以后退，但双脚不得同时越过剑道的端线。

t.14. 在剑道上要非常明显地画出与剑道长边垂直的**5条线**，即：

a. **一条中心线：**与剑道宽度等长，画为虚线；

b. **两条准备线：**在中心线两边各2米处，与剑道宽度等长；

c. **两条端线：**剑道两端，距中心线各7米处，与剑道宽度等长。

d. 此外，在剑道端线前**最后的2米区域**应做出明显标记——如有条件，可使用不同颜色的剑道加以区别——以便运动员更容易确定自己在剑道上所处的位置（图1、图2）。

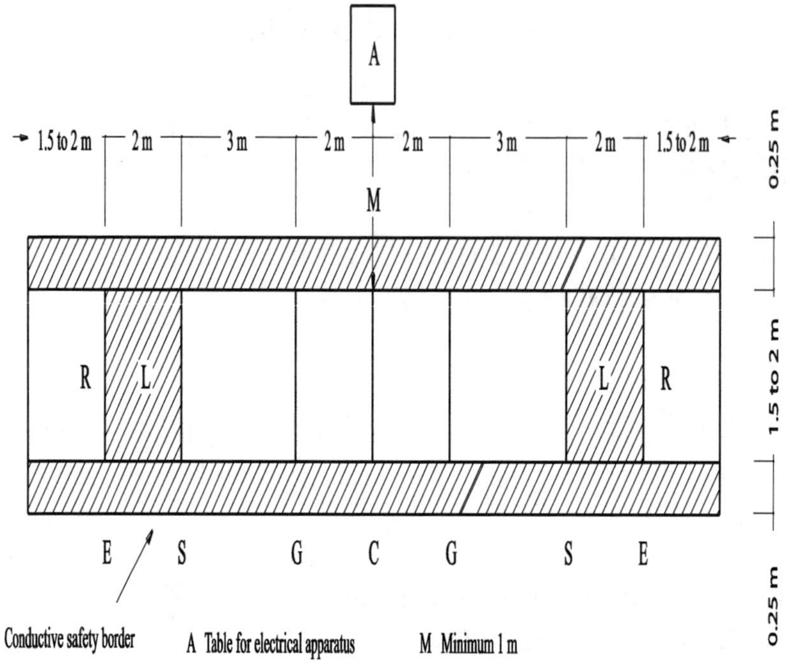

A Table for electrical apparatus
C Centre line
G On-guard lines
R Run back (extension of piste)

M Minimum 1 m
L Last 2 m of piste
E End of piste (rear limit)
S Start of 2 m signal area

For foil and épée the conductive surface must cover the whole of the length and breadth of the piste, including its extensions (run back) and its safety borders (cf. Article t.13s, m.57)

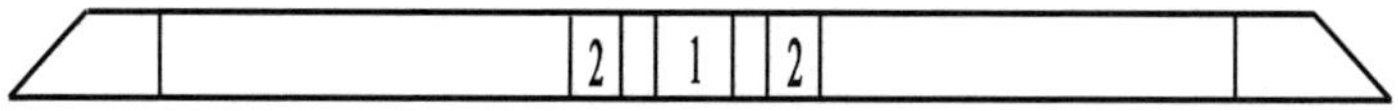

1 Scoring apparatus 2 Extension lamps

Figure 1 Piste for semi-finals and finals (maximum height 50 cm)

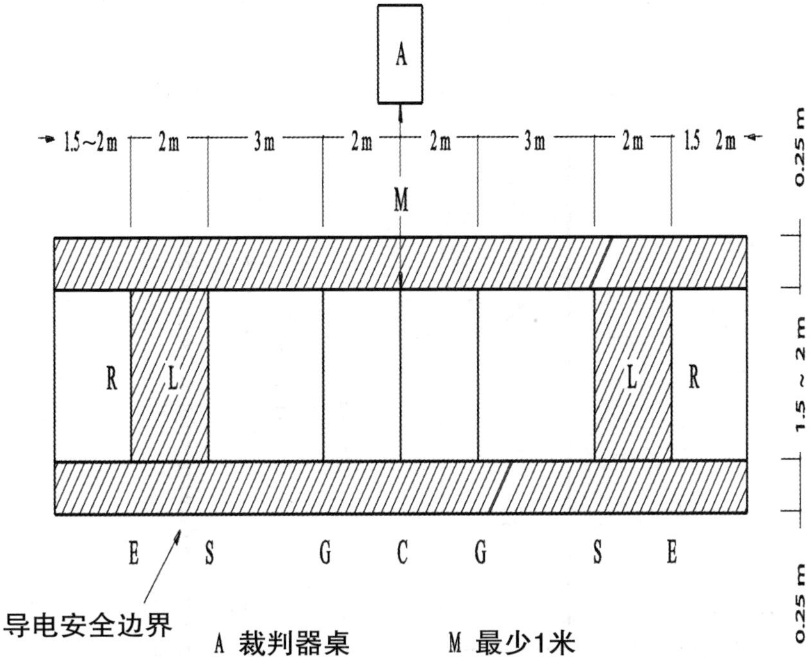

A 裁判器桌　　M 最少1米
C 中线　　L 剑道的最后2米
G 开始线　　E 端线
R 延长区　　S 警告线

对于电动花剑和重剑金属物必须覆盖着整个剑道、延长区部分及颜色不同的其他区域

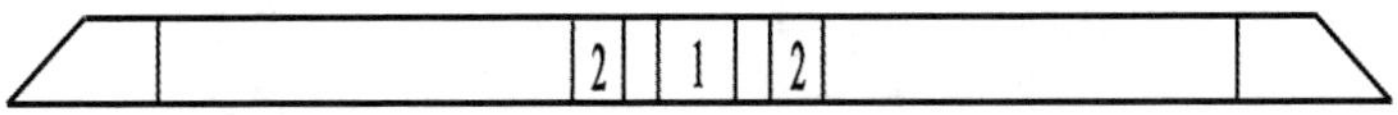

1裁判器　2 重复灯

图1　决赛半决赛剑道（剑道最高为50厘米）

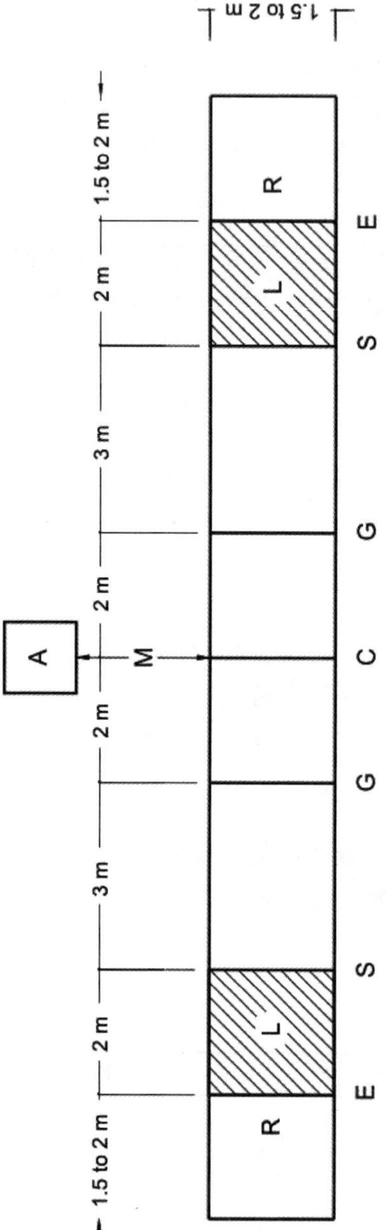

A Table for electrical apparatus
C Centre line
G On-guard lines
R Run back (extension of piste)
M Minimum 1 mm
L Last 2 m of piste
E End of piste (rear limit)
S Start of 2 m signal area

For foil and épée the conductive surface must cover the whole of the length and breadth of the piste, including its extensions (run back) (cf. Article t.13s, m.57)

Figure 2 Standard piste for all three weapons

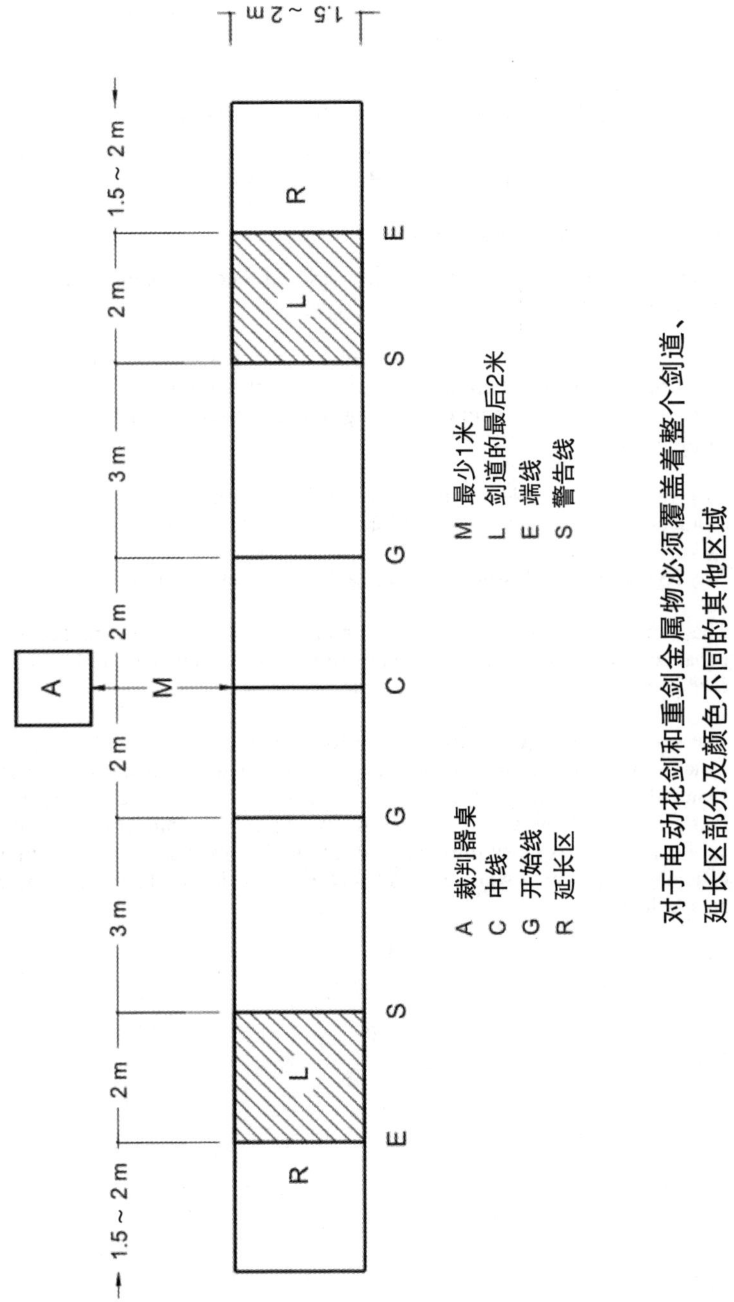

图2　三个剑种通用的普通剑道

CHAPTER 4. THE FENCERS' EQUIPMENT

(Weapons — Equipment — Clothing)

RESPONSIBILITY OF FENCERS

t.15. **1.** Fencers arm, equip and clothe themselves and fence **at their own responsibility** and **at their own risk**.

2. It is obligatory for any fencer who warms up or trains with another fencer on site at an official FIE competition (including in the training halls linked to the competition) to wear **fencing clothing and equipment** which conforms with the FIE regulations.

Any person giving a lesson must wear at least a fencing master's plastron as well as a fencing glove and a mask conforming with the regulations.

Any fencer taking a lesson must wear at least a mask and a glove.

The Supervisor of the competition or a member of the Directoire Technique must penalize any person not respecting this rule with a yellow card, followed by a black card in case of a repeated infringement.

3. The **safety measures** specified in the Rules and in the standards contained in the annexe to them and the methods of control laid down in the present Rules (cf. Material Rules) are only designed to ***reinforce*** the fencers' safety and cannot ***guarantee*** it. They cannot, therefore, whatever the manner in which they are applied, impart responsibility to the FIE, or to the organisers of competitions, to the officials or personnel who carry out such organisation, or to those who may cause an accident.

第四章　运动员器材
（武器、装备、比赛服）

运动员职责

t.15. 1. 运动员负责自身比赛所需的武器、装备、比赛服，并自主比赛、自担风险。

2. 任何一名运动员与另一名运动员在国际剑联正式比赛的场地（包括与比赛相关的训练馆）进行热身和训练时，必须穿着符合国际剑联标准的服装和器材。

带课人员必须至少着教练服，戴击剑手套和合格面罩。

上课的运动员必须至少戴面罩和手套。

比赛观察员或某名技术委员会成员须对违反上述规则的人员进行黄牌处罚，对于再次犯规人员给予黑牌处罚。

3. 现行规则及附属规定制定的安全措施与现行规则（参见器材规则）规定的器材检验措施，都只是为了加强运动员的安全，不能确保安全。因此，运动员不可用任何方式将安全责任转移给国际剑联、比赛组织者、官员、工作人员或其他可能造成事故的人员。

CHAPTER 5. FENCING

METHOD OF HOLDING THE WEAPON

t.16. 1. With all three weapons, **defence** must be effected exclusively with the guard and the blade used either separately or together.

2. If the **handle** has no special device or attachment or special shape (e.g. orthopaedic), a fencer **may hold it** in any way he wishes and he may also alter the position of his hand on the handle during a bout. However, the weapon must not be — either permanently or temporarily, in an open or disguised manner — transformed into **a throwing weapon**; it must be used without the hand leaving the handle and without the hand slipping along the handle from front to back during an offensive action.

3. When the handle has a **special device** or **attachment** or has a **special shape** (e.g. orthopaedic) it must be held in such a way that the upper surface of the thumb is in the same plane as the groove in the blade (at foil or at epée) and perpendicular to the plane of flexibility of the blade at sabre.

4. The weapon must be used **with one hand only**; a fencer may not change hands before the end of the bout, unless the Referee gives special permission in the case of injury to the hand or arm.

COMING ON GUARD

t.17. 1. The fencer **whose number is called first** should place himself on the **right** of the Referee, except in the case of a bout between a right- and a left-hander, if the left-hander is called first.

2. **The Referee places** each of the two competitors in such a way that the front foot of each is 2 metres from the centre line of the piste (that is, behind the 'on-guard' lines).

---

2. For foil and épée, the Referee places each of the two competitors in such a way that the front foot of each is 2 metres from the centre line of the piste (that is, behind the 'on-guard' lines).

For sabre, the Referee places each of the two competitors in such a way that the back foot of each is 2 m from the centre line of the piste (that is, in front of the "on-guard" lines).

Application: The replacement of t.17.2 will commence after the Olympic Games and be valid until December 31, 2016. Subsequently Comex will decide if the rule change will be permanently applied.

第五章　击剑

持剑的方法

t.16. 1. 在三个剑种中，防御动作只能借助于剑身和护手盘，分别或配合使用。

2. 如果没有专用装置、系扣带或专用（矫形）物等限制，运动员可以自由随意地握住手柄，可以在比赛中改变手握剑的位置或姿态。但是无论以持久或短暂的、明显或隐蔽的方式，都不得抛掷武器；武器必须紧握在手中，手不能离开手柄；在一个进攻动作过程中，手不能在手柄前后滑动。

3. 如果有专门装置、系扣带或专门（矫形）物存在，则握手柄的拇指指面（花剑和重剑）应与剑身凹槽方向一致；而佩剑中拇指应与剑身柔韧面垂直。

4. 武器只能用单手控制，一局比赛结束前不能换手。除非在手或手臂受伤时，在裁判员允许的情况下才能换手。

预备姿势

t.17. 1. 第一个被点名的运动员应站到裁判员的右侧，除非比赛是在一个右手持剑和一个左手持剑的运动员之间进行，而第一个被点名的又是左手持剑的运动员。

2. 裁判让比赛双方各就各位，双方前脚应站在离剑道中心线2米的位置（即在开始线后面）。

---

2. 略（译者注：该规则经试行后已取消）。

---

3. Competitors are always put on guard, whether at the beginning of the bout or subsequently, **in the centre of the width of the piste**.

4. When placed on guard during the bout, the distance between the two competitors must be such that, in the position 'point in line', **the points of the two blades cannot make contact**.

5. **After the scoring of a valid hit** the competitors are put on guard **in the middle** of the piste.

6. **If no hit is awarded** they are replaced in the position which they occupied when the bout was interrupted.

7. At the beginning **of each period** (in a direct elimination bout) and of any **additional minute** of fencing time, the fencers are placed on guard in the middle of the piste.

8. The competitors may not be replaced **on guard, at their correct distance**, in such a way as to place behind the rear line of the piste a fencer who was in front of that line when the bout was halted. If he already had one foot behind the rear line, he remains in that position.

9. If a fencer has crossed the **lateral boundaries of the piste**, with one or both feet, he must be placed on guard at the correct distance even if this means that he is placed behind the rear line and thus causes a hit to be awarded against him. (cf t.28, t.102).

10. Competitors come on guard when the Referee gives the order '**On guard!**', after which the Referee asks, '**Are you ready?**'. On receiving an affirmative reply, or in the absence of a negative reply, he gives the command for fencing to commence with the word '**Play!**'.

11. The fencers must **come on guard correctly** and remain **completely still** until the command 'Play!' is given by the Referee.

12. At foil and sabre fencers may not come on guard in the '**in line**' position.

3. 不管是比赛开始和还是重新预备时，运动员都应站于剑道宽度的中央处。

4. 实战中重新处于预备姿势时，两名运动员的距离应为，双方伸直手臂成击剑线，剑尖不能接触。

5. 在每次被视为有效的击中之后，运动员在开始线后恢复预备姿势。

6. 如果击中不被承认，他们应回到实战中断时各自所占据的位置上恢复预备姿势。

7. 在每一局及可能进行的加时赛开始时，运动员都应当在场地中央进入预备姿势。

8. 运动员双方恢复预备姿势时应相隔一段距离，但是在比赛“停”时站在端线以内的运动员不能被安排在端线以外恢复预备姿势。如果当时该运动员的一只脚已越出端线之外，那么他（她）站在原地不动。

9. 如果运动员的单脚或者双脚越出边线，则必须按照正确的距离恢复预备姿势，即使这将导致他（她）站在端线之外并被处罚一剑（参见t.28、t.102）。

10. 裁判员发出“预备！”命令时，运动员做预备姿势，然后裁判员询问“准备好了吗？”在得到肯定回答或者没有否定回答时，裁判员发出比赛信号“开始！”。

11. 运动员必须处于正确预备姿势，并且完全保持不动，直到裁判员发出“开始”口令。

12. 在花剑和佩剑中，预备姿势不得成“击剑线”。

BEGINNING, STOPPING AND RESTARTING THE BOUT

t.18 1. **The start** of the bout is signalled by the word 'Play!'. No movement made or initiated before the word 'Play!' is counted.

2. The bout **stops** on the word 'Halt!', except in the case of special events occurring which modify the regular and normal conditions of the bout (cf. also t.32.1/2).

3. Directly the order '**Halt!**' has been given, a competitor may not start a new action; only a movement which has been begun before the order was given remains valid. Everything which takes place afterwards is absolutely not valid (But cf. t.32.1/2).

4. If a competitor **stops** before the word 'Halt!', and is hit, the hit is valid.

5. The order 'Halt!' is also given if the play of the competitors is **dangerous, confused,** or **contrary to the Rules**, if one of the competitors is **disarmed** or **steps off the piste**, or if, while retiring, he approaches too near the spectators or the Referee (cf. t.26, t.54.5 and t.73.4.j).

At foil it is forbidden, during the course of fencing, to advance the shoulder of the non-sword arm in front of the shoulder of the sword-arm (cf.t.19). If a competitor does so he is liable to incur the penalties enumerated in Articles t.114, t.116, t.120. Any hits scored by the fencer at fault while committing this offence will be annulled.

Application: starting season 2016-2017.

---

6. The Referee may not allow a fencer to **leave the piste**, save in exceptional circumstances. If a competitor does so without permission he is liable to incur the penalties enumerated in Articles t.114, t.116, t.120.

FENCING AT CLOSE QUARTERS

t.19. **Fencing at close quarters** is allowed so long as the competitors can wield their weapons correctly and the Referee can, at foil and sabre, follow the phrase.

Corps à corps

t.20. 1. **Corps à corps** is said to exist when the two competitors are in contact; when this occurs the Referee must stop the bout (cf. t.25, t.63.1/2/3).

2. **At all three weapons** it is forbidden for a fencer to **cause corps à corps intentionally** to avoid being hit, or to jostle his opponent. Should such an offence occur, the Referee will penalise the fencer at fault as specified in Articles t.114, t.116, t.120 and any hit scored by the fencer at fault is annulled.

比赛开始、停止和重新开始

t.18. 1. “开始”口令的发出表明双方可以开始交锋。在此口令前发起的任何动作都无效。

2. 交锋的终止是以“停”口令为标志的，除非出现特殊情况，改变了正常的交锋条件。（参阅t.32.1/2）

3. “停”的口令一旦发出，运动员便不能再进行新的动作；只有在口令发出前已经开始的动作仍然有效。此后发生的一切均绝对无效（参阅t.32.1/2）。

4. 如果运动员一方在“停”口令前停下，并被击中，这一击中有效。

5. 如果运动员动作危险、混乱或违反规则，或者一方运动员武器脱落或离开剑道，或者后退时距离观众或裁判太近，都可以下达“停”口令。（参阅t.26、t.54.5和t.73.4.j）

花剑比赛中，运动员非持剑手的肩部不得超越持剑手的肩部（参照t.19），否则将接受规则t.114、t.116、t.120的处罚，并导致击中被取消。

6. 除特殊情况外，裁判不得准许运动员离开剑道。如果运动员未经允许擅自这样做，他将受到t.114、t.116、t.120之条款规定的处罚。

近战

t.19. 只要运动员能正常使用武器，并且在花剑和佩剑中裁判员能继续观察运动员的动作，就允许进行近战。

身体接触

t.20. 1. 两名对手在交锋时如身体互相接触，裁判应发令停止交锋。（参阅t.25、t.63.1/2/3）

2. 三个剑种的比赛均禁止为避免被击中而故意造成身体接触或挤撞对手。如发生此类犯规，裁判员应按条款t.114、t.116、t.120之规定处罚犯规运动员，同时该运动员可能击中的一剑将被取消。

DISPLACING THE TARGET AND PASSING THE OPPONENT

t.21. 1. **Displacing the target and ducking** are allowed even if during the action the unarmed hand or the knee of the rear leg comes into contact with the piste.

2. It is forbidden to **turn one's back** on one's opponent during the bout. Should such an offence occur, the Referee will penalise the fencer at fault as specified in Articles t.114, t.116, t.120 and any hit scored by the fencer at fault is annulled.

3. When a fencer **goes completely past** his opponent during a bout, the Referee must immediately call 'Halt!' and replace the competitors in the positions which they occupied before the passing took place.

4. When hits are made **as a fencer passes his opponent**, the hit made immediately is valid; a hit made after passing his opponent by the competitor who has made the passing movement is annulled, but the hit made immediately, even when turning round, by the competitor who has been subjected to the offensive action, is valid.

5. If during a bout a fencer who has made a flèche attack has a hit registered against him and he continues to run beyond the extreme limit of the piste sufficiently far to cause his spool or the connecting line to his spool **to be torn out**, the hit which he has received will not be annulled (cf. t.103).

SUBSTITUTION AND USE OF THE NON-SWORD HAND AND ARM

t.22. 1. The use of the **non-sword hand** and **arm** to carry out an offensive or defensive action is forbidden (cf. t.114, t.117, t.120). Should such an offence occur, the hit scored by the fencer at fault is annulled and the latter will be penalised as specified for offences of the 2nd group (red card).

2. At foil and sabre, it is forbidden to **protect** the target area or to **substitute** another part of the body for the target area, by covering it (cf. t.114, t.116, t.120); any hit scored by the fencer at fault is annulled.

   a) If, during the fencing phrase, there is protection or substitution of a valid surface, the fencer at fault will be penalised as specified for offences of the 1st group (cf. also t.49.1, t.72.2).

   b) If, during the fencing phrase, as a result of protection or substitution of a valid surface, a hit correctly given is registered as not valid , the fencer at fault will be penalised as specified for offences of the 1st group (cf. also t.49.1, t.72.2) and the hit will be awarded by the referee.

3. During the fight, the fencer must not, under any circumstances, **take hold of any part of the electrical equipment** with his non-sword hand (cf. t.114, t.116, t.120); any hit scored by the fencer at fault is annulled.

躲闪和超越

t.21. 1. 移动和躲闪是允许的，甚至非持剑手和后腿的膝盖可以接触地面。

2. 在比赛过程中，禁止转身背向对手。当发生这种犯规行为时，裁判员将按t.114、t.116、t.120的条款处罚犯规运动员。同时该运动员可能击中的一剑将被取消。

3. 在比赛过程中，当一个运动员完全超越他的对手时，裁判应立即发出“停”的口令，命令双方回到超越之前各自占据的位置。

4. 在超越过程中，如发生相互击中的情况，立即做出的击中被视为有效；而超越之后的击中则被视为无效，但是受到攻击而且被超越的运动员在转身时立即做出的击中应为有效。

5. 比赛过程中，当一名进行冲刺攻击的运动员显示被击中，同时他超越剑道范围很长距离，而引起拖线盘或拖线盘联接线被脱开，则他受到的击中不会被取消（参见t.103）。

遮挡和非持剑手与手臂的使用

t.22. 1. 禁止使用非持剑手和手臂进行攻击或防御动作（参阅t.114、t.116、t.120）。如发生此类犯规，该运动员刺中的一剑视为无效，并接受第二类犯规处罚（红牌）。

2. 在花剑与佩剑中，禁止用身体其他部位做出遮掩来保护或替代有效部位（参阅t.114、t.116、t.120），同时该运动员可能击中的一剑将被取消。

a. 交锋过程中，如果保护或替代有效部位，犯规的剑手将受到第一类犯规的处罚（参见t.49.1、t.72.2）。

b. 交锋过程中，如果由于保护或替代有效部位导致正确刺中的一剑被记录为无效，则犯规运动员将受到第一类犯规的处罚（参见t.49.1、t.72.2），正确刺中的一剑由裁判判得分。

3. 在比赛进行时，运动员非持剑手在任何情况下都不得抓握电动器材的任何部位（参阅t.114、t.116、t.120）。如有犯规，则该运动员可能击中的一剑将被取消。

t.23. **1.** If during a bout the Referee notices that one of the fencers is making use of his non-sword arm and/or hand, or is protecting or covering the valid target with a non-valid surface, he can call for the help of two **neutral judges** who will be designated by the Directoire Technique.

2. These judges, one on each side of the piste, will watch **all aspects of the fight** and will indicate, by raising their hand or when asked by the Referee, if the non-sword arm or hand has been used, or if the fencer has protected or covered the valid target with a non-valid surface (cf. t.49, t.72, t.114, t.116, t.120).

3. The Referee may also **make the fencers change places** so that the fencer committing this fault does not have his back to the Referee.

GROUND GAINED OR LOST

t.24. When the order 'Halt!' is given **ground gained** is held until a hit has been given. When competitors are replaced on guard, each fencer should retire an equal distance in order to keep fencing distance (cf. t.17.3/4).

t.25. However, if the bout has been stopped on account of **corps à corps**, the fencers are replaced on guard in such a position that the competitor who has sustained the corps à corps is at the place which he previously occupied; this also applies if his opponent has subjected him to **a flèche** attack, even without corps à corps.

CROSSING THE LIMITS OF THE PISTE

Stopping the bout

t.26. **1.** When a competitor **crosses one of the lateral boundaries** of the piste with **one or both feet completely off the piste**, the Referee must immediately call 'Halt!'.

2. If the fencer **goes off the piste** with **both feet**, the Referee must annul everything that has occurred after the boundary has been crossed, except a hit received by the competitor who has crossed the boundary even after he has crossed it, provided that this hit results from a simple and immediate action.

3. However, a hit scored by the fencer who **leaves the piste with one foot only** is valid provided that the action was started before the 'Halt!'.

4. If **one of the competitors** leaves the piste with **both feet**, only a hit made by the fencer who remains on the piste with at least one foot can be counted valid, even in the case of a double hit.

t.23. 1. 如果裁判员发现在一场比赛中两名运动员之一使用非持剑手或手臂，或者用无效部位保护或遮盖有效部位时，他可以请求技术委员会指定两名中立的助理裁判协助自己。

2. 两名助理裁判分别站在剑道两侧，观察整个比赛，助理裁判员可以主动举手或应主裁判要求，报告运动员是否使用非持剑手臂或手或无效部位保护或遮挡有效部位。（参阅t.49、t.114、t.116、t.120）

3. 主裁判也可以让两名运动员交换位置，使犯规者不背向自己。

获得和失去比赛场地

t.24. “停”口令发出后，该运动员获得的场地应得到承认，直到得分。当恢复预备姿势时，每个运动员应退回同样距离以保持预备距离。（参阅t.17.3/4）

t.25. 然而，当发生身体接触而中断比赛时，运动员将按照以下方式重新恢复预备姿势，即受到身体接触的运动员回到他原先占据的位置；这种方式对于受到对方运动员冲刺攻击但没有发生身体接触的情况也同样适用。

越出边界

停止交锋

t.26. 1. 当某一运动员的一只脚或双脚完全越出剑道的边线时，裁判员应立即叫“停”。

2. 当某一运动员双脚越出剑道的边线时，裁判要取消出界以后的一切动作。除非出界运动员被击中，即使击中是在出界以后，只要这个击中是由简单即时动作造成的。

3. 但是如果运动员只有一只脚越出边线，那么他的击中就是有效的，只要击中是在“停”口令之前发生。

4. 当双方运动员之一双脚出了界，即使双方互相击中，也只有留在剑道上的运动员（至少要有一只脚在界内）做出的击中视为有效。

Rear limits

t.27. Should a competitor cross the **rear limit** of the piste completely — i.e. with both feet — a hit will be scored against him.

Lateral boundaries

t.28. **1.** If a competitor crosses one of the lateral boundaries of the piste with one or both feet, he must step back one metre from the point where he left the piste; and if he goes off the piste during an attack he must return to the position he occupied when he started his attack and then step back a further metre (but cf t.29).

2. **If the exercise of this penalty** places a competitor with both feet beyond the rear limit of the piste, that competitor is considered as having been hit.

3. A competitor who crosses one of the lateral boundaries of the piste with both feet — e.g. when making a flèche — **to avoid being hit** will be penalised as specified in Articles t.114, t.116, t.120.

Leaving the piste accidentally

t.29. A competitor who **involuntarily** crosses one of the boundaries of the piste as the result of any accidental cause (such as jostling) incurs no penalty whatever.

DURATION OF THE BOUT

t.30. **1.** Duration of the bout is held to mean the **effective duration**, that is the total of the intervals of time between the orders 'Play!' and 'Halt!'.

2. The duration of the bout is **controlled** by the Referee or by a time-keeper. For the finals of all official competitions, as well as for all bouts for which a chronometer is visible to the spectators, the chronometer must be so placed that it is visible to the two fencers on the piste and to the Referee.

3. The effective **duration** of a bout is:

— For **pools**, 5 hits, maximum 3 minutes.

— For **direct elimination** bouts, 15 hits, maximum 9 minutes divided into 3 periods of 3 minutes, with one minute's pause between any two periods.

— For **team matches**, 3 minutes for each lap or bout.

t.31. **1.** The fencers may ask **how much time they have left** to fence each time that the fencing is interrupted.

2. Any fencer who attempts improperly to **cause or to prolong interruptions** to the bout is penalised as specified in Articles t.114, t.116, t.120.

端线

t.27. 当一名运动员双脚完全越出剑道端线，将判被击中一剑。

边线

t.28. 1. 如果运动员单脚或双脚出边线，则运动员须回到出边线的位置并后退1米；如果运动员在进攻时出边线，则须回到发起进攻的位置并后退1米（t.29. 情况除外）。

2. 运动员被执行这一处罚时，如双脚已被置于端线之外，则将判被击中一剑。

3. 运动员为避免被击中，尤其在冲刺时双脚越出边界，将受到t.114、t.116、t.120中规定的处罚。

意外出界

t.29. 运动员由于任何意外情况（如挤撞）而越出界线，不受任何处罚。

比赛时间

t.30. 1. 比赛时间应理解为实际比赛时间，即“开始”和“停”之间的总和，除去暂停的时间。

2. 比赛时间由裁判员或一名计时员控制。对于国际剑联正式比赛决赛及所有其他阶段的比赛都应配备计时装置，计时器应放置在剑道上两名运动员和裁判员都能见到的地方。

3. 有效比赛时间为：
—— 小组循环赛：击中5剑，最长3分钟；
—— 直接淘汰赛：击中15剑，最长9分钟，分成3局，每局3分钟，每两局之间休息1分钟；
—— 团体赛：每局3分钟。

t.31. 1. 击剑运动员在每次中断比赛时可以询问时间。

2. 如果一名运动员多次企图引起比赛中断或延长中断时间，裁判将按t.114、t.116、t.120中之规定对他进行处罚。

t.32. 1. **At the expiry of the regulation fencing time**, if the clock is linked to the scoring apparatus (obligatory standard for finals of official FIE competitions), it must set off automatically a loud audible signal, and automatically cut off the scoring apparatus, without cancelling hits registered before the disconnection. The bout stops with the audible signal.

2. **If the clock is not linked to the scoring apparatus**, the time-keeper must shout 'Halt!' (or operate a sound signal) which stops the fight; in this case even a 'coup lancé' is not valid.

3. **The referee must operate the time-keeping throughout the match.** Should there be a **failure of the clock**, the Referee must himself estimate how much fencing time is left. He must be able to reset the time manually and if necessary to reset the time to that previously shown to the nearest 1/100 of a second. [Application: season 2015/2016 for the World Championships and the Olympic Games only: season 2016/2017 for the World Cup competitions (Junior and Senior), the Grand Prix and the Zonal Championships (Junior and Senior).]

4. When wireless apparatus is used, no hits registered after the end of fencing time will be awarded even if a lamp is showing on the wireless apparatus.

INJURIES OR CRAMP, WITHDRAWAL OF A COMPETITOR

t.33. 1. For an **injury or cramp** which occurs in the course of a bout and which is properly attested by the delegate of the FIE Medical Committee or by the doctor on duty, the Referee will allow a break in the fight lasting no longer than 10 minutes. This break should be timed from the point when the doctor gave his opinion and be strictly reserved for the treatment of the injury or cramp which brought it about. If the doctor considers, before or at the end of the 10 minute break, that the **fencer is incapable of continuing** the fight, he will decide that the fencer should retire (individual events) and/or be replaced, if possible (team events) (cf. o.44.11.a/b).

Application: Proposal to reduce length of break from 10 minutes to 5 minutes will be trialled during the 2016 Junior and Cadet World Championships.

---

t.32. 1. 在规定时间终止时，如果计时器和裁判器联接在一起（这是国际剑联所有正式比赛的决赛必须遵守的规定），它应该自动发出响亮的声音信号，并自动切断裁判器的运行，但是在裁判器中止运转之前记录下的信号应固定地保留在裁判器上。一旦听到声音信号，比赛就终止。

2. 如果计时器没有和裁判器联接在一起，计时员应叫“停”或发出声音信号，这时比赛结束，此时即使做出刺中，也无效。

3. 比赛计时必须由裁判员全程操作。在计时器失灵的情况下，裁判须自己评估剩下的比赛时间。裁判员必须能够手工调整时钟，并能够精确到百分秒。此规则仅在2015/2016赛季世锦赛、奥运会中执行，从2016–2017赛季世界杯（含青年和成年）、大奖赛、洲际锦标赛（含青年和成年）开始执行。

4. 使用无线器材时，当比赛时间结束，即使无线器材的灯亮了，显示击中信号的剑也不计入比分。

创伤或痉挛，运动员退出比赛

t.33. 1. 对于比赛过程中意外发生的创伤或痉挛应当由医务委员会的代表或值班医生按规定出具证明确认。为此比赛最多可以暂停10分钟，并且应扣除医生诊断的时间。暂停的10分钟应严格用于治疗。在10分钟暂停结束时或之前，如果医生证明运动员没有能力继续比赛，他决定这个运动员退出个人比赛；如果是团体赛可以换人上场（参阅组织规则o.44.11.a/b）。

伤停时间由原来的10分钟缩短为5分钟，此规则将在2016年世青赛进行测试。

---

2. During **the remainder of the same day**, a fencer cannot be allowed a further break unless as a result of a different injury or cramp.

3. Should a fencer **demand a break** which is deemed by the delegate of the Medical Committee or by the doctor on duty to be **unjustified**, the Referee will penalise that fencer as specified in Articles t.114, t.117, t.120.

4. **In team events** a fencer judged unable to continue the bout by the doctor may, nevertheless, on the advice of the same doctor, fight in subsequent matches on the same day.

5. The Directoire Technique may **modify the order of bout**s in a pool in order to ensure the efficient running of the competition (cf. o.16.1).

2. 在同一天内，运动员只有发生不同于先前的伤病，才允许再次伤停。

3. 如果运动员无理要求暂停，经医务委员会的代表或值班医生按照规定手续证明无理，裁判将按规定的t.114、t.117、t.120条款给予犯规运动员以处罚。

4. 在团体比赛中，被值班医生判定没有能力继续比赛的运动员，仍然能够由同一名医生决定参加同一天中接下来的其他比赛。

5. 技术委员会可以更改小组循环赛比赛顺序，以确保比赛的顺利进行。（参阅组织规则 o.16.1）

CHAPTER 6. REFEREEING AND JUDGING OF HITS

t.34. 1. By accepting a position as referee or judge, the person so designated **pledges his honour** to respect the Rules and to cause them to be respected, and to carry out his duties with the strictest impartiality and absolute concentration.

2. Referees **may not combine** their function with any other activity during the tournament, such as member of the Directoire Technique, team captain, official delegate of their national federation, trainer, etc.

THE REFEREE

t.35. 1. All bouts at fencing in official FIE competitions are directed by a **referee** who must be an FIE referee licensed for the current season. For reasons of expedience, National category referees who are candidates for the FIE refereeing exams and have paid to take them are authorised to referee satellite competitions.

2. The Referee has many **duties**:

a) He **calls the roll** of the competitors (cf. t.86.1, t.86.5/6).

b) He **directs** the bout.

c) Before each bout he must **check** the weapons, clothes and equipment of the fencers, according to the regulations below.

d) He **superintends** the proper functioning of the electrical apparatus. Either on his own initiative or when asked to do so by a team captain or competitor, he implements tests necessary to check the apparatus and locate any faults which may be found. He will prevent the competitors from hindering the tests by unplugging or changing their equipment prematurely.

e) He **directs** the judges, time-keepers, scorers, etc.

f) He positions himself and moves in such a way as to be able to **follow the bout** while always being able to see the illumination of the signal lamps.

g) He **penalises** faults (cf. t.96.2).

h) He **awards** the hits (cf. t.40ss).

i) He **maintains** order (cf. t.96.1–4).

j) Whenever he considers it necessary, he should **consult** the experts concerning the electrical apparatus (cf. o.7).

第六章　击中的裁决和判定

t.34. 1. 作为裁判员或助理裁判员必须遵守规则并要求参赛者（在场的所有人）遵守规则，并且以最为公正和非常专心的态度来担任这个职务。

2. 裁判员不能在比赛中担任其他职务，例如技术委员会成员、领队、国家协会官员以及教练等。

裁判员

t.35. 1. 所有国际剑联正式的击剑比赛都是由一名拥有当年赛季国际裁判证的裁判裁决。为了便于组织，国家级裁判已报名并付款参加国际剑联裁判员考试的可以裁决国际剑联卫星赛。

2. 裁判员的工作有以下内容：

a. 运动员点名（参见 t.86.1、t.86.5/6）。

b. 指挥比赛。

c. 每场比赛前，根据规则规定检查运动员的武器、服装和器械。

d. 观察裁判器的运转情况。主动地或应队长或者运动员的要求派人进行检查并确定可能出现故障的地方；制止运动员以切断器材电源或擅自更换器材的方式阻碍检查工作的正常进行。

e. 指导助理裁判员、计时员、计分员等工作人员。

f. 为了能够准确观察比赛及裁判器的信号，应当根据情况站定或走动。

g. 对犯规进行处罚（参见 t.96.2）。

h. 判定击中（参见 t.40ss）。

i. 维持秩序（参见 t.96.1 ~ 4）。

j. 必要时咨询电动裁判器专家（参见组织规则o.7）。

JUDGES

t.36. **1.** The Referee fulfils his functions with the aid of an apparatus for the automatic registering of hits; he may also be assisted by **two judges** watching for the use of the unarmed hand or arm, substitution of the valid target, hits scored on the floor at épée, leaving the piste to the side or the rear or any other offence defined in the Rules (cf. t.120).

2. The judges are **obligatory** for all individual competition finals (4 fencers) and for the **final** (2 teams) of team events.

3. The judges are placed on each side of the Referee, on either side of the piste; they watch **all aspects** of the entire fight.

4. The judges must **change ends** halfway through each bout or after each period in direct elimination bouts and after each bout in team matches, so as not to watch the same fencer the whole time.

ATTRIBUTION OF REFEREES AND VIDEO CONSULTANTS

Olympic Games and World Championships

t.37. Whenever video refereeing is used, there shall be designated video consultants who will watch the match live, then, should the need arise, subsequently on the video screen, and interact with the referee as specified in t.42.3.

The video-consultant must:

a) be a referee holding an FIE licence for the year in question;

b) have been trained to assist with the video;

c) be of a different nationality from the fencers on the piste;

d) be of a different nationality from the main referee.

Individual competitions

1. For the rounds of pools and the direct elimination table, **the Refereeing Delegates** select the referees by drawing lots.

2. **For the pools**, the referee must be of a different nationality from that any of the fencers in the pool.

3. For the **direct elimination tables at each weapon**, the Refereeing Delegates establish, among the referees present, a list of the best referees at each weapon (according to the grades obtained during the season).

助理裁判员

t.36. 1. 裁判员借助于一台电动裁判器，有时也可在两名助理裁判的协助下，完成任务。助理裁判监督运动员是否使用非持剑手或手臂遮挡有效部位，重剑比赛中击中地面，越出剑道边线及端线，或规则中规定的其他一切犯规行为（参见t.120）。

2. 对于个人赛的所有决赛（前4名）和团体赛的前2名决赛，必须配备助理裁判。

3. 助理裁判员分别站在主裁判两侧，并且在剑道两边，观察整个比赛过程。

4. 助理裁判应在比赛中间或每局之后交换场地，以免始终观察同一名运动员。

裁判员和录像裁判的选派

奥运会与世界锦标赛

t.37. 使用录像裁判系统时，需指派录像裁判观看比赛实况。如需要，录像裁判将根据实况录像协助当执裁判员工作（详见 t.42.3）。

录像裁判需要：

a. 持有当年赛季的国际剑联裁判资格证；
b. 对录像系统做过培训；
c. 与比赛中的运动员不是同一国籍的；
d. 与主裁判不是同一国籍的。

个人赛

1. 对于小组循环赛和直接淘汰赛，裁判委员会代表通过抽签选定裁判。

2. 对于循环赛，裁判员要与该小组中的所有运动员的国籍不同。

3. 对于每一剑种的直接淘汰赛，裁判委员会的代表将所有出席裁判中最优秀的裁判列一个名单（根据赛季中获得的分数）。

For each quarter of the table, 4 referees are assigned by drawing lots from among at least of 4 to 5 referees, to referee the bouts in the order of the table. They must be of a different nationality from that of any of the fencers participating in that quarter of the table. Then, the video consultants will be assigned by drawing lots among a list of at least 4 to 5 referees.

As the table progresses, the referees will be switched around in a sequence established beforehand.

4. At the end of each round, the Refereeing Delegates can **withdraw** one or more referees whose performance was not satisfactory. This decision must be taken by the majority of the Refereeing Delegates present. However, a referee may not be changed during a bout except in exceptional circumstance. In such a case the decision, which must be well founded, must be taken by the majority of the Refereeing Delegates present (this rule is equally valid for team competitions).

5. **For the final of 4**, the Refereeing Delegates, immediately after the end of the direct elimination tables, select 4 referees by lot from among at least **a list of 4 to 5** referees, who must be of a different nationality from any of the fencers.

   15 minutes before the final, the Refereeing Delegates will draw lots to assign the referees for all the bouts at the same time, in the following order: 1st semi-final, 2nd semi-final.

   As soon as the two semi-finals are over, the Refereeing Delegates will establish a list of 4 to 5 referees and draw lots to assign the referee and vide consultant for the final as well as (at the OG) the referee and video consultant for the 3rd place bout.

6. The drawing of lots is done with the help of a computer for the whole of the competition right through to the final. The computer programme must record each drawing of lots so that it is possible to know which referees were submitted for each draw. The computer programme should also be able to indicate whether the draw for any round was subsequently redone.

7. In conformity with articles t.37.2 and t.37.3, the designation of the video-consultant must be made by drawing lots using a computer programme. The name and nationality of the video-consultant must also be written on the pool or match sheet, beside those of the referee.

Team competitions

t.38. The same rules as those in article t.37 3), 4), 5), 6) and 7) are applied to the team competitions, with two referees per match

World Cup competitions

t.39. Rules described in t.37 and t.38 above are applied by the Directoire Technique, assisted for the finals by the official FIE Refereeing delegate.

并按照抽签方式，从最少4~5名裁判员中随机抽取4名，作为表格上每四分之一区比赛的裁判，按对阵表顺序进行执裁。裁判国籍要与其所处的四分之一区参赛运动员国籍不同。录像裁判从最少4~5名裁判员中随机抽取。

随着直接淘汰赛的进行，裁判员将按照最初预定的顺序进行轮换。

4. 每轮比赛结束后，裁判委员会代表可以取消一名或几名表现令人不满意的裁判。这个决定要由在场的裁判委员会代表中的多数成员决定。然而，除了特殊情况外，一名裁判在比赛进行中是不能被替换下场的。在此情况下，将由所有在场的裁判委员会代表中的多数成员做出决定（此规则也适用于团体赛）。

5. 对于前4名的决赛，裁判委员会代表在直接淘汰赛对阵结束后，将从4~5名与运动员国籍不同的裁判员中随机抽取4名。

在决赛开始前15分钟，裁判委员会代表根据以下顺序随机抽取每场比赛的裁判：半决赛第一场、半决赛第二场。

半决赛结束后，裁判代表将从4~5名裁判中随机抽取决赛和铜牌赛（奥运会）的主裁判和录像裁判。

6. 所有比赛包括决赛都要借助电脑进行抽签。抽签软件要能够记录每次抽签，以便查询哪些裁判参加过哪次抽签。软件还要能够显示哪次抽签重新做过。

7. 根据技术规则t.37.2和t.37.3，录像裁判的指派也要通过抽签软件进行。录像裁判的姓名与国籍要同样标注在记分单主裁判的名字旁边。

团体赛

t.38. 团体赛按照规则t.37.3/4/5/6/7执行，每场比赛配备两名主裁判。

世界杯比赛

t.39. 技术委员会按照上述t.37、t.38的规定执行。在决赛中，由国际剑联正式裁判代表协助执行。

METHOD OF JUDGING HITS

Materiality of the hit

t.40. 1. The **materiality of the hit** is established according to the indications of the apparatus, and when necessary by consulting the judges (cf. t.36).

2. Only the **indications of the electrical apparatus** as indicated by its own lamps or by the extension lamps can be taken into consideration for judging hits. Under no circumstances can the Referee declare a competitor to be hit unless the hit has been properly registered by the apparatus (except as provided for in Article t.49.1 or when a penalty hit has been awarded).

t.41. On the other hand, the Referee should, in the cases enumerated for each weapon, **annul** a hit registered by the apparatus (cf. t.53ss, t.66ss, t.73).

Validity or priority of the hit

t.42. 1. As soon as the bout has stopped, the Referee briefly **analyses** the movements which composed the last fencing phrase.

2. After reaching his decision regarding the materiality of a hit, the Referee, **by applying the rules**, decides which fencer was hit, whether both were hit (épée), or whether there was no valid hit (cf. t.55ss, t.64ss, t.74ss).

Video Refereeing

t.42 3 **a)** Video-refereeing is compulsory at all three weapons at **Grand Prix, Senior World Cup individual and team competitions, the World Championships and Olympic Games, Zonal Championships** and qualification events for the **Olympic Games**. It is optional at the **Veteran World Championships**.

i) For World Cup individual, Grand Prix competitions, Zone Championships and qualification events for the Olympic Games, video-refereeing is compulsory and must be used as soon as the timetable allows the competition to be run on only 4 pistes, and in any case, **from the table of 64.**

ii) For World Cup team competitions, video-refereeing is compulsory **as soon as the timetable allows the competition to be run on only 4 pistes** including the match for 3rd place, but excluding the other ranking matches.

iii) For individual and team competitions of the open World Championships, video-refereeing is obligatory **as soon as the timetable allows the competition to be run on a maximum of 8 pistes, all equipped for video-refereeing.**

iv) For individual competitions of the Junior and Cadet World Championships, video-refereeing is compulsory as soon as the timetable allows the competition to be run on a maximum of 4 pistes, all equipped for video-refereeing.

击中的判定

击中的事实认定

t.40. 1. 裁判器显示的信号是认定击中的事实基础，必要时可以参考助理裁判员的意见（参见t.36）。

2. 只有裁判器或重复灯显示信号，才能判定击中。在任何情况下，只要裁判器没有正常显示击中信号，主裁判就不能判决一名运动员被击中（罚剑情况除外，参见t.49.1）。

t.41. 根据相关条款规定，主裁判将可取消裁判器正常显示信号的一次击中（参 t.53ss、t.66ss、t.73）。

击中的有效性和优先权

t.42. 1. 交锋一停止，裁判员简要地分析最后一个阶段的动作。

2. 在确定了击中的具体情况以后，裁判员运用规则，判定哪位运动员被击中，或者是否双方都被击中（对于重剑），或者是任何击中都无效（参见t.55ss，t.64ss，t.74ss）。

3. 录像裁判系统

a. 录像裁判系统在以下比赛中是强制要求使用的：3个剑种的大奖赛、世界杯个人赛及团体赛、世锦赛和奥运会、洲际锦标赛及奥运资格赛。世界老年人击剑锦标赛没有强制要求。

i） 对于世界杯个人赛、大奖赛、洲际锦标赛及奥运资格赛，只要时间允许比赛在4条剑道上进行，就必须使用录像裁判系统。

ii） 对于世界杯团体赛，只要时间允许比赛在4条剑道上进行，就必须使用录像裁判系统，其中包括第三名的比赛，其他排位赛可以除外。

iii） 对于世界成年锦标赛个人赛及团体赛，只要时间允许比赛在配备录像裁判系统的8条剑道上进行，就必须使用录像裁判系统。

iv） 对于世界青少年锦标赛个人赛，只要时间允许比赛在4条装有录像裁判系统的剑道上进行，就要使用录像裁判系统。

For team competitions in the conventional weapons, video-refereeing is compulsory **from the table of 16.** In epee, video-refereeing is compulsory **from the table of 8.**

v) For individual and team events at the Olympic Games, the video-refereeing system is mandatory **in all three weapons, at all stages of the competition.**

b) Appeals

Both in team and individual events, only the fencer on the piste has the right to request a video review.

i) **In the individual events**, the fencer has:

- in **pools**, one possible appeal during each bout;
- in **direct elimination** bouts, two possible appeals.

Should **the referee agree with the fencer** who appealed for the video-refereeing, the latter is entitled to retain the right of appeal.

ii) **In team events**, the fencers have one possible right to appeal to the video-refereeing per relay and they are entitled to retain this right should the referee agree with the appeal.

iii) **In the case of an appeal for video-refereeing**, the referee will walk over to **the video consultant**, they will watch the video together and after having **analysed the action**, the referee will give his final decision.

c) There shall only be a maximum of **4 repetitions of the action.** The referee can choose to review the action in real time or in slow motion, at any speed he wishes.

d) At all weapons and at any time, the referee may consult his monitor before making a decision.

e) If the fencers' scores are **equal at the end of the match**, for the decisive hit, the referee must use the video-refereeing **before even giving his decision, except in the case specified in article t.42.3.d.**

f) The video consultant may at any time request that the referee **use the video-refereeing**.

g) Once the referee, together with the video consultant, has analysed the action, whether it is :

- at the referee's initiative
- at the request of the athlete
- in case of a tied score, before the decisive hit
- at the video consultant's request

the decision given by the referee is final and no other review of the same action can be requested.

对于花剑和佩剑团体赛，从16表开始必须使用录像裁判系统。对于重剑，必须从8表开始使用。

v）对于奥运会个人和团体比赛，所有3个剑种的所有阶段比赛都必须使用录像裁判系统。

b. 申诉

不论是个人赛还是团体赛，只有比赛中的运动员可以要求查看录像回放。

i）个人赛中，运动员有权要求：

- 小组循环赛中，每场比赛一次回放；
- 直接淘汰赛中，每场比赛两次回放。

如果裁判判决同意申诉运动员的意见，则该运动员可保留这次申诉的权利。

ii）团体赛中，每局比赛运动员都有一次录像回放的权利，如果裁判判决同意申诉运动员的意见，则该运动员可保留这次申诉的权利。

iii）当接到录像回放申诉时，主裁判要来到录像回放屏幕前，与录像裁判一起观看录像内容，并在分析动作后，由主裁判做出最终决定。

c. 每次录像回放的次数不能超过4次，裁判可以选择常速或慢速回放。

d. 对于所有剑种，在任何时候，主裁判都有权在给出其裁决前观看录像回放。

e. 最后一剑时，如果双方比分相等，裁判员必须在做出决定之前观看录像内容，除了t.42.3.d中出现的情况。

f. 任何时候，录像裁判都有权要求主裁判使用录像裁判系统。

g. 在裁判和录像裁判根据录像内容做出分析后，不论是：

—— 主裁判自己决定查看的

—— 运动员要求的

—— 最后一剑前比分相等时

—— 录像裁判要求的

主裁判的判决将是最终的，且不可再要求针对同一剑查看录像回放。

4. The Referee must use the following **signals** (Figure 3,).

Figure 3 Referee signals and commands

For the fencers to adopt the on guard position

To find out if the fencers are ready

To start and restart the fencing

To stop the fencing before a hit is scored, because of the fencer on the Referee's right

Point in line position from the right towards the fencer on the left

Attack or stop hit (counter-attack) from the fencer on the Referee's right

A hit is given against the fencer on the Referee's left

One hit scored by the fencer on the Referee's right

An off-target hit on the fencer on the Referee's left

A parry or counter-time carried out by the fencer on the Referee's right

4. 裁判员使用以下手势（图3）

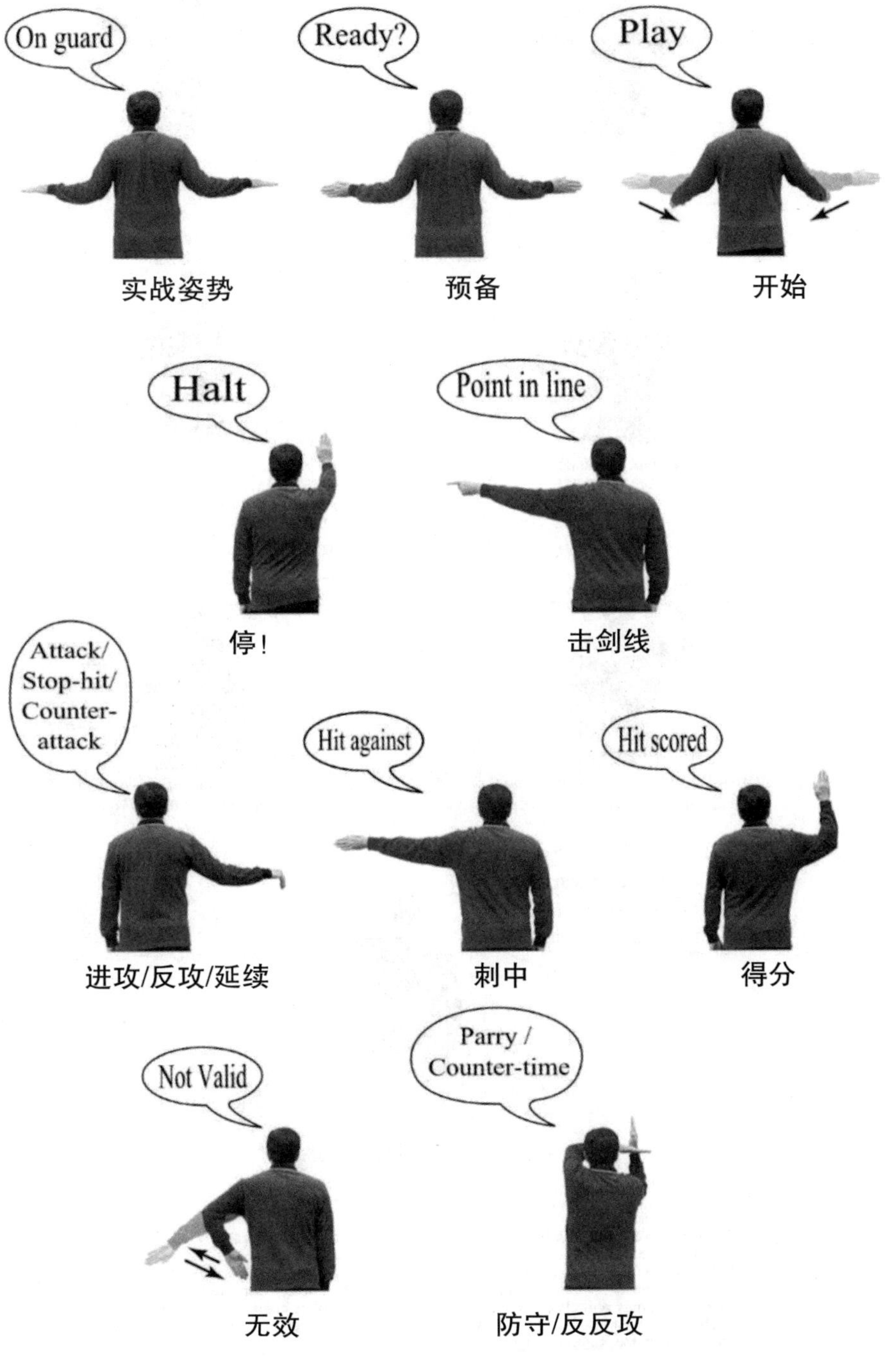

Both fencers are hit

Each fencer scores a hit

Simultaneous attacks

No hit or warning

Offensive action from the fencer on the Referee's right; too short and does not hit

Incorrect attack or riposte from the fencer on the Referee's right

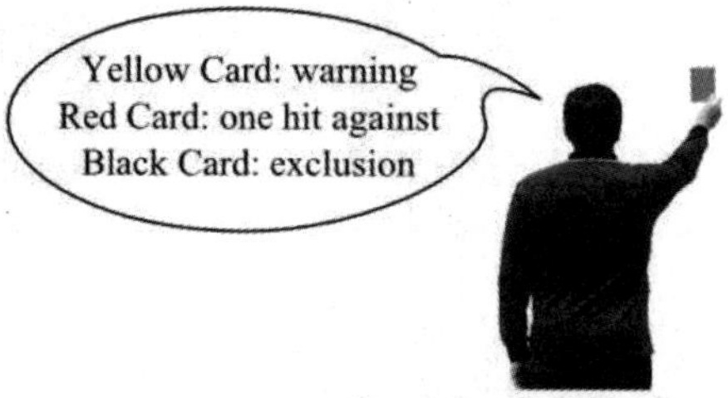

By mimicry, the Referee demonstrates the offence of the fencer on the right and shows the card corresponding to the offence concerned

NOTES

1. The Referee analyses the fencing and announces his decisions by means of the signals and words above.
2. In following the fencing phrase the Referee uses the following words without making the signals: "Riposte!", "Counter-riposte!", "Remise!", "Reprise!", "Redouble!"
3. The fencers may politely ask the Referee for a more complete analysis of the fencing phrase.
4. Each signal must last 1–2 seconds, be expressive and be correctly made. Above they refer to the fencer on the Referee's right.

互中！

双方得分

同时

没有

没有进攻

错误动作

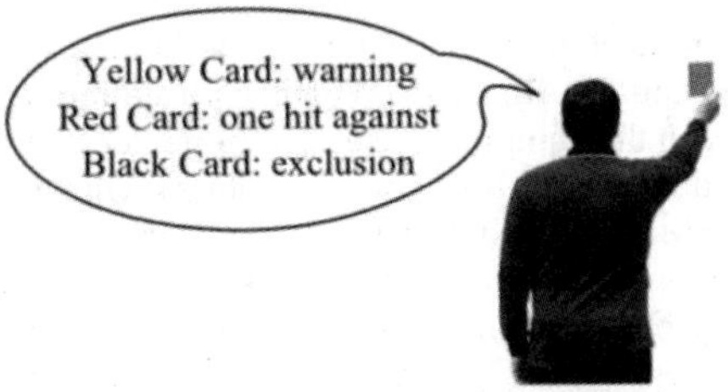

黄牌 / 红牌 / 黑牌

图3 裁判员手势图

说明： 1. 裁判用以上的手势和语言来宣布他的决定。

2. 分析交锋过程时，裁判还继续使用下面词语“还击”“反还击”，但是不再配合动作。“进攻”的示意动作同样适用于“延续”“重新进攻”“连续进攻”。
3. 运动员可以合理地请求裁判员做出更加详细的交锋分析。
4. 每个手势的都要有一定的表示时间（1~2秒），动作要准确易于理解。

以上是运动员在裁判右侧的手势。

REGULATION EQUIPMENT AND CHECKING OF EQUIPMENT BY THE REFEREE

t.43. **1. Before the start** of each pool, team match or bout by direct elimination, the Referee must assemble all the competitors and verify that (cf. t.35.2.c):

a) at all weapons, the **FIE guarantee label** is present on the fencers' equipment (clothing, masks).

b) at foil, the **conductive jacket** conforms to the provision of Article m.28 when each competitor is standing upright, is on guard and is in the lunge position;

c) at épée, the fencer is wearing a **jacket conforming to the regulations** and that the material from which the clothing is made has not too smooth a surface;

d) at sabre, the **conductive jacket** conforms to the provision of Article m.34 when each competitor is standing upright, is on guard and is in the lunge position;

e) at all three weapons, each fencer is wearing, under his jacket, a regulation **protective under-plastron**, made of cloth which can resist 800 Newtons.

f) at all three weapons, the fencer is not equipped with any **electronic communication equipment** which would allow a person off the piste to communicate with the fencer during the bout.

In pools, this checking must be done at the roll call of the fencers.

For bouts in the direct elimination and the finals this checking must be done in the assembly area.

The organisers of all official FIE competitions (junior and senior) must make provision in their set-up for an assembly area.

2. For bouts in the **direct elimination** and the **finals** at the **World Championships and the Olympic Games**, and for **finals of World Cup competitions**, the two fencers in each bout will go to the equipment checking zone, located near the piste, 30 minutes before they are due on the piste. Their equipment will be checked under the responsibility of the SEMI (or the designated expert for finals of World Cup competitions). If any anomaly is identified the equipment at fault will be changed at once, without any penalty being applied. The SEMI delegate will hand over the bodywires, the masks and the weapons that have been checked to the Referee for the bout. **Ten minutes before** they are due on the piste the fencers will report to the Referee designated for their bout. The Referee will hand over a bodywire to each of the fencers in the access zone for the piste. He will check that the fencers are wearing regulation under-jacket protection.

合格器材和裁判员对器材的检验

t.43. 1. 在每场循环赛或团体相遇，或每场淘汰赛开始之前，裁判员应集合参赛选手，进行以下检查（参见35.2.c）：

a. 在所有剑种中，运动员器材均具备国际剑联合格标志（服装、面罩）。

b. 花剑：在站立、准备及冲刺等各种姿势时，金属衣都严格符合器材规则m.28.规定。

c. 重剑；双方均穿着合格服装，其构成的面料没有过于光滑的表面。

d. 佩剑：在站立、准备及弓步等各种姿势时，金属衣都严格符合器材规则m.34的规定。

e. 三个剑种：每位选手在外衣里都穿着一件合格的保护背心，抗800牛顿的力。

f. 在三个剑种中，任何运动员都不允许在比赛过程中，通过佩戴电子交流设备，与场外的人进行交流。

小组循环赛，检查在点名的时候进行。

对于直接淘汰赛和决赛，检查在检录室进行。

所有国际剑联正式比赛（青少年或成年）的组委会都要设有检录室。

2. 对于世界锦标赛和奥运会的直接淘汰赛和决赛，以及世界杯决赛，每场比赛的双方选手都应在入场前30分钟时，到剑道附近的器材检验区去。他们的器材将由器材委员会（SEMI）负责检查（世界杯决赛中由指定的专家负责）。如果受检器材有问题，将立即更换，不受处罚。器材委员会代表将检查过的手线、面具及剑交给裁判。入场前10分钟，运动员到比赛指定的裁判处报到。裁判员在入场区把手线交给每位选手。他将检验运动员是否都穿着合格的保护背心。

3. The Referee and the fencers must **stay together** in the access zone until they go on the piste. **One minute** before they go on the piste the Referee will give a weapon to each fencer, for him to plug in his bodywire. No check will be carried out on the piste prior to the bout.

4. Competition organisers must organise a **waiting area where the fencers can warm up** during this checking procedure.

t.44. 1. **In addition to the checks mentioned above**, the Referee of a bout may at any time, on his own initiative or at the request of a fencer or of a team captain, carry out such checks, or verify the checks already carried out or even carry out, or have carried out, new checks (cf. t.35).

2. He will in any case, before each bout, ensure that the **guarantee label** is present on the clothing, the blade and the mask of each fencer, and that the **insulation of the wires** inside the guard and the **pressure of the spring** in the point of foils and épées conform with the Rules. Checking the insulation of the wires and the pressure of the spring will be repeated each time a weapon is changed. At all three weapons, he will check that the fencer is not equipped with **electronic communication equipment** which would allow a person off the piste to communicate with the fencer during the bout.

3. At épée he will check **the total travel and the residual travel** of the pointe d'arrêt:

— He will check the **total travel** by inserting a gauge measuring 1.5 mm between the barrel of the pointe d'arrêt and the tip. This gauge, provided by the Organising Committee, may have a tolerance of ± 0.05 mm, i.e. from 1.45 mm to 1.55 mm.

— He will check the **residual travel** by inserting a gauge measuring 0.5 mm between the barrel of the pointe d'arrêt and the tip. The apparatus should not register when the point is depressed. This gauge, provided by the Organising Committee, may have a tolerance of ± 0.05 mm, i.e. from 0.45 mm to 0.55 mm.

4. For details of the **weight** used for the check, cf. m.11.3, m.19.3, m.42.2.d.

5. At the beginning of the bout the Referee will place the **reserve equipment that has been checked** near the appropriate end of the piste for the fencer concerned.

3. 直到入场时刻为止，裁判和运动员应一起站在入场区中。入场前1分钟时，裁判给每位选手发一件武器，将手线插入插座。不必在剑道上预先进行任何检验。

4. 竞赛组织者应准备一块等候区，使选手们在检验程序进行时可以热身。

t.44. 1. 除上述检验措施外，一场比赛的主裁判还可以在任何时候主动地或应某一运动员或队长的要求，亲自检验比赛选手的器材，也可以核查已完成的检验，甚至可以进行或让人进行新的检验。

2. 总之，每场比赛之前，裁判员都应检验运动员的服装、剑和面罩上的检验标记，检查花剑和重剑护手盘内导线的绝缘性能和剑尖弹簧的压力。每次更换武器都要重复检查导线的绝缘性能和剑尖弹簧的压力。对所有三个剑种，都要检查运动员是否佩戴有电子交流设备，此类设备使得他们能够在比赛过程中与场外的人进行交流。

3. 对于重剑，裁判应检查电动剑尖的整个行程和剩余行程：

——整个行程：在剑尖底座和按钮之间插入一块1.5毫米厚的薄片。这块薄片由组委会提供，可以有0.05毫米的误差，即1.45 ~ 1.55毫米；

—— 剩余行程：在剑尖底座和按钮之间插入一块0.5毫米厚的薄片。对剑尖的压力不应引起裁判器显示信号。此薄片由组委会提供，可以有0.05毫米的误差，即0.45 ~ 0.55毫米。

4. 上述检验所需的配重细节，参见器材规则 m.11.3、m.19.3、m.42.2.d。

5. 检验过的备用器材由裁判员在开赛前放置在选手一侧的剑道附近。

NON-REGULATION EQUIPMENT

t.45. In whatever circumstances a fencer on the piste is found to be in possession of equipment which is **non-regulation or defective** (cf. m.8, m.9, m.12, m.13, m.16, m.17, m.23), this equipment will be immediately confiscated and submitted to the experts on duty for examination. The equipment in question will only be returned to the owner after the measures necessitated by this examination have been completed and, if appropriate, after the payment of any expenses for repairs. The equipment must be rechecked before it is used again.

1. If a fencer appears on the piste:

— with only **one** regulation **weapon** (cf. t.86.1/2); or

— with only **one** regulation **bodywire**; or

— with only **one** regulation **mask wire**; or

— with a weapon or a bodywire which does not work or which does not conform with the Rules; or

— without his **protective under-plastron** (cf. t.43.1.e); or

— with a **conductive jacket** which does not fully cover the valid target; or

— with **clothing** which does not conform with the Rules;

the Referee will apply the penalties stipulated in Articles t.114, t.116, t.120 (First Group).

2. When during a bout an irregularity is found in the equipment which could be caused by conditions **during the bout**:

Examples:

— conductive jacket with holes in which hits are registered as non-valid,

— weapon or bodywire no longer functioning,

— pressure of the spring in the point too weak,

— the travel in the point no longer regulation,

the Referee will apply **neither warning nor penalty** and any hit scored with the equipment which has become defective will be awarded.

However, even during the course of a bout, any fencer whose weapon, at the moment he presents himself on guard and ready to fence, has a **curve of the blade** which exceeds that permitted (cf. m.8.6, m.16.2, m.23.4) commits an offence in the first group and will be penalised in accordance with Articles t.114, t.116 and t.120.

3. a) If, when a fencer appears on the piste or during a bout, it is established that the equipment used by the fencer:

i) does not bear the marks applied at the preliminary check, the Referee will:

— annul the last hit, if any, scored by the fencer at fault;

— penalise him as specified in Articles t.114, t.117, t.120.

不合格器材

t.45. 无论在什么情况下，只要运动员持有不符合规则或有瑕疵的器材上场（参见器材规则 m.8、m.9、m.12、m.13、m.16、m.17、m.23），该器材将立即被扣留，并送交负责的专家检查。有问题的器材只有在因检查采取了措施以后，才能归还主人，如果发生这种情况（如有必要），要支付修理费用。再次使用以前，该器材将须重新接受检查。

1. 当运动员上场时：

—— 假如只带一支合格剑（参见 t.86.1/2）；

—— 假如只带一根合格手线；

—— 假如只带一根合格头线；

—— 假如所带的一支剑或手线不能正常运行，或者不符合规则条款；

—— 假如没有保护背心；（参见43.1.e）

—— 假如所穿金属衣不能完全覆盖有效部位；

—— 假如服装不符合规则。

裁判员将按 t.114、t.116、t.120（第一组）规定对他进行处罚。

2. 在比赛中，当证实可能是由交锋引起的器材不符合规则时，比如：

—— 金属衣有洞，击中时没有显示有效信号；

—— 手线或武器出现故障；

—— 弹簧压力变得不足；

—— 电动剑尖行程不再符合规定。

裁判员将不给予警告，也不给予处罚，且出现故障的剑做出的有效击中将被承认。

但是，即使在比赛中，当运动员声明可以开始比赛了，如果他的武器剑身的弓形不符合规定（参见器材规则m.8.6、m.16.2及m.23.4），将按照第一组违规进行处罚（参见技术规则t.114、t.116及t.120）。

3.

a. 如果在运动员上场时或比赛期间，其所使用的器材被发现：

i）不具备器材检查合格标记，裁判员将：

—— 取消犯规运动员可能击中的最后一剑；

—— 根据 t.114、t.117、t.120之规定给予其处罚。

ii) does not conform to the rules in a way **not covered by the preliminary check**, the Referee will:

— penalise him as specified in Articles t.114, t.116, t.120.

iii) has been passed by the preliminary check but is fraudulent;

iv) bears the marks of the preliminary check which have been **imitated or transferred**;

v) has been willfully altered (i.e. in a manner other than by accidental cause or by conditions during the bout) so that it would not pass a preliminary check;

vi) has been altered in any way to allow the recording of hits or the non-functioning of the apparatus **at will**;

vii) is equipped with **electronic communication equipment** permitting a person off the piste to communicate with the fencer during the bout; then,

— in cases **iii), v), vi) and vii) above**, the Referee must immediately **confiscate** the equipment (weapon, bodywire, if necessary conductive jacket, mask, protective under-plastron, breeches, etc.), and have it examined by the expert on duty.

b) After having obtained the **opinion of the expert** (a member of the SEMI Committee at the fencing events at the Olympic Games and at World Championships), who has established the facts (cf. m.33ss), the Referee will apply the following **sanctions**, without prejudice to the application of Article t.96.2/4;

— in cases **iii), v), vi)** and **vii)** the Referee will penalise him as specified for offences of the 4th group (cf. Articles t.114, t.119, t.120).

c) While awaiting the decision of the Referee that bout will be suspended but the other bouts in the pool may continue.

4. Every fencer must appear on the piste with clothing **conforming to the rules** as follows:

a) Name and nationality, in accordance with the rules, on the back of the jacket. *Application: all official FIE competitions, at all stages of the competitions.*

ii）不合规则，但又不属于预先检查范围，裁判员将给犯规运动员以t.114、t.116、t.120规定的处罚。

iii）通过弄虚作假的方式通过器材检查；

iv）伪造、挪用器材检查合格标记；

v）被故意改动（除突发情况或由交锋过程造成之外），以至于原本无法通过器材检查；

vi）经过改动，能够随意引起裁判器记录击中，或使裁判器不发生作用。

vii）或佩戴有比赛中可以与场外人员进行交流的电子通信设备。

——如出现ⅲ、ⅴ、ⅵ、vii其中任何一种情况，裁判员应当立即扣留其器材（武器、手线，如有必要：金属衣、面罩、保护背心、比赛服等），并且请当值专家检查。

b. 在听取做出证明的专家（世界锦标赛和奥运会击剑比赛为器材委员会的一名成员）的意见后（参器材规则m.33.ss），裁判员在不影响执行 t.96.2/4 的情况下，将给予以下处罚：

——对于ⅲ、ⅳ、ⅴ、ⅵ的情况，裁判员将对犯规运动员执行第4组违规处罚（参见t.114、t.119、t.120规定）；

c. 在等候裁判员的裁决时，当场比赛中止，但小组循环赛的其他比赛可以继续进行。

4. 所有运动员在剑道上就位时都要身着符合以下规定的比赛服：

a. 保护服的后背要印有运动员的名字及国籍（所有国际剑联官方比赛的所有阶段）。

b) Wearing his **national uniform and logo** (cf. m.25.3). *Application as follows:*

- **i)** **Senior, Junior and Cadet World Championships**, all bouts, whether in a pool, in the direct elimination or during a team match;
- **ii)** **Individual: Senior World Cup competitions** and **Senior Zonal Championships**, all bouts, whether in a pool or in the direct elimination;
- **iii)** **Teams: Senior World Cup competitions** and **Senior Zonal Championships**, all bouts in every match.

In case of violation of this rule:

— For the competitions mentioned in items **i)** and **iii)** above, the Referee shall **eliminate** the fencer at fault, and he will not be allowed to participate further in the event.

— For the competitions mentioned in item **ii)** above, the Referee shall penalise the fencer at fault with a Red Card (Articles t.114, t.117, t.120, Second Group). The fencer at fault shall however be **allowed to remain** on the piste and fence the bout concerned.

5. If the conductive jacket does not conform to the rules, the fencer must put on a spare jacket that does conform to the rules. If this jacket does not have his name and nationality on the back, the fencer has until the next stage of the competition (from the pools to the table of 64, the table of 32, etc) to get his name and nationality printed on it.

If this is not done and except in cases of 'force majeure' the referee will eliminate the fencer and he cannot continue to participate in the competition.

b. 按照以下要求身着国家队队服和标志（参见器材规则m.25.3）：

i）世界锦标赛及世界青少年锦标赛，所有小组循环赛比赛，直接淘汰赛及团体赛；

ii）个人赛：成年世界杯和成年洲际锦标赛，所有小组赛和直接淘汰赛；

iii）团体赛：成年世界杯和成年洲际锦标赛所有阶段比赛。

如果出现违反以上规定的情况：

——如果出现上述第ⅰ、ⅲ条的情况，裁判取消违规运动员比赛资格，他将不能参加以后的比赛。

——如果出现上述第ⅱ条的情况，裁判将判罚运动员红牌（参见技术规则t.114、t.117及t.120，第二组处罚），但运动员可以继续完成当前比赛。

5. 如果导电背心不符合规定，运动员要穿上备用背心。如果这件备用背心的后背没有印有运动员的姓名和国籍，则他可以在下一阶段比赛之前（从小组赛到64表，32表等）去印刷。

如果没有，除了不可抗外力，裁判员将会淘汰此名运动员，他将不能参加后面的比赛。

PART 2. FOIL

THE CONVENTIONS OF FENCING

METHOD OF MAKING A HIT

t.46. 1. The foil is a **thrusting** weapon only. Offensive actions with this weapon are made therefore with the point and with the point only.

2. **Pushing or letting drag** the point of the electric weapon on the electric piste is forbidden during the actual bout (between 'Play!' and 'Halt!'). Placing the weapon on the piste at any time to **straighten** it is also forbidden. Any breaking of these rules will be punished according to Articles t.114, t.116, t.120.

TARGET

Limitation of the target

t.47. 1. At foil, only hits which arrive **on the target** are counted as valid.

2. **The target** at foil excludes the limbs and the head. It is confined to the trunk, the upper limit being the collar up to 6 cm above the prominences of the collar bones; at the sides to the seams of the sleeves, which should cross the head of the humerus; and the lower limit following a horizontal line across the back joining the tops of the hip bones, thence by straight lines to the junction of the lines of the groin. It also includes the part of the bib beneath a horizontal line 1.5 - 2 cm below the chin which, in any case, may not be lower than the line of the shoulders (see Figure 4).

Figure 4 Valid target at foil

This diagram is for guidance purposes only.

In case of any doubt the wording of the appropriate text takes precedence

第二部分　花剑
交锋协定

击中的方法

t.46. 1. 花剑是仅使用刺击技术的武器。因此，这种武器的攻击动作是使用剑尖的，并且只能使用剑尖。

2. 在比赛过程中（“开始”与“停”口令之间）明确禁止用剑尖在金属场地上挤压或拖拉。同样禁止任何时候在剑道上矫正武器。任何犯规行为将根据 t.114、t.116、t.120 受到处罚。

有效部位

有效部位的限定

t.47. 1. 花剑中，只有击中有效部位才能得分。

2. 有效部位除去四肢和头部。限于躯干，向上至衣领顶端、直至锁骨顶端以上6厘米处为止；侧面至袖子缝线，应经过肱骨尖端；向下沿脊背上一条水平走向的线，经过胯骨顶端，并由此通过一条直线，在腹股沟折皱处的连接点相交（图4）。

图4　花剑有效部位

以上图示只用作示意，如有任何的疑虑，
以相关文字描述为准。

Hits off the target

t.48. A hit which is made on a part of the body **other than the target** (whether directly or as a result of a parry) is not counted as a valid hit (cf t.49).

Extension of the valid target

t.49. **1.** However, hits which arrive off the target are counted as valid whenever, by reason of an **abnormal position**, the fencer has substituted this non-valid target for the valid target.

2. The Referee may question the judges about this, but he **alone** must decide whether the hit is valid or not.

JUDGING OF HITS AT FOIL

t.50. Foil competitions are judged with an **electrical recording apparatus**.

Materiality of the Hit

t.51. **Only the indications of the recording apparatus** can be taken into consideration for judging the materiality of hits. The Referee cannot declare a competitor to be hit unless the hit has been properly registered by the apparatus (except as provided for in Article t.49.1, or when a penalty hit has been awarded).

t.52. When using the apparatus it should be noted that:

a) If a **non-valid hit** has been scored the apparatus will not register a possible valid hit scored on the same side of the apparatus.

b) The apparatus does not indicate whether there is any **priority in time** between two or more hits which it registers simultaneously.

Annulment of a Hit

t.53. **1.** The Referee will **disregard** hits which are registered as a result of actions:

— started before the word 'Play!' or after the word 'Halt!' (cf. t.18.1/3);

— which are made on any object **other than the opponent** or his equipment (cf. t.41).

2. A competitor who, **intentionally**, causes the apparatus to register a hit by placing his point on the ground or on any surface **other than that of his opponent** will be penalised as specified in Articles t.114, t.117, t.120.

3. Fencers are forbidden to place a **non-insulated part** of their weapon in contact with their conductive jacket with the intention of jamming the electrical apparatus and thus avoiding being hit.

击中无效部位

t.48. 击中无效部位（无论是直接或由于防守）不得分，但是要停止交锋，并因此取消随后的任何击中（参阅 t.49）。

有效部位范围的延伸

t.49. 1. 但是，当运动员通过不规范姿势，用无效部位代替有效部位时，该无效部位若被击中就算有效。

2. 主裁判可以询问助理裁判，但是他应当独自判定这一击中是否有效。

击中的判断

t.50. 比赛借助电动裁判器来判断。

击中的事实认定

t.51. 对于击中事实的认定，只能以裁判器显示信号为准。在任何情况下，只要裁判器没有记录击中信号，裁判员就不能宣布某一运动员被击中，规则规定的t.49.1和罚剑除外。

t.52. 使用裁判器时应注意以下情况：
a. 如果击中无效部位，裁判器将不记录在同侧可能做出的有效击中。
b. 如果两次或几次击中是同时的，但是在时间上各有优先，裁判器的信号无法显示。

取消击中

t.53. 1. 裁判员将不考虑由于以下情况产生的击中信号：
—— 在“开始”之前或“停”之后做出的动作（参阅 t.18.1/3）
—— 击中对手以外的任何其他物体或对手的器材（参阅 t.41）

2. 运动员如果故意用剑尖触及地面或对手以外任何表面，从而引起击中信号，将受到 t.114、t.117、t.120规定的处罚。

3. 禁止运动员用自己武器非绝缘的部分接触自己的金属背心，企图引起裁判器失灵，并因此避免被击中。

The penalty for committing such an offence is specified in Articles t.114, t.116, t.120. Any hit scored by the fencer at fault is annulled.

t.54. **1.** The Referee must, on the other hand, take into account **possible failures of the electrical equipment**, in particular:

a) He must **annul a hit which he has just awarded** as a result of a hit signalled as on the valid target (coloured lamp) if he establishes, by tests made under his personal supervision, before the bout has effectively recommenced (the command 'Play!') and without any of the equipment in use having been changed (cf. t.35.2/d):

— either that **a hit registered as 'valid'** against the competitor against whom the hit has been awarded can be made without there being in fact a valid hit;

— or that a **'non-valid' hit** made by the fencer against whom the hit was awarded is not registered by the apparatus;

— or that a **'valid' hit** made by the fencer against whom the hit was awarded does not cause any hit either valid or non-valid to be registered;

— or that the registration of hits **made by the competitor against whom the hit was awarded** does not remain recorded on the apparatus.

b) On the other hand, when the Referee has decided that a hit made by a competitor has priority, this hit **shall not be annulled** if subsequently it is found that a valid hit made by the opponent is registered as non-valid or that the weapon of the fencer against whom the hit was awarded is permanently registering a non-valid hit.

2. The Referee must also apply the following rules:

a) Only the **last hit** made before the fault was established can be annulled.

b) A competitor who **makes any modification in or who changes his equipment** without being asked by the Referee to do so, before the Referee has given his decision, loses all right to the annulment of the hit (cf. t.35.2.d).

c) **If the bout has effectively recommenced** a competitor cannot claim the annulment of a hit awarded against him before the said recommencement of the bout.

d) **The location of a fault** found in the equipment (including the equipment of the competitors) is of no importance for this possible annulment.

e) It is not necessary that **the failure found should repeat itself each time** a test is made; but it is essential that the fault should be observed by the Referee without the possibility of doubt at least once during the tests made by him or under his supervision.

如果犯此类错误，裁判员将对犯规运动员执行 t.114、t.116、t.120中的处罚。该运动员由此可能击中的一剑将被取消。

t.54. 1. 裁判员必须考虑到电动器材可能发生的故障，尤其是：

a. 在任何实际交锋重新开始之前（“开始”命令前），并且场上器材没有任何更换的情况下，经过主裁判认真监督下进行的测试后确认有以下情况，裁判员应当取消在出现了一次击中有效部位的（彩色灯）信号后自己刚刚认可的击中（参阅 t.35.2.d）。

—— 宣布被击中的运动员身上显示“有效”信号，而实际并未产生有效击中。
—— 被击中运动员做出一次无效击中，而裁判器没记录下来。
—— 宣布被击中的运动员做出的有效击中，没引起任何信号，既无“有效”，又无“无效”。
—— 宣布被击中的运动员引起的信号没有稳定出现在裁判器上。

b. 然而，如果经过测试确认，宣布被击中的运动员做出的一次有效击中被记录为无效，或者宣布被击中的运动员的武器一直显示无效信号，当裁判员已经判定其对手的击中有优先权时，就不必取消此次击中。

2. 裁判还应当执行以下规则：

a. 只有确认故障前的最后一次击中才能被取消。

b. 运动员未经裁判员的同意，在裁判员做出裁决前，就已着手改动或更换自己的器材，将失去取消击中的任何权利（参见 t.35.2.d）。

c. 如果实际交锋已重新开始，运动员就不能再要求取消重新开始之前已被确认对自己的击中。

d. 在设备中发现的缺陷所在之处（包括运动员自己的器材），对于可能产生的取消击中无关紧要。

e. 没有必要每次重复试验以确认缺陷；但毫无疑问该缺陷必须至少得到裁判本人的一次确认，测验过程由他自己或在他指挥下进行。

f) When a competitor against whom a hit has been registered has **broken his blade**, the hit must be annulled unless the breaking of the blade has occurred clearly after the hit has been registered.

g) The Referee must pay particular attention to **hits which do not register or which are registered abnormally**. Should such defects be repeated, the Referee must ask a member of the SEMI Committee or an expert technician on duty to verify that the equipment conforms to the Rules.

h) The Referee must ensure that **nothing is altered in the competitors' equipment** or in the whole of the electrical apparatus before the expert carries out his check.

3. Whenever accidental causes make it impossible to carry out tests, the hit will be considered **doubtful** and annulled.

4. If hits are registered simultaneously **on both sides of the apparatus**, and the Referee cannot establish the priority with certainty, he must replace the competitors on guard.

5. In accordance with the general rules (cf. t.18.5) the Referee must **stop the bout**, even if no hit is registered by the apparatus, whenever play becomes **confused** and he is no longer able to analyse the phrase.

6. The Referee should also supervise **the state of the conductive piste**; he must not allow the bout to commence or to continue if the conductive piste has holes in it which might affect the proper registering of hits. (The organisers must make the necessary arrangements to ensure the rapid repair or replacement of the conductive piste.)

VALIDITY OR PRIORITY OF THE HIT

Preface

t.55. The Referee **alone** decides as to the validity or the priority of the hit by applying the following basic rules which are the conventions applicable to foil fencing.

Respect of the fencing phrase

t.56. **1.** Every **attack**, that is every initial offensive action, which is correctly executed must be parried or completely avoided and the phrase must be continuous — that is to say, co-ordinated (cf. t.7.1).

2. In order to judge **the correctness of an attack** the following points must be considered:

a) **The simple attack, direct or indirect** (cf. t.8.1), is correctly executed when the straightening of the arm, the point threatening the valid target, precedes the initiation of the lunge or the flèche.

f. 显示被击中信号的运动员碰巧剑身折断这一事实，可以作为理由来取消对手对他的击中，除非剑身明显是在记录击中之后才断裂。

g. 裁判员应当十分注意裁判器没有显示或不正常显示的击中。在这些故障重复出现的情况下，裁判应当要求在场的器材委员会成员或专职技术专家帮助，以检查器材是否符合规则。

h. 在专家检查之前，裁判员务必注意到运动员的装备以及整个电动设备不能有任何改变。

3. 由于意外情况而不可能进行检查时，击中将被视为“可疑”并被取消。

4. 如果裁判器两侧同时显示有效信号，而裁判员无法准确判定优先权时，他应当让双方重新恢复预备姿势。

5. 在执行一般规则（参见 t.18.5）时，即使任何信号都不显示，每当一系列交锋变得混乱，在裁判员无法分析时，应当中止交锋。

6. 裁判员同样应该注意金属剑道的状况；如果剑道上有洞，可能扰乱记录时，他将不准许比赛开始或继续进行（组织者必须采取必要措施，进行修理或迅速更换金属剑道）。

击中的有效性和优先性

前言

t.55. 裁判员根据花剑特有的条款及其原则，必须单独对击中的有效性或优先性做出裁决。

交锋的准则

t.56. 1. 任何进攻，即任何开始的攻击动作正确完成时，应当被防守或完全避开，而一系列交锋应当连贯协调（参见 t.7.1）。

2. 为了判断一个进攻是否正确，应考虑到以下情况：

a. 直接或间接的简单进攻（参见t.8.1）的正确做法是：在做出冲刺或弓步动作之前，伸出手臂剑尖威胁有效部位。

b) **The compound attack** (cf. t.8.1) is correctly executed when the arm is straightened in the presentation of the first feint, with the point threatening the valid target, and the arm is not bent during the successive actions of the attack and the initiation of the lunge or the flèche.

c) The attack with a **step-forward-lunge** or a **step-forward-flèche** is correctly executed when the straightening of the arm precedes the end of the step forward and the initiation of the lunge or the flèche.

d) Actions, simple or compound, steps or feints which are **executed with a bent arm**, are not considered as attacks but as preparations, laying themselves open to the initiation of the offensive or defensive/offensive action of the opponent (cf. t.8.1/3).

3. To judge **the priority of an attack** when analysing the fencing phrase, it should be noted that:

a) If the attack is initiated **when the opponent is not 'point in line'** (cf. t.10), it may be executed either with a direct thrust, or by a disengage, or by a cut-over, or may even be preceded by a beat or successful feints obliging the opponent to parry.

b) If the attack is initiated **when the opponent is 'point in line'** (cf. t.10), the attacker must, first, deflect the opponent's blade. Referees must ensure that a mere contact of the blades is not considered as sufficient to deflect the opponent's blade (cf. t.60.5.a).

c) If the attacker, when attempting to deflect the opponent's blade, fails to find it (**dérobement**), the right of attack passes to the opponent.

d) **Continuous steps forward, with the legs crossing one another**, constitute a preparation and on this preparation any simple attack has priority.

4. Attacks by beats on the blade:

a) In an attack by beating on the blade, the attack is correctly carried out and retains its priority when the beat is made on the foible of the opponent's blade i.e. the two-thirds of the blade furthest from the guard.

b) In an attack by beating on the blade, when the beat is made on the forte of the opponent's blade i.e. the one-third of the blade nearest the guard, the attack is badly executed and the beat gives the opponent the right to an immediate riposte.

t.57. The parry gives the right to riposte: **the simple riposte** may be direct or indirect, but to annul any subsequent action by the attacker, it must be executed immediately, without indecision or delay.

t.58. When a compound attack is made, if the opponent **finds the blade during one of the feints**, he has the right to riposte.

b. 复杂进攻（参见 t8.1）的正确做法是，做第一个假动作时就伸出手臂，剑尖威胁有效部位，且在后续进攻动作和发动冲刺或弓步的过程中不收回手臂。

c. 通过向前一步冲刺或向前一步弓步发动进攻的正确方法是，在向前一步结束并发动冲刺或弓步之前就已伸出手臂。

d. 一个动作无论简单还是复杂，如果在向前一步或做假动作时，手臂已收回，就不算进攻，而只算一个准备动作，可能导致对手发动攻击动作或防御性的攻击动作（参 t.8.1/3）。

3. 为了判断一系列交锋时一次进攻的优先权，应注意以下几点：

a. 如果发动进攻时，对手不处于“击剑线”姿势（参见t.10），那么可以运用直刺、转移刺、交叉刺发动进攻或进攻之前运用一次击打或有效的假动作，迫使对手防守。

b. 如果发动进攻时，对手处于“击剑线”的姿势（参见t.10），进攻者应该预先打开对手的剑，裁判员应注意到轻轻地擦过不能视为足以打开对手的剑。（参 t.60.5.a）

c. 如果进攻者寻找对手的剑以便打开它，却没碰到（已被对手避开），优先权转移到对方。

d. 向前交叉步是一个准备动作，基于这个动作之上的一切简单进攻都有优先权。

4. 击打进攻

a. 实施击打进攻时，当击打在对手剑身弱部，即远离护手盘的三分之二部位，击打为有效且优先权得以保留。

b. 实施击打进攻时，当击打在对手剑身强部，即靠近护手盘的三分之一部位，击打为无效且对手获得及时还击的权利。

t.57. 防守时有权还击：简单还击可以是直接或间接的，但是为了防止进攻者随后的任何动作，还击应当毫不犹豫或没有停顿地立即完成。

t.58. 在一个复杂进攻中如果对手在做一个假动作时碰到武器，他有权还击。

t.59. When **compound attacks** are made, the opponent has the right to **stop-hit**; but to be valid the stop hit must precede the conclusion of the attack by an interval of fencing time; that is to say that the stop hit must arrive before the attacker has begun the final movement of the attack.

Judging of hits

t.60. In applying these basic conventions of foil fencing, the Referee should judge as follows:

1. When, during a phrase, both fencers are **hit simultaneously**, there is either a *simultaneous action* or a *double hit.*

2. The **simultaneous action** is due to simultaneous conception and execution of an attack by both fencers; in this case the hits exchanged are annulled for both fencers even if one of them has been hit off the target.

3. The **double hit**, on the other hand, is the result of a faulty action on the part of one of the fencers.

Therefore, when there is not a period of fencing time between the hits:

4. **Only the fencer who is attacked is counted as hit:**

   a) If he makes a **stop hit** on his opponent's simple attack;

   b) If, instead of parrying, he attempts **to dodge the hit** and does not succeed in so doing;

   c) If, after making a successful parry, he makes a **momentary pause** which gives his opponent the right to renew the attack (redoublement, remise or reprise);

   d) If, into a compound attack, he makes a **stop hit** without being in time;

   e) If, **having his 'point in line'** (cf. t.10) and being subjected to a beat or a taking of the blade (prise de fer) which deflects his blade, he attacks or places his point in line again instead of parrying a direct thrust made by his opponent.

5. **Only the fencer who attacks is counted as hit:**

   a) If he initiates his attack **when his opponent has his point in line** (cf. t.10) without deflecting the opponent's weapon. Referees must ensure that a mere contact of the blades is not considered as sufficient to deflect the opponent's blade.

   b) If he attempts to find the blade, does not succeed (is the object of **a dérobement**) and continues the attack.

   c) If, during a compound attack, his opponent **finds the blade**, but he continues the attack and his opponent ripostes immediately.

t.59. 在复杂进攻时，对手有权反攻，但是必须提前于进攻结束一个击剑时间，反攻才有效。也就是说，反攻必须在进攻者开始进攻的最后动作前击中。

判断击中

t.60. 在执行花剑的这些基本条款时，裁判员应当作如下判断：

1. 在一系列交锋中，当双方运动员同时被击中，或者视为同时动作，或视为相互击中。

2. 同时动作是由于双方运动员发动进攻的同时想法和同时动作；在这种情况下，即使其中一方击中无效部位，双方击中均被取消。

3. 相反的是，相互击中是一名运动员的一个错误动作的结果。

因此，如果在两次击中之间没有一个击剑时间，判定情况如下：

4. 只有被进攻者一方被击中：

a. 如果他对一个简单进攻进行反攻；

b. 如果他不防守而是竭力躲闪，但没有成功；

c. 如果他在一次防守成功之后，停顿了片刻，使对手得以再次进攻（转移、延续或重新进攻）；

d. 如果他对一个复杂进攻进行反攻，却没有一个击剑时间的优势；

e. 如果他处于“击剑线”姿势（参见t.10.），在对手一次击打或一个缠绕打开他的剑之后，他没有对进攻者直接做出的劈刺进行防守，而是出手进攻，或者重新做“击剑线”姿势。

5. 只有进攻者一方被击中：

a. 如果当对手处于“击剑线”时，他发动了进攻却没有打开对手的剑。裁判员应注意到，轻轻擦过不能视为足以打开对手的剑；

b. 如果他寻找对手的剑而没有碰到（因为已被对方避开）而继续进攻；

c. 如果在一个复杂进攻中，对手已碰到剑并立即进行还击时，他仍继续进攻；

d) If, during a compound attack, he makes **a momentary pause**, during which time the opponent makes a stop hit, while the attacker continues his attack.

e) If, during a compound attack, he is **stop-hit** in time before he begins his final movement.

f) If he makes a hit by a remise, redoublement or reprise when his original attack has been **parried and his opponent has made a riposte** which is **immediate**, simple, and executed in one period of fencing time without withdrawing the arm.

6. **The Referee must replace the competitors on guard** each time that there is a double hit and he is unable to judge clearly on which side the fault lies.

One of the most difficult cases to judge arises when a stop hit is made and there is doubt as to whether it was made sufficiently in time in relation to the final movement of a compound attack. Generally, in such cases, the double hit occurs through the fault of both fencers concerned, which justifies the Referee replacing them on guard. (The fault of the attacker consists of indecision, slowness of execution or the making of feints which are not sufficiently effective. The fault of the defender lies in delay or slowness in making the stop hit.)

d. 如果在一个复杂进攻中，他犹豫片刻，而在此刻对手做出反攻，而他继续进攻；

e. 如果在一次复杂进攻中，他在做最后一个动作前的击剑时间里遭到反攻；

f. 如果对于对手的一次防守，他采用延续、连续或重新进攻，而对手紧接防守之后，在相同时间内进行直接简单还击，且没有回收手臂。

6. 每当裁判员在发现互相击中时不能清楚判断错误属于哪一方时，便命令双方运动员恢复预备姿势。

最难判断的情况之一就是，当一个反攻击中可能令人怀疑其对于复杂进攻的最后动作是否有足够优势。通常在这种情况下，相互击中是双方运动员同时做出错误动作的结果，裁判便命令他们恢复预备姿势。错误在于进攻者犹豫不决、缓慢迟钝或假动作不奏效，被进攻者反攻击中延迟或缓慢。

PART 3. EPEE

THE CONVENTIONS OF FENCING

METHOD OF MAKING A HIT

t.61. **1.** The épée is a **thrusting weapon** only. Attacks with this weapon are therefore made with the point, and with the point only.

2. **Pushing** or letting the point of the electric weapon **drag** on the electric piste is forbidden during the actual bout (between 'Play!' and 'Halt!'). Placing the weapon on the piste at any time to **straighten** it is also forbidden.

Any breaking of this rule will be penalised according to Articles t.114, t.116, t.120.

THE TARGET

t.62. At épée the target includes the whole of the fencer's body including his clothing and equipment.

Thus any hit which arrives is counted, whatever part of the body (trunk, limbs or head), the clothing or the equipment it touches (see Figure 5).

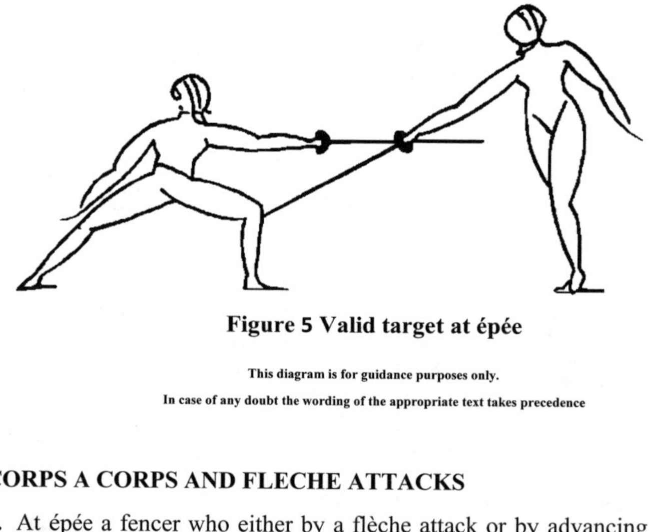

Figure 5 Valid target at épée

This diagram is for guidance purposes only.

In case of any doubt the wording of the appropriate text takes precedence

CORPS A CORPS AND FLECHE ATTACKS

t.63. **1.** At épée a fencer who either by a flèche attack or by advancing vigorously brings about a **corps à corps** even several times in succession (**without brutality or violence**) does not transgress the basic conventions of fencing and commits no fault thereby (cf. t.20.1/3, t.25).

第三部分 重剑

交锋协定

击中的方法

t.61. 1. 重剑是仅使用刺击技术的一种武器。因此这种武器的攻击动作是使用剑尖进行的，并且只能使用剑尖。

2. 在比赛过程中（“开始”与“停”之间），明确禁止将剑尖在金属剑道上挤压或拖拉。同样在任何时候都禁止在剑道上矫正武器。任何犯规行为将按照t.114、t.116、t.120受到处罚。

有效部位

t.62. 有效部位包括运动员整个身体、衣服与装备。因此，无论击中身体（躯干、四肢或头部）、服装或装备的哪一部分，都能得分（图5）。

图5　重剑有效部位

以上图示只用作示意，如有任何的疑虑，
以相关文字描述为准。

身体接触和冲刺

t.63. 1. 如果交锋一方由于冲刺或突然向前移动，多次造成身体接触（既不粗暴也不剧烈），并不违反击剑的基本协定，因此不构成任何犯规行为（参见 t.20.1/3、t.25）。

2. A fencer who **intentionally causes corps à corps** to avoid being hit or who jostles his opponent is penalised according to Articles t.114, t.116, t.120.

3. The 'flèche ending systematically in a corps à corps' referred to in this article must not be confused with the 'flèche resulting in a shock which jostles the opponent', which is considered as an act of **intentional brutality** at all three weapons and is punished as such (cf. t.87.2, t.120).

4. On the other hand the '**flèche** which is made by running, even going past the opponent', and **without a corps à corps**, is not forbidden: the Referee should not call 'Halt!' too soon, in order not to annul a possible riposte; if, when making such a running flèche without hitting his opponent, the fencer who makes the flèche crosses the lateral boundaries of the piste, he must be punished as laid down in Article t.28.3.

JUDGING OF HITS AT EPEE

t.64. 1. Epée competitions are judged with an **electrical recording apparatus**.

2. When both competitors are hit, and the apparatus registers both these hits as valid, there is a **double hit**, that is to say a hit is scored against each competitor.

Basic principle

t.65. Only the **indications of the electrical recording apparatus** can be taken into consideration for judging the materiality of hits. The Referee cannot declare a competitor to be hit unless the hit has been properly registered by the apparatus (except when a penalty hit has been awarded).

The annulment of hits

t.66. 1. In arriving at his judgement, the Referee will disregard hits which are registered as a result of actions:

— started before the word **'Play!'** or after **'Halt!'** (cf. t.18.1/3);

— caused by the **meeting of the points** of the épées or by a hit made on the **ground** where it is **not insulated**;

— or which are made on any object **other than the opponent** or his equipment (cf. t.36.1, t.67.e).

2. Any competitor who, intentionally, causes the apparatus to register a hit by placing his point on any surface **other than that of his opponent**, will be penalised as specified in Articles t.114,t.117, t.120.

t.67. The Referee must take note of **possible failures** of the electrical equipment and must annul the last hit registered in the following circumstances:

2. 如果运动员为了避免被击中，而故意引起身体接触或是挤撞对手，将受到 t.114、t.116、t.120 规定的处罚。

3. 本条款所指的有序冲刺造成的身体接触，不应该与导致挤撞对手的冲刺混为一谈，在三个剑种中，后者均被视为故意的粗暴行为，都要受到应有的处罚（参见 t.87.2、t.120）。

4. 相反，跑动中的冲刺，甚至超过对手而没有身体接触都是允许的，裁判员不应过早叫“停”，而不至于取消可能发生的还击；如果做冲刺时没有击中对手，而冲刺者越出了剑道边线，他应受到 t.28.3 规定的处罚。

击中的判断

t.64. 1. 重剑比赛借助一台电动裁判器来判断。

2. 当两名运动员都被击中，而裁判器记录的两次击中都有效，就出现“相互击中”，即每人都算击中一次。

基本规则

t.65. 判断击中只能以裁判器显示信号为准。在任何情况下，只要裁判器没有按常规显示击中信号，裁判就不能判决某一名运动员被击中（罚剑的情况除外）。

击中的取消

t.66. 1. 裁判员在裁决中不考虑由以下原因产生的刺中信号：

—— 在“开始”之前或“停”以后做出的刺中（参 t.18.1/3）；

—— 由于重剑剑头相碰撞或者击中非绝缘地面而引起的击中信号；

—— 刺中对手以外的其他物体或对手的装备（参见t.36.1、t.67.e）。

2. 运动员如果故意用剑尖刺击对手以外的任何部位而引起的信号，他将受到t.114、t.117、t.120规定的处罚。

t.67. 裁判员还应考虑到电动器材可能发生的故障，在下列情况中应当取消已显示击中信号的最后一剑：

a) If a hit **made on the guard** of the competitor against whom the hit was registered or on the **conductive piste** causes the apparatus to register a hit;

b) If a hit **properly made** by the competitor against whom the hit was registered does not cause the apparatus to register a hit;

c) If the apparatus **fortuitously registers a hit** on the side of the competitor against whom the hit was registered, for example, after a beat on the blade, by any movements of his opponent, or as a result of any cause other than a properly made hit;

d) If the registering of a hit made by the competitor against whom the hit was registered **is annulled** by a subsequent hit made by his opponent.

e) Special cases

— If a double hit is registered and **one hit is valid and the other is not valid** (such as a hit made on some surface other than on the opponent (cf. t.66.1) or a hit made after leaving the piste (cf. t.26ss), only the valid hit is scored.

— If a double hit is registered by **an established hit and a doubtful hit** (failure of the electrical apparatus) the fencer who has made the established hit may choose to accept the double hit or ask to have it annulled.

t.68. The Referee must also apply the following rules regarding the annulment of hits:

a) Only the last hit which precedes the establishment of the failure of the apparatus may be annulled and then only if it is the competitor against whom the hit was registered who is placed at a disadvantage by the failure.

b) The failure must be established by tests made immediately after the bout was stopped, under the supervision of the Referee and without changing anything whatever of the equipment in use.

c) With these tests, one is trying only to establish whether there is **material possibility** of a mistake in the judgement as a result of a fault. **The location of this fault** in the electrical equipment, including that of either of the fencers, is unimportant in reaching a decision.

d) A competitor who makes any **modification** in, or **changes** his equipment without being asked by the Referee to do so, before a judgement is pronounced, loses his right to the annulment of the hit (cf. t.35.2.d). Similarly, after again coming on guard and after the bout has effectively recommenced, a competitor cannot claim the annulment of a hit registered against him before the said recommencement of the bout.

a. 如果刺中运动员护手盘而显示击中的信号，或者刺中金属场地引起裁判器信号显示；

b. 如果显示被击中的运动员完成一次合乎规则的击中，而没有引起裁判器的信号显示；

c. 如果显示被击中信号的运动员一侧裁判器不正常显示，例如：由于对剑的击打，对手的几个动作，或者由于合理击中之外的任何其他原因。

d. 如果显示被击中信号的运动员做出一次击中所产生的信号被对手后来的一次击中所取代；

e. 特殊情况

——如果相互击中包括一次有效击中和一次无效击中（击中对手以外的地方见t.66.1，离开剑道后才击中见t.26ss），只保留有效击中。

——如果相互击中包括一个肯定击中和一个可疑击中（电动设备出故障），由肯定击中的运动员来选择接受或取消相互击中。

t.68. 裁判员还应该执行以下取消击中的规则：

a. 显示被击中的运动员，只有确实是由于器材故障而处于不利地位，才可以要求取消击中剑，而且只取消故障确认前的最后一剑。

b. 如果出现故障，应在比赛暂停后不更换使用器材的情况下，由裁判监督立即进行测试，以确认故障。

c. 测试只是力图确认是否真的存在由于某一故障而出现判断失误的可能性。至于这一故障在整个电动设备中的位置，包括运动员任何一方的个人装备中的位置，都不影响最后判断。

d. 运动员没有经过裁判员的同意，在做出裁决之前就着手改动或调换自己的器材，将失去取消击中的权利（参见t.35.2.d）。同样，在恢复预备姿势和重新开始实际交锋以后，运动员就不能再要求取消重新开始之前自己被击中的一剑 。

e) It is not necessary, in order to justify the annulment of a hit, that **the failure found should repeat itself** each time a test is made, but it is essential that the fault should be observed by the Referee without the possibility of doubt at least once.

f) If the incidents mentioned in Article t.67 occur as a result of the competitor's **bodywire being unplugged** (either near the hand or at the back of the fencer), they cannot justify the annulment of the hit registered.

However, if the safety device prescribed by Article m.55.4 is missing or not functioning, the hit should be annulled if the plug at the fencers' back has become unplugged.

g) The fact that the épée of a competitor has large or small **areas of insulation** formed by oxidation, by glue, paint or any other material on the guard, on the blade or elsewhere, on which his opponent's hits can cause a hit to be signalled, or that the **electric tip** is **badly fixed** to the end of the blade so that it can be unscrewed or tightened by hand, cannot justify the annulment of hits registered against that competitor.

h) When a competitor against whom a hit has been registered has **broken his blade**, the hit must be annulled unless the breaking of the blade has occurred clearly after the hit has been registered.

i) If a competitor **tears the conductive piste** by a hit made on the ground and, at the same time, the apparatus registers a hit against his opponent, the hit must be annulled.

j) Whenever, owing to some accidental cause, tests cannot be made, the hit must be considered as **doubtful** and must be annulled (but cf. t.67.e).

k) The Referee must pay particular attention to hits which **do not register** or which **are registered abnormally**. Should such defects be repeated, the Referee must ask the members of the SEMI Committee present or an expert technician on duty to verify that the equipment conforms to the Rules.

The Referee must ensure that **nothing is altered** either in the competitor's equipment or in the whole of the electrical apparatus before the expert makes the check.

t.69. The Referee must also supervise the **condition of the conductive piste;** he must not allow the bout to commence or to continue if the conductive piste has holes in it which might affect the proper registering of hits or cause accidents. (The organisers must make the necessary arrangements to ensure the rapid repair or replacement of the conductive pistes.)

e. 对于击中的取消来说，确认故障没有必要每次重复测试，但毫无疑问必须至少得到裁判员的一次确认。

f. 如果 t.67 指出的事件是由于运动员手线从接触插头上脱落而发生的（或在运动员手边，或在其背后），就不能取消击中。

然而，如果器材规则 m.55.4 规定的安全装置不起作用或不存在，在运动员背后插头断开情况下，应当取消击中。

g. 护手盘、剑身或其他地方出现一些由氧化物、胶水、油漆或任何一种物质形成的或大或小的绝缘斑点，对手击中这些斑点可能引起信号；同样，剑身顶端的电动剑头固定不牢，使人可以用手拧紧或拧松，这些不能成为理由来取消运动员已被记录的击中。

h. 显示被击中信号的运动员剑身断裂，这一事实可以作为理由，以取消自己被对手的击中，除非明显记录击中以后剑身才断裂。

i. 如果某一运动员在刺中地面后刺破金属场地，同时裁判器显示其击中对方，击中应取消。

j. 只要因偶然情况而不可进行检查时，击中将被视作可疑，并被取消。（参见 t.67.e）

k. 裁判员应十分注意裁判器没有显示或异常显示的击中。在这些故障重复出现的情况下，裁判员应求助于在场的器材委员会（SEMI）成员，或一名专职的技术专家，以核查器材是否符合规则。

在专家检查之前，裁判员应当注意，无论运动员装备还是电动设备都不能有任何改变。

t.69. 此外裁判员还应当注意金属场地的状况；如果场地有洞，可能扰乱信号或引起事故，将不准许比赛开始或继续进行（组织者应采取必要措施，以便能够迅速维修或迅速更换金属场地）。

PART 4. SABRE

THE CONVENTIONS OF FENCING

METHOD OF MAKING A HIT

t.70. **1.** The sabre is a weapon for **thrusting** and **cutting** with both the **cutting edge** and the **back** of the blade.

2. All hits made with the **cutting edge,** the **flat** or the **back** of the blade are counted as good (cuts and back-cuts).

3. It is forbidden to **hit with the guard**. Any hits registered by hitting with the guard must be annulled, the fencer so hitting being penalised as specified in Articles t.114, t.116, t.120.

4. Hits **through the blade**, that is to say those which touch at the same time the valid target and the sabre of the opponent, are valid whenever they arrive clearly on the target.

5. **Placing the weapon on the piste** at any time to **straighten** it is forbidden. Any breaking of this rule will be punished according to Articles t.114, t.116, t.120.

THE TARGET

t.71. Only hits which arrive on the target are counted as valid.

The **target** comprises any part of the body above a horizontal line drawn between the top of the hip bones and then horizontally round the fencer's trunk (see Figure 6).

Figure 6 Valid target at sabre

This diagram is for guidance purposes only.

In case of any doubt the wording of the appropriate text takes precedence

第四部分 佩剑
交锋协定

击中的方法

t.70. 1. 佩剑是一种使用刺击、劈砍技术的武器，可使用剑刃和剑背。

2. 用剑刃、扁平部分或剑背做出的任何劈打都算击中（正劈和反劈）。

3. 禁止使用护手盘劈打。因护手盘劈打而产生的一切击中均应被取消，做出这一动作的运动员将受到t.114、t.116、t.120规定的处罚。

4. 通过剑身的劈打，是指劈打时同时碰到对手的有效部位和剑，只要是明显击中有效部位，就算有效。

5. 任何比赛时间都禁止在剑道上矫正武器。任何犯规行为将根据 t.114、t.116、t.120规定受到处罚。

有效部位

t.71. 只有击中有效部位才能得分。

有效部位包括连接髋骨顶端并水平环绕于运动员躯干的水平线之上的任何身体部位（图6）。

图6 佩剑有效部位

以上图示只用作示意，如有任何的疑虑，
以相关文字描述为准。

t.72. **1.** A hit which arrives on a **non-valid part** of the target is not counted as a hit; it does not stop the fencing phrase and does not annul any subsequent hits.

2. If a fencer **substitutes a non-valid part of his target for a valid part**, either by covering it or by any abnormal movement, the Referee must penalise him by applying the penalties specified in Articles t.114, t.116, t.120, and any hit scored by the fencer at fault is annulled.

JUDGING OF HITS AT SABRE

Materiality and Annulment of Hits

t.73. Competitions at sabre are judged with the help of an **electric apparatus registering hits.**

1. To judge the materiality of a hit, **only hits signalled by the registering apparatus** may be taken into account. The Referee cannot award a hit unless it has been properly registered by the apparatus, except for penalty hits. He will not take account of hits scored by movements started before 'Play!' or after 'Halt!' (cf. t.18.1–3).

2. However, the Referee must take into account any **possible malfunctions** in the electrical equipment; in particular he must **annul a hit** he has just awarded in accordance with a signal from the apparatus if it can be established, by tests carried out under his attentive supervision, before the bout **has effectively re-started** and with no changes having been made to the equipment (cf. t.35.2.d):

— that a hit made by the fencer judged to have been hit **does not cause the apparatus to register**;

— that a hit made by the fencer judged to have been hit **does not remain fixed** on the apparatus;

— that the **signal of a hit** against the fencer judged to have been hit can be produced either without there having been in fact a valid hit, or by a hit on the weapon or on a non-valid surface.

3. If the **sabre** of the fencer judged to have been hit **does not conform** with Article m.24.6–8 (insulation of the interior and exterior of the guard, of the handle and of the pommel), there will be no annulment, even if a hit on the weapon causes a signal to register.

4. The Referee should also apply the following rules:

a) **Only the last hit** made before the fault was established can be annulled.

b) A competitor who makes any **modification to** or who **changes** his equipment without being asked by the Referee to do so, before the Referee has given his decision, loses all right to the annulment of the hit (cf. t.35.2.d).

t.72. 1. 击中了有效部位以外的地方，不算击中；不能因此停止一系列交锋，随后的击中也不取消。

2. 如果运动员通过遮掩或者不正常动作，用无效部位取代有效部位，裁判将按 t.114、t.116、t.120 的规定对其进行处罚，犯规队员做出的击中将被判定为无效。

击中的判断

击中的事实认定及其取消

t.73. 佩剑比赛由一种记录击中的电动裁判器辅助判决。

1. 击中只能以裁判器显示为准。如果裁判器不显示击中信号，裁判员就不能判决某运动员被击中，罚剑情况除外。“开始”前和“停”后的击中也同样不被认可（参见 t.18.1/3）。

2. 裁判员应该重视电动器材可能发生的故障，尤其是在任何重新实际交锋之前，且场上器材没有任何更换时，在裁判认真监督下进行测试后，确认有以下情况，他应当把自己在裁判器显示击中信号后刚刚认可的一次击中取消。（参 t.30.2.d）

—— 宣布被击中的运动员做出一击，但没有引起“击中”信号；

—— 宣布被击中的运动员引起的击中信号在裁判器上未保持稳定；

—— 显示被击中的运动员实际上没有被击中，或者其信号是由于碰到剑或者打在无效部位上而产生的。

3. 如果宣布被击中的运动员的剑不符合器材规则 m.24.6/7/8 的规定（护手盘内外侧、手柄及其剑头的内外部分应当绝缘），即使击中剑身而引起信号，击中也将不被取消。

4. 裁判员还应当执行下列规则：

a. **只有在确认故障前的最后一次击中可以取消；**

b. 运动员如果未经裁判员的同意在其做出裁决之前着手改动或更换自己的器材，就将失去取消击中的一切权利（参见 t.35.2.d）；

c) If the bout has **effectively recommenced**, a competitor cannot claim the annulment of a hit awarded against him before the said recommencement of the bout.

d) The **location of a fault** in the equipment (including the equipment of the competitors) has no bearing on whether or not a hit should be annulled.

e) It is not necessary that a fault should **repeat itself every time** a test is made; but it is essential that the fault should be observed by the Referee without the possibility of doubt at least once during the tests made by him or under his supervision.

f) When a competitor against whom a hit has been registered has **broken his blade**, the hit must be annulled unless the breaking of the blade has occurred clearly after the hit has been registered.

g) The Referee must pay particular attention to hits which **do not register** or are **registered abnormally**. Should such defects be repeated, the Referee must ask a member of the SEMI Committee or an expert technician on duty to verify that the equipment conforms to the Rules.

h) Whenever accidental causes make it impossible to carry out tests, the hit will be considered **doubtful** and therefore annulled.

i) If there are signals on **both sides of the apparatus**, the Referee will apply the rules in Article t.80.

j) In accordance with the general rules (cf. t.18.5) the Referee must **stop the bout**, even if no hit is registered on the apparatus, whenever the fencing becomes **confused** and he is no longer able to analyse the phrase.

VALIDITY OR PRIORITY OF THE HIT

Preface

t.74. The Referee **alone** decides as to the validity or the priority of the hit by applying the following basic rules which are the conventions applicable to sabre fencing.

Respect of the fencing phrase

t.75. 1. **Any attack properly executed** (cf. t.7) must be parried, or completely avoided, and the phrase must be continuous.

2. The attack is **correctly carried out** when the straightening of the arm, with the point or the cutting edge continuously threatening the valid target, precedes the initiation of the lunge.

c. 如果实际交锋已重新开始，运动员就不能再要求取消重新开始之前已被确认的被击中的一剑；

d. 在设备中（包括运动员自己的器材）发现缺陷的地方，对于可能发生的取消击中无关紧要；

e. 为确认故障，没有必要每次重复试验；但毫无疑问该故障必须至少一次得到裁判的亲自确认，试验过程由他自己或在他指挥下进行；

f. 显示被击中信号的运动员如果碰巧折断其剑身，可以因此取消对手对他的击中，除非剑身断裂明显在记录击中之后；

g. 裁判员应十分注意裁判器未显示或异常显示的击中情况。在这些故障重复出现的情况下，裁判应当向在场的器材委员会成员或专职技术专家求助，以便检查器材是否符合规则。

h. 由于意外情况而不可能进行检查时，击中将被视为可疑，从而被取消；

i. 如果裁判器两侧均显示信号，裁判将执行 t.80 的规定；

j. 在执行规则（参阅 t.18.5）时，即使无任何信号被记录下来，只要交锋一变混乱，使裁判无法分析一系列交锋时，他就应当停止交锋。

击中的有效性和优先性

前言

t.74. 裁判员应根据以下有关佩剑比赛的专项比赛规则，独立裁决击中剑的有效性或优先权。

交锋的准则

t.75. 1. 任何正确完成的进攻（参 t.7）应当被防守或完全避开，一系列交锋应该连贯。

2. 进攻的正确做法是，伸出手臂，在发动弓步进攻前用剑尖或剑刃连续威胁有效部位。

3. **An attack with a lunge is correctly carried out:**

   a) in a **simple attack** (Cf. t.8.1) when the beginning of the straightening of the arm precedes the launching of the lunge and the hit arrives at the latest when the front foot hits the piste;

   b) in a **compound attack** (Cf. t.8.1) when the beginning of the straightening of the arm, on the first feint (Cf. t.77.1), precedes the launching of the lunge and the hit arrives at the latest when the front foot hits the piste.

4. **An attack with a step-forward-lunge** is correctly carried out:

   a) in a **simple attack** (Cf. t.8.1) when the beginning of the straightening of the arm precedes the step-forward and when the hit arrives at the latest when the front foot hits the piste;

   b) in a **compound attack** (Cf. t.8.1) when the beginning of the straightening of the arm for the first feint (Cf. t.77.1) precedes the step-forward, followed by the lunge, and the hit arrives at the latest when the front foot hits the piste.

5. **The fleche and any forward movement** in which the rear foot completely passes the front foot is forbidden. Any offence will be penalised as specified for penalties in the 1st group (cf. t.114, t.116 et t.120). Any hit scored by the fencer at fault will be annulled. However, any hit correctly executed by his opponent is valid.

t.76. In order to judge as to the correctness of an attack the following points must be considered:

   a) If the attack is initiated when **the opponent has his point 'in line'** (cf. t.10) the attacker must first deflect his opponent's weapon. Referees must ensure that a mere contact of the blades is not considered as sufficient to deflect the opponent's blade.

   b) If, when attempting to find the opponent's blade to deflect it, the blade is not found **(dérobement)**, the right of attack passes to the opponent.

   c) If the attack is commenced when the **opponent's blade is not 'in line'**, the attack may be completed either direct, or by a disengagement or by a cutover, or else be preceded by feints (cf. t.77.1) which oblige the opponent to parry.

t.77. 1. In **compound attacks** the feint must be correctly carried out, i.e.:

   a) A **feint with the point**, with the arm straightened and the point threatening the target continuously.

   b) A **feint with a cut**, the arm straightened, the blade and the arm forming an obtuse angle of about 135°, with the cutting edge threatening a valid part of the target.

3. 弓步进攻的正确做法是：

a. 如果是简单进攻（参阅 t.8.1），即在发动弓步之前伸出手臂，最迟在前脚着地时劈刺击中；

b. 如果是复杂进攻（参阅 t.8.1），即在发动弓步之前，做出第一个假动作（参阅 t.77.1）时，伸出手臂，最迟在前脚着地时劈刺击中。

4. 向前一步弓步进攻的正确做法是：

a. 如果是简单进攻（参阅 t.8.1），即在向前一步之前伸出手臂，最迟在前脚着地时劈刺击中；

b. 如果是复杂进攻（参阅 t.8.1），即在做出第一个假动作时，伸出手臂，接着向前一步，之后弓步，最迟在前脚着地时劈刺击中。

5. 在向前移动、做弓步或任何向前的动作时，禁止后脚超过前脚。任何犯规都将受到第一组处罚（参见 t.114、t.116、t.120 规定）。犯规运动员可能完成的击中将被取消。相反，对手正确完成的击中将有效。

t.76. 为判断一次进攻正确与否，必须考虑到以下情况：

a. 如果发动进攻时，对手正处于“击剑线”姿势（参阅 t.10），进攻者应预先打开对手的剑。裁判们应当十分注意，如果只是轻擦了一下剑，不应视为足以打开对手剑。

b. 如果在寻找对手的剑以便打开它时，并没有碰到对手剑（已避开），动作的优先权转移到对方。

c. 如果在对手不处于“击剑线”姿势时发动进攻，可以运用直接进攻、转移进攻、交叉进攻，或在进攻前使用假动作（参阅 t.77.1），迫使对方防守。

t.77. 1. 在复杂进攻中，应当正确做出假动作，即：

a. 剑尖劈刺假动作：手臂伸出，剑尖连续威胁有效部位；

b. 剑刃劈打假动作：手臂伸出，剑身和手臂形成一个135° 左右的钝角，剑刃威胁有效部位。

2. If during a compound attack the opponent **finds the blade during one of the feints**, he has the right to riposte.

3. In a compound attack the opponent has the right to stop-hit; but, in order to be valid, the stop hit must precede the last movement of the attack by one period of fencing time, i.e. the **stop hit** must arrive before the attacker has started the last movement of the attack itself.

t.78. **Attacks by beats** on the blade:

a) In an attack by beating on the blade, the attack is correctly carried out and retains its priority when the beat is made on the **foible** of the opponent's blade, i.e. the two-thirds of the blade furthest from the guard.

b) In an attack by beating on the blade, when the beat is made on the **forte** of the opponent's blade, i.e. the one-third of the blade nearest the guard, the attack is badly executed and the beat gives the opponent the right to an immediate riposte.

t.79. 1. The parry gives the right to **riposte**; a simple riposte may be direct or indirect, but in order to annul any subsequent movement by the attacker, it must be carried out immediately, without any hesitation or pause.

2. Against cuts with the **cutting edge**, the **flat** or the **back** of the blade, the object of the parry is to prevent hits made by the opponent arriving on the valid target; therefore:

a) The parry is **properly carried out** when, before the completion of the attack, it prevents the arrival of that attack by closing the line in which that attack is to finish.

b) When a parry is properly executed, the attack by the opponent must be declared parried, and judged as such by the Referee, even if, **as a result of its flexibility**, the tip of the opponent's weapon makes contact with the target.

Judging of hits

t.80. In applying these basic conventions of sabre fencing, the Referee should judge as follows.

1. When during a phrase both fencers are hit simultaneously there is either a **simultaneous action** or a **double hit**:

The simultaneous action is due to simultaneous conception and execution of an attack by both fencers; in this case the hits exchanged are annulled for both fencers.

2. The double hit (coup double) on the other hand, is the result of a clearly faulty action on the part of one of the fencers.

Therefore, when there is not an interval of fencing time between the hits:

2. 在一次复杂进攻中，如果有一个假动作让对手碰到了武器，对手有权还击。

3. 在一次复杂进攻中，对手有权反攻，但是反攻必须提前于进攻的最终动作一个击剑时间，即反攻必须在进攻者已经开始的进攻最后一个动作终止之前击中。

t.78. 击打进攻：

a. 在击打进攻中，正确且保持其优先权的做法是，击打在对手剑的弱部，即剑身的上方2/3部位；

b. 在击打进攻中，错误的做法是，击打在对手剑的强部，即剑身下方1/3部位，同时对手因此得到了及时还击的优先权。

t.79. 1. 防守时有权还击；简单还击可以是直接的，也可以是间接的，但是为了取消进攻者随后的任何动作，必须立即、毫不犹豫或没有停顿时间地做出还击。

2. 对于正劈、反劈和平劈的防守，其目的在于阻止对手向自己有效部位做出劈打的击中，因此：

a. 防守的正确做法是，在对手攻击的最后动作之前，关闭相应的线，使得该攻击动作不得不结束，从而阻止对手劈刺的命中；

b. 当正确完成防守时，即使对手攻击的剑身顶端因其柔韧性已触及了有效部位，裁判必须宣布并判决攻击动作已被防开。

判断击中

t.80. 在执行佩剑的这些基本规则时，裁判应作如下判断：

1. 在一系列交锋中，当双方运动员同时被击中时，可以是“同时动作”，也可以是“相互击中”。

同时动作因双方运动员进攻的同时想法和同时动作而产生；在这种情况下，两人的命中均被取消。

2. 相反，相互击中则是某一运动员一个明显错误动作的结果。

因此，在两次击中之间没有一个击剑时间，判断如下：

3. **The fencer who is attacked** is alone counted as hit:

   a) If he makes a **stop hit** on his opponent's simple attack;

   b) If, instead of parrying, he attempts to **avoid** the hit and does not succeed in so doing;

   c) If, after making a successful parry, he makes a **momentary pause** (delayed riposte) which gives his opponent the right to renew the attack (redoublement, or remise or reprise);

   d) If, during a compound attack, he makes **a stop hit** without being in time;

   e) If, having his **point 'in line'** (cf. t.10) and being subjected to a beat or a taking of the blade (prise de fer) which deflects his blade, he attacks or places his point in line again instead of parrying a direct hit made by his opponent.

4. **The fencer who attacks is alone counted as hit:**

   a) If he initiated his attack when **his opponent had his point 'in line',** without deflecting the opponent's weapon. Referees must ensure that a mere contact of the blades is not considered as sufficient to deflect the opponent's blade.

   b) If he attempts to find the blade, does not succeed (because of a **derobement**) and continues the attack.

   c) If, during a compound attack, he allows his opponent to **find the blade**, and continues the attack while his opponent ripostes immediately.

   d) If, during a compound attack, he **bends his arm** or makes a **momentary pause**, during which time the opponent makes a stop hit or an attack while the attacker continues his own attack.

   e) If, during a compound attack, he is **stop-hit** one period of fencing time (temps d'escrime) before he makes his final movement.

   f) If he makes a hit by a remise, redoublement or reprise following a **parry by his opponent** which has been followed by a riposte which is immediate, simple and executed in one period of fencing time without withdrawing the arm.

5. When there is a double hit (coup double), and if the Referee is unable clearly to judge from which side the fault has come, **he must replace the competitors on guard**.

   One of the most difficult cases to judge arises when a stop hit is made and there is doubt as to whether it was made sufficiently in time in relation to the final movement of a compound attack. Generally, in such cases, the double hit occurs through the fault of both fencers concerned, which justifies the Referee replacing them on guard. (The fault of the attacker consists of indecision, slowness of execution or the making of feints which are not sufficiently effective. The fault of the defender lies in delay or slowness in making the stop hit.)

3. 被进攻者一方被击中：

a. 如果他对一个简单进攻进行反攻；

b. 本应防守，但是他却尽力躲闪，而没有成功；

c. 如果在一次防守成功以后，他停顿了片刻（不及时还击），便给了对手重新进攻的权力（连续、延续或重新进攻）；

d. 如果他对一个复杂进攻进行反攻，但没有一个击剑时间的优势；

e. 如果他处于“击剑线”姿势（参阅 t.10），在受到一次击打或者对手的剑打开自己的剑以后，他没有对进攻者做出的直接劈刺进行防守，而是出手进攻，或是重新提剑处于“击剑线”。

4. 进攻者一方被击中：

a. 当对手处于“击剑线”姿势（参阅 t.10）时，他没有打开对手的剑就发起进攻。裁判应特别注意，若只是轻擦一下，便不能视之为足以打开对手剑。

b. 如果他寻找对手的剑却未碰到（因为被避开），且继续进攻；

c. 如果在一次复杂进攻过程中，对手碰到剑时，他继续进攻而对手立即给予还击；

d. 如果在一次复杂进攻中，他手臂回收了一下或犹豫了片刻，此时对手做出反攻劈刺或进攻，而他却继续自己的动作；

e. 如果在一次复杂进攻中，他在做出最后一个动作前一个击剑时间之前，被对方击中；

f. 如果他对于对手的防守采取延续、连续或重新进攻并击中，而对手在防守以后在同一时间内进行直接、简单的还击，且没有回收手臂。

5. 在相互击中的情况下，每当主裁判不能明显判断哪一方有错时，则双方运动员恢复预备姿势。

最难判断的情况之一，就是一个反攻击中可能令人怀疑其对于复杂进攻的最后动作是否有足够优势。通常在这种情况下，双方运动员的一次同时错误导致了相互击中，从而不得不恢复预备姿势。这时进攻者的错误在于犹豫不决、缓慢迟钝或假动作不奏效，被进攻者错误在于反攻击中延迟或缓慢。

PART 5. DISCIPLINARY RULES
FOR COMPETITIONS[1]

CHAPTER 1. APPLICATION

PERSONS SUBJECT TO THESE RULES

t.81. **1.** The regulations laid down in this Part apply to **all persons** who take part in or attend a fencing competition, including the spectators.

2. In the following articles, all these persons are referred to as **fencers.**

MAINTENANCE OF ORDER AND DISCIPLINE

t.82. **1.** Fencers must **observe strictly and faithfully** the Rules and the Statutes of the FIE, the particular rules for the competition in which they are engaged, the traditional customs of courtesy and integrity and the instructions of the officials.

2. In particular they will subscribe, in an **orderly, disciplined and sporting manner**, to the following provisions; all breaches of these rules may entail punishments by the competent disciplinary authorities after, or even without, prior warning, according to the facts and circumstances (cf. t.113–t.120).

3. **a)** Everybody taking part in or present at a fencing competition must **remain orderly and must not disturb the smooth running** of the competition. During bouts no one is allowed to **go near the pistes**, to **give advice to the fencers**, to **criticise the Referee** or the judges, to insult them or to attempt to influence them in any way. Even the **team captain** must remain in the space assigned to him and he may only intervene in the situations and in the manner provided for in Article t.90 of the Rules. The Referee must stop immediately any activity which disturbs the smooth running of the bout which he is refereeing (cf. t.96.1–3).

b) Any person who, for any reason, threatens or insults an official commits an offence of the 4th group and is penalised according to article t.119.

4. **Smoking** in competition halls is forbidden. Smoking will be considered as a disturbance of the smooth running of the competition (cf. t.83).

Any breach of these rules will be punished as laid down in Articles t.114, t.118, t.120.

---

1 The penalties relating to the Publicity Code appear in that appendix.

第五部分　纪律规则

第一章　适用范围

适用对象

t.81. 1. 本篇的规定适用于所有参加或出席击剑比赛的人员，包括观众。

2. 所有这些人员在以下条款中一律被称为“击剑者”。

秩序和纪律的维护

t.82. 1. 击剑者必须严格、忠实地执行国际剑联的规则及章程，所参加比赛的具体规则，基于礼仪与忠实的传统准则和官方指令。

2. 尤其是在遵守秩序和纪律、发扬体育精神的同时，他们应服从以下规定，对任何违反规则的行为，主管纪律的机构将根据情况和环境，在给予警告或甚至不用事先警告，给予处罚（参阅 t.113 ~ t.120）。

3. a）所有参加或出席一场击剑比赛的人员，必须遵守秩序，不得扰乱比赛的正常进行。比赛过程中，任何人都不准走近剑道、为运动员出主意，不准批评或辱骂主裁判或助理裁判，不准以任何方式纠缠他们。甚至队长也必须坐在指定的座位上，只有在规则 t.90中规定的情况下，他才能以规定方式介入比赛。裁判有责任立即制止扰乱比赛正常进行的一切行为（参阅 t.96.1/3）。

b）所有人无论任何原因，威胁或侮辱官员，即犯了第4组错误，将受到 t.119惩罚。

4. 禁止在比赛大厅内吸烟。吸烟行为将被视为扰乱比赛秩序的行为（参阅 t.83）。任何违规行为将受到 t.114、t.118、t.120的处罚。

t.83. The Referee and/or the Directoire Technique, on their own authority or at the request of an official delegate of the FIE or of the Organising Committee, can decide to **expel from the competition venue**, with or without a warning, any person who by his gestures, attitude or language disturbs the good order or smooth running of the event.

THE COMPETITORS

Pledge of honour

t.84. By the mere fact of entering a fencing competition, the fencers **pledge their honour** to observe the Rules and the decisions of the officials, to be respectful towards the referees and judges and scrupulously to obey the orders and injunctions of the Referee (cf. t.114, t.116, t.120).

Refusing to fence an opponent

t.85. **1.** No fencer (individual or team) from an FIE member national federation may take part in an official competition if he **refuses to fence** against any other fencer whatsoever (individual or team) correctly entered in the event. Should this rule be broken, the penalties specified for offences of the 4th group will be applied (cf. t.114, t.119, t.120).

2. **The FIE** shall consider whether there are grounds, and to what extent, for taking sanctions against the national federation to which the disqualified competitor belongs (cf. FIE Statutes 1.2.4 and Rules Article t.120).

Presence on time

t.86. **1.** The fencers, completely equipped, with all equipment conforming with the regulations (cf. t.43–t.45) and ready to fence, must **be present at the time and place** appointed for the beginning of the pool, match, or bout of direct elimination, or at the time appointed for the checking of their equipment before their bout (cf. t.43.1–3), as well as during the competition, whenever the Referee requires it.

2. When presenting themselves to fence a bout, the fencers must arrive on the piste **completely ready to fence** — regulation clothing, jacket fastened, sword-hand gloved and holding the weapon, bodywire connected to the plug inside the guard. The mask should be carried in the unarmed hand.

Before the start of the bout, the fencers' hair must be fastened and placed inside the clothing and/or mask in such a way as to ensure that:

— it does not cover a valid surface (and thus prevent a hit from being scored).

— it does not conceal the name and nationality of the fencer.

— it does not need to be put back in place during the bout, thus interrupting it.

t.83. 主裁判和（或）技术委员会，可以自行决定或在国际剑联、组委会一名正式代表的要求下，警告或不事先警告，决定将任何以动作、姿势或语言干扰比赛正常进行或比赛秩序的人驱逐出比赛地点。

运动员

承诺

t.84. 只要运动员报名参加击剑比赛，他们便应承诺遵守规则和官方决定，尊重主裁判和助理裁判，严格服从主裁判的命令和指挥（参阅 t.114、t.116、t.120）。

拒绝与某一对手交锋

t.85. 1. 如果会员协会的任何一名击剑运动员（个人或团体）在参加正式比赛时拒绝与任何一名正式报名参赛的运动员（个人或团体）交锋，该运动员（个人或团体）将立即被取消比赛资格。这种行为将受到第四组犯规处罚（参见 t.114、t.119、t.120）。

2. 国际剑联将考虑是否有必要、何种程度上对被取消参赛资格的运动员所属的会员协会进行处罚（参阅国际剑联章程 1.2.4、t.120）。

准时到场

t.86. 1. 在完全装备好一套符合规则（参阅 t.43 ~ t.45）的器材并做好上场准备后，击剑者必须在小组循环赛、团体相遇或直接淘汰赛开始之前、在预定的赛前器材检查时间之前、以及在比赛过程中应裁判员要求，准时到达规定地点（参阅 t.43.1/2/3）。

2. 比赛开始前作介绍时，运动员要出现在剑道上完全做好比赛的准备：身着符合规定的服装，比赛服拉链拉好，持剑手佩戴手套，手拿武器，手线与护手盘内的插座插好。护面应拿在非持剑手中。

比赛开始前，运动员的头发要以合适的方式放在比赛服或护面里，以便：
—— 不能遮挡有效部位（影响击中）；
—— 不能遮挡运动员的姓名及国籍；
—— 不能因为在比赛过程中整理头发，而打断比赛。

In the case of violation of this rule, the referee will apply the penalties for group 1 offences (t.114, t.116, t.120).

3. Under no circumstances should the fencers **dress or undress in public** except in the case of an accident duly recognised by the doctor on duty or by the representative of the Medical Commission (cf. t.87.8, t.114, t.116, t.120).

4. The fencers must arrive on the piste, to fence their bouts, with **two weapons** (one as a spare), **two bodywires** (one as a spare) and two mask wires (one as a spare) which satisfy the regulations and are in perfect working order(cf. t.45.1, t.114, t.116, t.120).

5. **Before the start of the pool, the team match or the bouts of direct elimination (individual or team):**

   i) When a fencer or complete team **do not present themselves** to the Referee **at his first call**, ten minutes before the time indicated to come onto the piste for the start of the pool or team match, or the start of the bouts of direct elimination (cf. Article t.43.2), the fencer or team concerned will be **eliminated**.

   ii) **A team** is considered complete when at least three fencers are present.

   iii) In a team match only those members of the team (the fencers, the team captain and one trainer — cf. Article t.92.4) who are **present at the Referee's first call**, ten minutes before the time indicated for the start of the match, may take part in the match.

6. **During a competition, individual or team**, if a fencer **does not present himself** on the piste, ready to fence, when ordered to do so by the Referee:

   — The fencer or team member not present will be penalised with a **Yellow Card**;

   — A second call will be made, one minute after the first call, followed by a **Red Card** for the fencer or team member not present;

   — A third and last call will be made, one minute after the second call, followed by **elimination from the competition** for the fencer not present in an individual competition or for the whole team in a team competition.

7. Should a fencer **abandon a bout** by leaving the piste (cf. t.18.6), he will be penalised as specified in Articles t.114, t.116, t.120.

如果出现违规，裁判员将给予第一组违规处罚（参见 t.114、t.116、t.120）。

3. 任何情况下，运动员不能当众穿脱服装，除非是比赛医生和医疗委员会代表决定的意外情况（参见 t.87.8、t.114、t.116、t.120）。

4. 运动员应各自携带两支剑（一支备用）、两根合格的手线（一根备用）、两根头线（一根备用）到场，这些器材都应当完全运行正常（参阅 t.45.1、t.114、t.116、t.120）。

5. 在小组赛、团体赛或者直接淘汰赛（个人或团体）比赛前：

i）当主裁判在小组循环赛、团体相遇或直接淘汰赛开始前的10分钟点名时，如果运动员或全体团体赛成员没有按时到达，裁判员将取消其参赛资格。

ii）团体队伍至少有3名运动员到场，方可被认为完整。

iii）团体赛只允许比赛正式开始前10分钟裁判员第一次点名时到场的成 员参加（运动员、队长及一名教练，参见 t.92.4）。

6. 个人赛或团体赛比赛过程中：
在比赛过程中（团体或个人）,裁判员下指令时，运动员未能出现在剑道上，做好比赛的准备：
—— 未能出现的运动员或团体将受到黄牌处罚；
—— 在间隔1分钟后，再次点名，如仍未到场，则给予团队或个人红牌处罚；
—— 第三次即最后一次点名是在第二次点名后1分钟，如个人或团体仍旧未能到场比赛，裁判员将取消其个人或团体的参赛资格；

7. 如运动员离开比赛剑道放弃比赛（参见 t.18.6），将按照规则 t.114、t.116、t.120进行处罚。

Fencing etiquette

t.87. **1.** The competitors must fence **faithfully** and strictly **according to the rules** laid down in these Rules. All breaches of these rules will incur the penalties laid down hereinafter (cf. t.114–t.120).

2. All bouts must preserve the **character of a courteous and frank encounter**. All **irregular actions** (flèche attack which finishes with a collision jostling the opponent, disorderly fencing, irregular movements on the piste, hits achieved with violence, blows struck with the guard, hits made during or after a fall) or anti-sporting behaviour are strictly forbidden (cf. t.114–t.120). Should such an offence occur, any hit scored by the fencer at fault is annulled.

3. **a)** Before the beginning of each bout, the two fencers must perform **a fencer's salute** to their opponent, to the Referee and to the spectators. Equally, when the final hit has been scored, the bout has not ended until the two fencers have saluted each other, the Referee and the spectators: to this end, they must remain still while the referee is making his decision; when he has given his decision, they must return to their on-guard line, perform a fencer's salute and shake hands with their opponent. If either or both of the two fencers refuse to comply with these rules, the Referee will penalise him/them as specified for offences of the 4th group (cf. t.114, t.119, t.120).

b) During or after a bout**,** even if the fencer has already left the piste, any act against the spirit of sportsmanship such as violently or dangerously throwing one's mask (or any other piece of equipment) will be penalised as specified in article t.119 (c.f. t.82.1, 2 and 3).

4. When both fencers make clear their unwillingness to fight, the Referee will immediately call 'Halt!'

Unwillingness to fight (non-combativity)

If one of the two criteria below is present, there is unwillingness to fight:

1. criterion of time : approximately one minute of fencing without a hit

2. excessive distance (greater than the distance of a step-forward-lunge) during at least 15 seconds.

5. Individual events

a) If during the **first two periods** of a direct elimination bout both fencers make clear their unwillingness to fight, the Referee will proceed to the next period, without the minute rest.

击剑礼仪

t.87. 1. 运动员应当严格地遵守现行规则中的各条款进行交锋。任何违背这些规则的行为将使他们受到以下条款规定的处罚（参阅 t.114~ t.120）。

2. 所有比赛均应保持礼貌和忠实的原则。明确禁止任何异常行为（参阅 t.114 ~ t.120），比如：冲刺结束时挤撞对手；混乱动作；反常移动；粗暴劈刺；护手盘劈刺；跌倒时或跌倒后击中或违反体育道德的行为。如发生这类犯规行为，犯规运动员可能击中的一剑将被取消。

3. a）在一场比赛开始前，双方运动员应当向各自的对手、裁判及观众行击剑礼。同样的，当最后一剑打出后，只有在裁判已经给出判决意见，双方运动员回到开始位置并向对手、裁判及观众行击剑礼才标志着比赛的结束。在裁判做决定期间，运动员不可以擅自移动到开始线的位置，提前与对手行礼及握手。如果双方运动员不服从此规则，将受到第四组规定的处罚（参阅 t.114、t.119、t.120）。

b）一场比赛进行期间或结束后，即便运动员已经离开剑道，其所实施的违反体育道德的行为，例如：粗暴地或危险地扔掉面罩（或其他任何器材装备），该运动员将受到 t.119 规定的处罚（参见 t.82.1/2/3）。

4. 如果双方运动员表现出“消极比赛”，裁判应立即喊“停！”

消极比赛

出现以下两种情况中的任意一种，即为消极比赛：

（1）时间条件：大约有1分钟的比赛无击中。

（2）在至少15秒钟的时间内，双方距离过大（超过向前一步弓步的距离）。

5. 个人赛

a. 在个人赛直接淘汰赛前两局的比赛中，如果双方运动员表现出消极比赛，裁判要求进入下一局的比赛，并且没有1分钟的休息时间。

b) When both fencers make clear their unwillingness to fight during the **third period** of a direct elimination bout, the Referee will proceed to a last minute of fencing. This last minute, which will be fenced in its entirety, will be decisive and will be preceded by a drawing of lots to decide the winner should the scores be equal at the end of the minute.

6. Team events

a) If both teams make clear their unwillingness to fight during a team match, the Referee will proceed to the next bout.

b) If both teams make clear their unwillingness to fight during **the last bout**, the Referee will proceed to a last minute of fencing. This last minute, which will be fenced in its entirety, will be decisive and will be preceded by a drawing of lots to decide the winner should the scores be equal at the end of the minute

7. The fencer, whether on or off the piste, must **keep his mask on** until the Referee calls 'Halt!' He may under no circumstances address the Referee until the Referee has made his decision (cf. t.114, t.116, t.120).

8. Under no circumstances may fencers **remove** clothing on the piste, even to change their bodywire (cf. t.114, t.116, t.120).

9. At the end of a bout, the Referee must bring together the two fencers, **to announce clearly the score**, which will be transmitted to the Directoire Technique. He must say clearly: 'Mister X won against Mister Y with the following score…'

PERSONAL EFFORT

t.88. Competitors must **fence to their utmost ability** in a sportsmanlike manner until the end of the competition in order to obtain the best possible classification, without giving away hits or seeking to be favoured by being given hits by anyone (cf. t.114, t.119, t.120).

The team manager

t.89. In all competitions, all competitors of the same nationality must be under the direction of a **team manager** (who may or may not fence), who is responsible to the Directoire Technique or the Organising Committee for the discipline, conduct, and sportsmanship of the members of his team.

b. 如果双方运动员在个人赛直接淘汰赛最后一局的比赛中表现出消极比赛，裁判将抽取优先权并要求进入最后一分钟的比赛。这最后一分钟的比赛将一直打到时间结束。如果结束后出现比分相等的情况，则抽到优先权的一方获胜。

6. 团体赛

a. 如果在团体赛中，双方表现出消极比赛，裁判将要求进入下一局比赛。

b. 如果双方队伍在最后一局的比赛中表现出消极比赛，裁判将抽取优先权并要求进入最后一分钟的比赛。这最后一分钟的比赛将一直打到时间结束。如果结束后出现比分相等的情况，则抽到优先权的一方获胜。

7. 在剑道以内或以外的运动员应当一直戴着面罩，直到裁判发出“停”口令。在任何情况下，他都不能在裁判做出裁决之前干涉裁判（参阅 t.114、t.116、t.120）。

8. 在任何情况下，运动员都不能在剑道上脱衣服，即使是为了更换手线（参阅 t.114、t.116、t.120）。

9. 裁判在比赛结束后，要集合双方运动员，向他们清楚地公布比分，并将成绩单交到技术委员会。他要清晰的宣读“某某以比分……胜某某……”

自身努力

t.88. 运动员应当发扬体育精神，尽自身全力比赛，直至比赛结束，不给任何人让分，也不要求任何人让分，以尽可能取得优异的名次（参阅 t.114、t.119、t.120）。

领队

t.89. 在所有比赛中，同一国籍的运动员必须接受同一名领队（运动员或非运动员）的指挥。在本队纪律、行为和体育道德方面，领队向技术委员会和组委会负责。

The team captain

t.90. In team events, only the **team captain** has the right to be to approach the Referee and/or the refereeing delegates in order to decide with them any technical matters or to register protests. The procedure for claims is set out in articles t.122 and t.123.

The members of the team who have **scrupulously abided by his decisions** may not be held responsible by the relevant authorities. However, they are **personally responsible** for any actions they commit for which their team captain has not taken authority and for any offence committed by them in violation of the present Rules.

The referees and judges

t.91. The members of the jury must fulfil their duties not only with **total impartiality** but also with the **utmost attention** (cf. t.34.1).

The instructors, trainers and technicians

t.92. **1.** During the direct elimination of the individual events, the fencer's **coach, medical staff and technicians** are not allowed to remain near their fencers; **the coaches** are allowed to be inside the competition area in a place indicated by the organisers.

2. The Referee may, whenever he considers it necessary, authorise a person to **come briefly to the assistance** of a fencer.

3. Each nation which has a fencer taking part in the round of the competition in progress may designate a maximum of **two people** who have the right to be positioned near the Piste Enclosure, outside it but close to a point of access. The organisers must provide the necessary space for these people.

4. In team competitions, there must be enclosures reserved for the team members. Only the team captain and one coach have the right to be with the team fencers **inside the Team Enclosures**, which must be clearly marked out by yellow lines on the ground or some other method. They should be at least 9 m^2 in area and be located at a distance of between 2 m and 6 m from each end of and outside the Piste Enclosure, which is 18 m x 8 m.

5. During team matches, the team members not actually fencing must **remain within** their Team Enclosure.

6. During team competitions, no one has the right to **enter the Piste Enclosure** without the Referee's permission. In the case of such an offence, the Referee will penalise the offending team as provided for in Articles t.114, t.116 and t.120. A warning imposed on a team is valid for the complete team match. Should a fencer, within the same match, commit another offence from the First Group, the Referee will penalise him on each occasion with a Red Card.

The spectators

t.93. Spectators are obliged not to **interfere with the good order** of a competition, to do nothing which may tend to influence the fencers or the Referee, and to respect the decisions of the latter even when they do not agree with them. They must obey any instructions which the Referee may deem it necessary to give them (cf. t.82.3/4, t.118, t.120).

队长

t.90. 1. 在团体赛中，只有队长有权与裁判员或裁判代表交涉，解决所有技术问题，或提出抗议。相关程序在 t.122和 t.123中说明。

2. 所有严格服从队长决定的队员，可以不承担相应的责任。然而，除队长参与之外，他们个人将依然对各自的所有行为负责，对自己违反现行规则各条款的所有犯规行为负责。

裁判员和助理裁判员

t.91. 裁判员和助理裁判员必须履行其职责，不仅要绝对公正，而且要严格认真（参阅 t.34.1）。

教练员、队医和技师

t.92. 1. 在个人赛直接淘汰赛中，教练员、队医和技师在比赛过程中不得停留在运动员身边；教练员可以进入竞赛区域内组委会指定的位置。

2. 当裁判认为有必要，他可以允许一名人员对某一运动员给予暂时帮助。

3. 当运动员参加正在进行的比赛时，其参赛国可以共指定两名人员，他们有权在剑道隔离区外面靠近入口处就近坐下。组织者应为这些人员准备必要的位置。

4. 在团体赛时，要准备有团体区域。只有各队队长、一名教练及团体赛运动员才可以进入这片区域。团体区域要用黄线或其他设施明确区分出来，它的面积最少要有9平方米，要在剑道区域18 × 8米以外，并与剑道两端保持2~6米的距离。

5. 在团体比赛中，非比赛运动员要待在各队的等候区内。

6. 在团体比赛中，如果没有裁判员的允许，任何人不得进入剑道区域。如果出现这样的违规，裁判将按照规则 t.114、t.116、t.120处罚。警告处罚在该团队整个比赛期间都有效，如果在同一场团体赛中，运动员再次受到第一组犯规的处罚，则每次犯规都将受到红牌处罚。

观众

t.93. 观众不得干扰比赛的良好秩序，不做任何可能影响运动员或裁判员的事，即使并不赞成裁判员的裁决，也应当尊重。他们应服从裁判员下达的指令（参阅 t.82.3/4、t.118、t.120）。

CHAPTER 2. THE DISCIPLINARY AUTHORITIES AND THEIR COMPETENCE

The following articles only regulate discipline at competition venues. Depending on the gravity of the offences established, they do not exclude the application of the Disciplinary Code of the FIE (Chapter VII of the Statutes of the FIE) which completes or, if the case arises, takes priority over the following articles.

JURISDICTION

t.94. The following are the **competent disciplinary authorities**:

— the Referee (cf. t.96);

— the Directoire Technique (cf. t.97, o.56–o.62);

— the Refereeing Commission delegate(s), or the Supervisor if there is no delegate;

— the Executive Committee of the IOC at the Olympic Games (cf. t.98);

— the Bureau of the FIE (cf. t.99.1/4, t.127.h, o.63);

— the Executive Committee of the FIE (cf. t.99.5);

— the Disciplinary Commission of the FIE and its Tribunal;

— the Court of Arbitration for Sport and the Sports Arbitration Tribunal.

See also Disciplinary Rules of the FIE (Chapter VII of the FIE Statutes).

Principle of jurisdiction

t.95. **1.** Whatever juridical authority has taken a decision, this decision may be subject to an **appeal** to a higher juridical authority, but only to one such appeal.

2. No decision on a question of **fact** can be the subject of an appeal (cf. t.122.1/2).

3. An appeal against a decision only **suspends** that decision when it can be judged immediately.

The Referee

t.96. **1.** The Referee is responsible not only for the direction of the bout, the judging of hits and the checking of equipment, but equally for the **maintenance of order** in the bouts which he is refereeing (cf. t.35.2.i).

2. In his capacity as director of the bout and arbiter of hits, he can, in accordance with the rules, **penalise** the competitors, either by refusing to award a hit which they

第二章　纪律主管机构及其权限

以下条款仅适用于比赛场馆的纪律问题。根据违规的严重性，不排除进一步适用国际剑联纪律准则（国际剑联章程第七章）的可能，该准则完善以下条款，或在事态升级的情况下优先于以下条款。

具有纪律主管权限的机构

t.94. 符合资质的纪律主管机构有：

—— 主裁判（参阅 t.96）；
—— 技术委员会（参阅 t.97，组织规则 o.56~o.62）；
—— 裁判委员会代表，或者观察员（无裁判代表的情况下）；
—— 奥运会的国际奥委会执行委员会（参阅 t.98）；
—— 国际剑联执行局（参阅 t.99.1/4、t.127.h、o.63）；
—— 国际剑联执行委员会（参阅 t.99.5）；
—— 国际剑联纪律委员会及其法庭；
—— 国际体育仲裁法庭（CAS）和体育仲裁法庭。

参见国际剑联纪律准则（国际剑联章程第七章）。

仲裁原则

t.95. 1. 对于任何裁判机构做出的决定，它牵涉的当事人可以向上一级裁判机构提出“上诉”，但只能上诉一次。

2. 任何裁决一经做出，就不能撤消（参阅 t.122.1/2）。

3. 对于某一裁决的申诉，只有在可以立即仲裁的情况下，才可以使该裁决暂停执行。

主裁判

t.96. 1. 主裁判的职责，不仅是指挥比赛，裁决是否击中和检验器材，他还负责他所担任比赛的秩序维持工作（参阅 t.35.2.i）。

2. 作为比赛的指挥者和击中的判决者，主裁判可以依照规则处罚运动员，根据现场情况确定，警告或不事先警告；可以拒绝认可他们确实击中对手的一剑，可以将实际上他们并未被击中的一剑做出处罚，也

have in fact made on the opponent, or by awarding against them a hit which they have not in fact received, or by excluding them from the competition which he is refereeing, all, according to the circumstances, with or without prior warning. In these circumstances, and if he has judged on a matter of **fact**, his decisions are irrevocable (cf. t.122.1/2).

3. By reason of the right of jurisdiction which he has over all the fencers who participate in, or are present at a competition which he is refereeing, he can also **propose** to the Directoire Technique the **expulsion** from the venue of the competition of the spectators, trainers, instructors and other persons who accompany the competitors (cf. t.114, t.118, t.120).

4. Finally, he may **recommend** to the Directoire Technique all other penalties which he considers appropriate (exclusion from the whole competition, suspension or disqualification) (cf. t.97.3).

5. The Refereeing Commission delegate or the Supervisor (if there is no delegate) is the **authority competent to deal with appeals** against the decisions of the Referee.

The Directoire Technique at official FIE competitions (cf. o.56–o.62)

t.97. 1. The **Directoire Technique**, the refereeing delegates or the supervisor have jurisdiction over all the fencers who take part in or are present at a competition which they are running.

2. When necessary they can **intervene on their own initiative** in all disputes.

3. They are also **responsible for maintaining order** and discipline during competitions, and may use the penalties specified in the Rules.

4. The Directoire Technique is responsible for sending direct to the Central Office of **the FIE** announcements of disciplinary penalties pronounced during the competitions, as well as any requests for censure, suspension, extension of penalty or permanent suspension, and requests for ultimate appeals.

5. The Directoire Technique **activates** any penalty imposed against which no appeal is possible or which is not subject to suspension (cf. t.95).

6. The disciplinary decisions of the Directoire Technique, the refereeing delegates or the supervisor that they take spontaneously or in their own right (as the first level of authority) are **subject to appeal** to the Disciplinary Commission of the FIE.

7. All the decisions of the Directoire Technique, the refereeing delegates or the supervisor are **immediately enforceable**. No appeal against a decision can suspend that decision during the competition.

可以把他们开除出他任裁判的这场比赛。在这方面，如果他的裁决已经做出，就不可撤消。

3. 按照主裁判所拥有的权限，对于所有参加或出席他担任裁判的击剑比赛的击剑者，他同样可以向技术委员会建议勒令将观众、医护人员、教练员和其他陪伴运动员的人员清除出比赛场馆（参阅 t.114、t.118、t.120）。

4. 最后他还可向技术委员会提出他认为适当的任何其他处罚建议（开除出整场比赛，停赛或取消比赛资格）（参阅 t.97.3）。

5. 针对主裁判裁决进行的上诉，由裁判委员会代表或观察员（无裁判代表的情况下）处理。

国际剑联正式比赛的技术委员会（参阅组织规则 o.56~o.62）

t.97. 1. 技术委员会、裁判代表或观察员对所有参加或出席由它负责的比赛的击剑者行使裁判权。

2. 必要时，他们可以主动调解所有争端。

3. 他们负责维持比赛的秩序和纪律，并可以根据规则做出处罚。

4. 技术委员会负责向国际剑联总部提交在比赛中宣布的纪律处罚决定，以及任何审查、停赛、扩大处罚、禁赛和向最高裁判机构上诉的请求。

5. 技术委员会对一切不可上诉的处罚或非停赛处罚履行执行权（参阅 t.95）。

6. 对技术委员会、裁判代表或观察员自发或按规定权限（第一级权限）做出的裁决，可以向国际剑联纪律委员会提出上诉。

7. 技术委员会、裁判代表或观察员做出的所有裁决必须立即执行；任何上诉都不能使该裁决在比赛中暂停执行。

THE EXECUTIVE COMMITTEE OF THE IOC AT THE OLYMPIC GAMES

t.98. **The Executive Committee of the International Olympic Committee** (IOC) is the final arbiter for all disputes of a non-technical nature which may arise during the Olympic Games. It may intervene either on its own responsibility, or at the request of a national Olympic Committee, the FIE or the Organising Committee.

FIE Central Office, Disciplinary Commission, Executive Committee, Sports Arbitration Tribunal

t.99. **1.** All disciplinary matters referred to the FIE by a national federation, a Directoire Technique or any other competent body on the occasion of an official FIE competition are addressed to the **Central Office of the FIE**. This latter transmits them to the competent body.

2. **The Disciplinary Commission of the FIE** is the juridical body of the FIE that, within the limits of the territories over which the FIE has authority, settles all disciplinary matters referred to the FIE and judges all appeals against decisions taken by a Directoire Technique, the Refereeing Commission delegate or the Supervisor (if there is no delegate).

3. **The Sports Arbitration Tribunal in Lausanne** (TAS) judges all appeals against the decisions of the tribunals of the Disciplinary Commission.

4. In urgent cases, **the FIE Central Office** may take the administrative measures necessary for the suspension of the licence of the accused in accordance with the Disciplinary Code.

5. **The Executive Committee** ensures that the decisions of the Disciplinary Commission are respected and carried out.

See the Disciplinary Code of the FIE (Chapter VII of the FIE Statutes).

奥运会期间的国际奥委会执行委员会

t.98. 国际奥委会执行委员会终审裁决在奥林匹克运动会期间发生的一切非技术性争端。国际奥委会执委会将依据自身职责，或者应某一国家奥委会、或国际剑联、或者组委会的请求而介入。

国际剑联办公室、纪律委员会、执行委员会及体育仲裁法庭

t.99. 1. 所有由会员协会、技术委员会或任何其他权力机构向国际剑联提交的国际剑联正式比赛期间的纪律事项都应该直接递交国际剑联办公室，并由其转交至相关权力机构。

2. 国际剑联纪律委员会是国际剑联的仲裁机构，在国际剑联管理的范围内，裁决所有提交至国际剑联的纪律事项，以及所有针对技术委员会、裁判委员会代表或观察员（无裁判代表的情况下）的上诉。

3. 洛桑的体育仲裁法庭（TAS）裁决所有针对纪律委员会法庭决定的上诉。

4. 紧急情况下，国际剑联办公室可根据纪律准则采用行政手段吊销被裁决人的执照。

5. 执行委员会确保纪律委员会的决定得到遵守和实施。

参见国际剑联纪律准则（国际剑联章程第七章）。

CHAPTER 3. PENALTIES

CLASSIFICATION OF PENALTIES

t.100. There are distinct **categories** of penalty applicable to different sorts of offence (cf. t.114ss).

1. **Penalties related to fencing**, applicable to offences committed while fencing. These are:

   — the loss of ground on the piste
   — refusal to award a hit actually made
   — awarding a hit which has not in fact been received
   — exclusion from the competition

2. **Disciplinary penalties** applicable to offences concerned with maintenance of order, discipline or sportsmanship. These are:

   — awarding a hit which has not in fact been received
   — exclusion from the competition
   — exclusion from participation in the whole tournament
   — expulsion from the venue of the competition
   — disqualification
   — censure
   — fine
   — temporary suspension
   — permanent suspension

t.101. 1. All these penalties except permanent suspension **can be applied** by the competent authorities at a competition — the Referee and the Directoire Technique.

2. **Temporary suspension** can be applied by these authorities only in the case of a fencer refusing to salute (cf. t.87.3, t.120).

   See the Disciplinary Code of the FIE (Chapter VII of the FIE Statutes).

第三章 处罚

处罚的类别

t.100. 针对不同性质的犯规，有不同类别的处罚（参阅 t.114ss）。

1. 交锋处罚，适用于实战中的犯规，有以下几点：
—— 在剑道上失去场地；
—— 拒绝承认事实上已经击中的一剑；
—— 判定实际上并没有被击中的一剑；
—— 开除出比赛。

2. 纪律处罚，适用于破坏秩序、纪律或体育精神的犯规，有以下一些：
—— 判定实际上没有被击中的一剑；
—— 开除出比赛；
—— 开除出整个赛会；
—— 驱逐出比赛场馆；
—— 取消比赛资格；
—— 纪律通报；
—— 罚款；
—— 暂时停赛；
—— 永久禁赛。

t.101. 1. 除了永久禁赛以外的处罚都可以由裁判和技术委员会等具有资质的权力机构实施。

2. 只有运动员拒绝行击剑礼才可被相关权力机构实施暂时停赛的处罚（参见 t.87.3、t.120）。

参见国际剑联纪律准则（国际剑联章程第七章）

PENALTIES RELATED TO FENCING

Loss of ground on the piste (cf. t.28.1)

t.102. If a competitor crosses one of the lateral boundaries of the piste with one or both feet, he must step back one metre from the point where he left the piste; and if he goes off the piste during an attack he must return to the position he occupied when he started his attack and then step back a further metre.

Refusal to award a hit actually made

t.103. Although a competitor may in fact have hit his opponent on the target, **this hit may be disallowed**, either because it did not arrive during the period of time during which fencing is allowed, or because the competitor had crossed the boundaries of the piste, or because of defects in the electrical equipment, or because violence was involved in the making of the hit, or because of other reasons as laid down in the Rules (cf. t.18.1/3, t.20.2, t.21.2/4, t.22, t.26.2/4, t.32.2, t.41.2, t.45.3, t.53.3, t.60.2/6, t.66.1, t.67, t.68, t.70.3, t.73.1–4, t.80, t.87.2, t.96.2, t.114.2, t.120).

Award of a hit which has not in fact been received

t.104. A competitor may have **a hit awarded against him** which he has not in fact received, either because he has crossed the rear limit of the piste (cf. t.27), or because he has committed an offence which has prevented his opponent fencing (a flèche attack which jostles the opponent, the use of the unarmed hand while fencing, etc.) (cf. t.96.2, t.114.3.a/b, t.116, t.117, t.118.1, t.120).

Exclusion

t.105. **1.** A competitor who, while fencing, commits certain **violent or vindictive actions** against his opponent, or who does not **fence to his utmost ability**, or who **profits from a fraudulent agreement** with his opponent, may be excluded from the competition.

2. **A competitor who is excluded** from a competition may not continue to take part in that competition, even if he is already qualified for promotion to the next round. He loses the right to his individual classification and all the fencers ranked after the disqualified fencer move up one place in the results of the competition. If necessary the two third places are decided according to their ranking for the composition of the table. Under all circumstances, only fencers who have actually received points in the competition can move up a place in the competition's results.

交锋处罚

失去场地（参阅 t.28.1）

t.102. 如果运动员单脚或双脚出边线，则运动员须回到出边线的位置并后退1米；如果运动员在进攻时出边线，则须回到发起进攻的位置并后退1米。

拒绝承认事实上已经击中的一剑

t.103. 尽管一方运动员实际上已经击中对方的有效部位，但由于下列原因，他可能被拒绝承认这一击中：击中并非在交锋时间内完成；运动员已越出剑道边界；击中是由于电动设备故障；击中伴有粗暴行为；以及规则中规定的其他原因（参阅 t.18.1/3、t.20.2、t.21.2/4、t.22、t.26.2/4、t.32.2、t.41.2、t.45.3、t.53.3、t.60.2/6、t.66.1、t.67、t.68、t.70.3、t.73.1–4、t.80、t.87.2、t.96.2、t.114.2、t.120）。

判定实际并未被击中的一剑

t.104. 由于下列原因，可判罚某一实际上并未被击中的运动员被击中：越出剑道端线（参阅 t.27）；某一犯规阻碍对手击中（冲刺挤撞对手，花剑和佩剑中身体接触；非持剑手的介入等）。（参阅 t.96.2、t.114.3.a/b、t.116、t.117、t.118.1及t.120）

开除出比赛

t.105. 1. 运动员如果在交锋中对对手采用某些粗暴行为或报复性动作，或者未尽其全力比赛，或者与对手订立虚假比赛协议并从中获利，可被开除出比赛。

2. 被开除出某比赛的运动员即使有资格进入下一轮，也不能再继续参加该项比赛；他便失去了该比赛个人排名的权利，排名在其后的所有运动员的比赛成绩提高一个名次。如有必要，两个第三名将根据运动员在对阵表中的排位决定。任何情况下，只有在比赛中得分的运动员才能在比赛成绩中提升一个名次。

DISCIPLINARY PENALTIES

Exclusion from the competition

t.106. 1. **Exclusion from a competition** may also be imposed for a disciplinary offence (failure to appear on the piste as required, weapons not in accordance with the rules, reprehensible attitude towards an official, etc.).

2. The consequences of such exclusion for the competitor are the same as those described in Article t.105 above.

Exclusion from participation in the whole tournament

t.107. 1. **Tournament** is the name given to a number of competitions, individual and team, held at the same place, at the same period and under the same aegis.

2. A competitor who is excluded from a tournament will no longer be allowed to participate **in any competition** during that tournament, either at the same weapon or another.

3. When this penalty is imposed **on a team**, the position of each member of that team must be examined individually, and the members of that team may, according to the circumstances, have different penalties imposed on them (cf. t.90.2).

Expulsion from the venue of the competition or the tournament

t.108. All participants or non-competitors who participate in or are present at a competition (instructors, trainers, technicians, supporters, officials, spectators) **may be expelled**. Such expulsion has the effect of forbidding them access to the venue for the duration of the competition or tournament (cf. t.93, t.106.3, t.120). In no circumstances can the imposition of this penalty give cause for redress to anyone.

Disqualification

t.109. 1. **Disqualification** of a competitor (for example, because he does not conform to the rules regarding age, qualification, etc. required for the competition) does not necessarily incur his (temporary) suspension or permanent suspension, if he has acted in good faith; a request for supplementary penalties for fraudulent intention may, however, be made against the competitor.

2. A team **which has included a competitor who is disqualified** necessarily incurs the penalty of that member and is also disqualified.

3. The consequences of disqualification are the same as those for exclusion from the competition (see Article t.105 above).

纪律处罚

开除出比赛

t.106. 1. 开除出比赛的处罚也可以针对一个纪律性犯规而作出（未到比赛场地，武器不合格，对裁判员态度无礼，等等）。

2. 开除出比赛的结果与以上 t.105中的说明相同。

开除出整个赛会

t.107. 1. "赛会"这一名称是对在同一地点、同一时期、为同一目的而举行的多场比赛的总称。

2. 被开除出赛会的运动员将不再被准许参加赛会中的任何单场比赛，不管是同一剑种还是其他剑种的比赛。

3. 如果处罚的是一个队，那么应该对其每个成员的情况做个别分析，并且根据情况，该队的某一成员可能会受到不同于其他成员受到的纪律处罚。（参阅 t.90.2）

驱逐出当场比赛或整个赛会的比赛场馆

t.108. 除运动员以外的所有参加者或出席者（教练员、队医、技师、支持人员、官员、观众），都可能受到驱逐出比赛场馆的处罚，结果是禁止他们在单场比赛或赛会期间进入比赛场馆（参阅 t.93、t.106.3、t.120）。任何人不得因受此处罚而得到赔偿。

取消比赛资格

t.109. 1. 取消某一运动员的比赛资格（例如由于他不符合比赛的年龄、资格或其他条件），如果他不是故意的，不一定要停赛或除名；然而假如他有欺诈目的，可以要求对他进行补充处罚。

2. 已经使用了一名被取消比赛资格的运动员的队，必须受到与该运动员相同的处罚，也要被取消资格。

3. 取消资格的结果和开除出比赛的结果相同（参阅前面 t.105）。

Censure

t.110. In cases where a more severe disciplinary sanction is not justified, the fencer or the official may be sanctioned by **censure**.

Temporary suspension

t.111. 1. A competitor who is suspended cannot take part in any official FIE competition during the time he is suspended.

2. All other persons who are suspended are debarred from exercising their functions within the limits of time and place fixed when the suspension is imposed.

Permanent suspension

t.112. Permanent suspension involves the same consequences as suspension, but is permanent.

ANNOUNCEMENT OF PENALTIES

t.113. 1. The Directoire Technique is required to **inform** the Central Office of the FIE without delay of **penalties** applied during the competition and their reasons (cf. t.97.5).

2. At the Olympic Games, the Directoire Technique must advise the IOC via the Organising Committee.

纪律通报

t.110. 在不应判处更为严重的纪律处罚的情况下，运动员或其他人员可被处以纪律通报。

暂时停赛

t.111. 1. 被停赛的运动员不能在停赛期间参加国际剑联的任何正式比赛。

2. 被停赛的其他任何人不得在停赛期间和规定地点内履行职能。

永久禁赛

t.112. 永久禁赛的后果与停赛相同，但具有永久性。

处罚的公布

t.113. 1. 技术委员会必须把比赛中采取的处罚措施及其原因及时向国际剑联办公室通报（参阅 t.97.5）。

2. 在奥运会上，技术委员会应通过组委会通知国际奥委会。

CHAPTER 4. THE PENALTIES AND THE COMPETENT JURIDICAL AUTHORITIES

THE TYPES (GROUPS) OF PENALTY

t.114. 1. There are **three types of penalty** to be applied in the cases indicated in the table in Article t.120. If a referee has to penalise a fencer who has committed several faults at the same time, he should penalise the least serious fault first.

2. Penalties are **cumulative and they are valid for the bout** with the exception of those indicated by a BLACK CARD, which means exclusion from the competition, suspension for the remainder of the tournament and for the following two months of the active season (1 October – World Championships for the Juniors, and 1 January – World Championships for the Seniors), whether current or forthcoming.

However, a **team** excluded from a tournament because of a BLACK CARD imposed on one of its members is not excluded as a team from the following competitions, but it may not select the penalised fencer.

Certain offences can result in the **annulment of the hit** scored by the fencer at fault. During the bout, only hits scored in circumstances connected with the offence may be annulled (cf. t.120).

3. The **penalties** are as follows:

a) a **warning**, indicated by a YELLOW CARD with which the Referee identifies the fencer at fault. The fencer then knows that any further offence on his part will result in a penalty hit.

b) a **penalty hit**, indicated by a RED CARD with which the Referee identifies the fencer at fault. A hit is added to the score of his opponent and may, if the last hit is at stake, lead to the loss of the bout. Furthermore, a RED CARD can only be followed by another RED CARD or by a BLACK CARD, depending on the nature of the second offence (cf. t.120).

c) Exclusion from the competition, suspension from the remainder of the tournament and for the following two months of the active season, whether current or forthcoming, indicated by a BLACK CARD with which the Referee identifies the person at fault.

d) Expulsion from the competition venue (any person disturbing the order of the competition).

4. All warnings (YELLOW CARDS), penalty hits (RED CARDS) and exclusions (BLACK CARDS) must be **noted on the score-sheet** of the bout, the pool or the match, together with the group to which they belong.

第四章 处罚和仲裁权限

处罚的性质

t.114. 1. 有三种类型的处罚适用于 t.120 表格中列出的情况。如果一名裁判要处罚一名违反多条规定的运动员时，先从最轻的处罚开始判罚。

2. 对于同一场比赛的所有处罚都是可以累加的，除了黑牌，黑牌标志着取消其当场比赛的参赛资格、开除出整个赛会及本赛季或下赛季接下来两个月的比赛（对于青少年，是10月1日至世青赛；对于成年人，是1月1日至世锦赛）。

但是对于团体比赛，如果只是团队中的一名运动员收到了黑牌，并不代表取消整个团队的参赛资格，但是该团队不得再选择这名运动员为团队成员。

某些犯规可以使得犯规运动员击中的一剑被取消。在实战过程中，只有和犯规有关系的击中才可被取消（参阅 t.120）。

3. 处罚措施有如下：

a. 黄牌警告，由主裁判向犯规运动员出示。因此该运动员明白他做出的任何新的犯规都将带来被罚一剑的后果。

b. 处罚一剑，由主裁判向犯规运动员出示红牌。这时他的对手的比分上会被加上一次击中的分数，并且如果这是最后一次击中，那么他就输掉了比赛。另外，根据新犯规的性质，任何红牌出示后只能跟着出示另一张红牌或一张黑牌（参阅 t.120）。

c. 裁判判罚黑牌时，取消比赛参赛资格，开除出整个赛会及本赛季或下赛季接下来两个月的比赛。

d. 驱逐出比赛场馆（所有扰乱比赛秩序的人员）。

4. 任何警告（黄牌）、罚剑（红牌）和开除（黑牌），以及是哪些队伍受到了处罚，都应被记录在淘汰赛、小组循环赛或团体赛的记分表里。

Competence

t.115. The **offences and their penalties** which appear in different articles of the Rules are summarised in the table that follows in Article t.120; they are divided into four groups (cf. t.116–t.119). All these penalties are within the **competence of the Referee**, although the Directoire Technique still retains the right to intervene on its own initiative (cf. t.97.1–3).

The First Group of offences

t.116. The first infringement in this First Group is penalised by a YELLOW CARD (warning). If during the same bout the fencer commits the same or a different offence in this group the Referee penalises him on each occasion, with a RED CARD (penalty hit). If the fencer at fault has already been penalised by a RED CARD because of an offence listed in the Second or Third Group he receives a further RED CARD for his first infringement relating to the First Group.

The Second Group of offences

t.117. Every offence in the Second Group, including the first infringement, is penalised by a RED CARD (penalty hit).

The Third Group of offences

t.118. **1.** The first infringement in the Third Group is penalised by a RED CARD (penalty hit), even if the fencer at fault has already received a RED CARD as a result of offences in the First or Second Groups.

2. If during the same bout the fencer commits the same or a different offence in this group, he is penalised with a BLACK CARD (exclusion from the competition, suspension from the remainder of the tournament and for the following two months of the active season (1 October – World Championships for the Juniors, and 1 January – World Championships for the Seniors), whether current or forthcoming).

3. Any person **not on the piste** who disturbs the good order of the competition receives:

a) On the **first infringement**, a warning, indicated by a YELLOW CARD, valid for the whole of the competition, which must be noted on the bout score-sheet and recorded by the Directoire Technique;

b) At the **second infringement** during the same competition a BLACK CARD.

4. In the most serious cases concerning disturbance either on or off the piste, the Referee may exclude or expel the person at fault **immediately**.

权限

t.115. 规则里不同条款中列出的犯规行为及处罚措施，都概括在 t.120的表格里；它们被划分为四大类（参阅 t.116 ~ t.119）。所有处罚的决定都在主裁判的权限内，而技术委员会始终保留主动干预的权利（参阅 t.97.1/2/3）。

第一类犯规

t.116. 在第一类犯规中，运动员首次犯规（不管是什么犯规）被罚以黄牌（警告）。假如在同一场比赛中该运动员犯了同样的错误或同类型的另一个错误，每次主裁判都罚以一张红牌（罚剑）。假如犯规运动员因第二类或第三类犯规已经被罚了一张红牌，即使他首犯属于第一类的错误，仍将被罚一张新的红牌。

第二类犯规

t.117. 在第二类中，从第一次犯规起，每次都将被罚红牌（罚剑）。

第三类犯规

t.118. 1. 第三类犯规中的初犯被罚红牌，即罚一剑（即使犯规运动员因犯第一类或第二类错误已被罚一张红牌）。

2. 假如运动员在同场比赛中又犯了同样的错误或同类型的另一个错误，主裁判将罚他一张黑牌，取消当场比赛资格，开除出整个赛会及本赛季或下赛季接下来两个月的比赛（对于青少年，是10月1日至世青赛；对于成年人，是1月1日至世锦赛）。

3. 对于剑道以外扰乱秩序的任何人员，有以下处罚：

a. 初犯给予黄牌警告，对整场比赛都有效，记录在计分表上，并被技术委员会记录在案；

b. 在同场比赛中再犯，罚以黑牌。

4. 在最严重的情况下，即在剑道上或剑道以外引起混乱时，主裁判可以立即开除或驱逐犯规者。

The Fourth Group of offences

t.119. The first infringement in the Fourth Group, is penalised by a BLACK CARD (exclusion from the competition, suspension from the remainder of the tournament and for the following two months of the active season (1 October – World Championships for the Juniors, and 1 January – World Championships for the Seniors), whether current or forthcoming). However, **a team** excluded from a tournament because of a BLACK CARD imposed on one of its members is not excluded as a team from the following competitions, but it may not select the penalised fencer.

Offences and penalties

t.120. Table of Offences and Penalties

This table is intended to be a convenient summary: it is not a substitute for the full texts of the articles concerned which should be consulted in any case of doubt.

<table>
<tr><th></th><th>OFFENCE</th><th>ARTICLES</th><th colspan="3">PENALTIES</th></tr>
<tr><td>0.1</td><td>Absence of name and nationality on the back, absence of national uniform or logo when compulsory, at World Championships, Senior Team World Cup competitions and at team Zonal Championships</td><td>t.45.4 a), b) i and iii</td><td colspan="3" rowspan="3">Elimination from the competition</td></tr>
<tr><td>0.2</td><td>Absence of name on back due to changing a non-conforming conductive jacket</td><td>t.45.5</td></tr>
<tr><td>0.3</td><td>Non presentation when first called by Referee ten minutes before time indicated for start of pool/team match/bouts of direct elimination</td><td>t.86.5</td></tr>
<tr><td>0.4</td><td>Non presentation on the piste ready to fence when ordered by the Referee, after three calls at one-minute intervals</td><td>t.86.6</td><td>1st call</td><td>2nd call</td><td>3rd call Elimination</td></tr>
</table>

第四类犯规

t.119. 在第四类犯规中，初犯被罚黑牌，取消当场比赛资格，开除出整个赛会及本赛季或下赛季接下来两个月的比赛（对于青少年，是10月1日至世青赛；对于成年人，是1月1日至世锦赛）。但是对于团体比赛，如果只是团队中的一名运动员收到了黑牌，并不代表取消整个团队的参赛资格，但是该团队不得再选择这名运动员为团队成员。

犯规及处罚表

t.120. 此表是对规则的简便概括，并不能代替规则中相关的文本，在发生疑问时应查询原文。

<table>
<tr><th></th><th>犯规</th><th>条款</th><th colspan="3">处罚</th></tr>
<tr><td>0.1</td><td>在世锦赛、成年世界杯团体赛和成年洲际锦标赛团体赛上，缺少必须有的后背上的姓名和国籍以及国家队服装或标志。</td><td>t.45.4 a），b）i 和 iii</td><td colspan="3" rowspan="3">取消比赛资格</td></tr>
<tr><td>0.2</td><td>金属衣不合格更换后，后背缺少名字。</td><td>t.45.5</td></tr>
<tr><td>0.3</td><td>小组循环赛、团体赛及直接淘汰赛开始前10分钟，裁判员第一次点名不到场。</td><td>t.86.5</td></tr>
<tr><td>0.4</td><td>裁判三次点名、每次点名间隔1分钟后，仍不到剑道就位。</td><td>t.86.6</td><td>第一次点名</td><td>第二次点名</td><td>第三次点名
取消比赛资格</td></tr>
</table>

	1st group		1st offence	2nd offence	3rd offence and subseq.
1.1	Leaving piste without permission	**t.18.6**	YELLOW	RED	RED
1.2	Corps à corps to avoid being hit *	**t.20.2 ; t.63.2**			
1.3	Turning back on opponent *	**t.21.2**			
1.4	Covering/substitution of valid target *	**t.22.2 ; t. 49.1 ; t.72.2**			
1.5	Touching/taking hold of electrical equipment *	**t.22.3**			
1.6	Crossing lateral boundary of the piste to avoid being hit *	**t.28.3**			
1.7	Interruption of bout without valid reason	**t.31.2**			
1.8	Clothing/equipment not conforming. Curve of blade exceeding that permitted. Absence of regulation/spare weapon or bodywire	**t.45.1/2/3.a)ii ; t.86.4**			
1.9	Placing weapon on the conductive piste to straighten it	**t.46.2 ; t.61.2 ; t.70.5**			
1.10	At foil and épée, bending, dragging weapon point on conductive piste	**t.46.2 ; t.61.2**			
1.11	Bringing weapon into contact with conductive jacket *	**t.53.3**			
1.12	At sabre, hit made with the guard *, any forward movement crossing the legs or feet *	**t.70.3 ; t.75.5**			
1.13	Refusal to obey the Referee	**t.82.2 ; t.84**			
1.14	Hair not conforming to the Rules	**t.86.2**			
1.15	Jostling, disorderly fencing * ; taking off mask before the Referee calls ' Halt!'; dressing or undressing on the piste	**t.86.3 ; t.87.2/7/8**			
1.16	Irregular movements on the piste * ; hits made with violence or during or after falling *	**t.87.2**			
1.17	Unjustified appeal	**t.122.2/4**			
1.18	Entering the Piste enclosure without the Referee's permission +	**t.92.6**			
1.19	Reversing the line of the shoulders at foil * Application: starting season 2016-2017	t.18.5			

	2nd group		1st offence	2nd offence	3rd offence and subseq.
2.1	Use of non-sword arm/hand *	**t.22.1**	RED	RED	RED
2.2	Demanding a break for claimed injury/cramp deemed unjustified by doctor	**t.33.3**			
2.3	Absence of weapon control marks *	**t.45.3.a).i**			
2.4	Absence of name and nationality on the back, absence of national colours when compulsory, at individual Senior World Cup competitions and individual Senior Zonal Championships	**t.45.4 a), b) ii**			
2.5	Deliberate hit not on opponent *	**t.53.2 ; t.66.2**			
2.6	Dangerous, violent or vindictive action, blow with guard or pommel *	**t.87.2 ; t.103 ; t.105.1**			

	第一组	条款	第一次	第二次	第三次
1.1	未经允许离开剑道	t.18.6	黄牌	红牌	红牌
1.2	为避免被击中而身体接触（*）	t.20.3；t.63.2			
1.3	转身背向对手（*）	t.21.2			
1.4	遮掩/代替有效部位（*）	t.22.2；t. 49.1；t.72.2			
1.5	接触/抓握电动器材（*）	t.22.3			
1.6	为避免被击中越出边线（*）	t.28.3			
1.7	多次无合理原因使比赛中断	t.31.2			
1.8	器材及服装不合格。剑的弯曲度不符合规格。缺少符合规定的备用剑或备用手线。	t.45.1/2/3.a）ii；t.86.4			
1.9	在剑道上矫正剑	t.46.2；t.61.2; t.70.5			
1.10	花剑和重剑中，在金属剑道上弯折或拖拉剑尖	t.46.2; t.61.2			
1.11	使武器接触金属外衣（*）	t.53.3			
1.12	佩剑中用护手盘劈刺（*）；任何向前动作中双腿或脚交叉（*）	t.70.3；t.75.5			
1.13	拒绝服从裁判	t.82.2；t.84			
1.14	头发不符合规则	t.86.2			
1.15	挤撞、混乱动作（*）；在“停”口令之前摘掉护面；在剑道上穿脱衣服	t.86.3；t.87.2/7/8			
1.16	不正常移动（*）；粗暴击打或摔倒过程中和摔倒后的击中（*）	t.87.2			
1.17	无理申诉	t.122.2/4			
1.18	未经裁判允许进入剑道封闭区域 +	t.92.6			
1.19	在花剑比赛中后肩超前肩（*）从2016-2017赛季执行	t.18.5			

	第二组	条款	第一次	第二次	第三次
2.1	使用非持剑手、臂（*）	t.22.1	红牌	红牌	红牌
2.2	要求伤停，但伤病或痉挛经医生确认为不合理	t.33.3			
2.3	缺少器材检验标志（*）	t.45.3.a）.i			
2.4	在成年世界杯个人赛及洲际锦标赛个人赛时，缺少必须有的后背上的姓名和国籍以及国家队服装或标志。	t.45.4 a），b）ii			
2.5	故意击中对手以外的地方（*）	t.53.2；t.66.2			
2.6	野蛮、危险或报复性动作；用护手盘或手柄平衡锤劈刺（*）	t.87.2；t.103；t.105.1			

	OFFENCE	ARTICLES	PENALTIES (Cards)	
	3rd group		**1st time**	**2nd time**
3.1	Fencer disturbing order when on piste. In the most serious cases, the Referee may award a black card immediately (t.118.4).	**t.82.3 ; t.83 ; t.96.2**	**RED**	**BLACK**
3.2	Dishonest fencing *	**t.87.1**	**RED**	
3.3	Offence against Publicity Code	**Publicity Code**		
3.4	Any person not on piste disturbing good order. In the most serious cases, the Referee may award a black card immediately (t.118.4).	**t.82.3/4 ; t.83 ; t.96.3 ; t.118.3 ; t.118.4**	**YELLOW**	**BLACK**
3.5	Warming up or training without wearing fencing clothing or equipment that conforms to the FIE regulations.	**t.15.2**		
3.6	Anti-sporting behaviour	**t.87.2**		

	4th group		PENALTIES (Cards)
4.1	Fencer equipped with electronic communication equipment permitting him to receive communications during bout	**t. 43.1.f ; t.44.2 ; t.45.3.a).vii**	**BLACK**
4.2	Fraudulent equipment, control marks that are imitated or transferred	**t.45.3.a) iii) iv) v)**	
4.3	Equipment altered to allow the recording of hits or the non-functioning of the apparatus at will	**t.45.3.a) v)**	
4.4	Refusal of a fencer to fence another competitor (individual or team) properly entered	**t.85.1**	
4.5	Offence against sportsmanship	**t.87.2 ; t.105.1**	
4.6	Refusal of a fencer to salute his opponent, the referee and the spectators before the beginning of the bout or after the last hit	**t.87.3**	
4.7	Profiting from collusion, favouring an opponent	**t.88 ; t.105.1**	
4.8	Deliberate brutality	**t.105.1**	
4.9	Doping	**t.127**	

EXPLANATIONS	
*	**Annulment of any hit scored by the fencer at fault**
+	**Special YELLOW CARD for the whole team and valid for the whole team match. If, during the same team match, a fencer commits an offence of the 1st group the Referee penalises with a RED CARD each time.**
YELLOW CARD	**Warning** valid for the bout (whether one or several encounters). If a fencer commits an offence of the 1st group after having been penalised with a RED CARD, for whatever reason, he receives a further RED CARD.
RED CARD	**Penalty hit**
BLACK CARD	**Exclusion from the competition**, suspension from the remainder of the tournament and for the following 2 months of the active season (1st October – World Championships for the juniors and 1st January – World Championships for the seniors), whether current or forthcoming.
	A fencer only receives a BLACK CARD in the Third Group if he previously committed an offence in this Third Group (demonstrated by a RED CARD).

	第三组	条款	第一次	第二次
3.1	运动员在剑道上扰乱秩序，在极其严重的情况下，裁判员可立即处以黑牌（t.118.4）	t.82.3；t.83；t.96.2	红牌	黑牌
3.2	比赛中弄虚作假（*）	t.87.1	红牌	
3.3	违反广告规则	广告规则		
3.4	剑道以外的任何人扰乱秩序，在极其严重的情况下，裁判员可立即处以黑牌（t.118.4）	t.82.3/4；t.83；t.96.3；t.118.3；t.118.4	黄牌	黑牌
3.5	在训练或热身期间未根据国际剑联规则穿戴击剑服和装备	t.15.2		
3.6	反体育运动行为	t.87.2		

	第四组	条款	处罚
4.1	运动员佩戴可以在比赛时与外界交流的电子设备	t. 43.1.f；t.44.2；t.45.3.a）.vii	黑牌
4.2	欺诈，模仿或转移器材检查标记	t.45.3.a） iii） iv） v）	
4.3	对器材进行修改，以至于可以任意记录刺中或使设备不正常工作	t.45.3.a） v）	
4.4	运动员拒绝和正常报名的另一名运动员比赛（个人或团体）	t.85.1	
4.5	违背体育精神的犯规	t.87.2；t.105.1	
4.6	在比赛开始前和最后一剑击中以后拒绝向对手、裁判和观众行礼	t.87.3	
4.7	给对手让分，从私下串通中得益	t.88；t.105.1	
4.8	故意的粗暴行为（*）	t.105.1	
4.9	使用兴奋剂	t.127	

解　　释	
（*）	取消击中的一剑。
+	特殊的黄牌，对整个队伍和整个团体比赛有效。如果在同一场团体赛中，运动员实施了第一组中的犯规行为，则每次犯规裁判员将给予红牌处罚。
黄牌	警告，对该局比赛有效（无论包含几次相遇）。如果一名运动员无论因何原因被罚一张红牌以后又实施了第一组中的犯规行为，他将再次被罚一张红牌。
红牌	罚被击中一剑。
黑牌	开除出当场比赛、开除出整个赛会及本赛季或下赛季接下来两个月的比赛（青年：10月1日至世界青年锦标赛；成年：1月1日至世界锦标赛）。
	一名运动员只有在他已经实施了一次第三组犯规行为（已被罚过一张红牌）以后，才能在他又一次实施第三组犯规行为时给予黑牌处罚

CHAPTER 5. PROCEDURE

BASIC PRINCIPLE

t.121. The various penalties are **imposed by the competent authorities** who will reach their decisions in an equitable manner, and will take into account the gravity of the offence and the circumstances in which it was committed (cf. t.94ss, t.114ss, t.124ss, t.125, t.126).

PROTESTS AND APPEALS

Against a decision of the Referee

t.122. 1. No appeal can be made against the decision of the Referee regarding a point of fact (cf. t.95.1/2/4, t.96.2).

2. If a fencer infringes this principle, **casting doubt** on the decision of the Referee **on a point of fact** during the bout, he will be penalised according to the rules (cf. t.114. t.116, t.120). But if the Referee **is ignorant of or misunderstands a definite rule**, or applies it in a manner contrary to the Rules, an appeal on this matter may be entertained.

3. This **appeal** must be made:

a) in **individual** events, by the fencer,

b) in **team** events, by the fencer or the team captain,

it should be made courteously but without formality, and should be made **verbally** to the Referee **immediately** and before any decision is made regarding a subsequent hit.

4. If the Referee **maintains** his opinion, the Refereeing Commission delegate or the Supervisor (if there is no delegate) has the authority to settle an appeal (cf. t.97). If such an appeal is deemed to be **unjustified**, the fencer will be penalised in accordance with Articles t.114, t.116, t.120.

Other protests and appeals

t.123. 1. Complaints and protests which are not concerned with a referee's decision must be made **in writing without delay**; they must be addressed to the Directoire Technique.

2. If a complaint or protest contests a decision taken by the Directoire Technique or the official FIE delegate it should be addressed to the FIE Central Office.

第五章 诉讼程序

基本原则

t.121. 考虑到犯规的严重程度和犯规时的客观环境，各种不同的处罚措施均由权力机构在公正裁决后宣布（见 t.94ss、t.114ss、t.124ss、t.125、t.126）。

抗议与申诉

对主裁判决定的抗议与申诉

t.122. 1. 对主裁判已经做出的关于客观事实的决定，不能提出抗议（参阅 t.95.1/2/4、t.96.2）。

2. 如果运动员违背这一原则，在比赛过程中对主裁判已做出的关于客观事实的决定持怀疑态度，他将受到规则规定的处罚（参阅 t.114、t.116、t.120）。但是如果该主裁判不了解规则中某一明确规定，或者执行方式与规则相违背，那么该申诉是可以得到受理的。

3. 此申诉须由以下人员提出：

a. 个人赛中，运动员。

b. 团体赛中，运动员或队长。

申诉应礼貌地提出，但不需要履行正式手续，且必须在下一次击中的裁决做出之前，立即口头向主裁判提出。

4. 当主裁判坚持其决定时，裁判委员会代表或观察员（无裁判代表的情况下）有权处理申诉（参阅 t.97）。如果该申诉被驳回，则运动员将会受到 t.114、t.116、t.120规定的处罚。

其他抗议与申诉

t.123. 1. 与裁判员裁决无关的申诉与抗议应立即以书面形式提交至技术委员会。

2. 对于技术委员会或国际剑联官方代表的决定提出的申诉和抗议应提交至国际剑联办公室。

Investigation — Right of defence

t.124. No penalty can be imposed until after an **enquiry** has been held in the course of which the parties concerned have been called on to give their explanation of the occurrence either verbally or in writing, within a reasonable interval of time, suited to the time and place. After this time limit has expired, the penalty may be imposed.

Method of decision

t.125. The decisions of the juridical authorities of competitions are by **majority vote**, the chairman (president) having the casting vote in case of a tie.

Repetition of offence

t.126. **1.** For offences regarding sportsmanship, good order or discipline, a fencer is said to **repeat** an offence if he commits a new offence, other than violation of the rules governing bouts, within two years of being censured, or subjected to exclusion, disqualification or suspension.

2. For the repetition of an offence, the **penalty** which must be imposed is:

a) **Exclusion** from the competition, if the previous penalty was a censure.

b) **Disqualification** from participation in the whole tournament, if the previous penalty was exclusion or disqualification from a competition.

See also the Disciplinary Code of the FIE (Chapter VII, FIE Statutes).

调查——辩护权

t.124. 处罚只能在调查以后才可实施。在调查过程中，根据时间和地点的情况确定适当的期限，传唤当事人用口头或书面形式陈述原因。过了这一期限后，才可实施处罚。

裁决方法

t.125. 所有裁判机构的裁决要以多数票表决通过，若赞成与反对票数相等，主席的一票具有决定权。

重犯

t.126. 1. 对于违背体育精神、扰乱秩序或违反纪律的犯规，如果一名击剑者以前曾因这种犯规受到过纪律处分、开除、取消比赛资格或停赛的处罚，当他两年内又实施了一个新的除交锋犯规之外的犯规行为，这就属于重犯。

2. 在重犯情况下，将实施以下处罚：

a. 如前一次处罚是纪律通报，则开除出比赛；

b. 如前一次处罚是开除出比赛或取消比赛资格，则取消整个联赛资格。

参见国际剑联纪律准则（国际剑联章程第七章）。

CHAPTER 6. ANTI-DOPING CONTROLS

t.127. a) **Doping** is forbidden by the FIE. Any breaking of this rule will incur disciplinary action.

b) Doping is defined as the occurrence of one or more of the anti-doping rule violations set forth in **Articles 2.1 to 2.8 of the FIE Anti-Doping Rules**.

c) The FIE has committed itself to the **WADA Anti-Doping Code.** The FIE Anti-Doping Rules are based on the WADA 'Models of Best Practice' and adopt in their entirety the 'mandatory clauses' of the above document. The FIE also adopts in full the WADA 'Prohibited Classes of Substances and Prohibited Methods' document.

d) The FIE reserves the right to conduct doping control **during competitions** — that is, at any competition organised under its control — as well as **out-of-competition**.

e) The athletes who participate in FIE competitions undertake to respect the FIE anti-doping Rules, use neither prohibited substances nor prohibited methods and agree to submit to any anti-doping control, whether in- or out-of competition;

f) **All the details** concerning the doping controls at official FIE competitions, as well as out-of-competition, are to be found in the articles of the Anti-Doping Rules of the FIE.

g) The **penalties** and consequences of the penalties arising from violations of the anti-doping rules are those laid down in the Anti-Doping-Rules of the FIE.

h) Fencers found to have contravened these anti-doping rules will be subject to the **procedures provided for in the Anti-Doping Rules.** The publication of test results and decisions relating to application of penalties will be announced by the Central Office of the FIE, which alone has the right to bring them to the notice of all member federations.

i) Doping offences committed and penalised in any of the **member countries** of the FIE will be taken into account and the penalties ('sanctions') will be applied by all member countries of the FIE.

j) **Modification of the FIE Anti-Doping Rules** falls within the competence of the Executive Committee.

第六章　反兴奋剂

t.127. a. 国际剑联禁止使用兴奋剂，任何违犯这一规则的行为都会受到纪律处罚。

b. 使用兴奋剂被认为是违反了一条或多条反兴奋剂规则，这些条款在国际剑联反兴奋剂规则2.1~2.8中有说明。

c. 国际剑联承认世界反兴奋剂机构的世界反兴奋剂条例。国际剑联的反兴奋剂规则是建立在世界反兴奋剂机构的“最佳实践案例”基础之上的，并且采纳了材料中所有“必须的规定”。国际剑联采纳了世界反兴奋剂机构所有“禁用物质和禁用方法”的材料。

d. 国际剑联有权在其比赛期间进行兴奋剂检查——即只要是在国际剑联控制下举办的比赛，同时也有权进行赛外兴奋剂检查。

e. 参加国际剑联比赛的运动员要遵守国际剑联的反兴奋剂规则，不得使用禁用物质及禁用方法，并且接受赛内或赛外兴奋剂检查。

f. 所有关于国际剑联正式比赛赛内及赛外兴奋剂检查的具体方式都在国际剑联反兴奋剂规则中有所描述。

g. 对于违反反兴奋剂规则的处罚及处罚结果都在国际剑联反兴奋剂规则中说明。

h. 违反反兴奋剂规则的击剑者将按照反兴奋剂规则中规定的程序进行处理。只有国际剑联办公室有权公布检查结果及最终决定，并通知所有会员协会。

i. 在任何一个国际剑联会员协会发生兴奋剂违规行为及处罚，其处罚措施将在所有国际剑联会员协会生效。

j. 国际剑联反兴奋剂规则的修订权归国际剑联执委会。

组织规则

BOOK 2. ORGANISATION RULES

CHAPTER 1. COMPETITIONS

o.1. The **official competitions** of the FIE are organised according to the following rules.

o.2. 1. The official competitions of the FIE are open to fencers (individual or team) of all FIE member countries.

2. Every competitor or designated official in a competition, irrespective of his status, is required to be **licensed for the current season** (cf. Statutes, Chapter IX).

CHAPTER 2. BODIES RESPONSIBLE FOR ORGANISATION AND CONTROL

THE ORGANISING COMMITTEE

o.3. The Organising Committee is the group of persons responsible for organising the competition.

THE CENTRAL OFFICE OF THE FIE

o.4. The Central Office of the FIE controls the activities of the Directoire Technique at the Olympic Games, the World Championships and the Junior and Cadet World Championships, as described in Article o.63.

THE DIRECTOIRE TECHNIQUE

o.5. The technical organisation of competitions is entrusted to a Directoire Technique, the functions and scope of whose activities are described in the Rules (cf. t.97, o.56–62).

AUXILIARY PERSONNEL

o.6. **The organising committee will appoint:**

1. Scorers and time-keepers

The organisers will appoint, on their own responsibility, **scorers** whose duty it will be to keep the score-sheet for the bout, the pool or the match and maintain the score-boards, and a **time-keeper** whose duty it will be to keep time for the duration of the bouts (cf. t.30ss).

For **finals**, the Directoire Technique may appoint a delegate or a referee, neutral wherever possible, to supervise the time-keeper, the scorer and the person responsible for the scoring apparatus.

第一章　比赛

o.1.　国际剑联正式比赛根据本规则组织举办。

o.2.　1. 国际剑联正式比赛向所有会员国的击剑运动员（个人或团体）开放。
2. 每名运动员或被指派的官员，无论以何种身份参赛，都必须持本赛季有效的国际剑联会员证。（参见章程第四章）

第二章　组织机构

组织委员会

o.3.　负责组织比赛的所有人员构成组织委员会。

国际剑联总部办公室

o.4.　奥运会及世界成年、青年、少年锦标赛期间，国际剑联总部办公室依据o.63对技术委员会的工作进行监督。

技术委员会

o.5.　比赛的技术组织工作由技术委员会负责，其职责和权限已在规则中说明（参见技术规则 t.97和本规则 o.56 ~ o.62）。

辅助人员

o.6.　**组织委员会将指派以下人员：**

1. 记分员及计时员

组委会将全权负责指定记分员来进行循环赛及各场次比赛的记录并操作电子记分牌，并指定计时员负责比赛的计时工作（参见技术规则 t.30及以下内容）。

在决赛阶段，技术委员会可以指派一名尽可能中立的代表或裁判员负责监督计时员、记分员及电子记分牌操作人员的工作。

2. The Organising Committee must choose **qualified persons**, who pay careful attention to the signals given by the apparatus in order that they may be able to advise the Referee as to what the apparatus has registered, and warn him, even during the course of a bout, as to any abnormal phenomena which may occur.

3. Experts

   a) For each tournament, the Organising Committee must appoint **experts in matters relating to the electrical apparatus**. These experts are placed under the supervision of the Directoire Technique.

   b) The experts may be consulted, separately or conjointly, by the referees or by the Directoire Technique regarding all questions relating to the electrical apparatus.

   c) **Members of the Committee for Electrical Apparatus and Equipment** of the FIE (SEMI) who are present are ex officio qualified to act as experts.

4. Repairers

   For each tournament, the Organising Committee must ensure the presence of **competent repairers** to remedy faults in the electrical apparatus and, possibly, in the personal electrical equipment of the fencers.

CHECKING OF EQUIPMENT

o.7. The checking of the organisers' equipment, as well as the equipment of the fencers, must be carried out in accordance with the rules to be found in the Material Rules by qualified personnel designated by the organizing committee. If there are present designated members of the SEMI Commission, this function must be carried out by them or under their control.

CHAPTER 3. ENTRIES FOR COMPETITIONS

o.8. Entries must be sent to the organisers by the competitors' national federation (for the Olympic Games by their national Olympic Committee).

2. 组委会须选择合适的人选认真监督裁判器的运行，能够向裁判员报告裁判器记录的内容，一旦出现异常情况，即使是在比赛进行时，也要给裁判提示。

3. 专家
   a. 对于每项比赛，组委会须指派电气设备专家，这些专家在技术委员会监督之下工作。
   b. 裁判员或技术委员会可就所有电气设备问题个别或集体咨询这些专家。
   c. 国际剑联器材委员会的全体现任成员均有资格被指派担当此类专家之职。

4. 维修员
   每场比赛，组委会必须确保有合格的维修人员在场，以便修复损坏的裁判器及运动员个人的器材装备。

器材检查

0.7. 场地器材的检查和运动员个人装备的检查工作应根据器材规则由组委会指派的合格人员执行。如果现场有器材委员会成员，则这一工作须由他们执行或在他们的监督和指导下进行。

第三章　比赛报名

0.8. 运动员应通过各自国家（地区）的击剑协会向组委会报名参加比赛（奥运会的报名则要通过国家奥委会进行）。

CHAPTER 4. TIMETABLE

o.9. **1.** The **programme** must be displayed, communicated and respected and must take into account the time needed for the fencers to rest between bouts. It should be arranged in such a way that no fencer is obliged to participate in events for **more than 12 hours in 24**. In any case, no pool, bout or match may begin after midnight, or at any time when it can be foreseen with certainty that it will end after midnight.

2. Whatever programme is adopted, **the final** should start at a time which, having regard to local routines, will ensure that the results can be communicated to the media in sufficient time to allow them to be published.

3. In their timetable the organisers must allow sufficient time for it to be possible to carry out **the checking of the fencers' equipment**, i.e. a minimum of one day per weapon.

o.10. The first round of all the individual and team competitions for the World Championships and Olympic Games must be displayed by 4 p.m. at the latest the day before the competition (cf. t.123).

CHAPTER 5. INDIVIDUAL COMPETITIONS

o.11. Individual competitions may be organised:

a) **By direct elimination with a mixed system** consisting of one round of eliminating pools and a preliminary direct elimination table, followed by a main direct elimination table of 64 fencers to qualify 8 or 4 fencers for a direct elimination final.

b) **By direct elimination with a mixed system** consisting of one round of eliminating pools, followed by a direct elimination table to qualify 8 or 4 fencers for a direct elimination final.

c) **By direct elimination throughout**. (This formula, applicable at the Olympic Games, is contained in an annexe.)

GENERAL RULES FOR THE ROUND OF POOLS

o.12. 1. In **all competitions for which the formula includes a round of pools**, these pools will consist of **7** fencers if the number of participants is divisible by 7. Otherwise the pools will be of 7 and 6. In no case may the pools be of fewer than 6 fencers.

第四章　竞赛日程

O.9.　1. 竞赛日程须予以公布、通知并得到遵守，制定日程要考虑每两场比赛之间运动员的休息。运动员不得被迫在24小时内进行超过12小时的比赛。任何情况下，所有小组赛、比赛或团体赛都不得在午夜后开始，并且必须在午夜前结束。

2. 无论采用何种方式，决赛开始的时间应在尊重当地习惯的基础上，确保媒体能够及时获取比赛结果通知并拥有足够的时间予以发布。

3. 组委会必须安排足够的时间用于检查运动员的器材，即每个剑种至少有一天的时间。

O.10.　世界锦标赛及奥运会的所有个人赛及团体赛，第一轮比赛名单最迟必须在比赛前一天下午16：00以前公布（参见技术规则 t.123）。

第五章　个人赛

O.11.　个人赛可按以下方式进行：

a. 混合式直接淘汰制，包括一轮小组循环赛及预淘汰赛，接着进行64表直接淘汰赛决出8名或4名运动员参加直接淘汰赛决赛。

b. 混合式直接淘汰制，包括一轮小组循环赛，接着进行64表直接淘汰赛决出8名或4名运动员参加直接淘汰赛决赛。

c. 全程采用直接淘汰制（这种方式在奥运会时使用，参见附件）。

小组循环赛的基本规则

O.12.　1. 在所有包含小组循环赛的比赛中，如果运动员人数是7的整数倍，则每个小组由7名运动员组成；如果不是7的整数倍，则每个小组由7名或6名运动员组成。任何情况下，小组运动员人数不得少于6人。

If, however, as the result of the absence of one or more fencers, one or more pools were to be reduced to 5 or fewer fencers, the organisers must add to these pools one or more fencers from other pools of 7 fencers, taking into account the initial ranking of the fencer(s) being replaced.

2. **At World Cup competitions** the organising country may add the necessary number of fencers of their own nationality for all the pools to consist of 7 fencers.

Composition of pools

o.13. 1. **The pools are composed** taking account of the latest official FIE ranking and by drawing lots among any fencers who are not in the ranking.

2. **The allocation of fencers in the pools** must be made in such a way as to place fencers of the same nationality in different pools, as far as possible.

3. **The order of fencers** on the pool sheet is decided by drawing lots.

4. The pools must be fenced **up to the last bout.**

o.14. **The order of bouts in the pools is as follows:**

1. Pool of seven

1–4	5–1	3–5
2–5	4–3	1–6
3–6	6–2	2–4
7–1	5–7	7–3
5–4	3–1	6–5
2–3	4–6	1–2
6–7	7–2	4–7

2. Pool of six

1–2	5–4	6–4
4–3	1–6	2–3
6–5	3–5	1–4
3–1	4–2	5–2
2–6	5–1	3–6

o.15. **When there are several fencers from the same country in a pool:**

1. If they **do not form the majority** of the competitors in the pool, they must fence off the bouts between themselves before meeting competitors of another nationality.

2. If they **form the majority** of the competitors in the pool, the Directoire Technique may establish a special order of bouts, departing as little as possible from the principle laid down in (a) above, in order to obviate excessive fatigue or delays for the competitors who form the minority in the pool.

然而，如果由于一名或几名运动员的缺席，使得一个或多个小组的参赛运动员人数减少至5人或更少，组织者须从7人组中调剂出一名或几名运动员到这些组，并且要考虑被调整运动员的最初排名。

2. 世界杯赛中，东道主有权增加必要数量的本国运动员，以确保每个小组有7名运动员。

小组循环赛分组办法

O.13. 1. 小组循环赛的分组依据国际剑联最新排名进行，无积分排名的运动员，将采取抽签方式决定其位置。

2. 在进行小组循环赛分组时，必须按照同一国家的运动员尽可能不被安排在同一小组的原则进行。

3. 运动员在小组循环赛中的出场位次由抽签决定。

4. 小组循环赛必须完成所有对阵的比赛。

O.14. 小组循环赛中各场次对阵按照以下顺序进行：

1. 7人组

1–4	5–1	3–5
2–5	4–3	1–6
3–6	6–2	2–4
7–1	5–7	7–3
5–4	3–1	6–5
2–3	4–6	1–2
6–7	7–2	4–7

2. 6人组

1–2	5–4	6–4
4–3	1–6	2–3
6–5	3–5	1–4
3–1	4–2	5–2
2–6	5–1	3–6

O.15. 当一个小组中包含几名来自同一国家的运动员时：

1. 如果他们不占多数的话，他们相互之间必须先进行比赛。

2. 如果他们占多数，技术委员会可制定一则特别的比赛次序，以避免少数运动员比赛过于频繁或长时间轮空，同时必须尽可能不违背上述第1条原则。

3. Examples of the **order of fencers of the same nationality** in a pool of six:

a) When a pool contains, among its six fencers,

— **two fencers of the same nationality A**, or
— **two fencers of the same nationality A and two of the same nationality B**
— **two fencers of the same nationality A, two of the same nationality B and two of the same nationality C**

the fencers' names are placed on the pool sheet in such a way that those of the same nationality fence each other in their first bout and the order of bouts of a pool of six is that shown in Article o.14 above.

b) When a pool contains among its six fencers,

— **three fencers of the same nationality A**, or
— **three fencers of the same nationality A and two fencers of the same nationality B**, or
— **three fencers of the same nationality A and three fencers of the same nationality B**, the order will be as follows:

1–2	6–4	4–2
4–5	2–5	3–6
2–3	1–4	5–1
5–6	5–3	3–4
3–1	1–6	6–2

the fencers' names are placed on the pool sheet in the following way:
— the fencers of nationality A are given numbers 1, 2 and 3;
— the fencers of nationality B are given numbers 4 and 5 or 4, 5 and 6.
The order of bouts will be as laid down in Article o.14.

c) When a pool contains among its six fencers **four fencers of the same nationality A** and two others of different nationalities, the four fencers of nationality A are placed on the pool sheet as 1, 2, 3 and 4 and the order of bouts in the pool is as follows:

3–1	1–2	4–5
4–2	3–4	6–2
1–4	1–6	5–1
2–3	2–5	6–4
5–6	3–6	5–3

4. Example of the order of fencers of the same nationality in a pool of seven:

a) When this pool contains, among the seven fencers,

— **two fencers of nationality A**, or
— **two fencers of nationality A and two fencers of nationality B**, or
— **two fencers of nationality A, two fencers of nationality B and two fencers of nationality C**,

3. 含有相同国籍运动员的6人组比赛顺序示例如下：

a. 当该组6名运动员中：
—— 有两人来自同一队A，或
—— 有两人来自同一队A，两人来自同一队B，或
—— 有两人来自同一队A，两人来自同一队B，两人来自同一队C。

运动员的出场安排须保证同一队的两人之间首先进行比赛，同时依照上述 o.14 中说明的6人组比赛次序安排。

b. 当该组6名运动员中：
—— 有3人来自同一队A或；
—— 有3人来自同一队A，有2人来自同一队B或；
—— 有3人来自同一队A，另3人来自同一队B，比赛顺序安排如下：

1–2	6–4	4–2
4–5	2–5	3–6
2–3	1–4	5–1
5–6	5–3	3–4
3–1	1–6	6–2

运动员们按以下方式获得小组序号：
—— 来自同一队A的运动员分别为1、2、3号；
—— 来自同一队B的运动员分别为4、5号或4、5、6号。
运动员出场顺序按照上述 o.14 说明的次序安排。

c. 当该组6名运动员中有4人来自同一队A，另2人来自不同的队时，同一队的4名运动员小组中分列1、2、3、4位，比赛顺序安排如下：

3–1	1–2	4–5
4–2	3–4	6–2
1–4	1–6	5–1
2–3	2–5	6–4
5–6	3–6	5–3

4. 含有相同国籍运动员的7人组比赛顺序示例如下：

a. 当该组7名运动员中：
——有2人来自同一队A，或
——有2人来自同一队A，另有2人来自同一队B，或
——有2人来自同一队A，2人来自同一队B，另有2人来自同一队C，

the fencers of the same nationality are listed on the pool sheet so that they fence their first bout against each other while following the order of fights laid down in Article o.14 above for a pool of seven fencers.

b) When the pool contains

— **three fencers of nationality A**, or
— **three fencers of nationality A and two fencers of nationality B**, or
— **three fencers of nationality A, two fencers of nationality B and two fencers of nationality C**

the three fencers of nationality A must be listed 1, 2 and 3 on the pool sheet, the two fencers of nationality B, 4 and 5, and the two fencers of nationality C, 6 and 7.

The order of bouts for the pool of seven, detailed in Article o.14, is no longer valid and must be replaced by the following order:

1–2	6–2	1–4
4–5	3–4	2–7
6–7	7–5	5–3
3–1	1–6	6–4
4–7	4–2	7–1
2–3	7–3	2–5
5–1	5–6	3–6

o.16. **1.** If a bout in a pool is **interrupted by an accidental cause**, and this interruption is likely to be prolonged, the Referee may (with the consent of the Directoire Technique, or possibly the Organising Committee) alter the order of bouts in such a way as to allow the normal progress of the competition to proceed.

2. **The time allowed for a fencer to rest** between two consecutive bouts in a pool is three minutes.

o.17. **In the pools a bout ends when:**

1. **a)** One of the fencers **has scored 5 hits**. In this case the score registered on the score-sheet is the final score of the bout (*V*5 – *Dn*, where *n* = the number of hits scored by the losing fencer).

b) **At épée**, if the two fencers reach a score of 4–all, they must fence for a deciding hit, up to the time limit. Any double hit will not be counted (and the fencers will therefore remain where they are on the piste).

2. **Three minutes of effective fencing time** have passed. (There is no warning for the last minute.)

a) If **when the time limit expires** there is a difference of at least one hit between the scores of the two fencers, the fencer who has scored the greater number of hits is declared winner. The score registered on the score-sheet is the actual score achieved in the bout (*VN* – *Dn*, where *N* = the number of hits scored by the winning fencer and *n* = the number of hits scored by the losing fencer).

运动员的出场安排须保证同一队的两人之间首先进行比赛，同时依照上述 o.14中说明的7人组比赛次序安排。

b. 当该组7名运动员中：

—— 有3人来自同一队A，或

—— 有3人来自同一队A，有2人来自同一队B，或

—— 有3人来自同一队A，2人来自同一队B，余下两人来自同一队C，

来自A队的3名运动员在小组名单上须被排在1、2、3号，来自B队的2名运动员列4、5号，来自C队的2名运动员列6、7号。

上述 o.14中说明的比赛次序不再适用，将由下列顺序取代：

1–2	6–2	1–4
4–5	3–4	2–7
6–7	7–5	5–3
3–1	1–6	6–4
4–7	4–2	7–1
2–3	7–3	2–5
5–1	5–6	3–6

O.16. 1. 当小组循环赛的一场对阵因意外情况而中断，且中断状况有可能持续下去时，裁判员可以征得技术委员会或组委会同意，修改比赛顺序，以便小组循环赛能继续进行。

2. 小组赛中同一名运动员在连续两次对阵之间可休息3分钟。

O.17. 出现以下情况时，表示小组循环赛结束：

1. a. 一名运动员得5分。这种情况下，记录表上将记下比赛双方的最后得分（V5–Dn，n为负方击中剑数）。

b. 在重剑比赛中，当两名运动员的比分为4∶4时，他们须在规定的时间内加赛一剑决定胜负。所有新的互中都不再记录，运动员从原位置开始继续比赛。

2. 3分钟有效比赛时间结束（剩 1 分钟时没有提示）

a. 如果比赛时间结束，两运动员的比分差在一剑以上，那么击中剑数较多的运动员获胜。比赛记录表上记录的成绩为实际比赛结果（VN–Dn，N为获胜运动员击中剑数，n为负方击中剑数）。

b) If **at the end of regulation time the scores are equal**, the fencers fence for a deciding hit, with a maximum time limit of one minute. Before the fencing recommences, the Referee draws lots to decide who will be the winner if scores are still equal at the end of the extra minute.

c) In this case the score registered on the score-sheet is always the **actual score achieved in the bout**:

— $VN - Dn$ if a deciding hit is scored within the time limit for the bout.
— $V4 - D4$ or $V3 - D3$ or $V2 - D2$ or $V1 - D1$ or $V0 - D0$ if the winner is designated by drawing lots.

o.18. Before the competition starts, the Directoire Technique will decide on and announce the **number of fencers who will be eliminated based on the ranking established by the pools**.

o.19. 1. After the pools, a **single general ranking** will be established of all the fencers who have taken part in the pools, taking account, successively, of the indices V/M, $HS - HR$, HS.

(V = victories; M = bouts; HS = hits scored; HR = hits received.)

2. A **summary classification table** shall then be made in the following way:

a) The results written up on the summary table will be added up to ascertain the **two indices** required.

b) The **first index**, for the initial classification, shall be obtained by dividing the number of victories by the number of bouts fought, using the formula V/M.

c) The fencer with the **highest index** (maximum 1) will be seeded first.

d) In cases of **equality in this first index**, and to separate fencers with equal first indices, a second index will be established, using the formula $HS - HR$, the difference between the total number of hits scored and hits received.

e) **In cases of equality of the two indices V/M and $HS - HR$**, the fencer who has scored most hits will be seeded highest.

f) In cases of **absolute equality** between two or more fencers, their seeding order will be decided by drawing lots.

3. Should there be **absolute equality among the last to qualify** there will not be a barrage, and the fencers with equal indicators will all qualify, even if they are in excess of the number decided on.

Withdrawal

o.20. A fencer who **withdraws, or who is excluded**, is scratched from the pool, and his results are annulled as if he had not taken part.

b. 若比赛时间结束时为平分，则加赛1分钟，先击中一剑的运动员获胜，而加赛之前，裁判员将抽签产生一名有优胜权的运动员，若1分钟加时赛结束后仍为平分，则该运动员将获胜。

c. 在这种情况下比赛记录表中将记录两名运动员的实际得分：

—— 若加时赛中有一方击中一剑，记为VN-Dn；
—— 若通过抽签决定胜负，则记为V4-D4或V3-D3或V2-D2或V1-D1或V0-D0。

O.18. 比赛开始前，技术委员会将决定并宣布小组赛淘汰运动员比例。

O.19. 1. 小组循环赛结束后，将依次根据V/M，HS-HR，HS指数对所有参赛运动员进行总排名。
（V=获胜场数，M=比赛场数，HS=击中剑数，HR=被击中剑数）

2. 小组赛排名表将按以下方式制定：

a. 首先依据上述比赛成绩数据计算得出两项必要指数。

b. 第一指数为运动员比赛的胜率，记为V/M，作为第一排名依据。

c. 指数值最高（最大值为1）的运动员位列第一名。

d. 当第一指数值相同时，为决定运动员排名先后，将采用第二指数，即运动员击中总剑数和被击中的总剑数之差，记为HS-HR。

e. 如V/M及HS-HR两项指数均相同，则击中剑数较多的运动员列前。

f. 若两名或多名运动员所有指数都相同，则由抽签决定他们各自在小组赛排名表上的位置。

3. 在争夺最后一个继续比赛的资格时，若有两名或多名运动员各项指数完全相同，则不进行选择，并列名次的所有运动员都入选，即使总人数超出预定人数。

退出比赛

O.20. 弃权或被取消参赛资格的运动员名字将被删除，比赛成绩取消，该运动员将被视为未参加比赛。

GENERAL RULES FOR DIRECT ELIMINATION

o.21. The **direct elimination table (bout plan)** is established taking account of the classification table and the special rules for each competition (see Figure 7a). The principle of protection of nationality will not be applied.

o.22. The organisers of a competition must **publish the direct elimination bout plan**, showing on it the scheduled time for each bout from the table of 64 onwards.

o.23. **1.** The **direct elimination bouts** are for 15 hits or end when the three periods of three minutes, with a one-minute rest between each period, have passed. As an exception, **at sabre,** the first period ends either at the expiry of the three minutes or when one of the fencers has scored eight hits.

2. **During the one-minute rests** a person, named before the bout, may have access to the fencer.

3. **A clock, incorporated into the electrical scoring apparatus**, blocks the latter at the end of each period.

o.24. **1.** The **bout ends** when:

— One of the fencers has **scored 15 hits**; or

— **9 minutes of effective fencing time** have passed.

2. The fencer who has scored **the greater number of hits** is declared the winner.

3. If **at the end of regulation time the scores are equal,** the fencers fence for a deciding hit, with a maximum time limit of one minute. Before the fencing recommences the Referee draws lots to decide who will be the winner if scores are still equal at the end of the extra minute.

4. In this case the score recorded on the score-sheet is the **real score** achieved in the bout.

Withdrawal

o.25. When, for whatever reason, a fencer **cannot fence, or cannot complete his bout**, his opponent is declared winner of that bout. A fencer who withdraws does not lose his place in the overall classification of the competition.

Order of bouts

o.26. **1.** In each round of the direct elimination table (256, 128, 64, 32, 16, 8 or 4), the bouts are always called **in the order of the bout plan**, starting at the top and ending at the bottom.

2. This rule must also be applied for **each quarter of the table**, when the direct elimination is taking place simultaneously on 4 or 8 pistes.

3. A fencer must always be allowed a **rest period of ten minutes** between two consecutive bouts.

直接淘汰赛的基本规则

O.21. 直接淘汰赛对阵表根据小组赛排名和每项赛事的特殊规则指定（见附图7a）。同国籍运动员回避规则不再适用。

O.22. 赛事组织者须公布直接淘汰赛对阵表，并从64表开始标明预计比赛时间。

O.23. 1. 直接淘汰赛采用15剑制，或打满比赛时间，每场比赛3局，每局3分钟，每两局之间休息1分钟。佩剑例外，打满3分钟或其中一名运动员得到8分，第一阶段即结束。

2. 休息时间内，赛前指定的一名随队人员可以对运动员进行指导。

3. 与裁判器相连的计时器在每一阶段结束后都将终止裁判器工作。

O.24. 1. 比赛至以下情况即结束：

—— 一名运动员击中15剑；或者

—— 9分钟有效比赛时间全部用完。

2. 击中剑数多的运动员获胜。

3. 若在规定时间内出现平分，则需加赛1分钟，加时赛中击中第一剑的运动员即获胜。加时赛前，裁判员须先进行抽签决定优胜权归属，若平分情况持续至加时赛结束，则拥有优胜权的运动员获胜。

4. 在这种情况下，比赛记录表中将记录运动员的实际得分。

退出比赛

O.25. 无论出于何种原因，若一名运动员不能进行比赛或不能完成比赛，与其对阵的运动员将被宣布获胜。退赛运动员在比赛中的排名仍将被保留。

比赛顺序

O.26. 1. 对于直接淘汰赛（256，128，64，32，16，8或4人）中的每轮比赛，所有比赛都依照对阵表从头至尾按顺序进行。

2. 当直接淘汰赛同时在4条或8条剑道上进行时，每个四分之一表也必须执行该项规则。

3. 同一名运动员在连续两场比赛之间可休息10分钟。

The final

o.27. **1.** The final, which is by direct elimination, will preferably consist of 4 fencers.

2. The finals of both women's and men's events at the same weapon should preferably be held on the same day.

Classification

o.28. **1.** The **general classification** is obtained as follows:

First:	the winner of the bout for the first place
Second:	the loser of the bout for the first place

2. The two fencers who lose the semi-final matches are placed equal third, **when it is not necessary to separate them**.

3. When it is **necessary to separate them**, a bout for third and fourth places will be fought between the two losers of the semi-final matches.

4. The remainder are placed, within each round of the direct elimination, in accordance with their **classification for the composition of the direct elimination table**.

5. **The fencers eliminated in the round of pools** are ranked according to their classification in this round and they are placed after those who qualified for the direct elimination.

A. MIXED FORMULA - One qualifying round of pools, a preliminary direct elimination table, a main direct elimination table of 64 fencers to qualify for a final by direct elimination (Senior World Championships and Senior World Cup competitions)

o.29. This formula is used for the **individual competitions of the Senior World Championships** as well as for the **Senior World Cup competitions** and **Grand Prix competitions**.

o.30. Apart from the details that follow, the general rules for **pools and direct elimination** prescribed above apply.

o.31. **1.** The competition consists of **two phases**, a preliminary phase and a main phase, each of which are run on one day.

2. The day before the competition, the organizers must publish and send to the FIE the pools and relevant schedules, as well as the list of exempt fencers, at the latest at 3:00 p.m. (local time). To do so, they must download the entry file from the FIE web site at the latest the day before the competition. No addition may be made to pools already published unless they come from pools starting at the same time (cf o.12.1).

3. The **16 fencers entered, who are ranked highest in the most recent official FIE classification** are exempt from the preliminary phase.

决赛

o.27. 1. 决赛将按照直接淘汰赛的方式进行，最好应包含4名运动员。

2. 同一个剑种的男子和女子项目的决赛最好安排在同一天进行。

排名

o.28. 1. 总排名按照以下方式进行：

—— 争夺第一名的比赛中的胜者获得冠军；

—— 负者获得亚军。

2. 三、四名之间若无需决出名次，则两场半决赛中的负者获并列第三名。

3. 三、四名之间若需决出名次，则需要在两场半决赛的负者之间进行第三、四名的比赛。

4. 其余运动员的比赛名次根据直接淘汰赛对阵表初始排位来排列。

5. 对于小组循环赛中被淘汰的运动员，他们的比赛名次依据小组赛成绩排列，并排在所有获得直接淘汰赛资格的运动员之后。

A. 混合赛制（成年比赛）

小组循环赛，预淘汰赛，64表直接淘汰赛及决赛（成年世界锦标赛和成年世界杯赛）

o.29. 此赛制适用于成年世界锦标赛、世界杯赛及大奖赛的个人赛。

o.30. 除下列细则，上述小组循环赛和直接淘汰赛的基本规则同样适用。

o.31. 1. 比赛包括两个阶段，预赛和正式比赛，每阶段比赛时间为1天。

2. 比赛前一天，组委会须在当地时间15：00前公布小组赛名单、比赛时间以及免赛运动员名单，并发至国际剑联。因此最晚须在比赛前一天从国际剑联官网下载报名名单。小组赛名单公布后不得再增加运动员，除非运动员来自同时开始的小组赛（参见 o.12.1）。

3. 在所有报名参赛的运动员中，国际剑联排名最靠前的16名运动员将不参加预赛。

4. **Should a fencer who has been entered not turn up, a fine (cf o.86**, table of financial penalties and fines), payable to the FIE, will be inflicted on the Federation of the fencer at fault except in a case of force majeure which is duly justified.

5. **In the case of a tie** in the official FIE ranking between two or more fencers for the 16th exempt place, lots will be drawn to decide which of these fencers will benefit from exemption from the preliminary phase.

o.32. 1. **The preliminary phase** consists of one round of pools, from which 20%–30% of the participants in the pools are eliminated, based on the indices of all competing in them, and a preliminary direct elimination table. For Grand Prix competitions, the number of fencers eliminated on the indices of the pools must be 30%.

2. **After the round of pools,** the 16 fencers ranked highest on the general index (cf o.19) are exempt from the preliminary direct elimination table. Should there be a tie between two or more fencers for the 16th place, there will be a barrage for 5 hits to decide who is ranked 16th. Following the barrage, the ranking of the fencers is determined according to V, TD-TR, TD. (2016/17)

3. The remainder of the fencers qualifying from the pools will make up a **preliminary integral direct elimination table**. This will be based on the indices of the fencers in all the pools (in the case of a tie on indices, the fencers will be separated by drawing lots). This table, be it complete or incomplete, will be fenced until only 32 fencers remain.

o.33. 1. **The main phase** consists of an integral direct elimination table, which is fenced on four pistes, one quarter of the table per piste. The first round of the table of 64 may, however, if required for the organisation of the competition, be fenced on eight pistes. Grand Prix competitions must be fenced on (only) four pistes.

2. **The seeded fencers exempted from the preliminary phase** occupy places 1–16 in this table, drawing lots in pairs in the order of their official FIE classification.

3. **Should one of the 16 exempted fencers** who had been entered **not present himself** to fence (cf. o.31), his position in the table will remain empty and his federation will be required to pay to the FIE a fine (cf o.86, table of financial penalties and fines) unless his absence is caused by circumstances duly justified as being outside his control.

4. **The 16 fencers who have the highest indices after the round of pools** and who are thus exempt from the preliminary direct elimination table will take places 17–32, classified in the order of their indices (in the case of a tie on indices, the fencers will be separated by drawing lots).

5. **The 32 fencers qualifying from the preliminary direct elimination table** will occupy places 33–64, classified according to their indices after the round of pools.

o.34. There will be no bout for the third place. The two fencers who lose the semi-final matches will be placed **equal third**.

4. 若报名运动员最终未能参赛，则该运动员所属会员协会将须向国际剑联交纳罚款（参见 o.86经济处罚及罚款表）,经证实正当的不可抗力的情况除外。

5. 在确定可直接进入正式比赛的运动员时，若出现两名或多名运动员在国际剑联排名中并列第16位的情况，则以抽签方式决定其中一名运动员获得该资格。

O.32. 1. 预赛阶段包括小组循环赛和预淘汰赛，小组循环赛将根据比赛成绩指数淘汰20%至30%的运动员。大奖赛小组循环赛淘汰比例须为30%。

2. 小组循环赛后，指数位列前16名的运动员（见组织规则 o.19）不需参加预淘汰赛。如有两名或多名运动员同时位列第16名，将加赛5剑决定位次。运动员的排名将依次采用指数V,TD–TR,TD.

3. 其余运动员依据小组循环赛成绩指数组成预淘汰赛对阵表（成绩指数相同时由抽签决定位次）。无论该对阵表是否完整，都将决出前32名运动员。

O.33. 1. 正式比赛包括完整的直接淘汰赛对阵表，分四条剑道进行，每四分之一区安排在一条剑道。若出于竞赛组织需要，64表的第一轮比赛可同时在8条剑道进行。大奖赛只能同时在4条剑道上进行。

2. 未参加预赛阶段比赛的16名运动员依据其国际剑联初始排位分列对阵表第1–16号位，并两两抽签进行再排位。

3. 若16名已报名参赛的种子运动员中某名运动员最终未能参赛（参见 o.31），则其在对阵表中的位置将空缺，其所属会员协会须向国际剑联交纳罚款（参见 o.86，经济处罚及罚款表），经证实正当的不可控情况除外。

4. 小组循环赛决出的前16名运动员根据各自成绩指数分列直接淘汰赛对阵表第17–32号位（成绩指数相同时通过抽签决定位次），不参加预淘汰赛。

5. 预淘汰赛决出的前32名运动员，依据各自在小组循环赛中的成绩指数分列直接淘汰赛对阵表第33–64号位。

O.34. 不进行争夺第三名的比赛，半决赛中负于对手的两名运动员获并列第三名。

B. MIXED FORMULA - One qualifying round of pools, a direct elimination table to qualify for a final by direct elimination (Junior and Cadet World Championships and Junior World Cup competitions)

o.35. This formula is used for the **individual competitions of the Junior and Cadet World Championships** and the **Junior World Cup competitions**.

o.36. **Apart from the details that follow**, the general rules for pools and direct elimination described above apply.

o.37. The competitions are run on **one single day per weapon**.

o.38. The competition consists of **one round of pools**, in which **all the fencers present take part**, and an integral direct elimination table.

o.39. When drawing pools in the **World Cadet Championships**, the Directoire Technique will take account of the following orders of strength:

1. The **top 8** in the previous year's **World Cadet Championships**;
2. The **64 highest** ranked in the **official FIE junior ranking of the year in course**;
3. Those placed **9–32** in the previous year's **World Cadet Championships;**
4. Those ranked **65 onwards in the official FIE junior ranking of the year in course**;
5. The seeding provided by the **national federations;**
6. The **DT's decision**.

o.40. **1.** All the fencers qualifying from the round of pools are placed in a direct elimination table, complete or incomplete, according to the **indices resulting from the pools**. This table is fenced right through to the final.

2. From the last 32 the direct elimination bouts will take place:

- either **on 4 pistes**, with each quarter of the table fenced on one piste.

- or on 8 pistes, with each quarter of the table fenced on 2 pistes.

At the cadet and junior World Championships video refereeing is obligatory on these pistes.

o.41. There will be no bout for the third place. The two fencers who lose the semi-final matches will be placed **equal third**.

B. 混合赛制（青少年比赛）

小组循环赛，直接淘汰赛及决赛（世界青少年锦标赛及青年世界杯赛）

O.35. 此规则适用于世界青少年锦标赛及青年世界杯赛个人赛。

O.36. 除以下细则，上述关于小组循环赛及直接淘汰赛的基本规则同样适用。

O.37. 每个剑种比赛一天。

O.38. 比赛包括一轮由全部运动员参加的小组循环赛，以及完整的直接淘汰赛对阵表。

O.39. 在进行世界少年锦标赛小组赛排位时，技术委员会将依次考虑下列条件：

1. 上一年度世界少年锦标赛的前8名运动员。
2. 本年度国际剑联官方青年运动员排名的前64名运动员。
3. 上一年度世界少年锦标赛的9至32名。
4. 本年度国际剑联官方青年运动员排名的第65名至最后一名运动员。
5. 各会员协会提供的排名。
6. 技术委员会的决定。

O.40. 1. 所有小组循环赛选拔出的运动员根据其小组赛成绩指数进行排位，组成直接淘汰赛对阵表，无论是否完整，进行比赛直至决赛。

2. 从直接淘汰赛32表开始，比赛可以：
—— 在4条剑道进行，每四分之一区在一条剑道上；
—— 或者在8条剑道上进行，每四分之一区在两条剑道上。

世界青少年锦标赛中，上述剑道必须配备录像裁判系统。

O.41. 不进行争夺第三名的比赛，半决赛中负于对手的两名运动员获并列第三名。

CHAPTER 6. TEAM COMPETITIONS

A. SENIOR AND JUNIOR WORLD CHAMPIONSHIPS (AND OLYMPIC GAMES) TEAM EVENTS

o.42. At each weapon teams consist of **three fencers**, with or without a reserve.

A team may only begin a match **if it is complete**.

o.43. **1.** The competition is run by **integral direct elimination** with a direct elimination table which may be incomplete (see Figure 7b).

2. At the Junior and Senior World Championships the teams will occupy the places in the table according to the **most recent official team ranking of the FIE**. The teams that are not classified will occupy the last places in the table, and will be separated by drawing of lots.

3. At the Senior and Junior World Championships, all places in the table up to 16th place will be fought for. From 17th place onwards teams will be classified, within each round of the table, according to their initial place in the table.

o.44. The **formula** for the competition is as follows.

1. The **relay formula** applies to all weapons.

2. The three fencers of one team fence the three fencers of the opposing team (**9 relay bouts**).

3. The bouts of each match have to be fought in the following **order**:

3–6	2–5
1–5	1–4
2–4	2–6
1–6	3–5
3–4	

If this order is **altered**, intentionally or unintentionally, all the hits scored following the modification are annulled and the match is resumed in the correct order. (cf. t.86).

4. The position of each team on the match score-sheet is decided by drawing lots. **The order of the individual fencers** is then decided by the team captains.

5. Each 'lap' (bout) of the relay match consists of **five hits** (5, 10, 15, 20, etc.); the maximum time for each bout is **3 minutes**.

第六章　团体赛

A. 成年、青年世界锦标赛（及奥运会）团体赛

O.42. 对于每个剑种，参赛队须由3名运动员组成，有无替补队员均可。每队只有在人员齐整的情况下才可进行比赛。

O.43. 1. 比赛按照直接淘汰赛对阵表进行，无论是否完整（见附图7b）。

2. 青年和成年世锦赛团体赛对阵表中各参赛队排位依据最新的国际剑联排名进行。没有排名的队伍排在最后，并通过抽签的方式决定位次。

3. 成年和青年世锦赛的第1至16名均通过比赛决出，从第17名开始，按各队初始排位决定比赛名次。

O.44. 赛制如下：

1. 所有剑种的比赛均按照接力方式进行。

2. 每场比赛其中一个队的3名运动员将与另一个队的3名运动员进行比赛（共9局对阵连续进行）。

3. 每场比赛须按以下次序进行比赛：

3–6	2–5
1–5	1–4
2–4	2–6
1–6	3–5
3–4	

若以上次序被改变，无论有意或无意，所有改变次序后的得分将被取消，比赛将按照正确的顺序恢复（见技术规则 t.86）。

4. 各队在比赛记分牌上的位置通过抽签决定，运动员的出场次序由各队领队决定。

5. 每局对阵包含5次击中（5，10，15，20等），每局对阵比赛时间不超过3分钟。

6. The first two opponents fence until one of them has scored five hits, within the time limit of 3 minutes.

The next two opponents fence until one of their scores has reached ten hits, within the time limit of 3 minutes, and so on with successive bouts, cumulatively, of five hits.

7. If by the expiry of 3 minutes of fencing time **the intended score for the bout has not been achieved**, the next two fencers take up the score where it was left off and fence up to the maximum score intended for their bout as normal, within the time limit of 3 minutes.

8. **The winning team** is that which first reaches the maximum score of 45 hits, or that which has scored the greatest number of hits after the expiry of regulation time.

9. If **at the end of regulation time** for the last bout the scores are **equal**, the match continues for a deciding hit, with a maximum time limit of one minute, fought for by the fencers of the last bout in the match. Before the fencing recommences the Referee draws lots to decide who will be the winner if scores are still equal at the end of the extra minute.

10. a) In the course of a match the captain of a team may ask to **substitute** for a fencer the reserve nominated before the start of the match. This substitution may only be made at the end of a bout. (Until 09/15)The fencer who has been replaced may not fence again during that match in order to replace a fencer on the piste, (From 09/15) However, the fencer who has been replaced may fence one more time during that match, but only to replace the fencer who originally substituted him. This second replacement is not allowed if the first replacement has been made for the reasons listed in article o.44.11. No further substitution for a fencer on the piste is allowed, even in the case of an accident or unavoidable circumstances. **The announcement** that a fencer is to be substituted must be made at the latest before the beginning of the bout preceding the next bout of the fencer who is to be replaced and must be reported by the Referee to the opposing team captain.

At World Championships and Olympic Games, the referee must also report this immediately to the Directoire Technique.

b) If an **accident** occurs in the bout which follows the request for a substitution, the team captain may annul that request.

c) If the captain of the opposing team has also requested a substitution, this substitution may be **implemented or cancelled**.

11. a) If a member of a team is **obliged to retire** during a match as the result of **an accident** which has been **duly recognised** by a medical representative of the FIE, the captain

of his team may ask to put in a reserve to continue the match at the point where the competitor who was obliged to retire withdrew, even during a bout in progress.

b) However, **a competitor who is thus replaced** cannot again take his place in the team **during the same match**.

6. 两队的第一名运动员对阵，当一方运动员在3分钟内击中5剑后，该局对阵结束。

两队的第二名运动员对阵，当一方运动员在3分钟内累计击中10剑后，该局对阵结束；依此类推，每局对阵递增5剑。

7. 如果在3分钟内，双方运动员均未击中预定剑数，则下一局的两名运动员在现有比分基础上继续进行比赛，直至累计击中剑数达到该局预定剑数为止，限时也为3分钟。

8. 首先获得45分的一方或在规定时间内击中剑数较多的一方获胜。

9. 如果最后一局比赛的规定时间结束时，两队击中的剑数相同，则由最后一局的两名运动员进行1分钟的加时赛，首先击中的一方即获胜。加时赛前裁判将进行抽签决定优胜权归属，若1分钟加时赛结束时双方得分仍相同，则抽中优胜权的一方获胜。

10. a. 比赛中，领队可提出由赛前指定的替补队员替换场上另一名运动员。换人只可在一局比赛结束后进行。被替换下的运动员可以再次上场，但只可以替换最初替换他的运动员。如果第一次换人是由于组织规则 o.44.11 中说明的原因，则不可以进行二次换人。此后不可再换人，即使是出现事故或不可抗力状况。换人的决定须最晚于拟换人比赛局的前一局比赛开始前报告主裁判，并由主裁判通知对方领队。

在世锦赛和奥运会，裁判还须立即向技术委员会报告换人情况。

b. 如果在换人要求提出后进行的下一局比赛中突然发生意外情况，领队可以取消换人请求。

c. 如果对方领队也要求换人，此换人请求可继续执行或取消。

11. a. 当一名运动员在比赛中受伤且国际剑联医疗代表认为其不得不退出比赛时，该队领队可请求由一名替补队员继续进行比赛，即便一局比赛正在进行中。

b. 因该原因被替换的运动员在当场比赛中不得重新上场比赛。

12. If both a fencer and the reserve, if any, are forced to retire, or if a fencer is excluded, their team has **lost the match**.

13. When for any reason whatever a team does not complete an event in which it is taking part, the Directoire Technique will apply the rules laid down for a competitor who does not complete an event in an individual competition, **each team being considered in its entirety as being a single competitor**.

14. When a team **fails to appear** against another team it is considered:

a) as not completing the event in which it is taking part, if it has already fenced against another team (cf. o.25);

b) as not competing at all in the event, if it is its first match.

B. JUNIOR AND SENIOR WORLD CUP TEAM COMPETITIONS

o.45. Apart from the following aspects, the competition is run in accordance with rules laid down for the team events in the Junior and Senior World Championships respectively.

o.46. If a team **does not begin a match** they will be disqualified from the competition and thus will not receive any World Team Cup points, unless this is because of an injury or illness, duly attested by the duty doctor.

o.47. **1.** The **first four teams** will be placed in the direct elimination table according to the current official team ranking of the FIE (cf. o.86); the remaining ranked teams will be placed in the table by drawing of lots in pairs.

The **teams that are not classified** will occupy the last places in the table, and will be separated by drawing of lots.

2. The **table will be drawn up** based on the ranking of the teams entered, at the latest one hour after the quarter finals of the individual event.

12. 如果一名运动员及替补队员均被迫放弃比赛，或一名运动员被取消比赛资格，则该队将被宣布负于对手。

13. 当某参赛队无论出于何种原因不能完成已经开始的比赛时，技术委员会将参照个人赛中关于未完成比赛的规则执行，每个参赛队整体上视作为是一名运动员。

14. 当某支参赛队未到场比赛，则：

a. 如果该队已经与另一队进行过比赛（参见 o.25），则将被视为没有完成所参加的这一站比赛；

b. 如果这是该队的第一场比赛，则该队将被视为未参加该站比赛。

B. 青年和成年世界杯团体赛

o.45. 除以下特殊规则外，比赛将依据青年和成年世界锦标赛团体赛的各项规则进行。

o.46. 如果一支队伍没有开始任何一场团体赛，则将被取消比赛资格，并且不能获得世界杯团体赛的积分，除非由当值医生证明为受伤或生病。

o.47. 1. 排名前4的队伍将根据国际剑联当前团体积分排名排在直接淘汰对阵表中（参见 o.86）；其余有积分排名的队伍将按照两两抽签的方式进行再排位。

没有积分排名的队伍将排在最后，并通过抽签决定位次。

2. 团体赛对阵表将根据参赛队的积分排名制定，最迟在个人赛1/4决赛结束后1小时内完成。

CHAPTER 7. ORGANISATION OF OFFICIAL FIE COMPETITIONS

A. COMMON CONDITIONS

PROGRAMME OF COMPETITIONS

o.48. **1.** The programme of fencing events at the **Olympic Games** currently comprises ten events. Any change in the number of events must be approved by the Congress.

2. The programme of the **Senior World Fencing Championships** comprises twelve events, six individual and six team — male foil, female foil, male épée, female épée, male sabre and female sabre.

3. The programme of the **Junior and Cadet World Fencing Championships** comprises twelve individual events (six junior and six cadet), and six junior team events — at male foil, female foil, male épée, female épée, male sabre and female sabre. These begin with the cadet events, followed by the individual junior events and lastly the junior team events.

4. The organisers must submit the **programme of events** to the Executive Committee for its approval.

Venues, installations, equipment, accreditation, circulation of people in the competition enclosure, administrative organisation of the Organising Committee, personnel, various publications and the official programme

o.49. The Organising Committee must take note of the instructions in the **Specifications** ('Cahier des Charges') specific to each type of competition.

ENTRIES TO COMPETITIONS

Official invitation

o.50. **1.** For all the official competitions of the FIE except the Olympic Games, the **official invitation** is the letter in which the organising federation invites every FIE member federation to take part in the Championships.

2. For the **World Championships**, this invitation must be sent to all the member federations, without exception, at least six months before the competitions.

3. For **World Cup competitions**, it must be sent out at least two months before the competition in question.

第七章　国际剑联正式比赛的组织

A. 通用规则

项目设置

O.48. 1. 奥运会击剑比赛目前共设10个小项。所有关于比赛小项数量的变化都须经代表大会批准。

2. 世界成年击剑锦标赛共设12个小项，6项个人赛及6项团体赛：男子花剑、女子花剑、男子重剑、女子重剑、男子佩剑、女子佩剑比赛。

3. 世界青少年击剑锦标赛共设12项个人赛（6项青年赛及6项少年赛）和6项青年团体赛：男子花剑、女子花剑、男子重剑、女子重剑、男子佩剑、女子佩剑。首先进行少年组比赛，然后是青年组个人赛，最后进行青年组团体赛。

4. 组委会须将日程安排提交国际剑联执委会批准。

场地、设施、器材、制证、人员流线、组委会行政机构、工作人员、各类印刷品及秩序册

O.49. 比赛组委会必须按照比赛操作手册中关于不同类型比赛的详细要求组织比赛。

比赛报名

正式邀请函

O.50. 1. 除奥运会外，国际剑联的所有正式比赛，均由负责组织比赛的会员协会以信函形式向国际剑联各会员协会发出正式的邀请。

2. 世界锦标赛，组织者必须最晚于赛前6个月向国际剑联所有会员协会发出邀请，不得有例外。

3. 世界杯赛，邀请函必须最晚于赛前2个月发出。

Advance programme

o.51. A **brochure**, comprising an **'advance programme'** of the Championships, must be sent to the member federations together with the official invitation. It should contain at least the following information:

a) the official name of the Organising Committee, postal address, e-mail address and telephone and fax numbers;

b) the proposed timetable;

c) organisational details;

d) information on means of transport, visas, customs duties, etc.;

e) information on hotels, their price, their location relative to the competition venue.

ENTRY FORMS

Commitment to take part in the World Championships

o.52. The **forms** must be sent to all federations at the same time as the official invitation. The federations must indicate their **intention to participate** three months before the beginning of the Championships.

Entries for World Championships (all categories) and junior and senior zonal championships

o.53. **1.** Three months before the start of the World Championships, the federations will receive an **entry form** from the Organising Committee, on which they are required to specify the **number** of fencers and teams participating in each event of the competition's programme, two months before the start of the first event.

2. The entry of fencers and teams by name is to be made via the FIE website. This entry of the names of the fencers and all possible substitutes, and the entry of teams, must be made:

- fifteen days (by midnight, Lausanne time) before the first event of the World Championships at the latest.

- seven days (by midnight, Lausanne time) before the first event of the Zonal Championships at the latest.

3. Withdrawal of a fencer.

After the **cut-off date** for entries, there can be no further withdrawal of a name except in any case of force majeure duly justified.

Should a fencer or team who have been entered **not present themselves to fence**, their federation will be penalised by a **fine** (cf o.86, table of financial penalties and fines), payable to the FIE, except in cases of properly authenticated 'force majeure'.

比赛信息

O.51. 在发正式邀请的同时还须向各会员协会发放“比赛信息”手册，其中至少应包含以下信息：

a. 组委会的正式名称、通讯地址、电子邮件地址、电话及传真号码；

b. 初步日程安排；

c. 组织工作情况；

d. 有关交通、签证、海关等方面的信息；

e. 关于宾馆的价格及宾馆相对于比赛场馆的位置。

报名表

世界锦标赛报名表

O.52. 报名表须与正式邀请函同时发至各会员协会。各会员协会应在开赛3个月前表明其参赛的意向。

世界锦标赛（所有组别）及洲际青年及成年锦标赛的报名

O.53. 1. 世界锦标赛，各会员协会将在赛前3个月收到组委会发布的人数报名表。各会员协会应在第一个小项比赛开始前2个月确定其参加每个小项比赛的运动员及团体数量。

2. 运动员及团体的姓名报名将通过国际剑联网站进行。运动员和替补运动员的姓名报名以及团体报名最迟要在以下时间前完成：

—— 世界锦标赛第一个小项比赛开始前15天（洛桑时间零时）完成。

—— 洲际锦标赛第一个小项比赛开始前7天（洛桑时间零时）完成。

3. 运动员报名取消

报名截止后，除非由于被认可的不可抗力状况，任何运动员不得取消报名。

除非由于被认可的不可抗力状况，若已报名的运动员或团体未参加比赛，则需向国际剑联缴纳罚款（参见 o.86 经济处罚及罚款表）。

4. **Addition of fencer(s) after the cut-off date.**

   Nevertheless one or more fencers may be added, up until 10.00am (local time in the town hosting the World or Zonal Championships) on the day before the competition, after payment to the FIE of a penalty (cf o.86, table of financial penalties and fines) per fencer added. To do this the national federation must address a request to the FIE to add a fencer, together with immediate payment of the penalty.

5. **Changes of names**, only with the agreement of the FIE can only be made at the latest up to 24 hours before the start of each event.

Entries by name for Senior and Junior World Cup competitions, Grand Prix competitions, Satellite competitions, Junior and Senior World Cup team competitions.

o.54 1. **The entry of the names** of the fencers and all possible replacements, and the entry of teams, must be made via the FIE website 7 days before the competition at the latest (midnight Lausanne time).

   For team entries, the names of the fencers making up the teams may be changed, by informing the organisers, up to the day before the competition, at the latest at the end of the quarter finals of the individual competition. However, a replacement can be made after this stage, and at the latest at the end of the individual event, in the case of injury or illness duly certified by the competition medical doctor.

2. **Withdrawal of a fencer or team.**

   After the closing dead-line for entries, no named fencer or team may be withdrawn except for reasons of injury or force majeure: the national federation must inform the FIE and the organisers.

3. **Substitution of a fencer.**

   Until the Wednesday preceding the competition (midnight, Lausanne time), a fencer may be replaced by another. To do this, the national federation must send to the FIE, by fax or e-mail, a written request to substitute the fencer.

4. **Addition of a fencer or a team after the dead-line.**

   a) However, until the Tuesday preceding the competition (midnight, Lausanne time), one or more fencers and/or a team may be added by their national federation after payment to the FIE of a penalty (cf o.86, table of financial penalties and fines) for each additional entry.

   To do this, the national federation must send to the FIE (by fax or e-mail) a request for the additional fencer(s) and/or team and a written commitment to pay the penalty within 15 days.

   b) From the Wednesday preceding the competition until 12 noon (local time) on the day preceding the competition, one or more fencers and/or a team may be added by national federations after payment to the FIE of a higher penalty (cf o.86, table of financial penalties and fines) for each additional entry.

4. 报名截止后增加报名

在当地时间比赛前一天上午10点前（世界锦标赛或洲际锦标赛举办地当地时间），可以在向国际剑联缴纳罚款后（参见 o.86 经济处罚及罚款表），增加一名或多名运动员的报名。为此，相关会员协会须向国际剑联提出请求，并立即缴纳罚款。

5. 更换运动员，必须经国际剑联同意，最迟在运动员参加的小项比赛前24小时进行。

世界杯青年赛、成年赛、大奖赛、卫星赛、青年及成年世界杯团体赛的报名

O.54. 1. 运动员和替补以及团体的报名须通过国际剑联网站进行，最迟在比赛开始前7天完成（洛桑时间零时）。

团体赛换人，可最晚于比赛前一天个人赛1/4决赛结束前向组织者申请。若为因伤换人并取得了大会医生对运动员伤病的认可，则换人最晚时间为个人赛结束。

2. 运动员或团体取消报名

报名结束后，任何运动员及团体不得取消报名。因伤或不可抗力取消报名，则该运动员所属会员协会须通知国际剑联及组织者。

3. 替换运动员

直到比赛前的周三（洛桑时间零时），可以替换运动员。为此，相关会员协会须向国际剑联提交书面换人申请（传真或电邮）。

4. 报名截止后增加报名

a）直到比赛前的周二（洛桑时间零时），可以在向国际剑联缴纳罚款后（参见o.86经济处罚及罚款表），增加一名或多名运动员的报名。

为此，相关会员协会须向国际剑联提交关于增加运动员或团体的书面申请（传真或电邮），并承诺在15日之内缴纳罚款。

b）从比赛前的周三直到比赛前一天的中午12点（当地时间）前，可以在向国际剑联缴纳更高额的罚款后（参见 o.86 经济处罚及罚款表），增加一名或多名运动员和/或团体的报名。

To do this, the national federation must send to the FIE (by fax or e-mail) a request for the additional fencer(s) **and/or team and a written commitment to pay the penalty within 15 days.**

5. Should a fencer or team who have been entered **not present themselves to fence**, their federation will be penalised with a **fine (cf** o.86, table of financial penalties and fines), payable to the FIE, except in cases of properly authenticated 'force majeure'.

6. The organisers of all official competitions must, at risk of a penalty of a fine payable to the FIE (cf o.86, table of financial penalties and fines), refuse the entry of any fencers not appearing on lists conforming with the above, **any entry** not requested by a federation and any entry of either fencer or referee not in possession of an FIE licence valid for the current season.

Age of participants

o.55. 1. No fencer is allowed to take part in an official event of the FIE unless he or she is **at least 13 years old** on 1 January in the year of the competition.

2. Fencers taking part in all the official FIE Cadet competitions must be under 17 years old at midnight on the 31st December of the year preceding the year in which the competition takes place.

3. Fencers taking part in all the official FIE Junior competitions, individual or team, must be under 20 years old at midnight on 31st December of the year preceding the year in which the competition takes place (cf o.80).

4. Apart from the stipulations above, there is no maximum age limit for those taking part in any other official events of the FIE, except in regard to the different Veteran categories.

5. All participants in an official competition of the FIE who are under the age of majority in the country in which such competition is being held must either:

   1. be accompanied by a person who is a parent or guardian of the participant or who has **been delegated in a form valid in the country of the competition** from a parent or guardian of such participant to act on behalf of the participant regarding health related issues; or

   2. have such power of attorney issued to a person who has achieved his/her majority and who will be at the competition site during the competition and has agreed to accept the responsibility delineated in such power.

6. The age groups in veteran competitions are:

   a) Age group 50-59: Must be at least 50 years old and less than 60 years old in the year of the competition.

   b) Age group 60-69: Must be at least 60 years old and less than 70 years old in the year of the competition.

   c) Age group 70+: Must be at least 70 years old in the year of the competition.

为此，相关会员协会须向国际剑联提交关于增加运动员或团体的书面申请（传真或电邮），并承诺在15日之内缴纳罚款。

5. 除非由于被认可的不可抗力状况，若已报名的运动员或团体未参加比赛，则需向国际剑联缴纳罚款（参见 o.86 经济处罚及罚款表）。

6. 所有正式比赛的组织者必须拒绝不符合报名条件的运动员的报名、不是由会员协会提出的报名、没有当赛季国际剑联会员证的运动员及裁判的报名，否则将需向国际剑联缴纳罚款（参见 o.86 经济处罚及罚款表）。

参赛运动员年龄

o.55. 1. 截止比赛年度的1月1日，未满13岁的运动员均不得参加国际剑联正式比赛。

2. 参加国际剑联正式少年比赛的运动员年龄须在17岁以下，运动员年龄以比赛前一年12月31日零时计。

3. 参加国际剑联正式青年比赛个人赛及团体赛的运动员年龄须在20岁以下，运动员年龄以比赛前一年12月31日零时计（参见 o.80）。

4. 除了以上提到的几点，国际剑联正式比赛没有对运动员最高年龄的限制，老将赛不同组别的比赛除外。

5. 任何参加国际剑联正式比赛的未满举办国法定成年年龄的运动员须：

1）由父母一方或监护人陪伴，或由父母一方或监护人按照比赛举办国认可的方式授权的代表陪伴，以代表运动员处理健康相关的事宜；或

2）将运动员监护权授予某名比赛期间能够在现场并同意承担监护义务的成年人。

6. 老将赛年龄组别划分如下：

a）50~59岁组：在比赛年度年龄须至少满50岁并未满60岁。

b）60~69岁组：在比赛年度年龄须至少满60岁并未满70岁。

c）70岁以上组：在比赛年度年龄须至少满70岁。

DIRECTOIRE TECHNIQUE AND FIE DELEGATES AT OFFICIAL FIE COMPETITIONS

o.56. **a)** Apart from the specific areas of competence which are the responsibility of the other FIE technical delegates specified hereafter, the technical management of the official competitions of the FIE is entrusted to a **Directoire Technique**.

b) The members of the Directoire Technique and the other official delegates of the FIE cannot act in any other capacity at the competition, such as team captain, official delegate of their federation, referee, competitor, etc.

c) The Directoire Technique and the official delegates of the FIE must always attend events from beginning to end, so as to solve any problem which could arise and thus ensure that the event continues to run smoothly.

d) All the decisions of the Directoire Technique and the official delegates of the FIE must be displayed sufficiently in advance on a clearly visible notice-board to be consulted by the fencers and officials. In principle, fencers and officials are kept informed by their heads of delegation or captains, and they may not make any complaint against changes in the timetable or any other matter about which information has been displayed within the stipulated time limits.

Nomination of the Directoire Technique

o.57. The Directoire Technique is composed of people who have the experience and competence to organise competitions.

1. World Championships and Olympic Games.

a) The Directoire Technique is composed of **six** members of different nationalities, one of whom must represent the organising country.

b) The President of the Directoire Technique and the other members are appointed by the Executive Committee of the FIE.

2. World Cup competitions.

a) The Directoire Technique is composed of three qualified persons from the organising country or invited by them.

3. Veterans World Championships

a) The Directoire Technique is composed of four members of different nationalities, one of whom must represent the organising country.

国际剑联正式比赛的技术委员会及国际剑联官方代表

O.56. a）除属于其他国际剑联代表的特殊职责，国际剑联正式比赛的技术管理工作由技术委员会负责。

b）技术委员会成员及其他国际剑联官方代表不得同时在该比赛中担任其他职务，例如领队、会员协会代表、裁判员或运动员等。

c）技术委员会成员及其他国际剑联官方代表须全程参加比赛，以便时刻准备解决突发问题，确保比赛顺利进行。

d）技术委员会及其他国际剑联官方代表所做出的一切决定须充分提前、并醒目地张贴在通告栏中，以便参赛运动员及官员查阅。原则上，参赛运动员和官员通过其团长或领队获得比赛最新信息，他们不应对竞赛日程变更或其他任何已按照时间要求提前通知的事项提出异议。

技术委员会成员的指派

O.57. 技术委员会由具备比赛组织经验及能力的成员组成。

1. 世锦赛及奥运会

a. 技术委员会由6名不同国籍的成员组成，其中1名代表东道主。

b. 技术委员会主席及其他成员由国际剑联执委会指派。

2. 世界杯

a. 技术委员会由来自东道主的3名合格成员组成，或由东道主邀请。

3. 世界老将锦标赛

a. 技术委员会由4名不同国籍的成员组成，其中1名代表东道主。

Functions of the Directoire Technique

o.58. **1.** The functions of the Directoire Technique include the **strict organisation** of the different events, except the responsibilities of the other delegates of the FIE (cf o.61, o.62, o.63). It has the obligation to see that the Rules are adhered to and cannot decide on any departure from the Rules except when circumstances arise in which it is absolutely impossible to apply them.

2. The Directoire Technique is responsible for the **technical organisation** of the competitions and for ensuring their smooth running.

3. Hence:

- **a)** It ensures the co-ordination between the Organising Committee, the Directoire Technique, the official delegates of the FIE and the other functions of the FIE;
- **b)** It checks the **entries**;
- **c)** It draws up the **pool sheets** and **direct elimination table**;
- **d)** It allocates the pistes;
- **e)** It supervises the **progress** of the event(s);
- **f)** It checks **results** with the help of the Organising Committee;
- **g)** It prepares the **subsequent events** sufficiently in advance to be able to warn the fencers, officials and judges;
- **h)** It supervises the **dissemination** of results.

4. Furthermore the Directoire Technique has **disciplinary responsibility** at competitions but only as a collective entity. In the event of a tied vote within the Directoire Technique, the **vote of the Directoire Technique President is decisive**.

Operation

o.59. Designation of refereeing, SEMI, and medical delegates

Refereeing delegates must be members of the FIE Refereeing Commission. SEMI delegates must be members of the FIE SEMI Commission. Medical delegates must be a members of the FIE Medical Commission.

1. World Championships and Olympic Games

A chief Refereeing delegate and 5 more Refereeing delegates, a chief SEMI delegate and 2 more SEMI delegates and 2 Medical delegates are appointed by the FIE Executive Committee following the recommendations of the respective commissions.

2. Senior World Cup competitions

One Refereeing delegate is appointed by the Executive Committee following the recommendation of the Refereeing Commission.

3. Veteran's World Championships

One Refereeing delegate, one SEMI delegate and one Medical delegate are appointed by the FIE Executive Committee following the recommendations of the respective commissions.

技术委员会职责

O.58. 1. 除国际剑联其他代表承担的职责外（详见o.61、o.62、o.63），技术委员会负责严谨地组织不同类型的比赛，有义务监督规则是否得到执行，并且无权决定违背任何规则，除非在某些情况下，这些规则毫无实施的可能。

2. 技术委员会负责比赛技术组织，确保比赛顺利进行。

3. 因此，技术委员会具体职责包括：

a. 负责组委会、技术委员会、国际剑联官方代表及国际剑联其他职能之间的协调；

b. 审核比赛报名；

c. 制订小组循环赛分组名单及直接淘汰赛对阵表；

d. 分配剑道；

e. 监督比赛过程；

f. 在组委会的协助下核对比赛成绩；

g. 充分提前准备将要进行的比赛，以便通知运动员、官员及裁判；

h. 监督比赛成绩的分发。

4. 此外，技术委员会还应负责比赛纪律，但须集体行动。若技术委员会投票出现等额情况，则技术委员会主任的投票拥有决定权。

O.59. 裁判代表、器材代表、医疗代表的指派

裁判代表须为国际剑联裁判员委员会委员。器材代表须为国际剑联器材委员会委员。医疗代表须为国际剑联医疗委员会委员。

1. 世界锦标赛及奥运会

由执委会根据相关委员会的推荐确定人选：1名主裁判代表及其他5名裁判代表；1名主器材代表及其他2名器材代表；2名医疗代表。

2. 成年世界杯赛

执委会根据裁判员委员会的推荐确定1名裁判代表。

3. 老将世锦赛

执委会根据相关委员会的推荐确定1名裁判代表、1名器材代表及1名医疗代表。

o.60. Functions of the Refereeing delegates

1. The functions of the Refereeing delegates include the strict and complete organisation of the refereeing of events. They have the obligation to see that the Rules are adhered to and cannot themselves decide on any departure from the Rules except when circumstances arise in which it is absolutely impossible to apply them.

2. Refereeing delegates are responsible for organising the refereeing aspect of events and ensuring that they run smoothly.

3. Hence:

a) They organise the referee's meeting on the day before the championships or event.

b) They establish the list of referees the day before each competition.

c) They observe the referees at work and make selections as mandated in articles t.37, t.38 and t.39.

d) They review protests and provide solutions in conformity with the instructions in article t.122.

4. For questions concerning the rules during FIE competitions (including the World Championships and Olympic Games), the Refereeing Commission delegate(s) alone are competent to judge a referee's decision from the beginning to the end of the bout.

5. Furthermore, a Refereeing delegate is an entity who has disciplinary responsibility at competitions; Article t.97 defines the extent of his or her authority.

o.61. SEMI and medical delegate duties

1. The functions of the SEMI delegate include the strict and complete organisation of the weapon control and the installations of events. They have the obligation to see that the Rules are adhered to and cannot themselves decide on any departure from the Rules except when circumstances arise in which it is absolutely impossible to apply them

2. SEMI delegates are responsible for organising the aspects of equipment and installations at events and ensuring that they run smoothly.

3. Hence, SEMI delegates:

a) Organise the equipment control and oversee its operations.

b) Verify the technical installations and the homologation of the various items of equipment.

c) Assist referees over material problems during matches.

4. The functions of the medical delegates include the strict and complete organisation of the medical aspect. They have the obligation to see that the Rules are adhered to and cannot themselves decide on any departure from the Rules except when circumstances arise in which it is absolutely impossible to apply them.

O.60. 裁判代表的职责

1. 裁判代表的职责包括对比赛裁判工作的严谨全面的组织管理。他们有义务监督规则是否得到执行，并且他们自己无权决定违背任何规则，除非在某些情况下，这些规则毫无实施的可能。

2. 裁判代表负责比赛裁判方面的组织工作，以确保其运行顺利。

3. 因此：
   a）他们在锦标赛或比赛前一天组织召开裁判员会议。
   b）他们在每场比赛前一天制定裁判员名单。
   c）他们对裁判员的临场执裁进行监督并依据 t.37、t.38、t.39授权对裁判员进行挑选。
   d）他们根据 t.122 对抗议进行审查及处理。

4. 在国际剑联比赛中出现的关于规则的问题（包括世锦赛及奥运会），裁判员委员会代表有权对临场裁判员在整场比赛中的决定做出裁决。

5. 此外，裁判代表还负有比赛纪律方面的职责，t.97 描述了其在此方面的职能范围。

O.61. 器材代表及医疗代表职责

1. 器材代表的职责包括严谨全面地组织器材检查及比赛场地布置工作。他们有义务监督规则是否得到执行，并且他们自己无权决定违背任何规则，除非在某些情况下，这些规则毫无实施的可能。

2. 器材代表负责比赛器材及场地布置方面的组织工作，以确保其顺利运行。

3. 因此，器材代表：
   a）组织器材检查并监督该项工作。
   b）负责各项技术设备安装及调试。
   c）针对比赛中器材方面的问题协助裁判员工作。

4. 医疗代表的职责包括严谨全面地组织医疗方面的工作。他们有义务监督规则是否得到执行，并且他们自己无权决定违背任何规则，除非在某些情况下，这些规则毫无实施的可能。

5. Hence, medical delegates:

a) Verify the medical services and oversee their operation.

b) Supervise the anti-doping control.

c) Oversee the evaluation and treatment of an injury or cramp in accordance with t.33.

o.62. Supervisor

For questions concerning **the rules** during FIE competitions (including the World Championships and Olympic Games), the Refereeing Commission delegate(s) alone are competent to judge a referee's decision from the beginning to the end of the bout.

At competitions where there is no Refereeing Commission delegate, it is **the Supervisor** who fulfils these respective functions (cf o.77).

The Supervisor settles any other **disputes** that might arise in World Cup and Grand Prix competitions.

SUPERVISION BY THE FIE

o.63. With the aim of ensuring that the rules are observed at the World Championships and Olympic Games, the President and the members of the Bureau of the FIE have the right to **attend all meetings of the Directoire Technique** and of the official delegates of the FIE. The Directoire Technique is obliged to give them notice of such meetings.

It is the responsibility of the Bureau of the FIE or of its designated representative to settle any other disputes which arise at World Championships.

ANTI-DOPING TESTING

o.64. An **anti-doping test** must be carried out at all official competitions of the FIE in accordance with the regulations in Article t.127 and the Anti-Doping Rules of the FIE. It may begin from the start of the competition and applies to fencers who have finished fencing.

5. 因此，医疗代表：

a）核查比赛医疗服务工作并监督其运行。

b）监督反兴奋剂工作。

c）根据 t.33 对运动员伤病或抽筋的评估及治疗进行监督。

O.62. 观察员

在国际剑联比赛中出现的关于规则的问题（包括世锦赛及奥运会），裁判员委员会代表有权对临场裁判员在整场比赛中的决定做出裁决。

若比赛无裁判代表出席，则由观察员代行其相关职责（参见 o.77）。

观察员负责处理在世界杯及大奖赛中其他任何可能出现的纠纷。

O.63. 国际剑联的监督

为了保证世锦赛及奥运会比赛中规则的执行，国际剑联主席及执行局成员有权出席技术委员会及国际剑联官方代表的所有会议，技术委员会有义务向其提供会议通知。

国际剑联执行局或其指定的代表有责任处理在世锦赛期间发生的其他一切纠纷。

反兴奋剂检查

O.64. 国际剑联的所有正式比赛均必须根据 t.127及国际剑联反兴奋剂规则进行反兴奋剂检查。检查可以从比赛一开始起启动，在运动员结束比赛后实施。

B. WORLD CHAMPIONSHIPS

ANNUAL CHAMPIONSHIPS

Entries

o.65. At the **Senior World Championships**, entries are limited to four fencers per weapon per nation for the individual events and one team per weapon per nation for the team events.

Referees

o.66. **1.** **Refereeing** at World Championships is carried out by referees chosen by the Executive Committee of the FIE at the proposal of the Refereeing Committee.

2. Referees' travel and board and lodging **costs** are paid by the Organising Committee, who in return will receive all the entry fees.

3. Referees **must** attend the **refereeing meeting** that takes place the day before the World Championships.

Invitations for international officials

o.67. **1.** Any proposed **candidature for organising the World Championships** must be studied at the venue concerned by an ad hoc delegation designated by the Executive Committee, at the invitation of the candidate federation.

2. The organising committee of the World Championships, who will receive all the entry fees from the participating delegations, must, **at their own expense, invite** the following international officials (tourist-class return air fare, accommodation and daily allowances):

a) The **President of the FIE** or his representative, who presides over the World Championships and, in particular, controls the smooth running of the Directoire Technique.
b) A **head of protocol** designated by the President of the FIE.
c) **Six members of the Directoire Technique** appointed by the Executive Committee of the FIE, of whom one must belong to the organising country.
d) **Three members of the SEMI Committee**, appointed by the Executive Committee of the FIE.
e) **Four members of the Refereeing Committee**, one of whom is designated principal delegate, appointed by the Executive Committee of the FIE.
f) **Two members of the Medical Committee**, appointed by the Executive Committee of the FIE.
g) The **referees** designated by the Executive Committee (maximum 34).

B. 世界锦标赛

年度锦标赛

报名

O.65. 世界成年锦标赛个人赛，每国每剑种限报4名运动员参赛；团体赛，每国每剑种限报一个队。

裁判员

O.66. 1. 世界锦标赛裁判员由国际剑联执委会根据裁判委员会的提议选派。

2. 比赛组委会负担裁判员的差旅费及比赛期间的食宿费用，因而收取所有报名费。

3. 世锦赛裁判员必须出席赛前一天的裁判员会议。

国际官员的邀请

O.67. 1. 世界锦标赛申办单位必须经国际剑联执委会指派的临时代表团实地考察确认，其所属会员协会应负责发出邀请。

2. 组委会收取所有参赛队的报名费，同时须邀请下列国际官员并负担相关费用（飞机往返经济舱、食宿及每日补助）：

a. 国际剑联主席或其代表，负责主持世界锦标赛，尤其是监督技术委员会工作；
b. 国际剑联主席指派的1名礼仪主管；
c. 国际剑联执委会指派的6名技术委员会成员，其中须有1名来自东道主；
d. 国际剑联执委会指派的3名器材委员会成员；
e. 国际剑联执委会指派的4名裁判委员会成员，其中1名主要代表；
f. 国际剑联执委会指派的2名医疗委员会成员；
g. 执委会指派的裁判员（最多34人）。

C. REGIONAL GAMES

o.68. 1. The **Regional Games** recognised by the FIE are the same as those recognised by the International Olympic Committee, when fencing is on the programme (e.g. the Mediterranean Games, the Pan-American Games, the Central American and Caribbean Games, etc.) as well as the Commonwealth Games.

2. The **Rules of the FIE** are obligatory in cases which are not provided for by the Rules for Regional Games adopted by the International Olympic Committee.

Technical delegates of the FIE

o.69. 1. The Technical delegate of the FIE, who represents the FIE in accordance with the Olympic Rules for Regional Games, will be chosen by the President of the FIE, after consultation with the Executive Committee, according to criteria of recognised technical abilities.

2. The **expenses** incurred by this representative (tourist-class air fare, hotel and board) will be paid by the Organising Committee.

Technical officials and referees

o.70. The Olympic Rules for Regional Games stipulate that **the control of all the technical organisation of the Games**, including appointing referees and officials, must be entrusted to the international federations. The Organising Committee must pay the expenses (tourist-class air fare, hotel and board) for the following officials:

1. **Directoire Technique: Two foreign members** if the Directoire Technique has three members; **five foreign members** if there are six members. The Directoire Technique is appointed by the Executive Committee of the FIE.

2. **Checking of Equipment: One or two representatives of the SEMI Committee**, depending on the importance of the fencing events at the Games. These representatives are appointed by the Executive Committee of the FIE.

3. **Refereeing delegate: A representative of the Refereeing Committee**, appointed by the Executive Committee of the FIE.

4. **Neutral referees: At least two international referees** from countries outside the region of the Games, appointed by the Executive Committee of the FIE at the proposal of the Refereeing Commission.

C. 地区性运动

O.68. 1. 国际剑联承认的地区性运动会与国际奥委会相同（例如：地中海运动会、泛美运动会、中美洲及加勒比海运动会等）以及英联邦运动会。

2. 当出现国际奥委会采用的地区性运动会规则中没有涉及的情况时，必须执行国际剑联竞赛规则。

国际剑联技术代表

O.69. 1. 国际剑联技术代表依据地区性运动会奥林匹克规则代表国际剑联，该技术代表将由国际剑联主席根据技术能力评判标准，参考执委会意见后选派。

2. 组委会负担该代表所需费用（经济舱飞机往返及食宿）。

技术官员及裁判员

O.70. 地区性运动会奥林匹克规则规定，运动会的技术组织工作的管理，包括裁判员及官员的指派，由各国际单项体育联合会负责。组委会承担下列工作人员的费用（经济舱飞机往返、食宿）：

1. 技术委员会

若技术委员会由3人组成，其中须有2名外籍成员，若由6人组成，则须有5名外籍成员。技术委员会成员由国际剑联执委会指定。

2. 器材代表

根据比赛重要性指派1~2名国际剑联器材委员会代表。器材代表由国际剑联执委会指定。

3. 裁判代表

1名国际剑联裁判委员会代表，由国际剑联执委会指定。

4. 中立裁判员

至少2名来自非比赛地区国家的国际裁判，由国际剑联执委会根据裁判员委员会提议指定。

D. JUNIOR AND CADET WORLD CHAMPIONSHIPS

ANNUAL CHAMPIONSHIPS

Entries

o.71. The Junior and Cadet World Championships are open to all FIE member federations.

o.72. For the Cadet World Championships, entries are limited to three fencers per weapon per nation for the individual events

For the Junior World Championships, the entries are limited to four fencers per nation for each individual event, and one team per weapon per nation for the team events.

Referees

o.73. 1. **Refereeing at World Junior and Cadet Championships** is carried out by referees chosen by the Executive Committee of the FIE on the proposal of the Refereeing Committee.

2. Referees' travel and board and lodging **costs** are paid by the organising committee, who in return will receive all the entry fees.

3. Referees must attend the **refereeing meeting** that takes place the day before the World Championships.

Invitations for international officials

o.74. The organising committee of the World Championships, who receive all the entry fees from the participating delegations, must, at their own expense, invite the same list of international officials (tourist-class return air fare, accommodation and daily allowances) as is set out (cf. o.67) for the Senior World Championships.

D. 世界青少年锦标赛

年度锦标赛

报名

O.71. 国际剑联的所有会员协会均可报名参加世界青少年锦标赛。

O.72. 少年赛个人赛，每个国家每个剑种只能派3名运动员报名参赛。

青年组个人赛，每个国家每个剑种只能派4名运动员报名参赛；团体赛，每个国家每个剑种只能报1个队。

裁判

O.73. 1. 世界青少年锦标赛裁判工作由国际剑联执委会根据裁判员委员会提议选派的裁判员担任。

2. 比赛组委会负担裁判员的差旅费及比赛期间的食宿费用，因而收取全部报名费。

3. 裁判员必须出席世青赛比赛前一天的裁判员会议。

国际官员的邀请

O.74. 组委会收取所有参赛队的报名费，同时须邀请国际官员并负担相关费用（飞机往返经济舱、食宿和每日补助），邀请人员清单与世界成年锦标赛相同（参见 o.67）。

E. WORLD CUP COMPETITIONS

INTRODUCTION

o.75. The title 'World Cup Competition' applies to the following competitions:

— The individual competitions of the Senior World Cup and the Grand Prix competitions

— The individual competitions of the Junior World Cup

— The competitions of the Junior and Senior Team World Cups

CRITERIA

Admission

o.76. An individual competition can only be classed or kept as a World Cup competition if it satisfies the following criteria.

1. Participation must include fencers:

- **from at least eight countries**, for senior competitions in Europe;
- **from at least five countries**, for senior competitions outside Europe;
- **from at least five countries**, for junior competitions.

2. Participation must include a **minimum** of:

- **ten fencers listed in the top 32** in the official ranking of the FIE and representing at least **five different countries** for senior competitions in Europe (no requirement for competitions outside Europe).

3. The competition must be attended by at least **four FIE A or B Grade referees** of different nationalities.

4. The **Rules** of the FIE must be faithfully applied, as well as the specification for World Cup competitions. The organisers must use automatic judging equipment of which the prototype has been approved by the SEMI.

5. The **finals** must take place in a hall in which there is space allocated to the public.

6. There must be a sufficient number of pistes to allow the first round to take place in no more than **two series** of pools.

7. During the **finals**, the organisers must display signs on the piste indicating the names and nationalities of the fencers.

8. For the presentation of the **prizes**, the protocol rules of the FIE must be applied (cf. FIE Administrative Rules).

9. There must be a **medical doctor** present on the premises of the competition for the whole duration of the competition.

10. There must be an **anti-doping test** conforming to the regulations of the FIE (cf. t.127 and the FIE Anti-Doping Rules).

E. 世界杯赛

概述

O.75. 世界杯比赛包括下列赛事：

—— 成年世界杯及大奖赛个人赛

—— 青年世界杯个人赛

—— 成年及青年世界杯团体赛

比赛标准

认可

O.76. 一项个人赛只有在符合下列标准时才能够被认可为世界杯赛：

1. 参赛运动员：

—— 在欧洲举办的成年比赛，至少有来自8个国家的运动员参赛；

—— 在欧洲之外举办的成年比赛，至少有来自5个国家的运动员参赛；

—— 青年比赛，至少有来自5个国家的运动员参赛。

2. 欧洲成年比赛中，必须至少有10名运动员在国际剑联官方排名中位于前32位，且至少代表5个国家（欧洲之外的比赛无此项限制）。

3. 至少有来自不同国家的4名国际剑联A或B级裁判员执裁；

4. 严格执行国际剑联竞赛规则及世界杯赛特别规定。组织者必须使用器材委员会认证的裁判器。

5. 决赛须在设有观众席的场地进行。

6. 须有足够的剑道以保证小组循环赛最多不超过两轮。

7. 决赛中，组织者必须在剑道旁放置注明运动员姓名、国籍的标牌。

8. 颁奖仪式必须遵照国际剑联礼仪规则执行（参阅行政规则）。

9. 比赛全程必须配备一名医生在比赛现场待命。

10. 必须依照国际剑联相关规定进行反兴奋剂检查（参见 t.127 及国际剑联反兴奋剂规则）。

The Supervisor

o.77. **1.** The organisers of World Cup events, individual and team, must ensure the **presence of a supervisor of the FIE** from a country other than that of the organisers, whose task it will be to verify that the competition properly fulfils the World Cup criteria.

2. The **travel, board and lodging costs** of the supervisor are the responsibility of the organisers, in accordance with the standards updated from time to time by the Executive Committee of the FIE.

3. This supervisor is either :

- a member of a FIE Commission,
- a member of the FIE Executive Committee,
- a member of a group of persons, appointed by the Executive Committee, available and experienced in the organisation of competitions.

The Supervisor is appointed by the Executive Committee of the FIE, at the suggestion of the FIE Bureau.

Participation

o.78. 1. For **Grand Prix competitions and Individual World Cup competitions**, both Senior and Junior, at each weapon, each national federation may enter a maximum of 12 fencers. The organising country may enter up to 20 fencers plus the number needed to make up the pools.

2. For **Individual World Cup competitions outside Europe**, the organising country may enter up to 30 fencers plus the number needed to make up the pools.

o.79 For junior and senior Individual Zone Championship competitions, at each weapon, the federations may enter up to 4 fencers.

For junior and senior Team Zone Championship competitions, at each weapon, the federations may enter 1 team (consisting of three fencers with or without a reserve).

o.80. Only fencers who are **of an age to qualify** for the next Junior World Championships may fence in the official FIE Junior competitions, individual or team, of the current fencing season.

观察员

0.77. 1. 世界杯个人赛及团体赛组织者必须保证有一名来自东道主之外的国际剑联观察员出席比赛，观察员负责核查比赛是否满足世界杯赛标准。

2. 组织者根据国际剑联制定的标准承担观察员的差旅费及食宿费用，该标准将由国际剑联执委会适时调整。

3. 这名观察员可以是：

—— 国际剑联任意委员会的成员；
—— 国际剑联执委会成员；
—— 由执委会任命的一组人员，能参加工作且具备比赛组织经验。

观察员由国际剑联执委会根据执行局的提议指定。

参赛

0.78. 1. 对于大奖赛及青年组、成年组世界杯个人赛，每个会员协会每个剑种可报12名运动员参赛。东道主最多可报20名运动员参赛，另加上为补足小组赛名单而增加的运动员。

2. 对于欧洲之外的世界杯赛，东道主最多可报30名运动员参赛，另加上为补足小组赛名单而增加的运动员。

0.79. 对于青年组、成年组洲际锦标赛个人赛，每个协会每个剑种最多可报4名运动员。

对于青年组、成年组洲际锦标赛团体赛，每个协会每个剑种最多可报1支队伍（由3名运动员及替补组成，或没有替补）。

0.80. 只有符合当前赛季世界青年锦标赛年龄要求的运动员方可参加当前赛季的国际剑联正式青年比赛。

Referees — Veteran World Championships, A Grade and Candidate A Grade competitions and Grand Prix

o.81. 1. a) The number of FIE A or B Grade **referees** (cf. t.35) that must accompany teams to junior A Grade competitions and Veteran World Championships is:

1–4 fencers	No obligation to provide a referee
5–9 fencers	One referee
10 or more fencers	Two referees
1 Junior Team	One referee

For junior A Grade competitions, the name(s) of the referee(s) (who must have an FIE category in the weapon of the competition for which they are entered) must be notified via the FIE website 7 days before the competition (midnight, Lausanne time).

b) Should a national federation not provide the required number of referees, a fine (cf o.86, table of financial penalties and fines) will be inflicted on it.

2. For **Senior A-grade, Grand Prix and World Cup team competitions,** 8 referees, proposed by the Refereeing Commission, will be designated by the Executive Committee and delegations will not have to provide any referees. The additional referees required (not less than 5) will be provided by the organising committee. All the referees will be at the expense of the organisers who in return will keep the entry fees.

TEAM WORLD CUP

Application

o.82. 1. Junior and Senior Team World Cup competitions take place at the three weapons, both male and female.

Principles

2. a) The Senior Team World Cup tournament is composed of a maximum of **five integral competitions** (through to the first place) spread, if possible, across all continents. Points will be allocated at the end of each competition.

The Junior Team World Cup tournament is composed of **four integral competitions** and points will be awarded at the end of each competition.

b) The teams are made up of **three fencers**, with or without a substitute.

c) The matches proceed according to the **team-relay formula**, as provided for in Article o.44 of these Rules.

Participation

3. Team participation is open to all countries and limited to **one team per weapon per country**.

裁判员

老将世锦赛，A级赛及候选A级赛，大奖赛

o.81. 1. a）青年A级赛和老将世锦赛所需A级或B级随队裁判（参见技术规则t.35）人数如下：

1~4 名运动员	无要求
5~9 名运动员	1名裁判员
10名及10名以上运动员	2名裁判员
1支青年队	1名裁判员

青年A级赛随队裁判的姓名须于赛前7天通过国际剑联网站报名（洛桑时间零点），裁判员需在其报名执裁的剑种持有国际剑联裁判证。

b）如某会员协会无法提供随队裁判，则需缴纳相应罚款（参见o.86经济处罚及罚款表）。

2. 对于成年A级赛、大奖赛及世界杯团体赛，执委会将根据裁判员委员会的提议指派8名裁判，各参赛队不需要提供裁判。此外还需要的裁判（最少5名）由组委会提供。组委会负担所有裁判员的费用，因而收取报名费。

世界杯团体赛

实施

o.82. 1. 青年和成年世界杯团体赛包含三个剑种、男子和女子的比赛。

原则

2. a） 成年世界杯团体赛最多由5站比赛组成，各站比赛将尽可能安排到所有大洲举办，每站比赛结束后分配积分。

青年世界杯团体赛最多由4站比赛组成，每站比赛结束后分配积分。

b） 每支参赛队由3名运动员组成，有无替补运动员均可。

c） 团体赛按照 o.44说明的团体接力方式进行。

参赛

3. 比赛向所有国家开放，每个国家每个剑种只能报一支队伍。

INDIVIDUAL WORLD RANKINGS

o.83. 1. Official FIE individual ranking

Principles

a) **The official Senior ranking of the FIE** takes into account the best five results of the World Cup, Grand Prix or Satellite competitions in which the fencer has participated, irrespective of continent, plus the World Championships or Olympic Games and the Zonal Championships.

b) **The official Junior ranking of the FIE** takes into account the best six results of the World Cup competitions in which the fencer has participated, irrespective of continent, as well as the World Championships and the Zonal Championships.

c) For both Senior and Junior rankings, the ranking is **kept permanently up to date.**

The first Grand Prix event of the current year cancels out the first Grand Prix event of the previous year and so forth for the remainder of the Grand Prix events.

The first World Cup event (individual and team) of the current year cancels out the first World Cup event (individual and team) of the previous year and so forth for the remainder of the World Cup events in the season.

The points allocated for a competition cancel out the points attributed to the same competition in the previous season.

If a competition does not take place in the current season, the points obtained at the same competition in the previous season are deleted on the anniversary of the competition.

d) **In the event of equal points**, the ranking is based on who has gained the most first places, then second places, etc.

If there is a complete tie, the fencers are ranked equal.

e) After each competition which is taken into account to establish the ranking, this is updated automatically after verification of the results by the FIE.

f) Except where special rules apply, the official up-to-date FIE ranking is the **deciding factor** for all rankings, seedings, exemptions, etc.

Scale of points

2. a) The ranking is based on the **following points system**:

1st place	32 points
2nd place	26 points
3rd place *ex aequo*	20 points
5th–8th places	14 points

个人排名

O.83. 1. 国际剑联官方个人排名

原则

a. 国际剑联成年运动员官方排名根据运动员参加的各大洲世界杯赛、大奖赛或卫星赛中最好的5项成绩，以及世界锦标赛或奥运会和洲际锦标赛的成绩之和计算。

b. 国际剑联青年运动员官方排名根据运动员参加的各大洲世界杯赛中最好的6项成绩，以及世界锦标赛和洲际锦标赛的成绩之和计算。

c. 成年及青年运动员的排名会即时更新。

本赛季首站大奖赛取代上赛季首站大奖赛，依此类推。

本赛季首站世界杯赛（个人和团体）取代上赛季首站世界杯赛，依此类推。

本赛季某站比赛的积分取代上赛季相同站比赛的积分。

如果本赛季某站比赛未举行，则上赛季该站比赛所得积分将在本赛季同一日期被减去。

d. 若总积分相同，则依次比较获冠军、亚军次数决定先后次序，依此类推。若完全一致，则运动员获并列排名。

e. 每站比赛结束，比赛成绩经国际剑联审核后，积分排名将自动更新。

f. 除执行特殊规则的情况外，国际剑联最新官方排名将用于决定所有其他排名、种子位、免赛运动员等。

积分表

2. a. 用于计算排名的积分表如下：

第1名	32分
第2名	26分
并列第3名	20分
第5~8名	14分

9th–16th places	8 points
17th–32nd places	4 points
33rd–64th places	2 points
65th–96th places	1 point (from 09/15)

b) Points obtained in an **individual A Grade World Cup** competition are as listed above.

c) Points obtained in a **Grand Prix** competition of the FIE and a **Zonal Championship** are multiplied by a factor of 1.5.

d) Points obtained in the individual events of the **Senior World Championships and in the Junior World Championships** are multiplied by a factor of 2.5.

e) Points obtained in the individual events of the **Olympic Games** are multiplied by a factor of 3.0. At the **Olympic Games, fourth** place is awarded 54 points.

f) Only fencers who have **actually participated** in a direct elimination table can receive any points.

Honours

3. **The winner** (first ranked fencer) of each **senior** official ranking of the FIE will be announced at the end of the Senior World Championships or Olympic Games.

The winner (first ranked fencer) of each **junior** official ranking will be announced at the end of the Junior World Championships.

TEAM WORLD RANKINGS

o.84. **1.** Official team ranking of the FIE

Principle

a) The official Senior team ranking of the FIE takes into account a team's **best four results** in the Senior Team World Cup competitions, irrespective of continent, plus the Senior World Championships or the Olympic Games and the Zonal Championships.

The official Junior team ranking of the FIE takes into account a team's **best four results** in the Junior Team World Cup competitions, irrespective of continent, plus the Junior World Championships and the Zonal Championships.

b) The official team ranking of the FIE is **updated on a permanent basis**: the event which is held during the current year cancels out the corresponding event held the year before, just as the points obtained during the new event replace the points obtained the year before. If an event does not take place in the current season, the points obtained at the same event in the previous season are deleted on the anniversary of the event.

第9~16名	8分
第17~32名	4分
第33~64名	2分
第65~96名	1分（自2015年9月开始执行）

b. 世界杯A级赛个人赛的积分按照以上表格计算。

c. 国际剑联大奖赛及洲际锦标赛的积分为上述基础分值的1.5倍。

d. 世界锦标赛或世界青年锦标赛的积分为上述基础分值的2.5倍。

e. 奥运会个人赛的积分为上述基础分值的3倍。奥运会第4名得54分。

f. 只有实际参加了直接淘汰赛的运动员才能获得积分。

荣誉

3. 国际剑联各成年官方排名的优胜者（排名第一）将在世界锦标赛或奥运会后宣布。

国际剑联各青年官方排名的优胜者（排名第一）将在世界青年锦标赛后宣布。

团体排名

o.84. 1. 国际剑联官方团体排名

原则

a. 国际剑联成年组官方团体排名根据各队参加的各大洲世界杯赛中的4项最好成绩，以及世界锦标赛或奥运会和洲际锦标赛的成绩之和计算。

国际剑联青年组官方团体排名根据各队参加的各大洲世界杯赛中的4项最好成绩，以及世界锦标赛和洲际锦标赛的成绩之和计算。

b. 国际剑联官方团体排名保持即时更新：本赛季某站比赛取代上赛季同站比赛，本赛季某站比赛积分取代上赛季同站比赛积分。如本赛季某站比赛未举行，则上赛季同站比赛所得积分将在本赛季同一日期被减去。

c) Should several teams **have the same points**, the same rules shall apply as for the official FIE individual ranking (cf. o.83).

d) Except where special rules apply, the updated official team ranking is the **deciding factor** for all rankings, seedings, etc.

2. Team scale of points

a) The ranking will be based on the following scale of points:

1st place	64 points	10th place	24 points
2nd place	52 points	11th place	23 points
3rd place	40 points	12th place	22 points
4th place	36 points	13th place	21 points
5th place	32 points	14th place	20 points
6th place	30 points	15th place	19 points
7th place	28 points	16th place	18 points
8th place	26 points	17th–32nd	8 points
9th place	25 points		

b) For the World Team Championships, the points indicated above are multiplied by two.

c) Points obtained in a Zonal Team Championship have a factor of 1.0.

3. Honours

The winner (first ranked team) of each official Junior and Senior **team** ranking of the FIE will be announced at the end of the Senior World Championships or Olympic Games

F. NATIONS' GRAND PRIX

o.85. For the scale of points for the Nations' Grand Prix at the World Championships and the Olympic Games, please refer to the Administrative Rules of the FIE.

c. 如果多个队伍积分相同，将采取与个人排名规则（参见 o.83）相同的方式决定先后次序。

d. 除执行特殊规则的情况外，国际剑联最新官方团体排名将用于决定所有其他排名、种子位等。

2. 积分表

a. 用于计算排名的积分表如下：

第1名	64分	第10名	24分
第2名	52分	第11名	23分
第3名	40分	第12名	22分
第4名	36分	第13名	21分
第5名	32分	第14名	20分
第6名	30分	第15名	19分
第7名	28分	第16名	18分
第8名	26分	第17~32名	8分
第9名	25分		

b. 世界锦标赛团体赛，积分值为上述基础分值的2倍。

c. 洲际锦标赛团体赛，积分值为上述基础分值的1倍。

3. 荣誉

国际剑联青年组及成年组官方团体排名的优胜者（排名第一）将在世界锦标赛或奥运会后宣布。

F. 国家综合排名大奖

o.85. 世锦赛及奥运会国家综合排名大奖的积分计算方法，参见行政规则。

o.86 Table of Financial Penalties and Fines

	Article	Amount	Date of payment	To be paid to	By whom
Entry to World Championships after closing date	o.53.3	150 euros per entry	With the entry	FIE	By the National Federation
Entry to other FIE competitions after closing date until the Tuesday preceding the competition	o.54.4 a)	150 euros per entry	With the entry	FIE	By the National Federation
Entry to other FIE competitions after closing date, from the Wednesday and until the day (12 noon local time) preceding the competition	o.54.4 b)	250 euros per entry	With the entry	FIE	By the National Federation
If a fencer or team duly entered does not turn up	o.31.4, o.33.3, o.54.5	500 euros per fencer or team	On receipt of notification of the fine	FIE	By the National Federation
Participation of a fencer or team not properly entered	o.54.6	1000 euros per improper participation	On receipt of notification of the fine	FIE	By the organiser
Required number of referees not respected	o.81.1	1000 euros per referee	At the same time as the information is sent to the organiser	Organiser	By the National Federation

o.86. 经济处罚及罚款表

	条款	金额	付款时间	付款至	付款人
世锦赛截止日期后报名	o.53.3	150欧元/人	报名时	国际剑联	会员协会
国际剑联其他比赛截止日期后、比赛前的周二前报名	o.54.4 a）	150欧元/人	报名时	国际剑联	会员协会
国际剑联其他比赛截止日期后、比赛前的周三至比赛前一天中午12点（当地时间）	o.54.4 b）	250欧元/人	报名时	国际剑联	会员协会
报名运动员或队伍未参赛	o.31.4 o.33.3 o.54.5	500欧元/人或队	收到罚单时	国际剑联	会员协会
未正确报名的运动员或团体参赛	o.54.6	1000欧元/例	收到罚单时	国际剑联	组委会
未满足要求的随队裁判人数	o.81.1	1000欧元/裁判	通知组委会时	组委会	会员协会

Chapter 8

Veterans World Championships

o.87 **1.** The organisers must submit the programme of events to the Executive Committee for its approval.

2. The programme must be arranged in such a way as to allow any fencer to participate in all weapons. Team events must be held on the day following the last championship of the three categories of each weapon.

3. No changes of dates are allowed for any competition, after the release of the programme.

4. Each competition must be held in one single day, avoiding long periods of inactivity.

o.88 **Entries for competitions**

1. Entries must be sent to the organisers by the competitors' national federation. Entries must be sent not later than one month before the beginning of the championships.

2. However, up to two days before the competition at noon (local time), fencers may be added by their national federation after payment to the Organizing Committee of a penalty equal to 100 % of the registration fee.

3. Entries for team championships must be forwarded to the Directoire Technique not later than 4.00 pm (local time) of the day before the competition.

o.89 At the Veterans World Championships, entries for the individual events are limited to four fencers in each category per gender, per weapon and per nation. The names must be the same as those on the FIE licences.

o.90 **Composition of the pools for individual championships**

When drawing the pools, the Directoire Technique will take into account the following orders of strength:

1. The 64 highest ranked from the addition of the results in the previous two years Championships, irrespective of age category changes;

2. All other fencers in order of age, starting from the youngest.

3. The allocation of fencers in the pools must be made in such a way as to place fencers of the same nationality, as far as possible, in different pools, by moving them down the ranking as necessary.

4. If in any category there are fewer than ten competitors, the competition is held as a poule unique followed by direct elimination.

第八章　世界老将锦标赛

0.87. 1. 组委会须将比赛日程提交执委会批准；

2. 比赛日程的制定要遵循让所有参赛选手可以参加全部剑种比赛的原则，团体赛必须在各剑种3个年龄组别个人赛结束后第二天进行；

3. 比赛日程公布后，不允许再做改动；

4. 各项比赛须在一天内结束，避免出现长时间的空档期。

0.88. 比赛报名

1. 报名须通过参赛运动员所属会员协会向组织者提交，且不能晚于赛前一个月；

2. 赛前2天的中午12：00前（当地时间），各会员协会仍可增加报名，但须向组委会缴纳相当于报名费全额的罚款；

3. 团体赛报名须于该项团体赛开赛前一天的下午16：00前（当地时间）提交至技术委员会。

0.89. 世界老将锦标赛，每个国家每个剑种每个组别男女分别只允许4名运动员报名参赛。报名运动员的姓名必须与国际剑联注册的姓名一致。

0.90. 个人赛中的小组赛分组

小组赛分组时，技术委员会需考虑以下排名指标：

1. 前64名的排位由上两届世锦赛的名次之和的排名决定，不考虑年龄组别的变化。

2. 其他所有运动员，根据年龄由小到大排位。

3. 小组赛分组时要尽可能将同一国家的运动员安排在不同的小组，必要时可以降低他们的排位。

4.如果某组别参赛运动员不足10人，则只安排唯一1个小组，随后进行直接淘汰赛。

5. If in any category there are fewer than 6 competitors, they will fence with the next lower age category. A separate ranking for that category will be extrapolated from the combined categories' final rankings at the end of the competition.

6. If in any category there is only one competitor, the event in that category is cancelled.

7. No fencer is eliminated after the pools, all are entered into the direct elimination.

o.91 Duration of the matches

The direct elimination bouts are for 10 hits or end when two periods of three minutes, with one minute rest between the periods, have passed. As an exception, at sabre, the first period ends either at the expiry of the three minutes or when one of the fencers has scored five hits.

o.92 Team championships

1. Participation

Each country can enter one team per gender and per weapon, thus giving a total of 6 competitions.

2. The rules for team championships are applicable with the following exceptions:

a) For each weapon, the teams are composed of three fencers of the same nationality, one from category "A", one "B" and one "C" with or without a reserve for each category. A team cannot begin the match if it is not complete.

b) In the case of a team being short of a fencer in any of the weapons the team may use a fencer who has competed in the individual championships at another weapon, but his/her ranking will be deemed to be the last ranking at that weapon plus 1.

c) The teams are placed in the pools according to the ranking of the three fencers in the individual championship, the highest place for the team having the lowest total. All the fencers registered for the team event must be present at the piste before the start of the match.

d). Each team may ask to substitute a fencer before the start of a bout, except in case of injury duly recognized by the Medical delegate, when the substitution can be immediate. There can be only one substitution per match.

3. A fencer who has been replaced because of an injury may not fence again during that match. If both a fencer and the reserve, if any, are forced to retire, or if a fencer is excluded, their team is deemed to have lost the match.

4. The relay system is always applied. The three fencers of a team fence against their opponent of the same category. Each fencer fences his/her opponent twice giving a total of 6 bouts. The bouts are for 5 hits (5-10-15-20- etc.); the maximum time for each bout is 3 minutes.

5. 如果某组别参赛运动员不足6名，则这些运动员将并入相邻的低年龄组别比赛，比赛结束后再根据合并组别的比赛成绩为这些运动员单独排名。

6. 如果某组别只有1名运动员参赛，这该组别比赛将取消。

7. 小组赛不淘汰运动员，所有运动员均进入直接淘汰赛。

O.91. 比赛时间

直接淘汰赛采用10剑制，或者是打满两局3分钟的比赛，中间休息1分钟。对于佩剑，打满3分钟或其中一名运动员得5分，第一局比赛即结束。

O.92. 团体赛

1. 参赛

每个国家每个性别每个剑种可报1支队伍，即每个国家最多可以参加6项团体赛。

2. 团体赛特殊规则

除以下特殊规则，其他采用锦标赛规则。

a. 每个剑种的参赛队均由来自同一国家不同年龄组的3名运动员组成，1人来自“A”年龄组，1人来自“B”年龄组,1人来自“C”年龄组。替补可有可无并用于任一年龄组。如队伍不完整则不可参赛。

b. 某剑种团体组成缺1人的情况下，可从同性别已参加其他剑种个人赛的运动员中补充，补充运动员的排位按此剑种个人赛名次最后一名加1计算。

c. 团体排位依据团体组成运动员的个人赛名次之和计算，数值越小则排位越高，团体赛运动员在比赛开始前须在剑道集体亮相。

d. 更换替补须在每局比赛的开赛前提出。如果有比赛医疗代表认定的受伤情况，可立即更换替补。每场比赛每支队伍只有一次换人机会。

3. 由于受伤被替换下场的运动员当场比赛不可再上场。如果某队的一名队员和替补都无法比赛，或一名队员被取消比赛资格，则该队本场比赛判负。

4. 团体赛始终按照接力原则进行。一队的3名运动员与另一队相同年龄组的对手比赛。团体赛共6局，每名队员与其固定对手比赛2局，每局比赛比分达到5的倍数时结束（5–15–20……），每局比赛时间为3分钟。

5. The team that first reaches the maximum score of 30 hits, or that which has scored the greatest number of hits after the expiry of regular time, is the winner.

6. The order of categories for each match is established by the referee with the captains on the piste prior to the start of the match: The referee will "toss a coin" and the winning captain will choose the first category in the order. The losing captain will choose the second category.

7. The competition consists of a round of pools of 3 or 4 teams, in which all the teams participate, and a direct elimination phase for a maximum of 16 teams; the other teams will be classified according to their place after the round of pools.

8. If there are fewer than 6 teams, they all fence in a poule unique; a match for the 3rd and 4th places is then held, followed by a match for the first place between the teams who came 1st and 2nd in the pool.

o.93 Referees

Participating countries must notify at least one month in advance whether they will either bring the required number of referees or pay the penalty, in order to allow enough time to the organisers to recruit other referees.

o.94 Invitations for international officials

1. Any proposed candidature for organising the World Championships must be studied at the venue concerned by a delegate designated by the Executive Committee, at the invitation of the candidate federation.

2. The organising committee of the World Championships, who will receive all the entry fees from the participating delegations, must, at their own expense, invite the following international officials (tourist-class return air fare, accommodation and daily allowances):

   a) The President of the FIE or his representative, who presides over the World Championships and, in particular, controls the smooth running of the Directoire Technique.

   b) Four members of the Directoire Technique appointed by the Executive Committee of the FIE, one of whom must belong to the organising country.

   c) One member of the SEMI Committee, appointed by the Executive Committee of the FIE.

   d) One member of the Refereeing Committee, appointed by the Executive Committee of the FIE.

   e) One member of the Medical Committee, appointed by the Executive Committee of the FIE.

These officials should preferably be selected from the Zone in which the Championships are being held.

5. 先获得30分或打满比赛时间分数领先的队伍获胜。

6. 每场团体赛的上场顺序由当场裁判和双方领队在开赛前以掷硬币的方式决定，猜中硬币的队伍选择第一个上场的年龄组，另一队选择第二个上场的年龄组。

7. 团体赛要进行小组循环赛和直接淘汰赛。所有参赛队都要参加小组循环赛，小组赛由3至4支队伍组成一个小组；直接淘汰赛最多有16支队伍参加，其余队伍的最终名次依据小组循环赛后的排名决定。

8. 如参赛队少于6支，则编为一个小组进行循环赛。小组赛后排名第3位和第4位的队伍进行铜牌赛，然后排名第1位和第2位的队伍进行金牌赛。

O.93. 裁判

各参赛队要在赛前一个月通知组委会是否能够按要求提供随队裁判，或缴纳罚款，以便组委会有充分的时间邀请其他裁判员。

O.94. 国际官员的邀请

1. 世界锦标赛申办单位必须经国际剑联执委会指派的代表实地考察确认，其所属会员协会应负责发出邀请。

2. 世锦赛组委会收取所有参赛队的报名费，同时须邀请下列国际官员并负担相关费用（飞机往返经济舱、食宿及每日补助）：

   a. 国际剑联主席或其代表，负责主持世界锦标赛，尤其是监督技术委员会工作；
   b. 国际剑联执委会指定的4名技术委员会成员，其中须有1名来自东道主；
   c. 国际剑联执委会指定的1名器材委员会成员；
   d. 国际剑联执委会指定的1名裁判委员会成员；
   e. 国际剑联执委会指定的1名医疗委员会成员。

以上官员最好能从比赛举办的区域选派。

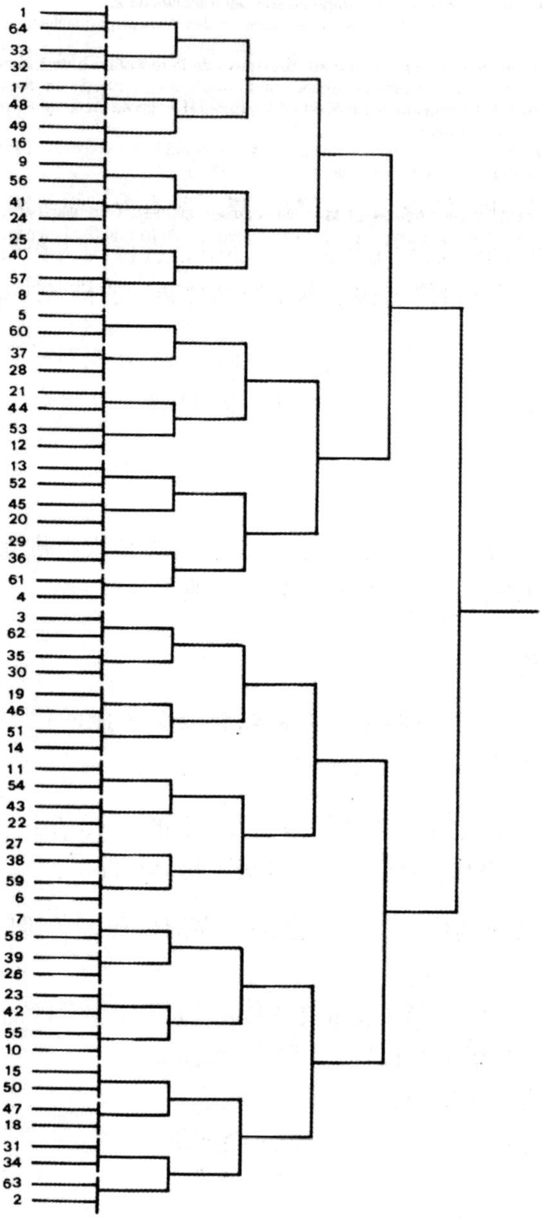

Figure 7a. Bout plan for individual direct elimination (table for 64 fencers)

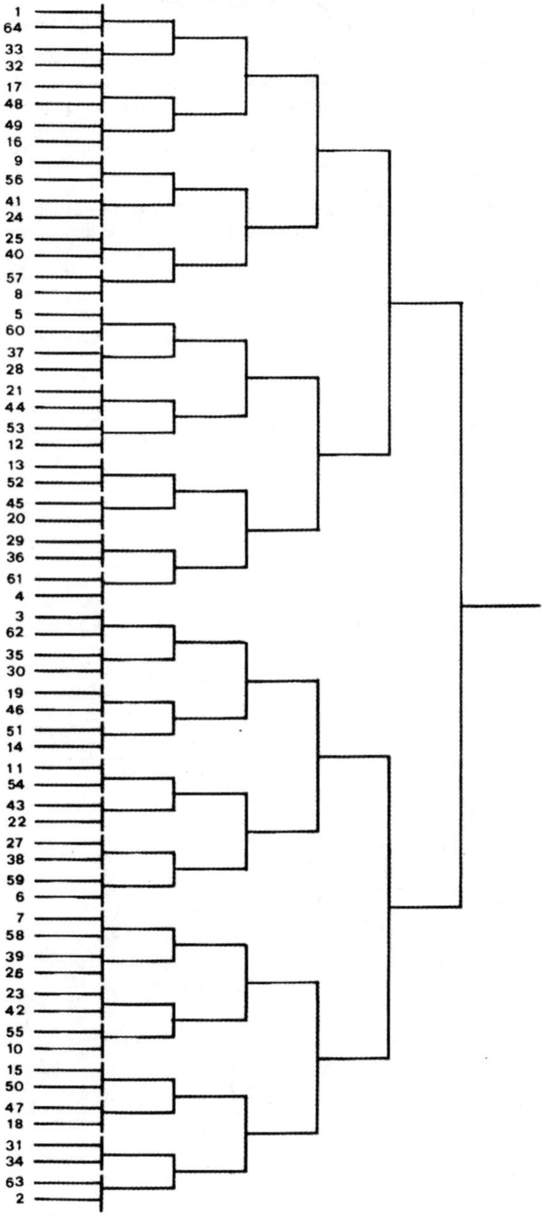

图7A　个人赛直接淘汰赛对阵表（64名运动员）

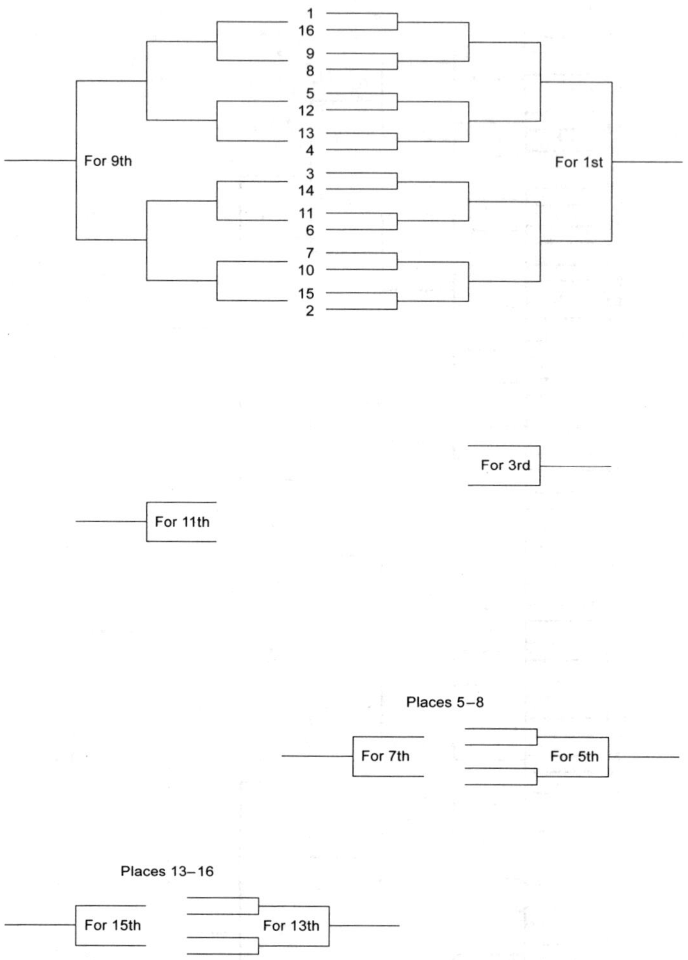

Figure 7b. Bout plan for direct elimination for team competitions (16 teams)

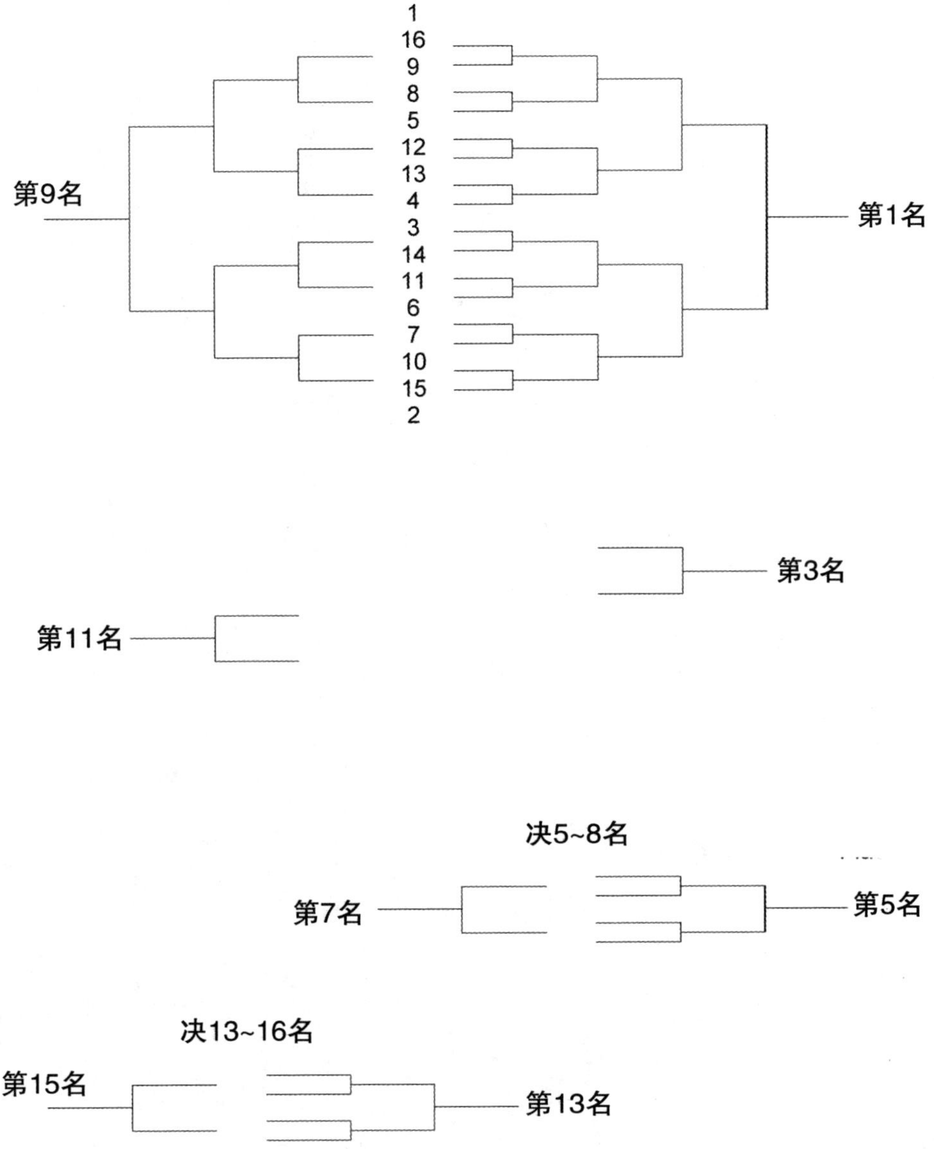

图7B　团体赛直接淘汰赛表（16支队伍）

器材规则

BOOK 3. MATERIAL RULES

PART 1. FENCERS' WEAPONS AND EQUIPMENT

CHAPTER 1. WEAPONS

CHARACTERISTICS COMMON TO ALL WEAPONS

m.1. **1.** There are three types of weapon: foil, épée and sabre.

2. All weapons are authorised providing only that they conform to these regulations and to the safety standards which are annexed.

3. The weapon should be so constructed that it cannot normally injure either the user or his opponent. All methods of treating a blade between the guard and the tip (button), by grinding, filing or other methods, are forbidden.

4. Sharpening the edges or angles of the point is forbidden.

General description

m.2. All weapons are composed of the following parts.

1. A flexible steel **blade** completed at its forward extremity by a **button** and at the rear by the **tang** (the latter included in the handle when the weapon is mounted).

2. A **handle** within which the tang of the blade is fixed by a **locking nut** or in any other way, and which enables the fencer's hand to hold the weapon. It may be composed of one or several parts: in the latter case it is divided into a **grip** (which is normally held in the hand) and a pommel (rear portion of the handle which locks the handle onto the tang).

3. A metal **guard** fixed (with the convex face towards the front) between the blade and the handle, serving to protect the sword hand. For foil and épée, the guard must contain a **padding** or cushion (cf. m.5/2) to reduce the effect of blows. It will also contain a **socket** to which the **bodywire** can be connected.

Dimensions (cf. m.7ss, m.15ss, m.21ss)

m.3. Each weapon has its particular design and measurements.

1. The **length** of the blade includes the button and everything which is added in front of the convex surface of the guard whether or not it is fixed to the latter.

2. The **total length** of the weapon and its various parts corresponds to the distances between lines (planes) drawn parallel to each other and perpendicular to the axis of the blade. These lines are situated:

第一部分　运动员的武器和装备

第一章　武器

所有剑种的共同特点

m.1.　1. 击剑运动中有三个剑种：花剑、重剑和佩剑。

2. 所有剑种的武器只有在符合本规则和所附的安全准则的条件下，才被准许使用。

3. 武器的构成，目的是在正常情况下不能击伤自己和对手。禁止通过磨、锉或其他方式对护手盘和剑头之间的剑身部分进行任何矫正。

4. 禁止将剑头磨利。

一般说明

m.2.　任何武器均由以下几个部分组成：

1. 一个柔韧的钢制剑身。最前端是剑头，最后端是柄芯（当武器装配好后柄芯插在手柄内）。

2. 一个手柄。柄芯通过螺母扣紧或其他方法固定在手柄内，以使运动员能够用手抓住武器。手柄可以由一个或数个部件构成。当由数个部件构成时，可分解为柄颈（手握的地方）和平衡锤（把柄颈紧固在柄芯上的手柄后面部分）。

3. 一个金属护手盘。固定在剑身和手柄之间，其凸起部分朝前，用于保护持剑手。花剑和重剑的护手盘必须安装一个软垫作为缓冲设备（参见 m.5/2）。另外，护手盘内还须安装一个用于连接手线的插座。

规格（参阅m.7ss，m.15ss，m.21ss）

m.3.　各个剑种的武器都有其特有的形状和标准。

1. 剑身的长度包括剑头、护手盘前面的附加部件，无论该部件是否固定在护手盘上。

2. 武器在总长度是其各部分之和，等于垂直于剑身中心轴的各平行面间的长度之和。这些平面位于：

a) A at the forward extremity of the weapon

b) B at the point where the blade leaves the front, convex, surface of the guard

c) C at the back of the aforesaid guard

d) D between the grip and the pommel

e) E at the rear extremity of the handle

3. The **total length** of the weapon is the distance between lines A and E; the **length of the blade** that between A and B; the **length of the handle** that between B and E; and the **depth of the guard** that between B and C.

4. The **maximum total length** of the weapon must be less than the greatest permissible length for the blade and the handle added together. These two latter lengths must, therefore, complement each other to arrive at the total length of the weapon.

5. In order to **measure** either the total length of the weapon or the length of the blade, it is essential that the latter should be without any curve. When measurements are being made, the blade should therefore be held straight on a flat surface.

6. Only the **pommel or the locking nut** may be placed between lines D and E.

The handle

m.4. 1. **The maximum length** of the handle at foil and épée is 20 cm, measured between lines B and E, and 18 cm, measured between lines B and D. At sabre the maximum length of the handle is 17 cm (see Figures 8, 9 and 13).

2. The handle must be able to pass through the same **gauge** as the guard. It must be so made that normally it cannot injure either the user or his opponent.

3. All types of handle are allowed providing that they conform to the regulations which have been framed with a view to placing the various types of weapons on the same footing. However, at **épée**, orthopaedic handles, whether metal or not, may not be covered with leather or any material which could hide wires or switches.

4. The handle must not include any device which assists the fencer to use it as a **throwing weapon**.

5. The handle must not include any device which can increase in any way the **protection** afforded to the hand or wrist of the fencer by the guard: a cross bar or electric socket which extends beyond the edge of the guard is expressly forbidden.

6. If the handle (or glove) includes any **device** or **attachment** or has a **special shape** (orthopaedic) which fixes the position of the hand on the handle, the handle must conform to the following conditions.

a) It must determine and fix one position only for the hand on the handle.

a. 武器的最前端；

b. 护手盘的凸面与剑身连接处；

c. 护手盘的后端；

d. 柄颈和平衡锤之间；

e. 手柄的末端。

3. 武器的总长度为a和e平面间的距离；剑身的长度为a和b间的距离；手柄长度为b和e间的距离；护手盘深度为b和c间的距离。

4. 武器的最大总长度应短于剑身和手柄最大准许长度的和，因此这两部分长度互补之和形成武器的总长度。

5. 为测量武器的总长度或剑身长度，剑身不得弯曲；在测量时，剑身应放在一个平面上并保持平直。

6. 在d与e之间只能有平衡锤或固定螺母。

手柄

m.4. 1. 在花剑和重剑中，手柄最大长度为：b、e平面间距不超过20厘米，b、d平面间距不超过18厘米。在佩剑中手柄的最大长度为17厘米（参见图8,9和13）。

2. 手柄应能穿过用于测量护手盘的量规。手柄的构成方式，在正常情况下不能伤害自身和对手。

3. 符合规则的手柄形式都可以使用，规则的目的是平等地对待各个不同的剑种。然而，在重剑中，金属或非金属的枪柄不能覆盖皮革或其他可能遮盖导线或插座的材料。

4. 手柄的各部件不得包含有助于把武器当作投射武器使用的装置。

5. 手柄的各部件不得增强护手盘对运动员手或手腕的保护作用。禁止十字形柄的横臂或插头超越出护手盘边缘。

6. 如果手柄（或手套）包括一种可将手固定在手柄上的装置、系扣用品或专用产品（矫形），这种手柄应符合以下两个条件：

a. 手必须固定在手柄的唯一位置；

b) When the hand occupies this one position on the handle, the extremity of the thumb when completely extended must not be more than 2 cm from the inner surface of the guard.

The guard (cf. m.9, m.17, m.24)

m.5 1. The **convex face** of the guard must have a shape and surface which is both smooth and not too shiny. It must be so made that it can neither hold nor catch the opponent's point. It must not have a raised rim.

2. a) For foil and épée, inside the guard there must be a cushion (padding) sufficiently wide to protect the electric wires from the fencer's fingers. The padding on the inside of the guard must be less than 2 cm thick and must be arranged in such a way as not to increase the protection which the guard affords the hand.

b) **The connections** must be so arranged that it is impossible for the fencer to break or make contacts while fencing.

c) On **foils**, the wire must be protected by an insulating sheath.

d) On **épées**, the two wires must be protected by two insulating sheaths, one on each wire.

e) Both the **wire** and the **insulating sheath** must go right up to the socket.

f) In no case may **uninsulated wires** project beyond the point where they are attached to the socket (cf. m.29, m.31).

3. Any system of attachment inside the guard is allowed, provided that it conforms to the following requirements.

a) It must be **easy to detach** or **attach** the bodywire.

b) It must be possible to **check it** by a simple method such as using a penknife or a coin.

c) It must be **easy to apply** the pointe d'arrêt of the opponent's weapon to the earth circuit connected to the blade.

d) It must have a **security device** which prevents the bodywire from becoming unplugged during the bout. In the absence of a security device being fitted to the weapon, a security device must be fitted to the plug of the bodywire.

e) It must ensure the **complete connection** of the electric wires; it must be impossible for even a momentary break of contact to occur while the plugs are connected.

f) It must not include any part which allows electrical contact to be made between the plug sockets.

b. 当握住此位置时，拇指伸直，指尖距护手盘内侧的距离不得大于2厘米。

护手盘（参见m.9、m.17、m.24）

m.5. 1. 护手盘的凸面表面光滑，稍有亮光，不能卡住对手的剑也不能阻滞对手剑尖。护手盘的边缘不能翻卷。

2. a. 在花剑和重剑中，护手盘内部必须装有一个足够大的软垫，用以保护运动员的手线。垫料厚度小于2厘米，其放置方式不得增加护手盘对手的保护作用。

b. 插座的安装应使运动员在比赛中不能折断或断开接触。

c. 在花剑中，导线被一个绝缘套保护。

d. 在重剑中，两根导线被两个绝缘套分开保护。

e. 导线和绝缘套接到固定接线柱时的长度要几乎是一样的。

f. 在任何情况下，非绝缘的线不能越出固定接线柱（参阅m.29、m.31）。

3. 在护手盘内部，联接方式自由灵活，但须符合以下条件：

a. 易于拆卸和安装；

b. 能够借助简单工具进行检查，如小折刀或硬币；

c. 便于对手的剑尖接触连接于地线的部分；

d. 配有防止比赛过程中插头断开的安全装置；如果武器本身不含有这样的安全装置，则手线必选安装有这样的装置。

e. 保证电路的触点正常，在电路保持联通时，绝不允许中断；

f. 不能包括可使各部份形成回路的部件。

4. **a)** The maximum **electrical resistance** allowed for foil and épée is 2 ohms.

b) Those who wish to assemble electric weapons, but who are not equipped to undertake electrical tests, are advised that the limits for the electrical resistance for the circuits laid down for each weapon have been fixed so that they can be attained by anyone who is reasonably careful.

c) They are advised:

i) thoroughly to **de-oxidise** the external surface of the guard and the connecting surfaces inside it;

ii) **not to damage** the insulation of the wires, especially where they pass along the groove in the blade at the point and at the guard;

iii) to avoid **accumulations of glue** in the groove of the blade.

Equipment and Checking of Weapons

5. **a)** At foil and épée, only traditional or homologated pointes d'arrêt are accepted. No other kind of pointe d'arrêt, notably new ones that are not homologated, will be accepted at the weapon control.

In order to make the identification easier, please note that a traditional pointe d'arrêt has two screws to fix the tip of the pointe d'arrêt to the base, the whole is in metal and there is no plastic in the base.

To make the checking of weapons easier and allow the complete observation of the tip and its base, foil fencers are requested to present their foils at the weapon control with bare points not covered with adhesive tape over the first 15cm.

b) In order that the registering of hits by the contact of the point on the opponent be correctly registered by the scoring device, the pointes d'arrêt must be clean. The electrical resistance measured in ohms must not exceed the limit of two ohms (m.5.4.a).

c) The blades and the guards at épée, foil and sabre must be totally of metal. Apart from at sabre where the part of the guard next to the pommel is insulated (insulating sheath), their exteriors must not be covered by any material (plastic or other).

The guard may not feature any advertising. This is also the case for the insulated part of the sabre guard.

d) Any fencer or other person who tries to register hits in a way that does not comply with the rules, either with the weapon or by manipulating the scoring device, will be excluded from the competition or from the competition zone and, after identification, will be liable to further penalty.

4. a. 花剑和重剑的电阻最大为 2 欧姆。

b. 安装电动武器时，即使不具备电路检查手段，仍然发现只要是稍加注意就可以成功安装完成，因为各剑种的电阻选择已经考虑到了这一点。

c. 安装时注意以下几点：

i） 护手盘的外表面及内部接触面须脱氧；

ii） 不要损坏导线外部的绝缘体，尤其在导线经过剑身的凹槽进入剑头和护手盘的位置；

iii） 避免剑身凹槽里堆积胶水。

器材装备与检查

5. a. 花剑和重剑中，只有传统和得到认证的剑头才能被接受。其他任何剑头，包括新款没有被认证的剑头都是不能被检查通过的。

为了便于识别，记住只有一种传统剑头，它包含两个固定剑头按钮和底座的螺丝，整个底座都是金属的，没有任何塑料成分。

为了便于器材检查以及全面观察剑头及其底座，请花剑运动员检查武器时，整个剑头都要裸露在外面，不要在剑头部分15厘米的范围缠绕胶带。

b. 为了使剑头刺中对手接通电路并正确地被裁判器记录，剑头必须是干净的。欧姆表检测出来的电阻值不能超过2欧姆（m.5.4.a）。

c. 花剑、重剑和佩剑的剑身及护手盘都必须是金属的。

除了佩剑护手盘平衡锤一边是绝缘的（绝缘的套子），它的外部不能再被任何材料（塑料或其他）覆盖。

护手盘上不能再带有任何广告，此规则同样适用于佩剑护手盘绝缘的部分。

d. 运动员或其他人员尝试通过不符合规则规定的方式来获取比分，不论是在武器还是在裁判器上做手脚，将被禁止参加比赛或地区比赛，一经证实，将会受到进一步处罚。

FOIL

Weight

m.6. The **total weight** of the foil ready for use must be less than 500 g.

Length

m.7. The **maximum total length** of the foil is 110 cm.

The blade

m.8. **1.** The blade, which is **rectangular in section**, must be made of steel complying with the safety standards described in Annexe A to the Rules.

2. The **edges** must be smoothed off so that they cannot cut, and must be chamfered at an angle of 45° (± 5°), 0.5 mm on each side (± 0.1 mm), so that they will neither cut nor become capable of cutting.

3. The blade **is mounted** with the widest face placed horizontally.

4. The **maximum length** of the blade is 90 cm (cf. m.3).

5. The blade should have a **flexibility** equivalent to a bend of minimum 5.5 cm and maximum 9.5 cm measured in the following way.

a) The blade is fixed horizontally at a point 70 cm from the extremity of the button.

b) A 200 g weight (tolerance +/- 1 g) is suspended 3 cm from the extremity of the button.

c) The bend of the blade is measured at the extremity of the button between the non-weighted and weighted positions (see Figure 8).

d) The groove in the blade must be uppermost.

6. The blade should be as straight as possible. **Any curve** of the blade must be uniform and the maximum bend must in any case be less than one cm; it is only permitted in the vertical plane and must be near the centre of the blade.

The curve of the blade must be measured as follows:

i) the blade is placed on a flat surface so that the curve is uppermost;

ii) the maximum distance between the flat surface and the blade is measured: this distance is deemed to be the curve of the blade (cf Fig 8).

花剑

重量

m.6. 准备好可以使用的花剑总重量要低于500克。

长度

m.7. 花剑的最大长度为110厘米。

剑身

m.8. 1. 剑身截面呈四角形，根据附录A的安全准则，剑身应用符合标准的钢制造。

2. 棱边应打磨，使其变钝；打磨形成的斜面应呈45度（±5度）角。（每边0.5±0.1毫米）使其钝化或不易变得锋利。

3. 剑身的安装应使得最宽的边水平放置。

4. 剑身的最大长度为90厘米（参见m.3）。

5. 剑身应具有一定柔韧性，弯曲度最小为5.5厘米，最大为9.5厘米，用以下方法测定：

a. 在距剑头顶端70厘米处固定剑身。

b. 将一个200克（±1克）的砝码挂在距剑头顶端3厘米处。

c. 剑头顶端不负重和负重的位置之差即为弯曲度（图8）。

d. 剑的凹槽面在上方。

6. 剑身应尽量保持平直：剑身曲线应当是均匀的，在任何情况下弯曲度应小于1厘米；弯曲的位置应出现在靠近剑身中央的垂直方向。

剑身的弯曲度按以下方式进行测量：

i）将剑身置于一个平面上，弧度朝上。

ii）测量平面到剑身的最大距离，这个距离就是剑身的弯曲度（图8）。

The guard (cf. m.5)

m.9. 1. The **guard** must be able to pass through a straight cylindrical gauge having a diameter of 12 cm and a length of 15 cm, the blade being parallel with the axis of the cylinder.

2. Eccentric mounting is forbidden, that is to say that the blade must pass through the centre of the guard. The diameter of the guard must be between 9.5 cm and 12 cm.

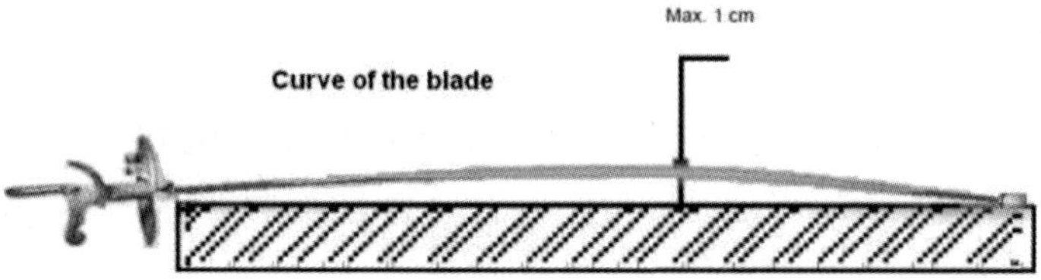

DIMENSIONS OF THE FOIL
(Articles m.3–m.8)

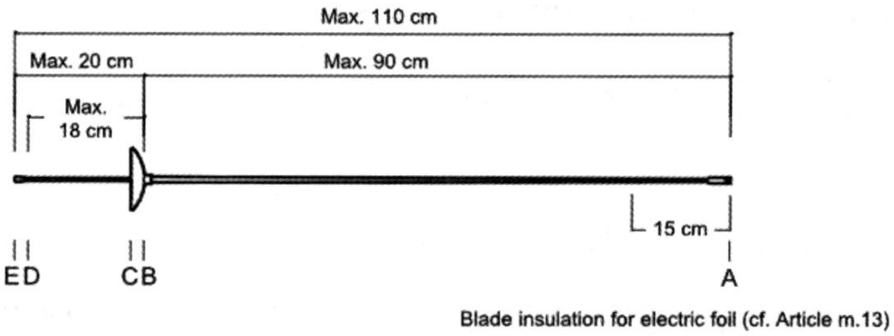

FOIL GUARD
(Article m.9)

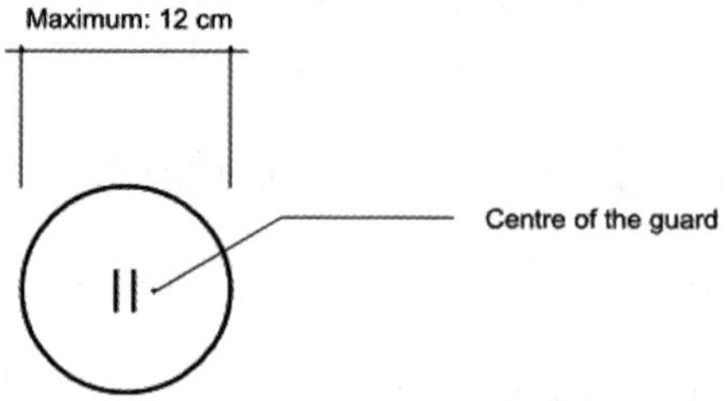

护手盘（参见m.5.）

m.9. 1. 护手盘应当能够穿过一个直径12厘米，长15厘米的圆柱形直管（量规），剑身与圆柱中轴线平行。

2. 禁止中心偏移，也就是说剑身应从护手盘中心穿过。护手盘直径应在9.5~12厘米的范围内。

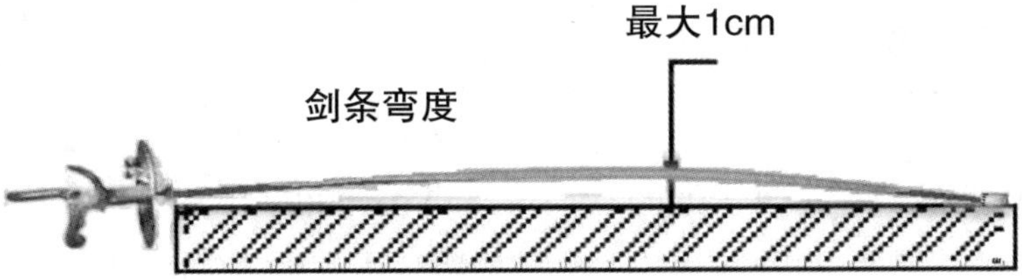

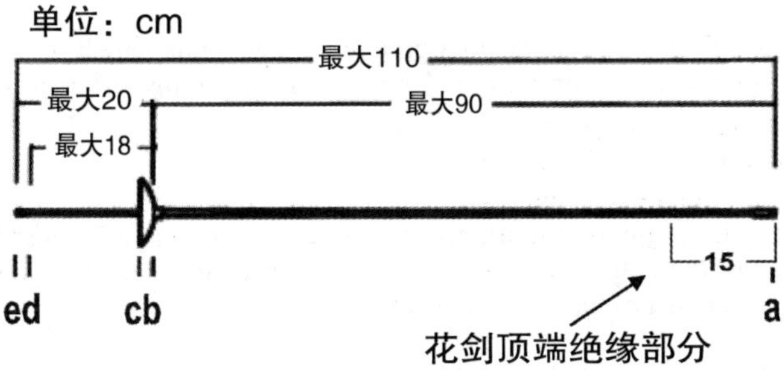

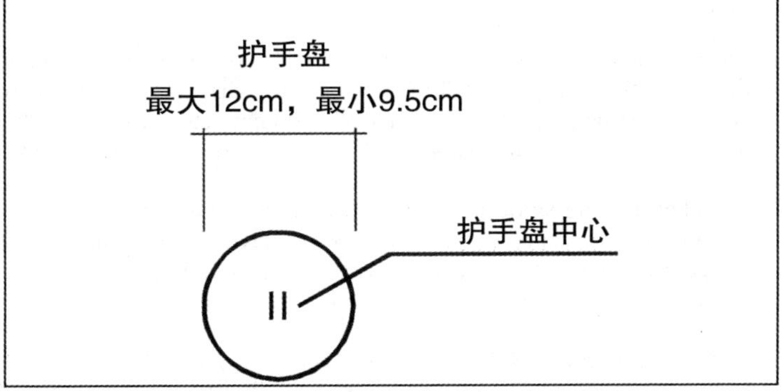

THE FOIL

The total weight of the foil must be less than 500 g (Article m.6)

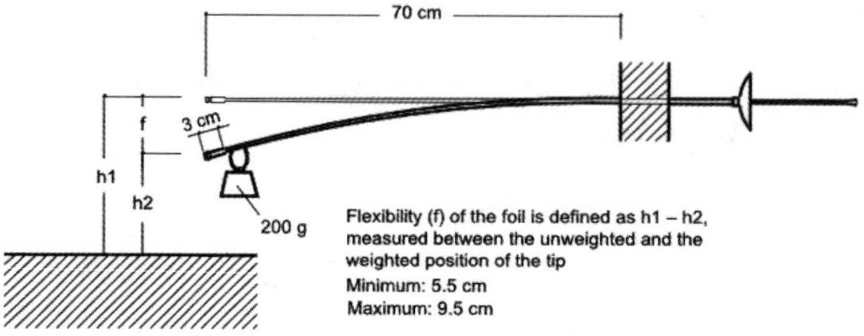

Figure 8. Foil dimensions and flexibility

This diagram is for guidance purposes only. In case of any doubt the wording of the appropriate text takes precedence

Electric wire

m.10. The foil has a single **wire**, glued in a groove cut the whole length of the blade, which permanently connects the pointe d'arrêt to the corresponding socket inside the guard.

Pointe d'arrêt

m.11. 1. The diameter of the **pointe d'arrêt** is between 5.5 mm and 7 mm; the diameter of the body of the button including its exterior insulation must not be more than 0.3 mm less than that of the pointe d'arrêt.

2. The pointe d'arrêt must be **cylindrical; its front surface** is flat and perpendicular to its axis.

Its edge will either be rounded with a radius of 0.5 mm or have a chamfer of 0.5 mm at 45°.

3. The **pressure** required on the pointe d'arrêt, in order to break the contact and cause the apparatus to register a hit, must be more than 500 g, that is to say that this weight must be lifted by the spring of the point. The weight of 500 g supplied by the Organising Committee may have a tolerance of ± 2 g, i.e. 498–502 g.

4. The **course** or travel of the pointe d'arrêt required to cause the electrical apparatus to register a hit, called the *lighting stroke*, may be infinitesimal: the total travel of the pointe d'arrêt must not be greater than 1 mm. The gauge used should have a tolerance of a maximum of +/- 0.05mm.

5. The pointe d'arrêt must be **retained in the button** in at least two places equidistant from each other, or by any other method which has been approved by the SEMI Committee of the FIE.

花剑总重量应低于500克

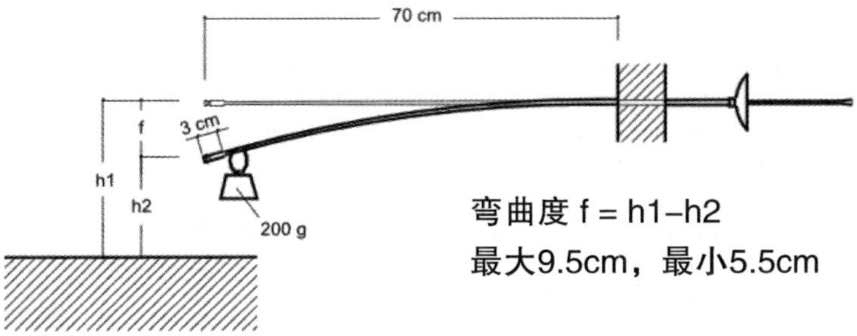

图 8　花剑的规格与弯曲度

以上的图示只用作示意，如有任何的疑虑，以相关文字描述为准。

导线

m.10. 花剑在剑身的凹槽内贴有唯一一根导线，该导线在护手盘内部通过相应的插头与剑头连接在一起。

剑头

m.11. 1. 剑尖的直径介于5.5到7毫米之间；剑头的直径，包括外部的绝缘材料，不能比剑尖直径小0.3毫米以上。

2. 剑尖呈圆柱形。它向前的一面平滑，并垂直于中轴线。
剑尖的边缘呈半径为0.5毫米的弧形，或为0.5毫米宽的45° 角斜面。

3. 施加在剑尖上的压力必须超过500克方能接通并启动裁判器发出信号。就是说剑头上的弹簧必须能顶起500克砝码。由组委会提供的500克砝码可以有 ± 2克的误差。即：498克到502克。

4. 启动裁判器发出信号所需剑尖行程，即“亮灯”行程可以非常小，剑尖的总行程最大为1毫米。用于测量的卡尺误差最大为 ± 0.05mm。

5. 剑尖必须固定在剑头上，固定点是至少两个相隔同样距离的点，或在器材委员会（SEMI）认可后用其他方法固定。

6. When not depressed the pointe d'arrêt is in contact with the **earth circuit of the foil**. When a hit is made, this contact must be broken.

Method of affixing the button

m.12. 1. If the **base** of the button is not made in one piece with the blade, or if it does not permit the flattened piece at the tip of the blade to be retained, it must be screwed onto the end of the blade, which must be cut and threaded for this purpose respecting the following conditions.

2. Normally, only **fixing** by metal to metal is allowed. However, fixing by any insulating material of great mechanical strength may be authorised after approval by the SEMI Committee of the FIE.

3. All methods of **soldering or brazing** or in general any heating which may affect the temper of the blade are forbidden. Only solder of very easily melted tin, used with a soldering iron, to prevent the tip from coming loose, is authorised.

4. The end of the blade before cutting the thread must not have a **diameter** at any point of **less** than 3.5 mm, and this without anything being wrapped round it, a process which is strictly forbidden.

5. The diameter of the **core of the thread** must not be less than 2.7 mm (thread SI 3.5 x 0.60). The threading must be very tight.

6. The **part of the blade** on which the button is fixed should be of a length of 7–8 mm entirely covered by the button. It is recommended that only the half of this length at the extremity of the blade be threaded. For the other half the button will have a smooth surface of 3.5 mm diameter into which it should take some force for the corresponding part of the blade to be introduced.

7. When a button made of **light alloy** is used, instructions should be sought from the SEMI Committee of the FIE.

8. At the point at which the wire passes into the button, the **width of the groove** must not exceed 0.5 mm, and its depth must not exceed 0.6 mm measured on the diameter of the core of the thread, in order to weaken as little as possible the section of the blade.

9. Only the members of the **SEMI Committee** of the FIE or the **Directoire Technique** can require the verification of the above points.

The insulation of the button, the blade and the handle

m.13. 1. The body of the button and the foil blade for a length of 15 cm from the button must be entirely covered with **insulating material** (insulating tape, gummed paper, Sellotape, plastic material or varnish).

2. The **flange** of the sleeve which slides in the base of the point and within which is fixed the pointe d'arrêt must be of a smaller diameter than the insulated head of the pointe d'arrêt itself, to obviate an accidental contact being made with the conductive jacket when a hit is made.

6. 在休息时，剑尖连接在地线上，当击中时，这一连接应断开。

剑头的固定

m.12. 1. 如果剑头的基座与剑身不成一体，或是剑身顶端不能保持平直，就应在遵循以下条文的情况下，在切断的剑身顶端加工螺纹，用螺钉固定住：

2. 正常情况下只允许把金属固定在金属上。不过，在器材委员会许可后，可准许用一种机械强度很大的绝缘材料来固定。

3. 任何焊接、钎焊或通常能影响剑身淬火加热的操作，均禁止使用。只准使用一种用于防止螺丝松动，用烙铁操作的易熔锡焊。

4. 在加工螺纹之前，剑身顶端直径不能小于3.5毫米，且加工中严禁用任何填料。

5. 对于剑头，螺纹内核直径最小为2.7毫米（螺纹反向旋转3.5 × 0.60）。螺纹应加工得十分紧密。

6. 剑身上用以安装剑头的长度应有7至8毫米，并完全被剑头覆盖。建议只在半段加工螺纹。在另半段上，剑头呈现直径为3.5毫米的光滑面，而剑身的相应部分应在一定的压力下进入这一光滑面。

7. 如果使用轻合金材料的剑头，应呈报器材委员会。

8. 在导线进入剑头之处，凹槽宽度不能超过0.5毫米，深度不能超过0.6毫米。应在加工螺纹内核的直径上测量，以便尽量减小截面。

9. 只有器材委员会成员或技术委员会可以要求核查上述几点。

剑头、剑身及手柄的绝缘

m.13. 1. 剑头主体和花剑剑身直至距剑头15厘米处，将全部被绝缘材料覆盖（绝缘胶布、橡皮膏、透明胶带、塑料或清漆）

2. 承受剑尖的颈圈，其直径应小于剑尖的绝缘头直径，这样在击中时，就不会与导电上衣产生意外接触。

EPEE

Weight

m.14. The **total weight** of the épée ready for use is less than 770 g.

Length

m.15. The **total maximum length** of the épée is 110 cm (cf m.3).

The blade

m.16. 1. The blade, which is **triangular in section** without cutting edges, is made of steel and must comply with the safety standards described in Annexe A to the Rules.

There are two methods of manufacture (see Figure 9):

— By forging a steel cylinder (Cross-section of blade, A);

— By folding a sheet of steel (Cross-section of blade, B).

2. It should be as straight as possible and mounted with the groove uppermost. **Any curve of the blad**e must be uniform and the maximum bend must in any case be less than 1 cm; it is only permitted in the vertical plane and must be near the centre of the blade.

The curve of the blade must be measured as follows:

i) the blade is placed on a flat surface so that the curve is uppermost;

ii) the maximum distance between the flat surface and the blade is measured: this distance is deemed to be the curve of the blade (cf Fig 9).

3. The **maximum length** of the blade is 90 cm.

4. The **maximum width** of any of the three sides of the blade is 24 mm.

5. The blade should have a **flexibility** equivalent to a bend of 4.5 cm minimum and 7 cm maximum measured in the following way.

a) The blade is fixed horizontally at a point 70 cm from the extremity of the button.

b) A 200 g weight (tolerance +/- 1 g) is suspended 3 cm from the extremity of the button.

c) The bend of the blade is measured at the extremity of the button between the non-weighted and weighted positions (see Figure 9).

重剑

重量

m.14. 准备好可以使用的重剑总重量要低于770克。

长度

m.15. 重剑的最大长度为110厘米。

剑身

m.16. 1. 剑身为钢制，截面为三角形，棱边不锋利，根据附录的安全准则制作。共有两种制作方式（图9）：

——锻造钢制圆柱体（参见图示a）

——折叠钢板（参见图示b）

2. 剑身应尽可能平直；安装时凹槽朝上。可能出现的弓形应是均匀的，弓形的高应小于1厘米；只允许在垂直方向产生，且弓形应靠近剑身中央处。

剑身的弯曲度按以下方式进行测量：

i） 将剑身置于一个平面上，弧度朝上（参照图9）。

ii） 测量平面到剑身的最大距离，这个距离就是剑身的弯曲度。

3. 剑身最大长度为90厘米。

4. 剑身三个棱面的任一面最大宽度为24毫米。

5. 剑身应具有一定柔韧性，其弯曲度最小为4.5厘米，最大为7厘米，按以下方式测量：

a. 在距剑头顶端70厘米处水平固定剑身；

b. 在离剑头顶端3厘米处悬挂一个200克砝码（允许有±1克的误差）；

c. 剑头顶端不负重和负重的位置之差即为弯曲度。

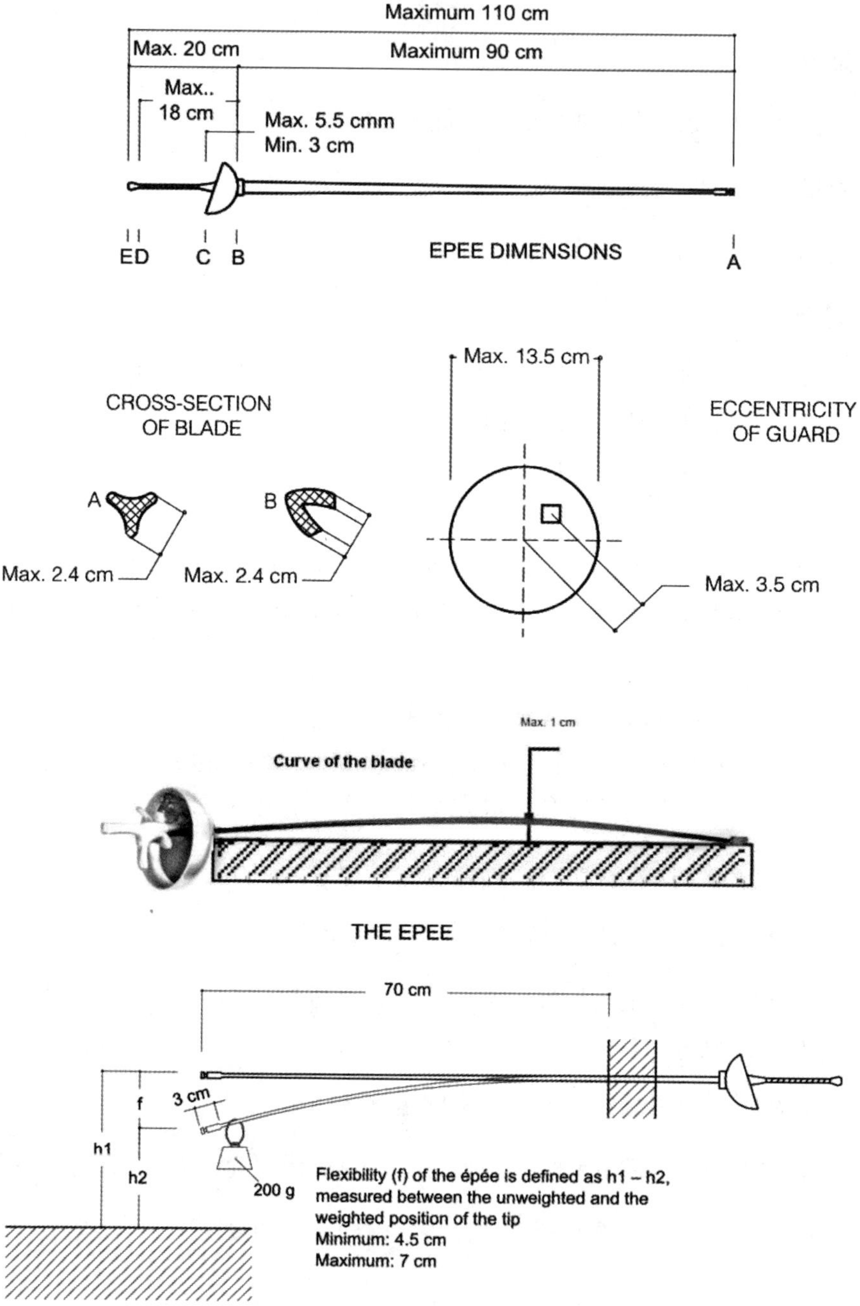

Figure 9. Epée dimensions and flexibility

This diagram is for guidance purposes only. In case of any doubt the wording of the appropriate text takes precedence

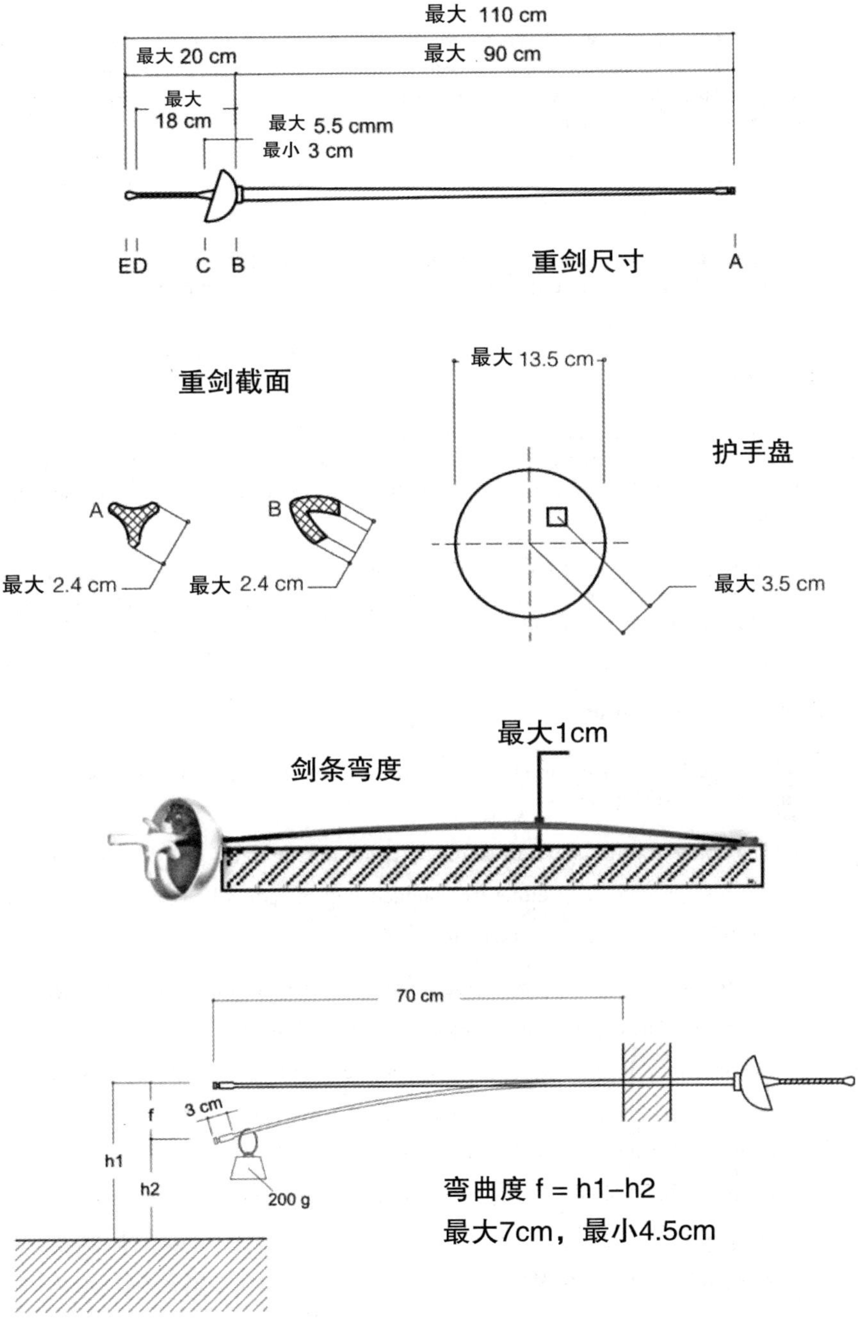

图 9　重剑的规格与弯曲度

以上的图示只用作示意，如有任何的疑虑，以相关文字描述为准。

The guard (cf. m.5)

m.17 1. The **guard**, which must have a circular edge, must be able to pass through a cylindrical gauge having a diameter of 13.5 cm and a length of 15 cm, the blade being parallel to the axis of the cylinder. The depth of the guard (the distance between lines B and C) must be between 3 cm and 5.5 cm (cf. m.3).

2. The **total length** between lines A and C must never be greater than 95.5 cm (cf. m.3).

3. **Eccentric mounting** is allowed provided the distance between the centre of the guard and the point where the blade passes through the guard does not exceed 3.5 cm.

Electric wires

m.18. 1. The épée has **two electric wires**, glued in a groove in the blade, which connect the button to two of the three sockets situated inside the guard and which form the active circuit of the épée. The earth circuit of the épée is connected to the third socket.

2. The handle must have, at the end which is in contact with the guard, a notch of 2 mm minimum depth, which allows the electric wires and their insulating sheaths to pass towards the sockets inside the guard without being squashed. (cf m.31.7)

Pointe d'arrêt and button

m.19. 1. The electric button is completed by a **pointe d'arrêt** which must conform to the following specifications.

a) The pointe d'arrêt is **cylindrical. Its front surface** is flat and perpendicular to its axis. Its edge will either be rounded with a radius of 0.5 mm or have a chamfer of 0.5 mm at 45° (see Figure 10).

b) The **diameter** of the crown of the pointe d'arrêt is 8 mm with a tolerance of ± 0.05 mm. The diameter of the base must not be less than 7.7 mm.

c) The **flange** (collar) which guides the pointe d'arrêt as well as the insulating washer must be sufficiently recessed in relation to the crown (it is recommended that it be reduced in diameter by 0.3–0.5 mm in relation to the crown) so that it shall not be possible to cause a hit to be registered merely by sliding the depressed pointe d'arrêt against the convex surface of the guard (see Figure 11) (cf. t.67.a).

护手盘（参见m.5.）

m.17. 1. 护手盘应呈圆形，并能穿过一个直径13.5厘米，长15厘米的圆柱（量规），剑身与圆柱中轴线平行。护手盘深度（b与c之间的距离）在3到5.5厘米之间（参见m.3）。

2. a 和 c 之间的总长度不能超过95.5厘米（参见m.3）.

3. 允许不超过3.5厘米的偏心距（护手盘中心与剑身穿过处之间的距离）。

m.18. 导线

1. 重剑装有两根贴在剑身凹槽中的导线，这两根导线接在护手盘内部插座的两个插芯上，与剑头相通，并形成重剑的有效电路。重剑的地线连接在插座的第三个插芯上。

2. 手柄顶端与护手盘相连接的地方有一个至少2毫米深的凹槽，可以使电线和绝缘护套在不被压扁的情况下连接护手盘里面的插座（详见m.31.7）。

m.19. 剑尖和剑头

1. 剑头的末端为剑尖，它应符合以下条件：

a. 剑尖是圆柱体。顶端平直，垂直于中轴线。其边缘为半径0.5毫米的圆弧形外廓，或是宽0.5毫米的45° 斜面。（图10）

b. 剑尖直径为8毫米，误差在 ± 0.05毫米范围内。基座直径不能小于7.7毫米。

c. 剑尖的颈圈以及任何绝缘层应缩进足够深处（建议直径缩小0.3~0.5毫米），以免因为剑尖在对护手盘“凸面”的压力作用下滑动而触发信号（参见技术规则 t.67.a）。（图11）

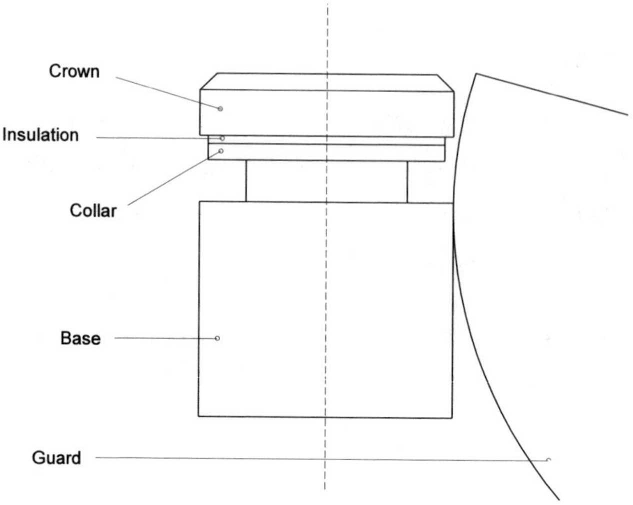

Figure 10. Epée: details of the electric button

This diagram is for guidance purposes only. In case of any doubt the wording of the appropriate text takes precedence

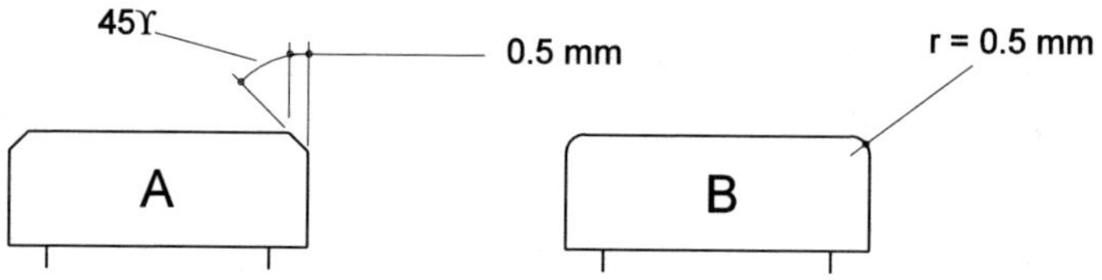

Figure 11. Epée: details of tip of point

This diagram is for guidance purposes only. In case of any doubt the wording of the appropriate text takes precedence

2. The **pressure** required on the pointe d'arrêt in order to complete the circuit in the épée, and thus cause the apparatus to register a hit, must be more than 750 g, that is to say that this weight must be lifted by the spring of the point.

3. The **weight** used to check competitors' épées on the piste consists of a metal cylinder drilled part of the way along its axis with a hole parallel to its sides; this hole, into which is inserted the end of the blade, must have an insulating lining to prevent its metallic parts coming into contact with the earthed mass of the épée which might then give a false result to the test.

   This weight of 750 g, which is supplied by the Organising Committee, may have a tolerance of ± 3 g, i.e. 747–753 g.

4. **a)** The **course** or travel of the pointe d'arrêt required to complete the circuit in the épée and thus cause the apparatus to register a hit, called the *lighting stroke*, must be greater than 1 mm. The further course which the pointe d'arrêt may travel must be less than 0.5 mm. (This requirement is just as essential as that for the lighting stroke). The gauge used should have a tolerance of a maximum of +/- 0.05mm.

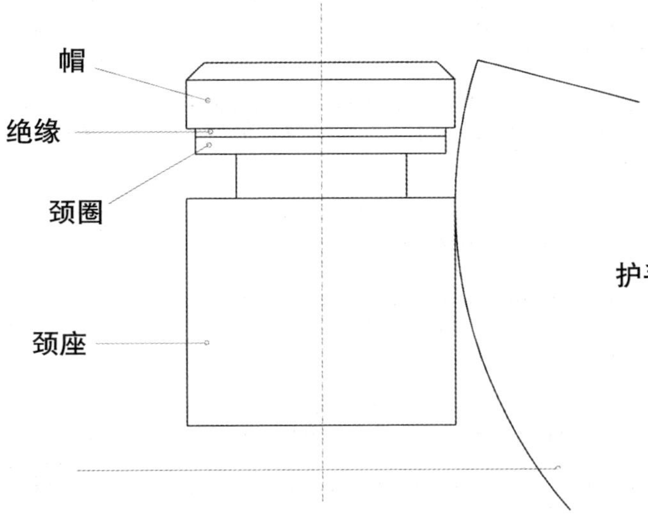

图 10　重剑的剑头结构

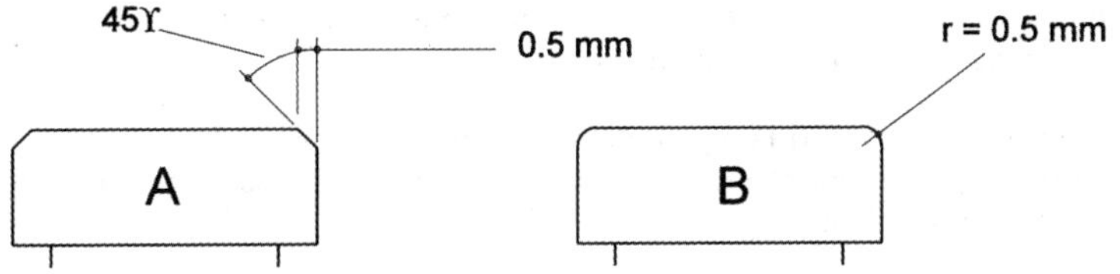

图 11　重剑的剑尖规格图

2. 用以接通重剑电路，导致电动裁判器启动所需剑尖压力应大于750克，也就是说剑头弹簧应该弹开这一重量。

3. 用于检验场上运动员重剑的砝码是一个金属圆柱体，其内部开有一个与剑身纵向平行并有一定深度的孔；该孔配有一个绝缘套，使得剑身顶端插入孔后，不会与地线接通，也就不会导致检验结果错误。这一750克的砝码由组委会提供，允许误差 ± 3克。即：747~753克。

4. a. 用于接通重剑电路，启动裁判器所必需的剑尖行程，即“亮灯行程”，应大于1毫米。剑尖的剩余行程应小于0.5毫米（此规定与亮灯行程之规定同样是强制性的）。用于测量的卡尺误差最大为 ± 0.05mm。

b) To enable a check to be made on the piste, the **total course** or travel of the point must be greater than 1.5 mm (cf. t.43). The gauge used should have a tolerance of a maximum of +/- 0.05mm.

c) Adjusting the lighting stroke by means of **screws or any other external fixing device**, once the point has been assembled on the weapon, **is forbidden** (cf t.44.3).

d) An external screw or similar fixing device is only allowed if it is actually part of the assembling of the point.

e) The **head of the screw** or fixing device must never project beyond the flat top surface of the point and its housing in the flat surface may not exceed 2 mm in diameter.

5. The pointe d'arrêt must be **retained in the button** at at least two points equally spaced, or by any other system approved by the SEMI Committee of the FIE.

6. When there is a **hit**, the electrical contact must be established.

Method of affixing the button

m.20. If **the base of the button** is not made in one piece with the blade, or if it does not permit the flattened inset piece at the tip of the blade to be retained, the button must be screwed onto the end of the blade, which must be cut and threaded for this purpose respecting the following conditions.

1. Normally, only **fixing by metal to metal** is allowed. However, fixing by any insulating material of great mechanical strength may be authorised after approval by the SEMI Committee of the FIE.

2. Only **solder** of very easily melted tin, used with a soldering iron, to prevent the tip from coming loose, is authorised.

3. The end of the blade, **before cutting the thread**, must not have a diameter at any point which is less than 4 mm and this without anything being wrapped round it, a process which is strictly forbidden.

4. **a)** The **diameter of the core** of thread at the end of the blade must not be less than 3.05 mm (thread SI 4.0 x 0.70).

b) The **part of the blade** on which the button is fixed should be of a length of 7–8 mm entirely covered by the button. It is recommended that only the half of this length, at the extremity of the blade, be threaded. For the other half the button will have a smooth surface of 4.0 mm diameter into which it should take some force for the corresponding part of the blade to be introduced.

5. The **groove** necessary to enable the wires to enter the button must be cut in such a way that it weakens as little as possible the section of the blade.

6. Only the members of the **SEMI Committee** of the FIE or the **Directoire Technique** can require the verification of the above points.

b. 为了能够在场地上进行检验，全部行程应大于1.5毫米（参阅技术规则 t.43）。用于测量的卡尺误差最大为 ± 0.05mm。

c. 剑尖由螺丝或任何其他外接装置连接在剑身上时，禁止调节亮灯行程。

d. 外接螺丝或类似装置只允许用来使剑尖装配得更牢固。

e. 螺丝或类似的加固装置的顶部绝不能超越剑尖前部的平直面，该平面的凹槽直径不得超过2毫米。

5. 剑尖应在剑头中至少两个相等间距的点上固定，或者在器材委员会同意后，采用其他方法固定。

6. 当发生击中时，应当引起电流回路。

剑头的固定

m.20. 如果剑头基座与剑身不成一体，或不能使剑身保持平直，就应当按照以下规定，在切断的剑身顶端加绞螺纹后用螺钉固定剑头。

1. 在正常情况下只允许把金属固定在金属上。不过，经过器材委员会同意，可以允许用一种机械强度很大的绝缘材料来固定。

2. 只允许一种用烙铁操作的易熔锡焊，且只能用于防止螺丝松动。

3. 在加工螺纹之前，剑身顶端任何部位的直径不能小于4毫米，并且加工中严禁用任何填料。

4. a. 剑身顶端加工螺纹内核直径不能小于3.05毫米（螺纹反向旋转 4 × 0.70）。

b. 剑身上安装剑头的部分长度应在7至8毫米，并完全被剑头覆盖。建议只在半段加工螺纹。在另半段上，剑头呈现出直径为4毫米的光滑表面，剑身的相应部分应在一定压力下进入这一表面。

5. 剑头导线经过的凹槽应尽可能少地减小截面。

6. 只有器材委员会或技术委员会可以要求核查上述几点。

SABRE

Length

m.21. The **total maximum length** of the sabre is 105 cm (cf m.3).

Weight

m.22. The **total weight** of the sabre ready for use is less than 500 g.

The blade (see Figure 13)

m.23. 1. The blade, which must be of steel, is **approximately rectangular** in section. The **maximum length** of the blade is 88 cm. The minimum width of the blade, which must be at the button, is 4 mm; its minimum thickness, also measured immediately below the button, must be at least 1.2 mm.

2. The end of the blade must be folded over onto itself or be fashioned in one piece to form a **button** which, viewed end on, must have a square or rectangular section of 4 mm minimum and 6 mm maximum. The maximum dimension must be not more than 3 mm from the end of the blade.

3. The **end of the blade** may also be formed by a solid button which must have the same section as the button which is folded over (Figure 12).

4. If the blade has a **curve**, it must be a distinct curve which must be continuous, and the deflection must be less than 4 cm. Blades with sharply bent extremities or which curve in the direction of the cutting edge are forbidden.

The curve of the blade must be measured as follows:

i) the blade is placed on a flat surface so that the curve is uppermost;

ii) the maximum distance between the flat surface and the blade is measured: this distance is deemed to be the curve of the blade (cf Fig 13).

5. The sabre blade must have a **flexibility** equivalent to a bend of minimum 4 cm and maximum 7 cm measured in the following way.

a) The blade is fixed horizontally at a point 70 cm from the tip of the blade.

b) A 200 g weight (tolerance +/- 1 g) is hung 1 cm from the tip.

c) The curve is measured at the tip of the blade between the weighted and unweighted positions (see Figures 12 and 13).

佩剑

长度

m.21. 佩剑的最大长度是105厘米（参见m.3）。

重量

m.22. 准备好可以使用的佩剑总重量要低于500克。

剑身（参见图13）

m.23. 1. 剑身钢制，截面近似长方形。其长度最大为88厘米，剑身宽度最小处在剑头部位，为4毫米；同样紧接在剑头下面的剑身厚度，应至少有1.2毫米。

2. 剑身顶端卷曲合拢或独立一体，形成剑头。从顶端看，剑头应呈现一个正方形或长方形截面，最小4毫米，最大6毫米，最大规格应位于距剑头顶端最多3毫米处。剑身顶端的边缘或者是剑头要进行至少0.5mm范围的削边处理，以便处理掉所有的锋利棱边。

3. 剑身末端也可用与折拢剑头呈相同截面的实心剑头制作（图12）。

4. 如果剑身呈现弓形，弓形应明显、持续，且弯曲度小于4厘米。禁止剑身顶端形成钩状，或剑身朝剑刃方向弯曲。

剑身的弯曲程度按以下方式进行测量：
ⅰ）将剑体置于一个平面上，弧度朝上；
ⅱ）测量平面到剑身的最大距离，这个距离就是剑身的弯曲度（图13）。

5. 佩剑剑身应具有一定的柔韧性，其弯曲度最小4厘米，最大7厘米，用以下方法测量：
   a. 在距剑头顶端70厘米处水平固定剑身；
   b. 在距剑头顶端1厘米处悬挂一个200克（允许有±1克的误差）的砝码；
   c. 剑头顶端不负重和负重的位置之差既为弯曲度（参图12、图13）。

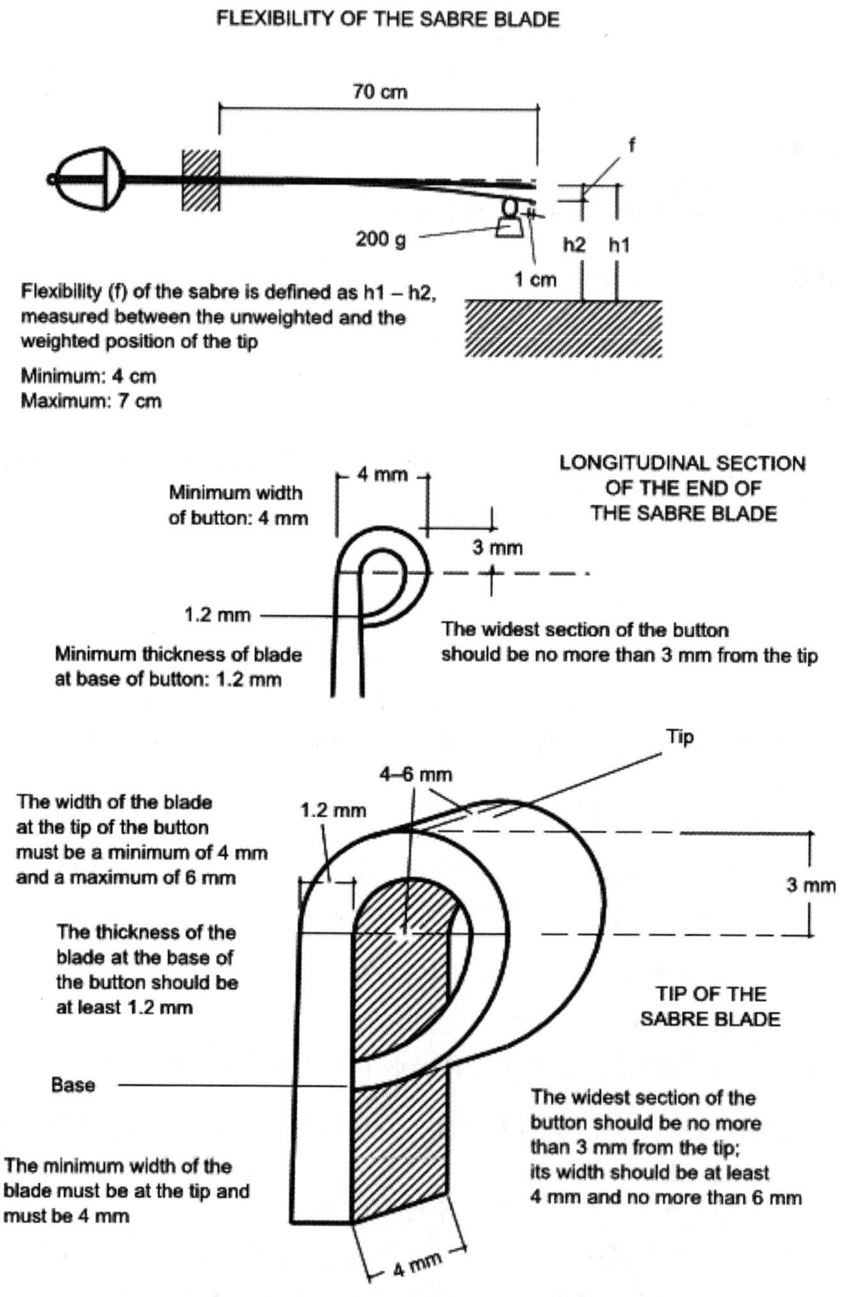

Figure 12. Sabre dimensions and flexibility

This diagram is for guidance purposes only. In case of any doubt the wording of the appropriate text takes precedence

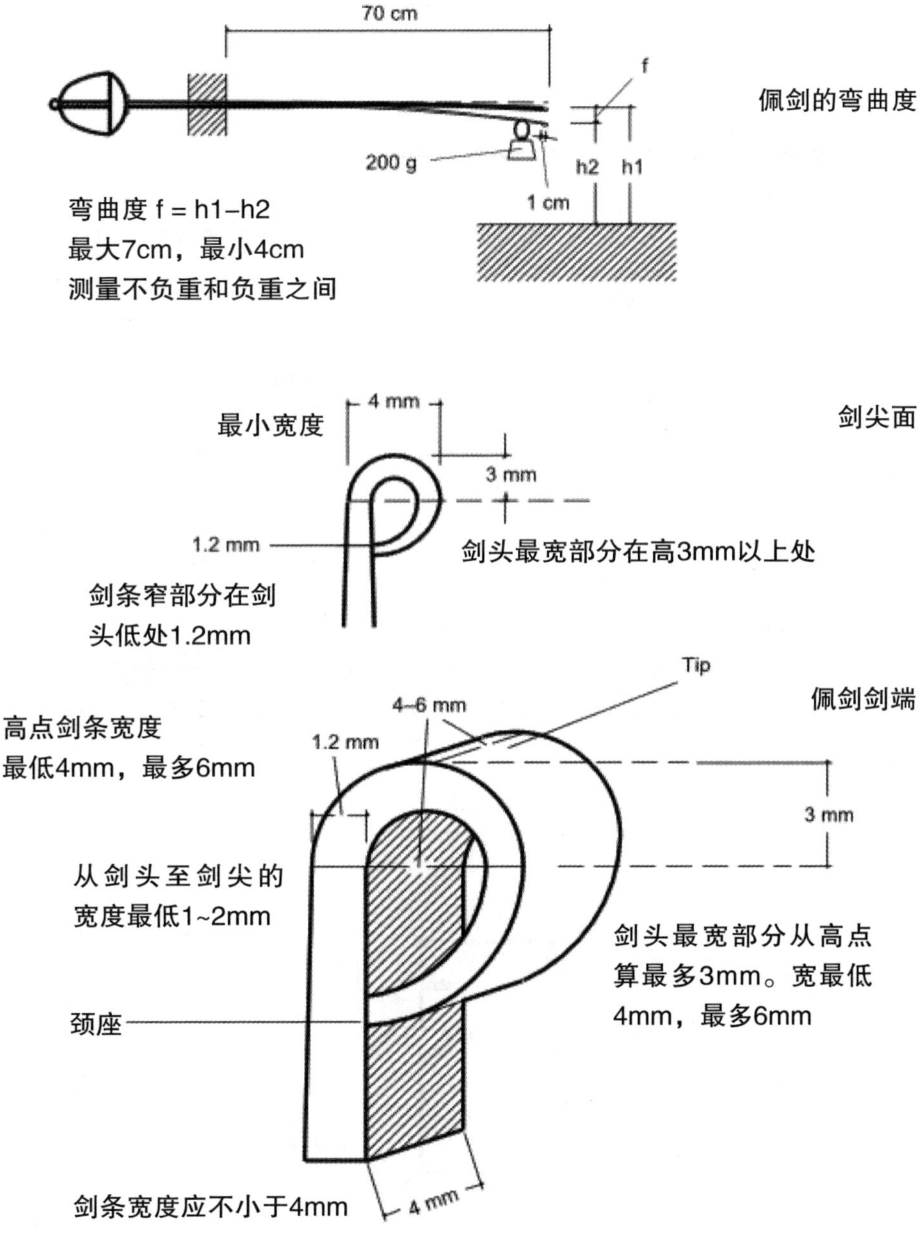

图 12　佩剑的规格与弯曲度

以上的图示只用作示意，如有任何的疑虑，以相关文字描述为准。

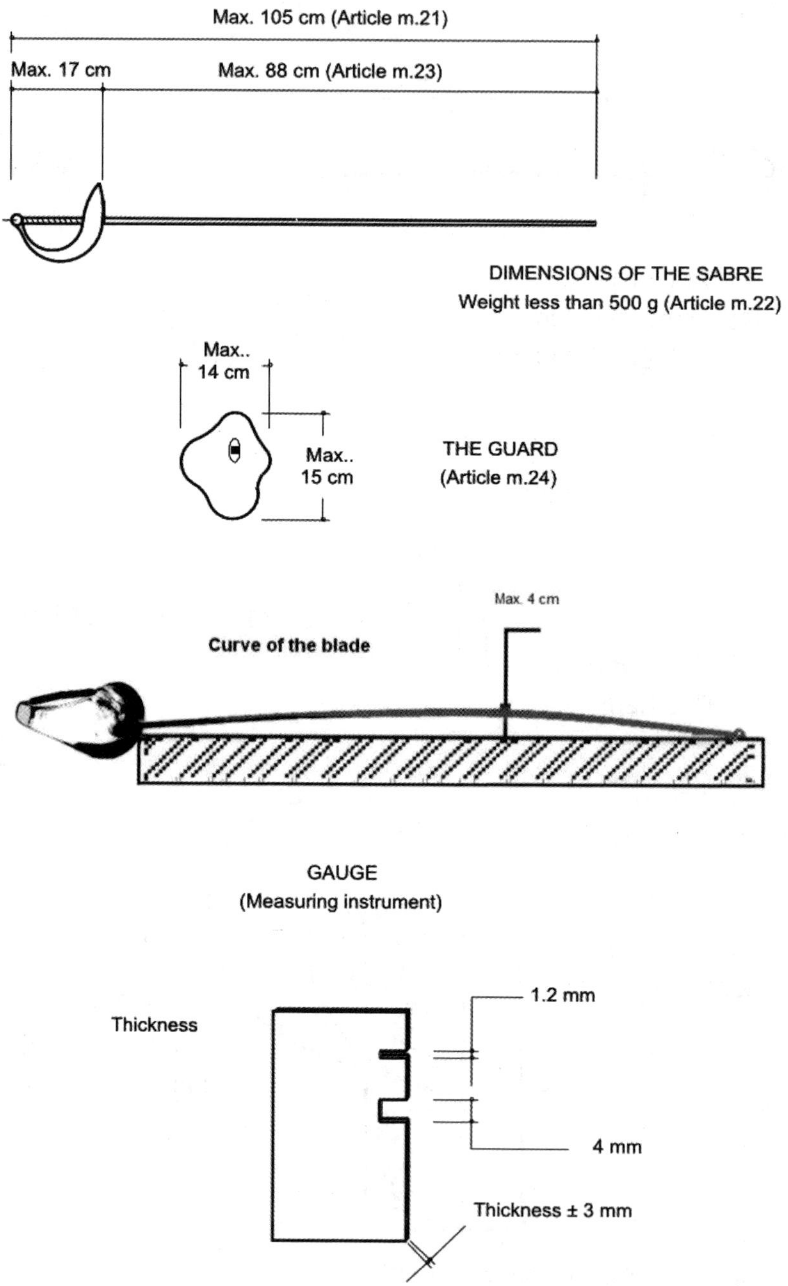

Figure 13. Sabre dimensions (contd.)

This diagram is for guidance purposes only. In case of any doubt the wording of the appropriate text takes precedence

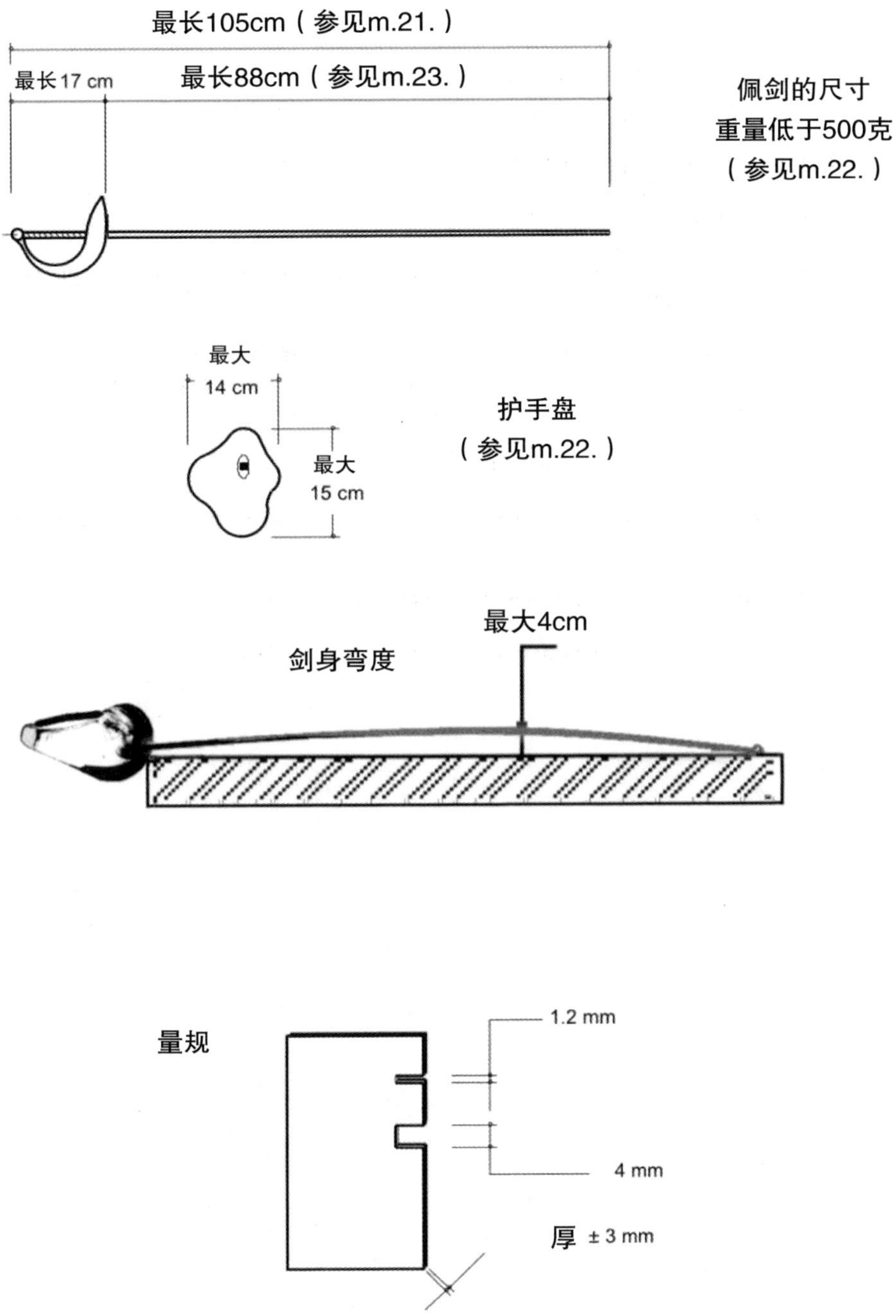

图 13　佩剑的规格尺寸

以上的图示只用作示意，如有任何的疑虑，以相关文字描述为准。

The guard (cf. m.5)

m.24. 1. The **guard** must be full in shape, made in one piece and externally smooth. It must have a convex form which is continuous, without rim or holes.

2. It must be able to **pass through** a rectangular gauge measuring 15 cm by 14 cm in section, with a length of 15 cm, the blade being parallel with the longitudinal axis of the gauge.

3. Inside the guard there must be a **socket** into which the bodywire is plugged, whatever system is used.

4. The two sockets of the bodywire plug must be in **direct contact** with the body of the guard, making a closed electrical circuit through the bodywire, the spool and the cable connecting the spool to the scoring apparatus.

5. The **resistance** in the weapon must not exceed 1 ohm.

6. The **interior of the guard** must be completely **insulated** by means of insulating paint or a pad.

7. The **exterior of the guard** must be **insulated** for 7–8 cm from the pommel.

8. The **handle and the pommel** must be completely **insulated**.

护手盘（参见m.5.）

m.24. 1. 护手盘是实心的，用整块材料制成，外表光滑。呈现出连贯的凸面，不得有翻边和破损。

2. 护手盘应穿过一个截面为15 × 14厘米的长方形、长15厘米的量规，剑身应与量规中轴线平行。

3. 护手盘内应当有一个插座以便按规定的方法插上手线的插头。

4. 手线插头的两根插芯应插在手线插座里，经过手线、拖线盘、过桥线（或挂线）和裁判器形成一个闭合电路。

5. 佩剑的电阻不得超过1欧姆。

6. 护手盘内部应使用绝缘清漆或一层垫子，保证完全绝缘。

7. 护手盘外部距平衡锤7~8厘米之间应绝缘。

8. 手柄和平衡锤应完全绝缘。

CHAPTER 2. EQUIPMENT AND CLOTHING

GENERAL CONDITIONS

m.25. The national uniform includes the socks, the breeches and the jacket.

1. **Protection**: The equipment and clothing must provide the competitor with the **maximum protection** compatible with the freedom of movement necessary for fencing.

2. **Safety:** It must not be possible for the opponent to be **obstructed or injured** by the equipment, nor for it to have either buckles or openings in which the opponent's point may be caught up — except accidentally — and thus held or deflected. The jacket and its collar must be completely buttoned or done up.

3. **Characteristics of the clothing**

    a) Fencers' clothing must be made of sufficiently **robust** material and be clean and in good condition.

    b) The material from which the equipment is made must not have a **surface which is smooth** enough to cause the pointe d'arrêt, the button or the opponent's hit to glance off (cf. m.30).

    c) Clothing must be made entirely in cloth able to **resist a pressure of 800 Newtons.** Very particular attention must be paid to the way the seams under the armpits, if there are any, are made. An **under-garment** consisting of a protective under-plastron covering the vital upper areas of the body (following the design given in Annexe A to these Rules, 'Safety norms for manufacturers') resistant to 800 Newtons is also obligatory.

    d) Fencers' clothing may be of different colours, **apart from black**.

    e) There shall be **only one** national uniform per country with the exception that the manufacturers' marks and sponsors' logos may be different.

    f) Logos (national strips) worn on the national clothing must be approved by the **FIE Executive Committee** at least 30 days before they are used for the first time in an official FIE competition; they are then published on the FIE website.

    g) For the following events, the wearing of national strips (logos) is **compulsory** on both legs, optional on the arm(s) (cf. t.45.4). All the logos worn by any one fencer must be identical.

        i) Senior Junior and Cadet World Championships: all bouts, whether in a pool, in the direct elimination or during a team match;

第二章　装备和服装

通 则

m.25. 国家队比赛服包含袜子、裤子和上衣。

1. 保护作用：装备和服装应提供最大限度的保护作用，同时又能使运动员在做动作时保持自由灵活。

2. 安全性：装备和服装不管以什么方式，都不得有妨碍或伤害对手的危险，不得有环状扣或开口（意外情况除外），以保证对手剑尖不被卡住或刺偏。上衣和衣领须完全扣住或封闭。

3. **服装的特点**

a. 服装材料要足够结实，干净且使用状态良好。

b. 服装的材料不得有引起对方剑尖、剑头或劈刺打滑的光滑表面（参阅m.30.）。

c. 服装的所有材料要能够抵抗800牛顿的抗力。要特别注意腋窝下接缝处（如有）的保护强度。上半身保护服内用于防护要害部位的保护背心（参见附件“制造商的安全规范”中的示意图）同样要有800牛顿的抗力。

d. 剑手可以穿各种颜色的击剑服，除了黑色。

e. 国家队比赛服是唯一的，除了生产商或赞助商的图标可以有所不同。

f. 国家队比赛服上使用的国家队标识要在国际剑联官方比赛第一次使用前至少30天得到国际剑联执行委员会的同意，之后国际剑联将会在其网站上公布。

g. 在以下比赛中，运动员的两条腿上必须要有国家队标识，手臂上（一只或两只）可有可无，同一名运动员使用的标识须相同：

i）世锦赛及世界青年锦标赛所有比赛，包括小组循环赛，直接淘汰赛和团体赛；

ii) Individual Senior World Cup competitions and in individual Senior Zonal Championships: all bouts, whether in a pool or in the direct elimination bouts;

iii) Teams: Senior World Cup team competitions and Senior Zonal Championships: all bouts in every match.

They must be **identical** for all fencers of the same federation for the competitions i) and iii) above.

h) The **name** of the fencer must be displayed on the back of the jacket, with the abbreviation of the national federation below it, at the level of the shoulder blades. They must be printed directly onto the jacket or onto a cloth entirely sewn onto the jacket. The letters must be in **dark blue**, in capitals, between 8 cm and 10 cm high, and between 1 cm and 1.5 cm wide, according to the length of the name.

4. Jacket

a) At all weapons, for men and ladies, the lower edge of the jacket must **overlap the breeches** by at least 10 cm when the fencer is in the on-guard position (cf. m.28, m.34).

b) The jacket must include a **lining** making a double thickness of material for the sleeve down to the elbow of the sword arm and covering the flank up to the region of the armpit. At épée the fencer is required to wear a regulation jacket, which covers the whole of the surface of the trunk.

c) The use of a **breast/chest protector** (made of metal or some rigid material) is compulsory for women and optional for men. At foil, this breast/chest protector must be worn below the protective plastron.

The entire outside of the chest protector (the side facing the opponent) must be covered with a soft material. (The material can be attached to the current plastic models or incorporated into the manufacture of new chest protectors.) The hardness of the outside of the material must be 20-30% hardness. This is the typical hardness of wet suit material for scuba diving (neoprene). This measure will be obligatory for the 2015/2016 season: the SEMI commission is to supply the specifications and testing procedures.

5. Breeches

a) The **breeches** must be fastened below the knees.

b) With breeches, the fencer must wear **socks** which cover the legs right up to the breeches. These socks must be held up in such a way that they cannot fall down.

c) The fencer is permitted to wear socks with a 10cm turn-over showing the **colours of his national team**.

ii）世界杯及洲际锦标赛成年个人赛，所有比赛，包括小组赛及所有直接淘汰赛；

iii）世界杯及洲际锦标赛团体赛所有比赛；

对于以上 i 和iii两类比赛，同一击剑协会所有运动员使用的标识必须统一。

h. 运动员上衣背后的肩胛骨位置处要有其姓名，名字下方要有其所属会员协会简写字母。可以直接印刷在上衣上，也可以将印好名字的面料整体缝在上衣上。所有字母都必须大写，颜色为深蓝色，高度为8至10厘米，根据姓名长短，笔画粗细可在1~1.5厘米间变化。

4. 上衣

a. 在所有剑种中，当运动员处于预备姿势时，上衣的下摆必须遮盖裤子至少10厘米的幅度（参阅 m.28.、m.34.）。

b. 上衣必须包括一件保护背心，自衣袖直到肘弯处、肋部直到腋下区加一层衬里。重剑运动员必须穿一件覆盖整个躯干表面的合格上衣。

c. 女子运动员必须佩戴一件金属或其他坚硬材料制成的硬质护胸，男子运动员可自由选择是否佩戴。花剑比赛中，护胸要穿在保护外衣里面。

护胸的外侧（面向对手的一侧）必须使用软质材料覆盖（该材料可附着在现有塑料模型上或者直接作为制造新型护胸的材料）。该材料的硬度须为20%至30%，此硬度相当于潜水员使用的防寒泳衣材料的硬度。器材委员会将提供技术细节和检查程序。

5. 长裤

a. 长裤应在膝盖以下被系紧固定。

b. 必须穿戴长袜。袜子须完全遮盖小腿直到长裤下方，比赛时系牢，不能下滑。

c. 准许运动员在长袜顶端留上一道长10厘米的代表国旗颜色的翻边。

6. Glove

At all weapons, the **gauntlet of the glove** must, in all circumstances, fully cover approximately half the forearm of the competitor's sword arm to prevent the opponent's blade entering the sleeve of the jacket.

7. Mask

a) The **mask** must be made with meshes (space between the wires) of maximum 2.1 mm and from wires with a minimum gauge of 1 mm diameter. The mask must include two different safety systems at the rear.

b) Masks, at all weapons, must be made in accordance with the **safety standards** described in Annexe A to these Rules and must carry the quality label specified in those standards.

c) When the **checks** are carried out the person responsible for them may, if in doubt, ensure that the mesh of the mask, both at the front and at the sides, is able to withstand, without permanent deformation, the introduction of a conical instrument, the angle of the surface of the cone being at 4° to the axis and at a pressure of 12 kg.

d) A mask which does not comply with the safety requirements laid down in this article will be rendered **visibly unusable** by the weapon checking personnel or the Referee in the presence of the person who presented the mask to the weapon check or the team captain of the fencer concerned.

e) The **bib** of the mask must be made with cloth resistant to 1600 Newtons.

f) The mask must contain a two different safety systems at the rear of the mask, with the two ends of the straps of the systems firmly affixed to the two sides of the mask. These straps may be elastic or of any other material that may be approved by the S.E.M.I. Commission.

Please refer to the examples in the drawings below:

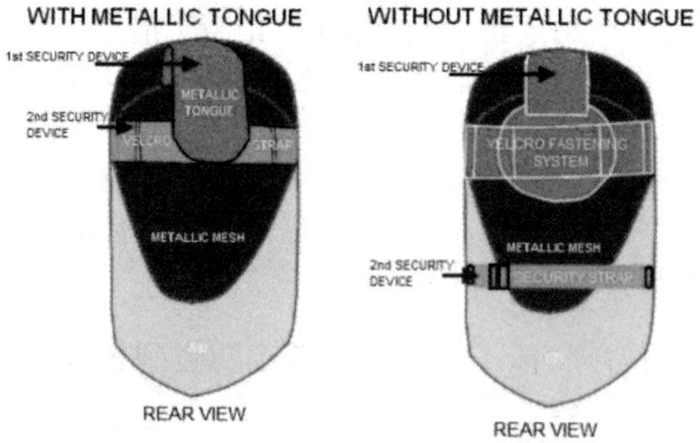

These images are only provided for information. When in doubt, the wording of relevant text prevails.

6. 手套

在所有剑种中，长筒手套的筒部在任何情况下都应完全覆盖运动员持剑前臂的一半，以避免对手的剑尖进入上衣的袖口。

7. 面罩

a. 面罩应当由金属网制成，其网眼（金属丝之间的孔）最大为2.1毫米，金属丝直径至少为1毫米，面罩后部必须有双重安全装置。

b. 所有剑种里的面罩必须按附录里的安全守则制作，并具备这些守则规定的质量标记。

c. 在检验时，负责人可以检查面罩的金属网正前面及侧面能否承受一个锥度（母线与中轴线之间的角度）为4° 的圆锥形铁扦插入网眼并负荷12公斤的压力，而长时间不变形。

d. 不符合本规则安全规定的面罩将被器材检查人员或裁判长视为不能使用，该决定将在送检人员或运动员所在队领队在场的情况下做出。

e. 面罩的护颈部分应当用能抗1600牛顿压力的面料制成。

f. 面罩后面需有双重安全装置，两个装置的绑带两端要牢固地固定在面罩的两侧。这些绑带可以是松紧或者是其他通过器材委员会认证的材料。

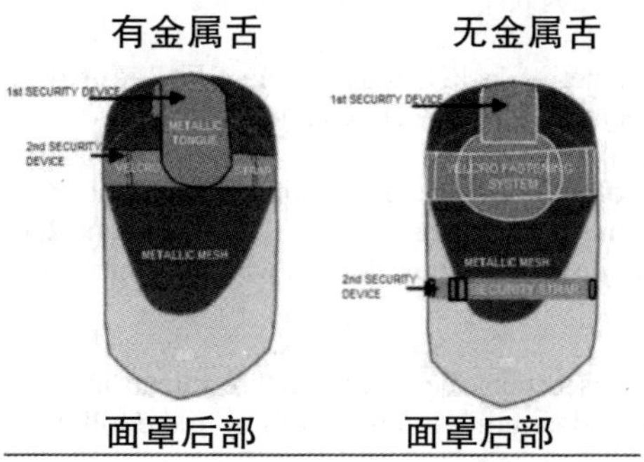

图片仅供参考，若有异议以相关文字描述为准。

RULES SPECIFIC TO FOIL

Glove (cf. m.25)

m.26. The **glove** may be slightly padded.

Mask (cf. m.25)

m.27. 1. The **mesh of the mask** must not extend below the chin. It must be insulated internally and externally by a plastic material resistant to impact.

2. The part of the bib that is beneath a horizontal line 1.5 - 2 cm below the chin, must be entirely covered with a material that has the same conductive characteristics as the conductive jacket.

3. Means of connection: the electrical contact between the conductive jacket and the bib of the mask must be ensured by means of a white coloured or clear covered wire with two crocodile clips. The wire must be attached to the bib of the mask with one crocodile clip and to the jacket with the other. This wire must be between 30cm and 40cm long.

A coiled mask wire is not allowed.

Conductive jacket and conductive T-shirt

m.28. 1. The conductive surface of the **conductive over-jacket** which is worn over the protective jacket must cover the valid target of the fencer (cf. t.47) entirely and without omission when in the on-guard position. The jacket must have a conductive flap, minimum 2 cm by 3 cm, near the middle of the back, just below the collar, to which the crocodile clip from the mask can be attached

2. Whatever the **means of fastening** used, the conductive material must cover a sufficient area to ensure that it covers the valid target in all positions of the fencer. The overlap must always be on the sword-arm side.

3. The interior of conductive jackets must be electrically **insulated** by a lining or by an adequate treatment of the conductive lamé material.

4. The conductive **collar** must have a minimum height of 3 cm and the foil conductive jacket must have a conductive flap, minimum 2cm by 3 cm, near the middle of the back, just below the collar, to which the crocodile clip from the mask can be attached.

5. The **lamé** material used must be of conductive thread in both warp and weft. As regards electrical conductibility it must conform to the following requirements.

花剑的特有规则

手套

m.26. 手套内部可以衬少许垫料。

面罩

m.27. 1. 面罩的金属网延伸到运动员下巴部位终止，并从面罩内部及外部均使用一种抗冲击的塑料来绝缘。

2. 护舌在下巴下部1.5至2厘米水平以下的部位要采用和金属背心一样导电特征的材质。

3. 连接方式：金属背心与面罩护舌的电路接通依靠一根白色或淡色的电源线以及两个鳄鱼夹。这根电源线依靠一个鳄鱼夹固定在面罩的护舌上，依靠另一个鳄鱼夹固定在金属背心上。电源线要有30~40厘米的长度。

不允许使用螺旋式头线。

金属衣与导电背心

m.28. 1. 运动员在上衣外还要穿一件导电背心，在预备姿势时其导电表面应完整且毫无遗漏地覆盖住整个有效部位（参见技术规则t.47）。在金属衣的背部中央位置附近，衣领下方，须有一个最小为2cm × 3cm的舌状金属织物，以便与来自面罩的鳄鱼夹连接。

2. 不管使用的是什么式样的闭合方式，导电面料叠放起来应有足够宽度，可以确保在所有姿势中都能覆盖住有效部位，被叠放的部位必须在持剑手臂的一侧。

3. 导电背心的内部应当用一层衬里或金属丝织物绝缘。

4. 金属衣领的高度最小为3cm，花剑金属衣的背部中央位置附近衣领下方处须有一个最小为2cm × 3cm的导电的金属舌，以便与来自面罩的鳄鱼夹连接。

5. 所用的金属丝织物应当用金属线双向编织；从导电性角度看，该织物应符合以下条件：

a) The **electrical resistance** measured between any two points of the lamé material must not be greater than 5 ohms. The resistance will be measured by using a 500g conductive metal weight which has a hemispherical end with a radius of 4 mm. This weight, placed on this end and moved about on the lamé, must maintain continuous contact with a maximum resistance of 5 ohms.

b) In no circumstances must the use of a conductive jacket be allowed if it has **holes** in it, or **patches of oxidation** or other defects which may prevent the registration of a valid hit.

c) A conductive jacket which is considered to be **unusable** will be so marked with a very visible coloured paint by a member of the SEMI Committee of the FIE.

6. The conductive jacket **must be so made** that when it is laid flat there is a straight line between the point of junction of the lines of the groin and the two points corresponding to the tops of the hip bones (ilium).

7. The band of **non-conductive material** passing between the legs must be at least 3 cm wide (see Figure 14).

8. For compliance of the T-shirt's electrical resistance with a wireless manufacturer's requirements, the maximum electrical resistance:

a) between any two points of the electrically conductive belt on the T-shirt (including both flaps for crocodile clip connection) should be not more than 15 Ohms;

b) between any two points on the electrically conductive fabric-belt portion of the T-shirt (including both flaps for the crocodile-clip connection) and any point of the electrically conductive fabric on the sleeves or on the neck, should be not more than 50 Ohms;

c) these checks must be carried out by a wireless equipment manufacturer.

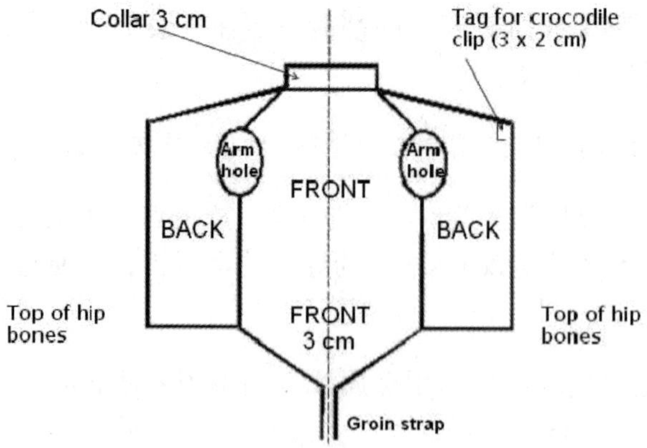

a. 在织物表面任意两点间测量的电阻不得大于5欧姆。为测量织物电阻，可使用一个铜或黄铜做的500克砝码，末端为半径4毫米的半球体，这一砝码的末端放在金属丝织物上来回移动，在保证持续接触的情况下，最大电阻为5欧姆。

b. 在任何情况下，导电背心都不容许出现可能妨碍有效击中的小洞、氧化斑点或其他情况。

c. 如果一件导电背心的面料被判定为不能使用，将被器材委员会一名成员涂上一种显眼的颜料，从而无法再使用。

6. 当导电背心平放时，其下部分的外形应该是，一条直线将两侧胯骨顶端对应的点与腹股沟交汇处对应的点连接起来。

7. 从双腿间穿过的不导电带状面料应至少有3厘米宽（参见图14）。

8. 导电T恤的电阻需符合无线装置制造商的要求，最大电阻为：

a. 导电T恤上导电区域中的任意两点（包括连接鳄鱼夹的金属舌）之间的电阻不能超过15欧姆。

b. 导电T恤上（包括连接鳄鱼夹的金属舌）导电织物区域中的任意两点以及衣袖或衣领上导电织物的任意点间的电阻不能超过50欧姆。

c. 以上检测须由无线器材制造商进行。

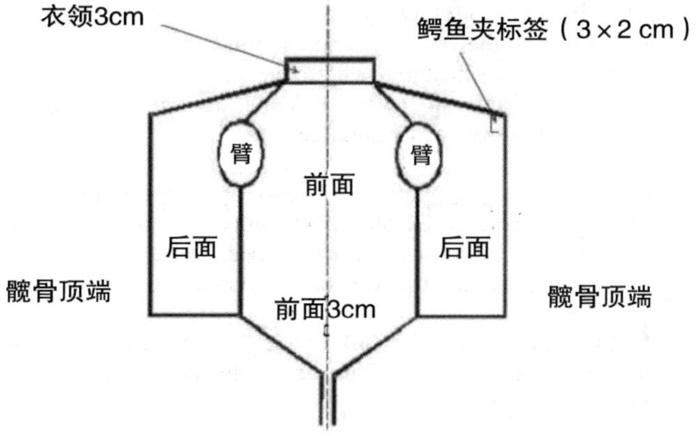

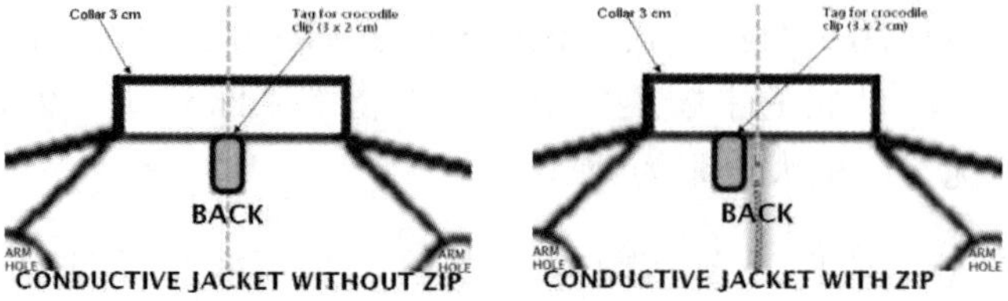

Figure 14. Foil: conductive jacket

This diagram is for guidance purposes only. In case of any doubt the wording of the appropriate text takes precedence

m.29. Bodywire and attachment plugs

1. **a)** The conductive wires of the **bodywire** (the fencers' personal equipment) must be well insulated electrically from each other, twisted or joined together, and not be affected by humidity.

   b) This bodywire has a **connecting plug** at each end. In the absence of a security device being fitted to the weapon, a security device must be fitted to the plug of the bodywire.

   c) The **electrical resistance** of each of these conductive wires (plug to plug and plug to crocodile clip) must not exceed 1 ohm.

2. **a)** At the **spool end** the three-pin male plug, which must comply with the conditions of manufacture and assembly laid down in Article m.55, will be attached to the wires in the following manner:

   — the pin at 15 mm from the centre pin to the conductive jacket;

   — the central pin to the wire in the weapon;

   — the pin at 20 mm from the centre pin to the foil earth circuit or the conductive piste.

   b) The wire which joins the rear connection of the bodywire to the conductive jacket by a **crocodile clip** must be separate for at least 40 cm. This wire must be soldered to the crocodile clip and this soldering must not be covered by any insulation or any material whatsoever. However, any method of fixing which presents the same guarantees as soldering may be used, provided it has been accepted by the SEMI Committee.

   c) The crocodile clip must be robust and ensure **perfect contact** with the conductive jacket. Its width at the point of contact must be at least 10 mm; the inside of the clip must leave a free space at least 8 mm long by 3 mm high. It must be clipped onto the back of the conductive jacket on the **sword-arm side**.

3. **a)** **At the end nearest the foil**, inside the guard, any method of attachment is allowed but the method adopted must always conform to the specification laid down in Article m.5.

   b) In addition, the pins of the plug must in no circumstances be able to **touch the metal part** of the guard.

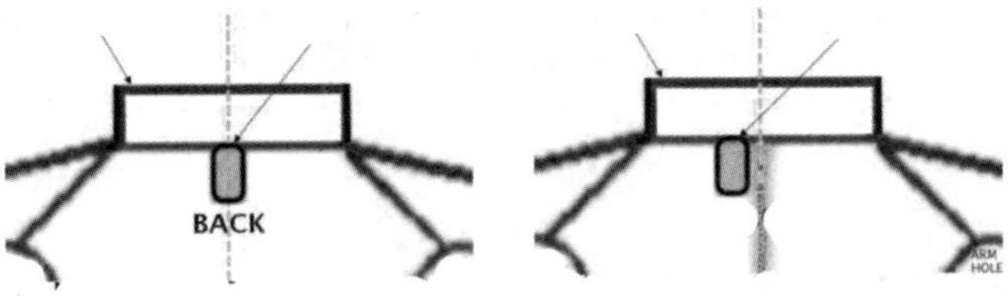

图 14　花剑导电背心

以上的图示只用作示意，如有任何的疑虑，以相关文字描述为准。

m.29. 手线和连接插头

1. a. 手线（运动员专用器材）完全绝缘，防潮，集束或拧成绳索状。

   b. 手线的每一端是一个连接插头。如果武器上没有安全锁扣装置，则手线需要有一个这样的安全锁扣装置。

   c. 手线每根导线的电阻，从插头到插头，以及从插头到鳄鱼夹，不能超过1欧姆。

2. a. 在连接拖线盘的一端，三相连接插头应符合m.55中规定的制造与装配规定，并按以下方法连接在拖线盘的导线上：
   —— 15毫米插芯：连接导电背心；
   —— 中央插芯：连接花剑导线；
   —— 20毫米插芯：连接花剑地线或金属剑道。

   b. 借助鳄鱼夹将手线后插头和导电背心连接起来的导线应至少有40厘米的长度。这根导线应焊接在鳄鱼夹上，且焊缝不得被绝缘材料或其他材料覆盖。在器材委员会同意后，可以准许其他具有同样保障的固定方法。

   c. 鳄鱼夹应坚固，且确保与导电背心接触良好。接触点宽度应至少有10毫米，夹子内部应具有一个至少8毫米长、3毫米高的自由空间。它应夹在持剑手臂一侧的导电背心背部。

3. a. 在花剑护手盘内部，连接方式是灵活的，但都应符合 m.5的规定。

   b. 另外，在任何情况下，插头上的插芯都不能触及护手盘的金属部件。

c) The wire from the point will be protected by an **insulated sheath** from the place where it enters the guard right up to the insulated connection on the plug socket. Under no circumstances may the non-insulated wire extend beyond this insulated plug connection (cf. m.5, m.9).

RULES SPECIFIC TO EPEE

Mask

m.30. 1. The mask must not be covered, in whole or in part, by material which can **cause the point to glance off** (cf. m.25).

2. The mask must be so shaped that the **bib** reaches below the prominences of the collar bones (clavicles).

Bodywire

m.31. 1. a) The **conductive wires** of the bodywire (the fencers' personal equipment) must be well insulated from each other, insensitive to humidity, and either joined or twisted together.

b) The maximum **electrical resistance** allowed for each of these conductive wires from plug to plug is 1 ohm.

2. The bodywire has a **connecting plug** at each end. In the absence of a security device being fitted to the weapon, a security device must be fitted to the plug of the bodywire.

3. At the **spool end**, a three-pin male plug is connected to the wire as follows:

a) the pin 15 mm from the centre pin to whichever wire is most directly connected to the pointe d'arrêt;

b) the centre pin to the other wire on the épée;

c) the pin 20 mm from the centre pin to the épée's earth circuit and to the conductive piste.

4. This plug must conform to the conditions of manufacture and mounting specified in Article m.55.

5. **Inside the guard** the choice of system is free but the system chosen must comply with the conditions of Article m.5.

6. In addition, the pins of the plug must not on any account permit **contact with the metal** of the guard.

7. The two wires coming from the tip must be protected by **two insulating sheaths**, one for each wire, from the point where they enter the guard right up to the two insulated connections on the plug socket. In no case may uninsulated wires extend beyond the plug connections (cf. m.5, m.9).

c. 来自花剑剑尖的导线从进入护手盘直到接线柱为止，都应用一个绝缘套包住保护起来。不绝缘电线不得超出接线柱（参见m.5、m.9）。

重剑特有规则

面罩

m.30. 1. 面罩不能全部或部分地覆盖有可能导致剑尖打滑的材料（参阅m.25）。

2. 面罩的护颈部分应延伸到锁骨以下。

手线

m.31. 1. a. 手线（运动员专用器材）完全绝缘，防潮，彼此集束或拧成绳索状。

b. 从插头到插头的每根导线的最大电阻为1欧姆。

2. 手线的每一端分别是一个连接插头。如果剑身没有安全装置，则手线需要有一个这样的安全装置。

3. 在连接拖线盘的一端，三相连接插头按以下方式连接：
a. 15毫米的插芯：连接重剑剑尖最直接的一根导线；
b. 中央插芯：连接重剑的另一根导线；
c. 20毫米的插芯：连接重剑地线和金属场地。

4. 这个插头须符合 m.55规定的制造、装配条件。

5. 在护手盘内部，连接方式可自由选择，但应符合m.5的规定。

6. 此外，插头上的插芯在任何情况下都不能触及护手盘的金属部件。

7. 来自剑尖的两根导线从进入护手盘直到插头支架的两个接线柱为止，应用两个绝缘套分别包裹保护起来。不绝缘导线不能超出接线柱（参阅m.5、m.9）。

RULES SPECIFIC TO SABRE

Mask

m.32. 1. The **metal mesh of the mask** must not be insulated and must ensure electrical conductivity.

2. The **bib and any trim** must be entirely covered with conductive material with the same electrical characteristics as the conductive jacket.

3. The **trim** may also be made of conductive material.

4. The **electrical contact** between the conductive jacket and the mask must be ensured by means of a white coloured or clear covered wire with one or two crocodile clips. The wire must be attached to the mask with one crocodile clip or by soldering and to the jacket with a crocodile clip. This wire must be between 30cm and 40cm long. A coiled mask wire is not allowed.

5. The **electrical resistance** between the crocodile clip and any point on the mask must be less than 5 ohms. The crocodile clip(s), the design and size of which must conform to the conditions laid down in Article m.29.2(c), must be soldered to the end(s) of the wire. In addition, the electrical resistance in this wire (between crocodile clip and crocodile clip or crocodile clip and soldering) must not exceed 1 ohm. The wire must be white-coloured or clear.

Glove

m.33. 1. The material of the fencing glove must have a level of protection of 800N on the areas shown in the diagram below, the seams a minimum strength of 200N and cuff a level of protection of 350N. The conductive material, which can be removable or fixed, must cover all of the gauntlet of the glove down to below the external cubital styloid (small prominent bone of the wrist), both when the fencer is in the 'on-guard' position and when the sword arm is straight. Inside the glove there must be

fixed the FIE quality label, granted after the homologation procedure, with the year of manufacture and stating 800N.

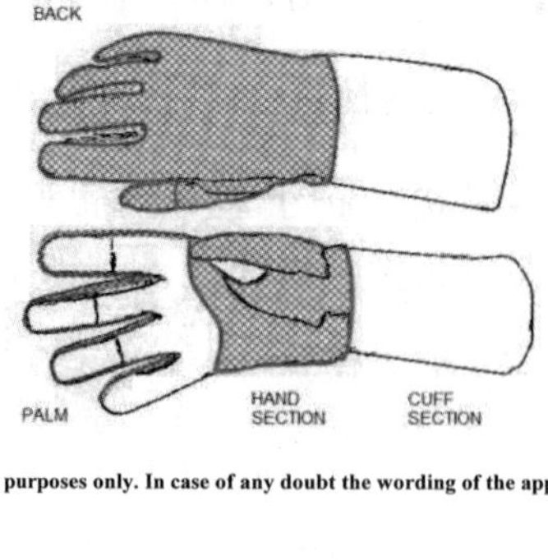

This diagram is for guidance purposes only. In case of any doubt the wording of the appropriate text takes precedence

佩剑特有规则

面罩

m.32. 1. 面罩的金属网不能被绝缘，须确保导电性。

2. 护颈及附件应被导电材料完全覆盖，须具有与导电上衣相同的导电特性。

3. 附件也可以由导电材料制作。

4. 金属上衣与面罩的电路接通依靠一根白色或透明的电源线以及两个鳄鱼夹。这根电源线可以依靠一至两个鳄鱼夹固定，或者焊接到面罩金属网上。电源线要有30到40厘米的长度。禁止使用螺旋式头线。

5. 鳄鱼夹与面罩上任意一点间的电阻应小于5欧姆。鳄鱼夹的形状及大小要符合器材规则 m.29.2.c的规定，要焊接到电源线头上。另外，这根电源线（鳄鱼夹之间或鳄鱼夹及焊接点之间）的电阻不能超过1欧姆。电源线须为白色或淡色的。

手套

m.33. 1. 击剑手套必须在以下图示位置处至少具备800N的保护强度，接缝强度至少为200N，袖口处保护强度至少为350N。导电材料应使用可拆卸或者固定方式，须覆盖整个长手套直至持剑手手臂腕骨外侧突出部位，在实战姿势和伸直手臂时均应保持此位置。手套内部必须带有经国际剑联授权的FIE认证标识，标明生产年份和800N字样。

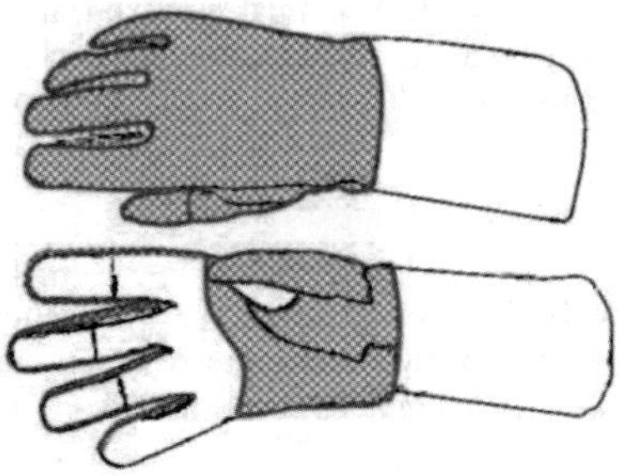

以上的图示只用作示意，如有任何的疑虑，以相关文字描述为准。

2. The **conductive material** must be turned over into the inside of the gauntlet to a depth of at least 5 cm.

3. In order to guarantee **a good contact** with the sleeve of the conductive jacket, it is necessary to use an elastic band, a popper button or any system which will guarantee conductivity and which has been approved by the SEMI Committee. When a conductive overlay is worn, the overlay must contain a device which fixes the position of the overlay on the arm so that its position on the arm cannot be changed during the bout.

4. The conductive tissue (lamé) must satisfy the specified control conditions (cf m.28.5)

Conductive jacket and conductive t-shirt

m.34. 1. The fencer must wear, over his jacket, a **conductive over-jacket**, the conductive surface of which must cover entirely and without omission the valid surface of the body above a horizontal line which, when the fencer is on guard, joins, round the fencer's trunk, the tops of the two hip bones. At wireless sabre the fencer must wear a **conductive t-shirt**. The conductive part is made of a conductive fabric: the maximum electrical resistance between any two points of the electrically conductive t-shirt fabric (including both flaps for crocodile clip connections) must be not more than 15 Ohms. These checks must be carried out by a wireless equipment manufacturer.

2. The **conductive surface** must cover the arms as far as the wrists. The jacket must have a collar which is at least 3 cm high. The jacket must have a conductive flap, minimum 2 cm x 3 cm in the middle of the back, just below the collar, to which the crocodile clip from the mask can be attached.

3. Whatever means of **fastening** is used, the conductive material must be ample enough to guarantee covering the valid target area in any position.

4. The **conductive material** (lamé) must satisfy the conditions laid down for testing (cf. m.28).

5. The **sleeves** of the conductive jacket must be fixed at the wrist by means of an elastic band. There must be a strap passing between the fencer's legs to keep the jacket in place (see Figure 15).

Bodywire and plugs

m.35. The fencer must use the **bodywire** specified for foil, plugged into the guard plug socket by means of any system which conforms with the conditions for manufacture and assembly laid down in Articles m.5, m.29 and m.55.

2. 导电面料应向手套筒部内侧翻边，翻边宽度至少5厘米。

3. 经过器材委员会允许，可以使用一根松紧条、一个按扣或者一种可以保证导电性的方法，以便能够确保手套与金属外衣袖口的良好接触。佩戴导电袖套时，袖套要能够用某种设置固定其在胳膊上的位置，以便即使是在交锋的过程中，袖套的位置仍不会发生变化。

4. 导电面料要符合明确的检查要求（参见m.28.5）。

导电上衣和导电T恤

m.34. 1. 运动员在上衣外穿一件导电上衣，其表面应完全且无遗漏地覆盖身体的有效部位，即在“预备”姿势时，从运动员大腿与躯干形成的褶痕顶端通过的水平线以上部分。使用佩剑无线设备时，剑手要身着导电T恤。导电部分是由导电织物构成：导电T恤导电织物上（包括连接鳄鱼夹的金属舌）任意两点间的电阻不能超过15欧姆。这些检测由无线器材制造商进行。

2. 导电面积遮盖双臂直至手腕。上衣衣领应至少有3厘米高。导电上衣背部衣领下正中央处应备有一块3厘米长2厘米宽的舌状金属织物，用来连接面罩上的鳄鱼夹。

3. 不管使用何种闭合式样，金属面料应有足够宽度，可以确保在所有姿势中都能覆盖住有效部位。

4. 导电面料应符合器材检测规定。（参阅 m.28）

5. 导电上衣的衣袖须用松紧带固定在手腕上。上衣须通过一根从运动员双腿间穿过的带子固定在原位（图15）。

手线和连接插头

m.35. 运动员应使用花剑规则中规定的手线，手线可用任何方式连接在护手盘上，但是应符合m.5、m.29、m.55中规定的制造和装配要求。

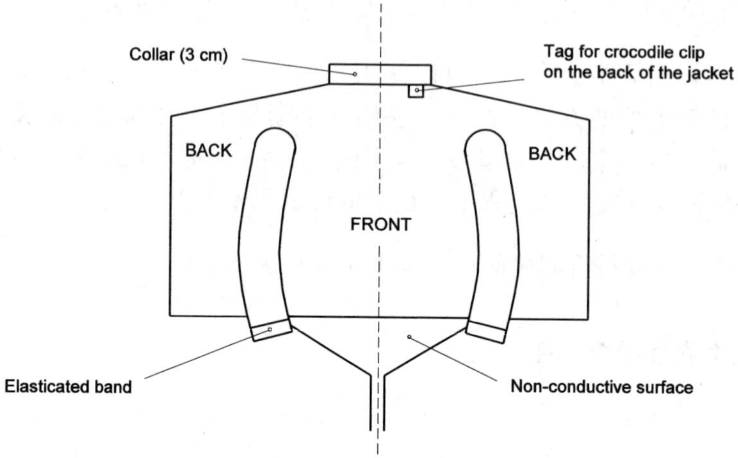

Figure 15. Sabre: conductive jacket

This diagram is for guidance purposes only. In case of any doubt the wording of the appropriate text takes precedence

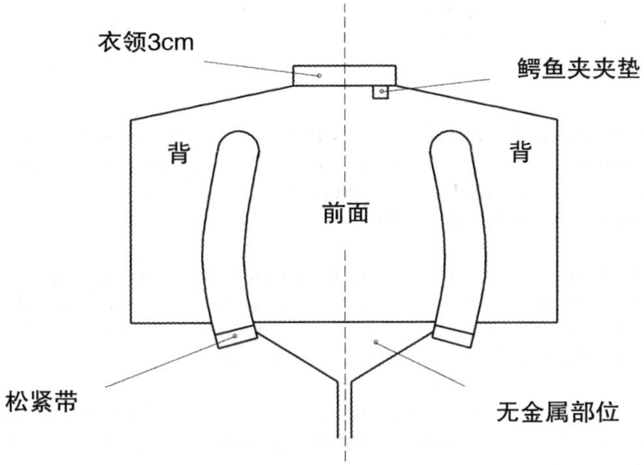

图 15　佩剑导电背心

以上的图示只用作示意，如有任何的疑虑，以相关文字描述为准。

CHAPTER 3. CHECKING OF MATERIAL

COMPETENCE

m.36. 1. The **checking of the electrical material** used by the organisers for the World Championships (Open, Junior and Cadet) and the fencing competitions of the Olympic Games, as well as the checking of the fencers' equipment, must be supervised by the SEMI Committee.

2. To carry out this supervision, **three members** of the above-mentioned Committee must be appointed and put in charge of this work. However, when the organising country possesses somebody competent, recognised as such by the SEMI, two members of the above Committee will be appointed.

3. The delegates of the SEMI Committee of the FIE **have the right** at any time to seize a weapon, a bodywire, a conductive jacket or any item of equipment or clothing for examination.

CHECKING OF FENCERS' EQUIPMENT

m.37. 1. In all official FIE competitions **the fencers are responsible** for their equipment (including weapons and clothes) at the moment they present themselves on the piste.

2. In particular blades, masks and clothing must all carry the **label of guarantee** specified in the safety standards annexed to these Rules.

3. **The forms of checking** laid down by these Rules are only intended to help organisers who must apply the Rules and fencers who must always respect these Rules. These checks can, therefore, in no way absolve any fencers who break the Rules from responsibility.

Presentation of equipment to the Weapon Checking Centre

m.38. 1. Fencers are obliged to **present themselves** at the Weapon Checking Centre, at the time advised in the timetable of each official competition of the FIE, with the equipment they intend to use during the event in question. The number of articles handed to the Checking Centre is limited to four weapons, three bodywires, two conductive jackets, two masks and three mask-to-jacket leads per fencer.

2. Each competitor must **submit his weapons** in a fencing bag at the Weapon Checking Centre reception. An inventory of the equipment is made by an organising official and a label is put on the bag, indicating the name of the country of the competitor. The bags are stored in the order in which they arrive, and are checked in the same order.

3. Provision should be made for weapons and clothing to be submitted on the **morning of the day before the competition**. Having been checked, the material will be returned to the delegations at the end of the day.

Weapons, equipment and clothing presented to the Checking Centre after 5 p.m. on the day before each event may be refused.

第三章　器材的检验

权 限

m.36. 1. 对于世界成人、青年和少年锦标赛以及奥运会击剑比赛，在器材委员会监督下，由组织者对使用的电动器材和运动员的装备进行检验。

2. 为完成这一监督工作，器材委员会指派3名该委员会的成员负责此项工作。当东道主拥有经器材委员会认可的合适人员时，将只指派该委员会的2名成员。

3. 器材委员会的代表有权在任何时候抽检一件武器、一根手线、一件金属上衣、装备或服装的任意一个部件。

运动员器材的检验

m.37. 1. 在国际剑联所有正式比赛中，运动员比赛时，对自己的器材（武器、装备和服装）负责。

2. 特别是剑身、面罩和服装应贴有附录的安全准则里规定的保证标志。

3. 本规则制定的检验措施只是为了帮助组织者执行规则，并帮助运动员遵守规则。因此，这些措施绝不能解脱违犯规则运动员的责任。

器材送检

m.38. 1. 运动员必须在国际剑联正式比赛的日程计划表中所规定时间内，携带在比赛期间将要使用的器材，前往器材检验中心。每位运动员送交给检验中心的物品数量限定在4件武器、3根手线、2件金属上衣和2件面罩和面罩的3根导线。

2. 参赛者把武器送往器材检验接待室外，放进一个击剑包里。清点工作由一名组织工作人员完成，并在包上贴上一张标明参赛者名称、国籍的标签。击剑包将按顺序存放，并按同样顺序接受检验。

3. 应在比赛前一天早上进行武器和服装的检验，检验好的器材要在当天下午交还给各个参赛队。在比赛前一天17点以后送交检验的武器、装备、服装可以被拒绝检验。

4. Each **head of delegation** must indicate where he can be contacted should a serious fault be detected while the equipment belonging to his fencers is being checked.

5. If a weapon is found to be **defective** at the first check a form is attached indicating the fault: e.g. the length of the blade, the insulation, the spring of the point, cutting edges, etc. This form is completed at the second check. However, when a weapon is rejected, it must go through the entire cycle again.

m.39. 1. If material or equipment presented to the Checking Centre appears **to have been assembled** in such a way that the fencer can control at will the registering of hits or the malfunctioning of the judging apparatus, the representative of the SEMI Committee may, after the examination of the irregular items, require a penalty against the person who submitted them.

2. The fencers or the team captain can only insist on the **return of the equipment which has been checked** one hour before the start of the event.

3. **Any repairs** to equipment rejected during the checking can be carried out in the repair workshop. Repaired equipment will, however, only be tested again after the first set of checks of the other fencers' equipment has been completed.

Body responsible for checks

m.40. 1. The **Executive Committee** of the FIE will appoint the member(s) of the SEMI Committee to be responsible for the checking of weapons, clothing and equipment of the fencers at the fencing competitions of the Olympic Games and for the World Championships.

2. For other official FIE competitions the **Organising Committee** will appoint one or more persons to be responsible for this checking.

m.41. The items of equipment which have been thus checked will be **distinctively marked**. A fencer must not, on pain of penalties (cf. t.120), use any equipment which does not bear this check mark.

Personnel and equipment required for checking

m.42. 1. In order to allow those carrying out the checking to fulfil their task, the organisers are required to make available the **equipment** (gauges, weights, scales, electrical measuring machines, etc.) and the personnel necessary to carry out the work.

2. The Organising Committee must provide the FIE technical delegates responsible for checking the weapons and equipment with at least **the following apparatus:**

a) Two **gauges** allowing the lengths of blades and the depths and diameters of the guards at all weapons to be measured quickly.

b) Devices for measuring the **flexibility of blades** and the **resistance of the mesh** of masks.

c) An electrical checking device to check quickly that the electrical **resistance** of the point is not too high, and that the bodywire and the weapon are **correctly assembled.** Devices enabling these measurements to be taken easily are, in fact, commercially available.

4. 在器材检查确认有严重缺陷时，将告知该代表队的领队。

5. 如果一件武器在第一次检验时就被发现有缺陷，须附清单说明缺陷：剑身长度、绝缘、剑头的弹力、锋利的棱边等；第二次检验将对照此清单进行。如一件武器被发现有缺陷，必须重新接受一次完整的检验。

m.39. 1. 如果送交检验的器材或装备进行了改装，有明显的舞弊行为，器材委员会代表可通过检测确认后，要求处罚送交该器材的人员。

2. 运动员或队长只能在分项比赛开始前一小时要求归还检验过的器材。

3. 在检验过程中退回的器材，如要修理，可以在修理室进行修理。修理过的器材只有在其他运动员器材第一轮检验结束后才能被检查。

检验机构

m.40. 1. 对于奥运会击剑比赛和世界锦标赛，国际剑联执行委员会将指定器材委员会一名或几名成员负责运动员武器、装备和服装的检验工作。

2. 对于国际剑联的其他正式比赛，组委会指定一名或几名检验工作负责人。

m.41. 器材被检验合格后，将被标上明显的记号；运动员不得使用无检验标志的器材比赛，否则就要受到规则规定的处罚（参阅技术规则t.120）。

检验人员及检验用具

m.42. 1. 为了便于检验者完成其任务，组织者必须提供必要的检验用具（量规、砝码、天平、万用表等等）和人员。

2. 组委会向负责检验武器和器材的国际剑联技术代表们至少提供以下检验仪器：

a. 两个可以快速检查所有剑种的剑身长度，护手盘深度和直径的量规。

b. 用以测量剑身柔韧性、面罩金属网强度的装置。

c. 一个电子检验仪器，可以快速检查剑尖电阻以及手线和武器的装配。市场上常见这样的检验仪器。

d) **Weights** of 750 g and 500 g to test the springs of the points in épée and foil, in the workshop and at each piste.

e) A device allowing the **lighting stroke** and **residual travel** of épée points to be accurately measured, in the workshop and at each piste.

f) **Labels** to indicate that a weapon has been checked and that it satisfies the regulation, or has been rejected.

g) In the world championships and Olympic Games the control of blades by Foucault current is mandatory.

h) The organisers must provide a **special stamp** to be affixed to each conductive jacket to enable the referees to verify that its resistance in ohms has been checked by the technical delegates of the FIE. Nevertheless, this compulsory checking mark is not sufficient to justify the use of the jacket. In effect, it is the task of the Referee to check, before each event, that the conductive jacket, having been checked and marked, entirely covers the valid target area, and accordingly to make the final decision whether it may be used.

i) A special **ink or paint** must be provided to mark the guards, blades and points of weapons which have been checked. Nevertheless, those responsible may use other methods to mark the weapons and conductive jackets.

m.43. 1. To carry out the checks properly and rapidly, **'workshop' teams of three people** should be used. (At least three such workshops should be provided.)

2. The first person checks that all the weapons are normal with respect to their **dimensions** by passing them through a gauge.

3. The second does all **electrical** tests.

4. The third affixes the **checking marks** and replaces the weapons in the fencing bag.

d. 500克和750克砝码，用于检查室和每个场地的花剑和重剑检查剑头的弹力。

e. 在检查室和每个场地，提供可以精确检查重剑剑尖的亮灯行程和剩余行程的装置。

f. 标签，用以标明武器已被检验，合格或被退回。

g. 世锦赛和奥运会上，必须使用涡流探测器检测剑条。

h. 组织者应准备一个专门印章，加盖在每件导电上衣上，使得主裁判可以核实其电阻已被国际剑联的技术代表们检查。然而，检验标志并不足够证明参赛者可以使用这些导电上衣参赛。而是在每场比赛前由主裁判核查导电上衣是否完全覆盖了有效部位，最后决定它们是否可以被使用。

i. 应准备专门的墨水或颜料，用来标明检查过的护手盘、剑身及武器剑尖。不过，技术代表也可以用其他方式来为武器和导电上衣作标记。

m.43. 1. 为稳妥、快速检验器材，应组成3人检查小组（至少配备3个这样的检查小组）；

2. 检查小组中的第一人负责从尺寸方面，使所有武器通过量规，检查它们是否正常；

3. 第二人负责进行有关电气方面的所有检查；

4. 第三人负责添加检验标记，并将武器放回击剑包。

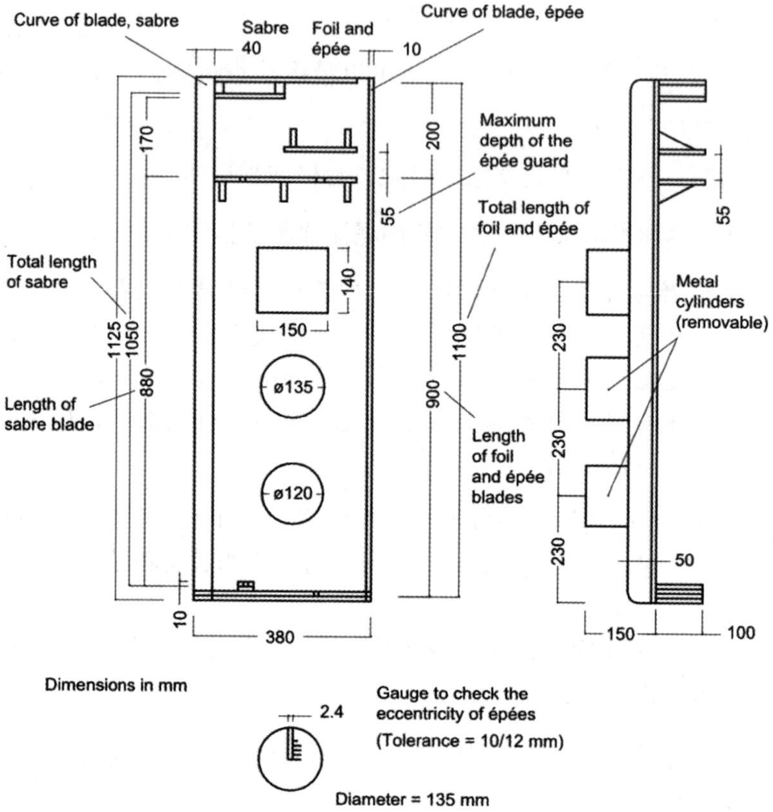

Figure 16. Gauge for checking weapons

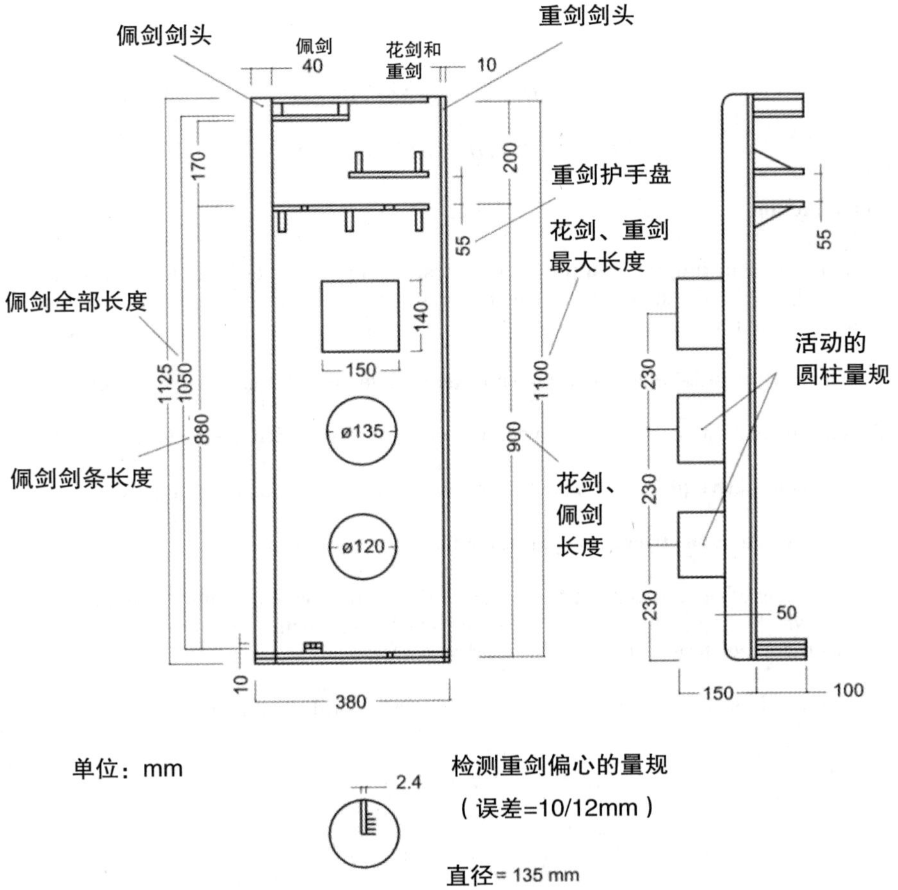

佩剑剑头
佩剑
40
花剑和
重剑
10
重剑剑头
170
200
重剑护手盘
55
花剑、重剑
最大长度
佩剑全部长度
140
150
1125
1050
1100
ø135
880
900
花剑、
佩剑
长度
佩剑剑条长度
ø120
10
380
55
活动的
圆柱量规
230
230
230
50
150
100
单位：mm
检测重剑偏心的量规
（误差=10/12mm）
2.4
直径= 135 mm

图 16　检验武器的量规

PART 2. FITTINGS AND MATERIAL

PROVIDED BY THE ORGANISERS

Introduction

m.44. 1. All **electrical judging equipment** includes, in addition to the equipment provided by the fencers themselves, the material provided by the organisers of a competition, which is:

2. The **central judging apparatus**, with extension lamps (cf. m.51, m.59, Annexe B);

3. The **spools**, with cables and connections, or cables suspended overhead (cf. m.55);

4. The **conductive piste** which neutralises hits made on the ground (cf. m.57);

5. The **source of electrical current** (accumulators) (cf. m.58);

6. For finals of official competitions of the FIE, a **clock** which counts down the time and which can be linked to the apparatus which controls the audible signal and the electrical registering of hits (cf. m.51, Annexe B).

7. The wireless apparatus is optional at the Veteran World Championships.

第二部分 组织者提供的设备和器材

概述

m.44. 1. 所有的得分电子显示设备包括，除运动员自己的器材外，比赛组织者应提供以下器材，即：

2. 外部带有重复灯的裁判器（参阅m.51，m.59，附录“B”）。

3. 拖线盘及连线，或挂线（参阅m.55）。

4. 金属剑道，以保证击中地面不显示信号（参阅m.57）。

5. 电源（蓄电池）（参阅m.58）。

6. 对于国际剑联正式比赛的决赛，一台计时器，可以连接发声控制装置和电动信号裁判器。（参阅m.51，附录“B”）

7. 世界老将锦标赛不要求必须使用无线设备。

CHAPTER 1. SCORING APPARATUS

Authorised designs

m.45. Only electrical apparatus designed with **wires connecting** the fencers to the central apparatus and registering hits by light signals with auxiliary sound signals are authorised, except for apparatus without wires using encoded waves authorised by the SEMI. This **excludes other apparatus based on wireless waves** and those which register sound signals only.

Approval of designs of apparatus

m.46. 1. Judging apparatus for use in a **World Championship or the Olympic Games** must have been approved by the SEMI Committee of the FIE.

2. In order to obtain this approval, the apparatus which it is proposed to use must be submitted **complete**, with spools, connections, etc., for an examination by the said Committee, at a place and on a date to be agreed with the Committee, at least six months before the date of the competition.

3. The apparatus must be accompanied by a **detailed drawing** showing its construction.

m.47. Approval is given for the use of the apparatus in one specific official competition only. The SEMI Committee is willing, as far as it is able, and without charge, to examine prototypes of apparatus submitted by constructors even if the use of such apparatus is not envisaged for an imminent official competition.

m.48. 1. Approval is given for only one **established design** of apparatus which conforms to the drawing submitted, and is not given as a general approval for all the products made by any manufacturer. The latter may state in their publicity only the fact that the design of apparatus which they offer for sale has been used at a specific official competition (if this in fact is the case); but they themselves must guarantee that the apparatus conforms to the design for which approval was given.

2. Every approved apparatus must carry, on its base, a **metallic plate** identifying its specific characteristics: manufacturer, year of manufacture, model, technical information, etc.

m.49. The **approval of an apparatus by the SEMI Committee** as well as its acceptance implies no guarantee against possible faults of construction, or against its use with a source of electrical current other than accumulators (cf. m.58).

m.50. All **expenses** incurred by the SEMI Committee for the examination of apparatus are the responsibility of the persons submitting the apparatus.

第一章　电动信号裁判器

准许使用的类型

m.45. 符合规则裁判器须具备以下条件：配有将运动员的武器连接在裁判器上的导线，带有主要的灯光信号及辅助信号；无线裁判器和仅基于声音信号的裁判器除外。

裁判器型号的批准

m.46. 1. 用于世锦赛或奥运会的裁判器应得到器材委员会的批准。

2. 送检裁判器应成套，有拖线盘、连接附件等，在比赛开始前至少6个月，在该委员会认为合适的时间和地点，送交该委员会检查。

3. 裁判器应附有一张详细的结构图。

m.47. 裁判器的检测与批准通过某场官方比赛进行。即使制造者提供的裁判器样品并不准备用于即将进行的下一次正式比赛，器材委员会也可根据其自身条件免费对其进行检测。

m.48. 1. 批准文件只能给予与提供图解相符的某一确定型号的裁判器，而并非笼统地给予任意一个制造厂商的任何产品。厂商们在广告中只能注明提供出售的裁判器型号已在某某正式比赛中使用过（如果情况确实如此）；但是他们自己应保证他们生产的裁判器与批准的型号相符。

2. 任何被批准的裁判器的底座上应带有一块金属铭牌，上面标明：制造商、制造年份、型号、技术信息等等。

m.49. 器材委员会对某种裁判器的批准及许可，并不能保证在生产中没有任何缺陷，或是可以使用除蓄电池以外的其他电源（参阅m.58）。

m.50. 器材委员会因检查裁判器而引起的一切费用由送检方承担。

Requirements for all electrical equipment (cf. Annexe B)

m.51. 1. A hit made on the **conductive piste or on the metallic parts of the weapon** must not be registered by the apparatus, nor may it prevent the registering of a hit made simultaneously by the opponent. At foil a hit made on a part of the foil may register if an uninsulated part of the weapon of the fencer is in contact with his conductive jacket.

2. The apparatus must not have any device whereby anyone other than the person detailed to supervise it **can interrupt its working** during a bout.

3. Hits are registered by **light signals**. The signal lamps must be placed on the top of the apparatus, in order that they may be visible to the Referee, the competitors and the superintendent of the apparatus. They must be so positioned that they show clearly from which side the hit was made. It must be possible to attach **extension lamps** to the exterior of the apparatus, in order to increase the visibility of the signals.

4. Once the signal lamps are alight, they must **so remain** until the apparatus is reset, without having any tendency to go out or flicker either when subsequent hits are made or if the apparatus is subjected to vibrations.

5. The visual signals must be accompanied by **audible signals** (cf. Annexe B).

6. The **resetting switches** must be placed either on top of or on the front part of the apparatus.

7. **a)** For official competitions of the FIE, the **source of power** must always be accumulators. The wiring of the box to be powered in this way must be designed so that it is impossible for the box to become connected by mistake to the mains supply.

b) All fencing salles, clubs, etc., and the organisers of training sessions or competitions involving weapons using electrical equipment, may use the current supplied by the mains on condition that they adhere strictly to the technical standards laid down on the subject by their countries and international communities.

8. **a)** During the last 10 seconds of each period in an individual bout and of each bout in a team match, the clock must show: the time to a tenth of second when the scoring apparatus is running and to a hundredth of second when the scoring apparatus is stopped. The timer should be provided with a remote start/stop device (see Annex B for technical specifications). [Application: season 2015/2016 for the World Championships and the Olympic Games only - season 2016/2017 for the World Cup competitions (Junior and Senior), the Grand Prix and the Zonal Championships (Junior and Senior).] If the **clock** is not incorporated in the electrical judging apparatus, the apparatus must have a

system for linking in an external clock. This clock must be powered by electricity from a 12 volt accumulator. A disconnection of the wiring which links the clock to the apparatus must cause, simultaneously, the blocking of the apparatus which registers hits, in a manner which preserves what it has registered up to that point, and the stopping of the clock.

所有电气设备须满足的条件（参阅附录“B”）

m.51. 1. 击中金属场地或武器的金属部分不得显示信号，也不得妨碍对手同时击中时信号的显示。对于花剑，如果运动员武器的非绝缘部分与其导电背心接触，那么对手击中其武器部分也会显示信号。

2. 裁判器不得带有使技术人员以外的任何其他人员可以在比赛期间中断其工作的装置。

3. 击中通过灯光信号显示。信号显示灯安装在裁判器上方，以便让主裁判、运动员及裁判器工作人员都能看见。信号显示灯通过其发光位置的不同，应清楚地表明哪一方已被击中。为增加信号的可见度，应能够在外部增加重复指示灯。

4. 一旦亮灯，显示的信号应保持稳定，直到裁判器重置为止，不能由于随后的击中或震动而产生熄灭或闪烁。

5. 灯光信号发出的同时须伴有声音信号（参阅附录“B”）。

6. 重置键须位于裁判器上方或前面。

7. a. 对于国际剑联的正式比赛，须用蓄电池供电。裁判器的电源插头要设计成不能因为错误连接而导致直接与主电源相连。

b. 所有击剑馆、俱乐部等，以及电动武器训练或比赛的组织者，只有严格遵守其所在国和国际组织规定的有关技术标准，才可以使用普通电网供电。

8. a. 在个人及团体赛每轮的最后十秒，计时器需显示：十分之一秒（当裁判器在工作中），百分之一秒（当裁判器停止工作）。计时器需配备远程起停遥控设备（详见附件B）。（适用于：2015–2016赛季：仅世锦赛及奥运会；2016–2017赛季：世界杯（青年及成年）、大奖赛、洲际锦标赛（青年及成年）。

如果裁判器内没有装入计时器，那么它与外接计时器之间应有一个连接系统。计时器必须由一台12伏特的蓄电池供电。如果计时器与裁判器之间的连接中断，须同时使裁判器停止运行，且保留已经记录的信号，计时器也停止运转。

b) To allow the apparatus to be used **when it is not connected to the clock**, there must be a switch in the interior of the apparatus which can change its operating mode (cf. t.32, m.44).

9. For the **finals** of official competitions of the FIE, the clock must be equipped with a system which connects it to some external extension clocks displaying large luminous numbers, and with another system for the connection of the audible signal. These two connection systems must be separated from the circuits situated inside the central judging apparatus by means of opto-couplers (cf. t.32, m.44).

10. When the cable connecting the audible-signal apparatus to the clock is **disconnected**, the audible-signal apparatus must emit a sound of between 80 and 100 decibels (measured at the centre line of the piste) lasting between 2 and 3 seconds, but the central judging apparatus must not be blocked and the clock must not be stopped (cf. t.32, m.44, m.51/9).

Number and quality of judging apparatuses

m.52. 1. For official FIE competitions, the organising committee must provide a **minimum number of electrical judging apparatuses** equal to the number of pistes plus at least two spares. All the apparatuses must be in perfect working order, and of a type approved for the World Championships.

2. As soon as a member federation is **selected to organise** an official FIE competition, it would do well to contact the President of the SEMI Committee immediately in order to obtain the names of manufacturers whose electrical apparatus is accepted by the Committee.

3. The Organising Committee usually prefers combined apparatus, which can be used for all three weapons. The Organising Committee must choose a manufacturer who will provide good quality equipment for the smooth technical running of competitions; this equipment must be approved by the SEMI Committee.

4. For official FIE competitions, it is compulsory that the apparatus be powered by **accumulators** without any connection to the main electrical supply.

b. 为了使裁判器在不连接计时器时也可以使用，裁判器内部应装有一个用于变换操作方式的按钮。（参阅技术规则 t.32，器材规则m.44）

9. 对于国际剑联正式比赛的决赛，计时器应配有一套连接显示大图像数字的外部扩展时钟的系统，和另一套连接声音信号发生器的系统。这两套连接系统应通过光电耦合器与裁判器的内部线路分开。（参阅技术规则 t.32，本规则 t.44）。

10. 当连接声音信号发生器与计时器的电缆电源被切断时，声音信号发生器发出的声音音量应在80至100分贝之间（在剑道中线上测量），持续2至3秒钟。但是裁判器主体不应停止运转，计时器也不得停止（参阅技术规则t.32，本规则m.44、m.51/9）。

裁判器数量与质量

m.52. 1. 对于国际剑联的正式比赛，组委会应提供至少与剑道数目相等的裁判器，加上至少2台备用裁判器。所有裁判器应完全调节好，并且是经批准可用于世界锦标赛的型号。

2. 一旦国际剑联某一会员协会被选定举办国际剑联正式比赛，该协会有义务立即与器材委员会主席取得联系，以便获得由该委员会批准的裁判器生产厂商的名单。

3. 一般来说，组委会更愿意选择可在三个剑种中兼用的裁判器。组委会应选择能够提供经器材委员会批准的优质裁判器并可以保证竞赛中技术服务的厂商。

4. 对于国际剑联的正式比赛，裁判器必须由蓄电池供电，且与主电网没有任何连接。

Checking of apparatuses

m.53. 1. Having chosen the manufacturer with which it wants to deal, the Organising Committee of a World Championship immediately advises the President of the SEMI Committee of the FIE who in turn contacts this firm to obtain, as soon as possible, a **prototype** of the desired model.

The control of the fencing apparatuses must be done before the competition using a checking device that is able to verify that the fencing apparatuses fulfil all requirements related to reaction times and electrical resistances.

2. The report on the **checking** of the apparatus is always presented to the manufacturer by the President of the Committee within one month of the apparatus being received.

3. There are then two possibilities:

a) The proposed apparatus is accepted by the Committee, in which case the other apparatuses can be manufactured like the prototype.

b) The apparatus does not conform to the requirements, in which case it must be modified and re-submitted to the Committee for a new examination.

4. When all the apparatuses are ready and before they are sent out, the President of the SEMI Committee must be notified, so that he can document the **checking of the apparatuses** before they leave the factory. Each apparatus comes with a test report giving the different specifications concerning the registering time in milliseconds and the resistance in ohms of the external circuits before registering a non-valid hit.

The person in charge of verification ticks off every apparatus and makes a note of its number.

m.54. 1. Before every World Championship or Olympic Games, a delegate of the SEMI Committee must check the **proper working of the apparatuses** to be used and that they conform to the type registered. This is independent of the registration of the type of apparatus mentioned above (cf. m.52).

2. The apparatuses must be **made available to this delegate** at least 48 hours before the beginning of the competition.

裁判器的检查

m.53. 1. 当世锦赛组委会已选定某厂商，应立即通知器材委员会主席，以便从该企业获得一台预选裁判器的样品。裁判器检查工作需在赛前完成。使用检查装置检测裁判器反应时间、电阻等是否符合要求。

2. 裁判器检验报告将在收到裁判器样品后一个月内，由器材委员会主席提供给制造厂商。

3. 这时会出现两种可能性：

a. 推荐的裁判器被器材委员会接受，在此情况下，其他裁判器可以按样品同样方式制造；

b. 裁判器不符合条件，在此情况下，应对其进行修改，并重新送交到器材委员会以进行新的检查。

4. 当所有裁判器制作完成后，应在发货前通知器材委员会主席，以便让他能够在裁判器出厂前，进行检验并建立档案。每台裁判器都配有一份检查报告，上面标明了在一次无效击中记录之前裁判器外部电路的电阻以及以千分之一秒为单位的记录时间。

检验者逐一检验每台裁判器，并记录其序列号。

m.54. 1. 在世锦赛或奥运会之前，器材委员会的一名代表须检验比赛将使用的裁判器运行是否良好，以及是否符合批准的型号。而这一检查应独立于上述对裁判器型号的批准。（参阅m.52）

2. 这些裁判器应至少在比赛开始前48小时准备好，供这名代表检验。

CHAPTER 2. SPOOLS, CABLES AND THEIR CONNECTIONS

m.55. 1. The maximum **electrical resistance of each wire of the spool**, measured from socket to socket, must be 3 ohms.

2. There must be no **interruption of electrical contact** even when the spool is being rotated at full speed. To ensure this the contact rings must have double brushes. The wire connected to the earth circuit of the weapon will be connected to the frame of the spool.

3. The spools must allow 20 m of cable to be **unwound** without straining the springs.

4. The socket which terminates the spool cable, and is designed to receive the plug of the bodywire at the fencer's back, must include a **safety device** which fulfils the following requirements:

— that it is impossible to use it unless the plug is correctly put in;

— that it is impossible for it to become separated during the bout;

— that it is possible for the competitor to verify that the two foregoing requirements are satisfied.

5. The **resistance** of each of the three wires in the connecting cables must not exceed 2.5 ohms.

6. The plugs used to **connect the bodywire** to the spool wire and the connecting cables to the spools and to the apparatus must have three pins of 4 mm diameter arranged in a straight line. The outer pins must be spaced 15 and 20 mm respectively from the centre pin. The bodywire and the connecting cables have plugs, the spool wires and the central electrical apparatus have sockets to them.

7. The use of **suspended cables** instead of spools is permitted, provided that the conditions already mentioned are satisfied.

m.56. 1. The organisers must ensure that the spools have cables of at least **20 m in length** so that they do not get ripped out in the event of a flèche made at the end of the piste.

2. It is desirable for the **spools to be placed** close to the pistes, but outside them so that fencers do not trip over them.

3. The **cables** connecting the spools to the apparatus should be of the three core type and be covered with rubber to protect them from humidity and blows.

4. Conductive pistes **should be earthed** at the centre of the piste.

5. Those in charge of checking equipment during competitions must have a simple and practical device at their disposal to allow them to **check quickly** that there are no breaks or short-circuits in the three wires of the spools.

第二章 拖线盘、连接电缆和连接插头

m.55. 1. 拖线盘每根导线各插孔之间测定的最大电阻为3欧姆。

2. 拖线盘即便在全速转动时，也不得出现任何接触中断。为此，接触环将有一对滚动式集电器。通过拖线盘地线，连接武器的地线。

3. 拖线盘应备有放线后达20米长的电缆，弹簧能承受放线后的拉力。

4. 用于插接运动员背后手线插头的拖线盘导线插孔，应具备以下条件：
—— 若未进行正确连接，就不可能连接上；
—— 在交锋过程中，不能脱落；
—— 使运动员有可能检验上述两点是否均已落实。

5. 连接电缆的三根导线中每根的电阻不能超过2.5欧姆。

6. 手线连接在拖线盘导线上的插头，电缆连在拖线盘和裁判器上的插头，都包括三个直径为4毫米的插芯，直线排列，两边的插芯与中间的插芯分别相隔15毫米与20毫米。手线与连接电缆带有插头，拖线盘和裁判器则带有插孔。

7. 准许使用悬挂电缆代替拖线盘，同时上述段落的规定仍然适用。

m.56. 1. 拖线盘导线应至少有20米长，以避免在剑道尽头做冲刺时导线被拔断。

2. 拖线盘最好放在剑道附近但在剑道以外，以免运动员被这一障碍绊倒。

3. 连接拖线盘和裁判器的导线将有三根，用橡胶包住，以保护导线防潮及避开劈刺。

4. 接地插头要设在剑道中央。

5. 在比赛期间检验器材的工作人员应当可以支配使用一台简单实用的仪器，能够迅速检验在拖线盘3根导线中是否有断裂或短路现象。

CHAPTER 3. CONDUCTIVE PISTES

m.57. 1. The **conductive piste** must be made from metal, metallic mesh or some substance that is conductive. The resistance of the piste, from one end to the other, must not exceed 5 ohms.

2. The conductive piste must **cover** the whole of the length and breadth of the piste including its extensions, in order to neutralise floor hits.

3. a) When the piste is mounted on a **platform** the conductive piste must cover the whole width of the platform.

b) The platform must not exceed **50 cm in height**, and must be wider than the fencing piste itself by at least 25 cm on each side. Each end of the podium must be equipped with a **gentle slope** right down to ground level.

4. Because the amount of wire which the spools can carry is limited, the conductive piste is designed for use on a **piste 14 m long**; an extension of 1.50–2 m is added at each end of the piste to allow the fencer crossing the rear limits of the piste to retire on an even and unvarying surface. The conductive piste must therefore have a length of 17–18 m.

5. a) It is preferable to lay the conductive piste on a **wooden base** with some flexible material between. It must be provided with some device which enables it to be kept well stretched.

b) The wooden bases are **12–15 cm** above ground level. Their sides must not be sloping.

c) It is preferable to have a **metal strip**, screwed down if possible, which will keep down the edges of the conductive piste along the entire length of the base on both sides.

d) Pistes made of **metallic mesh** must never be placed directly on a floor of reinforced concrete or tiles.

6. The **paint** used to draw the lines on the conductive piste must not prevent its electrical conductibility, so that a hit made on it at a point where a line occurs is also neutralised.

7. The organisers must have equipment for the immediate **repair** of the piste available on the spot.

8. There must be no roller or any sort of **obstacle** at the ends of the conductive pistes which could prevent the fencers from retreating normally.

9. Pistes used in the World Championships and in the Olympic Games must be tested before competition by SEMI Commission Delegates using the Slip-Meter.

10. The specifications of the Slip-Meter must fulfil the specifications defined in the homologation manual.

第三章　金属剑道

m.57. 1. 金属剑道由金属、金属网或导电的材料制成。从剑道一端到另一端的金属剑道的电阻不能大于5欧姆。

2. 金属剑道应覆盖住剑道，包括延伸部分，以抵消对地面的劈刺。

3. a. 如果剑道设在决赛台上，金属剑道应覆盖决赛台的整个宽度。

b. 决赛台高度不得超过0.5米，同时其两侧应比剑道宽至少25厘米。决赛台两端各配一块坡度平缓的斜板，延伸到地面。

4. 拖线盘导线长度有限，因而金属剑道按14米长的剑道设置；为了使越出边界的运动员能后退到一块平坦的场地上，剑道两端各增加1.5米到2米的长度。因此金属剑道将有17到18米长。

5. a. 金属剑道最好铺设在木地板上，木板上铺有软质垫料。金属剑道配有一种收紧器，可以保持其良好的拉紧状态。

b. 木地板放置于地面以上0.12至0.15米高处，侧面不铺任何斜板。

c. 最好使用金属条，如有可能用螺钉把它固定在木板两侧。

d. 金属网剑道绝不可以直接铺在钢筋混凝土和瓷砖地面。

6. 在金属剑道上划线使用的颜料成分不能妨碍剑道的导电性能，以使得击中于剑道划线上时同样不产生信号。

7. 组织者应在现场备有可以立即修理剑道的器材。

8. 在金属剑道末端，不得有妨碍运动员正常后退的障碍物。

9. 世锦赛和奥运会使用的剑道，器材委员会代表必须在赛前用摩擦力测试仪进行检测。

10. 摩擦力测试仪的规格必须符合认证手册规定的相关要求。

CHAPTER 4. SOURCE OF ELECTRICAL CURRENT

m.58. 1. The apparatus must be based on a **12 volt supply** (± 5%) or, if the sources of current for each side of the apparatus are separate, on 2 x 12 volts or 2 x 6 volts. (The separation of the supply for each side of the apparatus is recommended because it can simplify a number of problems met in the construction of apparatus for foil.)

2. The apparatus may include warning lights to indicate that it is switched on. Such lights should be colourless.

3. If the apparatus is constructed to operate with **dry batteries**, it must be equipped with a voltmeter or some other device enabling the power in the batteries to be checked at any moment. However, the apparatus must always be e**quipped with a socket**, as described above, to allow it to be powered by accumulators.

4. Generally, there should be **two batteries** available per apparatus: 12 volt car batteries are used, of 60 or 90 amps/hour.

第四章　电源

m.58. 1. 裁判器应使用12伏特的电压（±5%），或者在两侧分开供电的情况下，电压为2×12伏特，或者也有可能是2×6伏特（推荐供电分开，可以解决花剑裁判器制造中遇到的若干问题）。

2. 裁判器可以装有一些指示灯，以表示是否通电。这些灯是无色的。

3. 若裁判器构造是以干电池进行运转的，应装备电压表，或是可以检查电压的其他装置，以便随时检查。为了通过蓄电池供电，裁判器应配有上文规定的电源插座。

4. 每台裁判器必须至少配备两个蓄电池组。使用12伏特，60或90安培/小时的汽车蓄电池组。

CHAPTER 5. EXTENSION LAMPS

m.59. 1. a) **Extension lamps** outside the apparatus are obligatory for the official competitions of the FIE.

b) The lamps should be placed at a minimum of **1.80 m** above the piste. (When the fencers fence on a 0.50 m high podium, the extension lamps must be 2.30 m above ground.)

c) The extension lamps signalling **valid hits** are coloured, one red, the other green, and they should if possible be of 150 watts.

2. a) The **white lights** indicating non-valid hits need be of only 75 watts.

b) The two lamps of the same group must not be **further apart** than 15 cm and each group must be at least 50 cm from the other.

3. **The white and coloured extension lamps** must be arranged on either side of the apparatus, either horizontally or vertically, and must be visible from all directions (cf. Annexe B, paragraph A.1.(a).2).

4. Lamps recording the **number of hits** scored may not be located alongside the extension lamps.

m.60. 1. The exterior lamps of high intensity may be connected to the main electrical supply, but in this case the signals of the recording apparatus have to be separated from the circuits of these lamps by phototransistors or by opto-couplers.

2. Light indicators recording the **number of hits** scored by each fencer are obligatory. These illuminated indicators may operate direct from the main electrical supply.

3. For World Championship and Grand Prix finals and Masters, it is obligatory to make use of a **display board** of the type shown in the drawing in Annexe C, providing instantaneous information on the fencers' names, the score, the time and other matters necessary for a good understanding of the bout.

4. This score-board must, if possible, be used for **A Grade finals** as well.

第五章　重复信号灯

m.59. 1. a. 对于国际剑联正式比赛，必须在裁判器外部安装重复信号灯。

b. 信号灯将位于剑道上方至少1.80米处。（当运动员在高0.5米的决赛台上比赛时，重复信号灯必须位于地面以上2.30米处）。

c. 显示有效击中的重复灯一盏红色，另一绿色，最好有150瓦的功率。

2. a. 表明无效击中的白色灯可以只有75瓦。

b. 同一组的两盏灯相距不能超过15厘米，两组灯相距至少50厘米。

3. 白色或彩色重复信号灯应水平排列，或是在裁判器两侧垂直排列，并从各个方向都可见（参阅附录“B”，段落A.1.（a）.2）。

4. 显示击中次数的灯不能与重复信号灯并排安装。

m.60. 1. 高强度的外接信号灯可以通过普通电网发光，但是在这种情况下，裁判器的脉冲必须通过光电晶体管或光耦合器与这些灯的电路分开。

2. 必须使用发光指示器指示每名运动员击中的得分。这些发光指示器可以直接通过电网工作。

3. 对于世锦赛，大奖赛决赛及大师赛，必须使用符合附录C图示类型的显示屏（参阅附录“C”），以便即时显示选手姓名、比分、时间以及其他便于观众了解比赛的信息。

4. 如有可能，这种显示屏也应用于世界杯A级赛决赛。

ANNEXE A TO THE MATERIAL RULES

Manufacturers' Safety Standards for Fencers' Weapons, Equipment and Clothing

Introduction:

Fencing material used in official FIE competitions and carrying the FIE logo must, without exception, have obtained a certificate of homologation, certifying that a specific item of fencing material complies with FIE Rules.

The homologation procedure is carried out by the FIE SEMI Commission under the supervision of an Executive Committee representative.

The homologation certificate is delivered following the successful passing of the homologation process described hereafter.

The manufacturer must wait for the result of the homologation process to be published and for the certificate to be issued prior to beginning production and/or commercialization.

The FIE SEMI Commission is composed of 10 elected members and the FIE COMEX representative and, in case of need, the SEMI Commission may consult experts from different fields to ensure the quality and expertise of the homologation process.

For software homologation, a delegate from the Rules Commission is mandatory.

For video-refereeing, a delegate from the Refereeing Commission is mandatory.

Field of application:

Homologation is compulsory for blades, points, protective clothing (jackets, breeches and under-plastrons) including masks and gloves, fencing scoring apparatuses (both with wires and wireless), pistes, video refereeing systems and competition management software.

This list is not exhaustive and can be extended at any time by the Executive Committee.

Homologation process:

1) The homologation request must be addressed in written form to the President of the SEMI Commission. The request must contain all the documents requested in the appropriate technical handbook.

2) The President of the SEMI checks the request for theoretical conformity (completeness of the file, complying descriptions…) and replies within 14 days to the person making the request. An application which fails is sent back to the person making the request with explanations for the rejection. A successful application is forwarded to the FIE SEMI Commission members with a copy to the person making the request.

附录A：运动员武器、装备及服装生产商安全标准

前 言：

在国际剑联正式比赛事使用的带有国际剑联标识的击剑器材必须经过国际剑联认证，以说明击剑器材的标准符合国际剑联规则要求。

认证程序由国际剑联器材委员会在执委会代表的监督下执行。

通过以下所述认证程序后发放认证证书。

制造商须等到认证结果公布及认证证书下发后才能进行产品生产和商业运营。

国际剑联器材委员会由10名选举产生的成员和国际剑联执委会代表组成，如需要，器材委员会还将聘请不同领域的专家参与，以确保认证程序的高质量和专业化。

软件认证须有一名规则委员会的代表参加。

录像裁判系统认证须一名裁判员委员会代表参加。

适用范围：

认证范围包括：剑条，剑头，保护服（上衣、短裤和背心）面罩和手套，裁判器（含有线和无线），剑道，录像裁判系统和成绩软件。

该清单尚未包含所有器材，执委会可随时对该清单进行补充。

认证程序：

1）认证申请以书面形式发送给器材委员会主席。申请应包含所有技术手册中要求的文件。

2）器材委员会主席从理论一致性（文件的完整性、描述的一致性等）的角度对申请材料进行审核并在14天内给予申请人答复。没有通过审核的，将说明被拒绝的原因并随申请材料一并返还给申请人。通过的申请将发给国际剑联器材委员会成员并抄送申请人。

3) The Manufacturer and the independent Institute of his choice should both send the laboratory compliancy test results to the President of the SEMI Commission, together with the request for homologation. The only specialized institutes approved by the SEMI are CRITT, Denkendorf and IFTH for clothing (jackets, breeches and under-plastrons) and masks; and CRITT, Sofranel and Visti for blades.

   Equipment failing to pass the tests may be modified following SEMI instructions and submitted again for the homologation process.

4) Equipment needing to be tested in a competition will be given a provisional homologation to be used at a specific competition, agreed with the representative of the Executive Committee and the organizer of the chosen competition at the proposal of the SEMI President.

5) After successfully passing all tests a sample of each piece of equipment should be sent to the President of the SEMI for analysis and reference; if the results of this analysis are satisfactory the specification of the equipment is given FIE homologation

6) Every step in the homologation process is documented in conformity with the technical handbooks. The person making the request has free access to the documentation. Every member of the SEMI Commission must receive the full documentation. However, to protect intellectual property these documents are not available to the public at large.

7) The final homologation is published on the FIE website.

8) CE certificates and tests are given by specialized institutes. The SEMI provides lists of equipment which has received homologation, published on the FIE website and with the appropriate certificates.

Modification management:

1) The homologation is valid for the duration specified in the technical handbooks as long as no modification is made to the equipment or its manufacturing process.

2) Any change must be reported to the FIE SEMI Commission President.

3) The modified equipment must pass the whole homologation process again.

In particular, if a manufacturer intends to change the material or the manufacturing of his FIE certified equipment, he must submit it to a new homologation process and wait for the result.

Technical handbooks:

1) Technical handbooks are elaborated by the SEMI and submitted to the Executive Committee.

2) Technical handbooks are specific to each item of equipment.

3）制造商及其选择的独立机构需将实验室标准检测结果连同认证申请一起发送给器材委员会主席。器材委员会批准的专业机构有：
服装（上衣、短裤和背心）和面罩：CRITT, Denkendorf和IFTH；
剑条：CRITT, Sofranel 和 Visti。

没有通过检测的器材要按照器材委员会的相关说明进行改进并再次申请认证。

4）器材如需在比赛中进行测试，由器材委员主席提议并征求执委会代表及组委会同意后，发给用于指定比赛的临时认证。

5）通过检测后，器材样本将发给器材委员会主席进行分析和参考。如果分析结果符合国际剑联认证要求将颁发国际剑联认证书。

6）认证程序的每个步骤在技术手册中都是有明文规定的。申请人可以查阅文件。器材委员会的每名成员都需接收到完整的文件材料，然而，为了保护知识产权，这些文件仅作为内部资料，不对外公布。

7） 最终认证将在国际剑联网站上公布。

8） 专门机构负责颁发CE证书和进行检测。器材委员会将在国际剑联网站上公布经过检测合格的器材清单及证书。

器材改动规定：

1）如果器材及其生产过程没有改动，则认证将在技术手册中详述的时间段内一直有效。

2） 所有改动都要向国际剑联器材委员会主席报告。

3）经过改动的器材必须重新进行认证。

尤其是当制造商想要改变已获国际剑联认证器材的材质和制作工艺时，他们必须重新申请认证并等待结果。

技术手册：

1）技术手册由器材委员会制定，并提交执委会。

2）技术手册对每项器材作了详细规定。

Marks:

The FIE emblem is a registered trademark.

It can only be used on equipment that has successfully undergone the FIE homologation process.

By affixing the FIE label of quality to their equipment manufacturers guarantee that such marked equipment fulfils FIE technical and security requirements.

Expenses:

All the expenses and costs related to the homologation of the equipment (masks, blades, breeches, jackets, under-plastron), pistes and apparatus, software and video systems are chargeable to the requester.

Withdrawal or suspension of a homologation:

- Homologation can be withdrawn or suspended when the SEMI Commission becomes aware that:

a) the homologated material no longer conforms with the Rules; or

b) after the homologation has been granted, the material has been modified significantly and the modifications have not been submitted for a new homologation.

Random quality control of Fencing Equipment

Whenever it deems necessary, the FIE SEMI Commission may obtain a random sample of any specific item of fencing equipment available on the market. Having obtained the equipment, the SEMI will submit it to technical analysis for quality control purposes. Should there be any doubt as to the quality of the item, the SEMI may send it directly to an agreed independent institute for testing; tests will be carried out in accordance with the existing FIE material rules and with CE/EC standards. Should the tests reveal any non-conformity or any lowering of quality level, the SEMI will take appropriate action, which may involve the application of a penalty. In extreme cases, the manufacturer may lose a previously awarded FIE homologation.

标记：

国际剑联徽章是注册商标，仅用于通过国际剑联认证的器材。

制造商要保证印有国际剑联质量标记的器材符合国际剑联技术与安全的要求。

费用：

所有器材（面罩、剑条、短裤、上衣、背心），剑道，裁判器，成绩软件和录像系统的认证费用由申请人承担。

认证的暂停和撤销：

—— 在以下情况下，器材委员会可以撤销或暂停认证：

a）原先经过认证的材料不再符合规则。

b）经过认证后，材料做了显著改变，未进行重新认证。

击剑器材的随机质量检查：

必要时，国际剑联器材委员会就市场流通的某一特定击剑器材进行随机抽取样本。获得该击剑器材后，器材委员会从质量检查的角度对其进行技术分析。一旦有疑问，器材委员会可将其直接交给被认可的独立机构进行测试，测试需符合国际剑联器材规则和CE/EC标准。如发现不符合标准或质量出现问题，器材委员会将采取措施，其中可能包含处罚，生产商有可能失去之前已经获得的国际剑联认证。

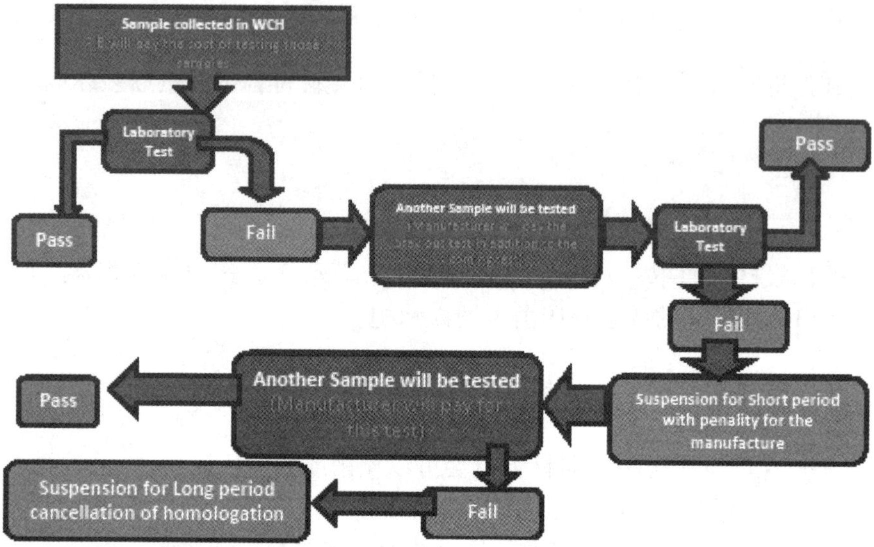

Occasional check

The SEMI alone may:-

- carry out occasional checks on blades (three blades);
- at World Championships, obtain a selection of blades bearing the official FIE guarantee stamp;
- have the blades tested at the approved laboratories, distributing the work evenly between them;

Should the blades fail the tests, the manufacturers will pay for the blades and the costs of the tests, their homologation will be annulled and the manufacturer will have to submit ten further blades for a new homologation process. There will be no certificate issued for the occasional check.

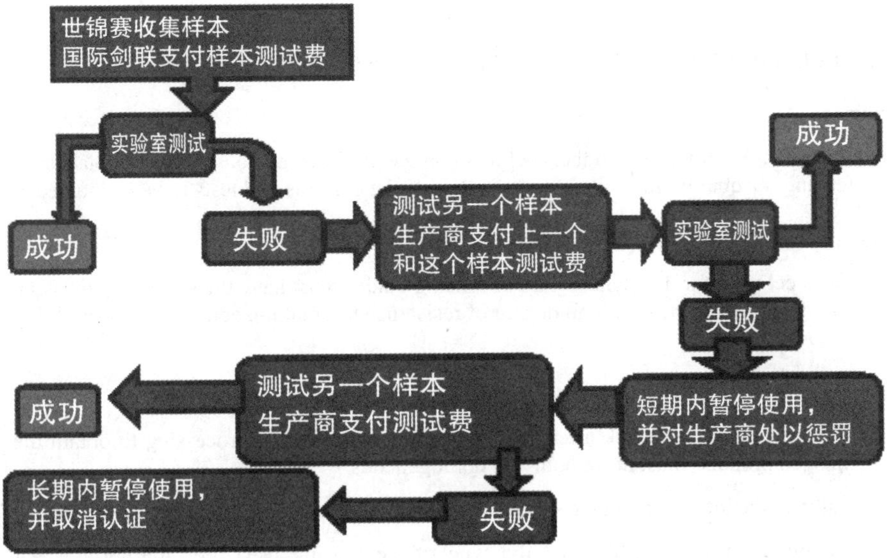

临时检查：

器材委员会可独立进行：

—— 每年对剑条（三个剑种）进行临时检查；

—— 世锦赛时，获得印有国际剑联印章的剑条；

—— 将这些剑条分配给认可的实验室进行测试。

如出现剑条未通过测试的情况，生产商需支付剑条和测试的费用，认证将被取消，且生产商将须另提供10个剑条进行新的认证程序。临时检查不发放证书。

1. WEAPONS

BLADES

SPECIFICATION FOR THE MANUFACTURE OF FENCING BLADES

1. Purpose

This specification refers to the steel that may be used for the construction of blades for fencing, its quality, its manufacturing process, the controls and tests to be conducted.

2. General conditions

The steel used for the manufacture of fencing blades must have the ability to withstand high levels of exertion, a high degree of resistance to breaking and a low susceptibility to corrosion.

3. Characteristics of the material

The structure of the steel, after treatment and manufacturing processing to obtain the finished product, must be smooth and homogeneous.

Faults in the interior or on the surface of the finished product itself are not permitted.

Having definitively established the type of steel being used, the appropriate heat treatments are compulsory.

3.1. Mechanical characteristics

The mechanical characteristics of the steel, after heat treatment, must conform to the requirements in Table I.

Table I. Mechanical characteristics of steel

Rp 0.2 N/mm²	Rm N/mm²	A %	Z %	KCU Joule/cm²	KIC Mpay m	HV
>= 1900	>= 2000	>= 7	>= 35	>= 30	>= 120	>= 500

3.2. Chemical analysis

The allowable limits of the composition of the different elements and impurities for the different types of steel are listed in Table II.

Table II. Chemical composition (in percentage terms)

Element	Type of steel		
	GMG	*	*
C	<= 0.03		
S	<= 0.0005		
P	<= 0.005		

1. 武 器

剑 身

剑身制造必须依据的规格

1. 内容

现行规格涉及可用来制作击剑剑身的钢材其质量、生产过程，要进行的检验和试验。

2. 一般条件

用于制作击剑剑身的钢材应具有高度的抗拉紧能力，抗断裂的高韧性，以及抗腐蚀能力。

3. 器材特点

对钢材进行处理和加工后，其结构应当纯粹且均质。

不允许在产品本身内部和外表出现物质突变现象。

一旦钢材型号被最终确定下来，钢材就应接受热处理。

3.1. 机械特性

热处理后的钢材的机械特性应符合表1中规定的指标。

表1 钢材的机械特性

Rp 0.2 N/mm²	Rm N/mm²	A %	Z %	KCU Joule/cm²	KIC Mpay m	HV
>= 1900	>= 2000	>= 7	>= 35	>= 30	>= 120	>= 500

3.2. 化学分析

表 2 中规定了关于不同型号钢材所含不同元素及混杂物的限定含量。

表2 钢材所含不同元素及混杂物的限定含量

Element 化学成分	Type of steel 钢材类型		
	GMG 百分比	*	*
C 碳	<= 0.03		
S 硫	<= 0.0005		
P 磷	<= 0.005		

Si	<= 0.10
Mn	<= 0.10
Cr	<= 0.50
Ni	18 - 20
Mo	4 - 5
Cu	<= 0.30
Sn	<= 0.005
Al	0.05 - 0
B	<= 0.003
Co	8 - 13
Ti	0.5 - 2.0
Ca	0.005
Zr	<= 0.02

* Types of steel still the subject of experiment must be included in this table, as they must conform to the characteristics detailed in point 3.1 of the specification.

3.3. Manufacturing process

The products must be subjected to a manufacturing process corresponding to those indicated for the different types of steel in Table III.

Table III. Manufacturing process

Type of steel	Process
GMG	1. Forging at temperatures between 1150°C and 950°C 2. Air-cooling with the blades spaced apart 3. Mechanical machining (removal of extra thickness by reworking) 4. Homogenisation at 950°C ± 10°C for 1 hour 5. Immersion heat treatment at 820°C ± 10°C for 1 hour 6. Air-cooling with the blades spaced apart 7. Ageing at 480°C for 9 hours 8. Air-cooling with the blades spaced apart 9. Cold finishing
*	
*	

* Types of steel still the subject of experiment must be included in this table, as they must conform to the characteristics detailed in point 3.1 of the specification.

Si	硅	<= 0.10
Mn	锰	<= 0.10
Cr	铬	<= 0.50
Ni	镍	18 - 20
Mo	钼	4 - 5
Cu	铜	<= 0.30
Sn	锡	<= 0.005
Al	铝	0.05 - 0
B	硼	<= 0.003
Co	钴	8 - 13
Ti	钛	0.5 - 2.0
Ca	钙	0.005
Zr	锆	<= 0.02

（*）目前正处于试验阶段的钢材型号，它们应当符合3.1中提供的规定。

3.3. 加工周期

产品应当受到为表3中不同型号钢材指定的相应的加工周期。

表3　加工周期

钢材型号	加工周期
GMG	1. 在温度1150℃到950℃之间进行锻造 2. 在空气中冷却，剑身拆开 3. 机械加工（通过磨削除去厚度余量） 4. 在950℃到10℃间均质加工1小时 5. 在820℃到10℃间增溶溶解1小时 6. 剑身拆开，在空气中冷却 7. 在480℃下进行9小时的老化处理 8. 剑身拆开，在空气中冷却 9. 冷磨削
*	
*	

（*）目前正处于试验阶段的钢材型号，它们应当符合3.1中提供的规定。

4. Tests and examinations (material)

The tests and examinations to which the steel must be subjected are as follows:

— Chemical analysis
— Traction test
— Ductility tests
— Fracture resistance tests

4.1. Chemical analysis

The sample must have a minimum mass of 50 g. The chemical composition in percentage terms must conform to that laid down in Table II for the corresponding type of steel.

4.2. Traction test

The test must be conducted on a test sample of circular section whose dimensions are indicated at the end of this annexe (Figure A.8), taken from materials that have been subjected to the same heat treatment as specified for materials for the manufacture of the blades.

The tensile strength values must conform to those laid down in Table I.

4.3. Tensile test

The test must be conducted on a test sample with a groove in the form of a V, whose dimensions are indicated at the end of this annexe (Figure A.8), taken in the longitudinal direction from materials that have been subjected to the same heat treatment as specified for materials for the manufacture of the blades.

The value must conform to that laid down in Table I.

4.4. Test of fracture toughness, KIC

The KIC value of the steel must be measured by traction on a CT sample which has the dimensions indicated at the end of this annexe (Table VIII), made from materials subjected to the same thermal treatment as required for the blades, notched mechanically initiating a fatigue crack at the apex of the notch. The test must be conducted according to the methods indicated by the standard ASTM E 399. The value must conform to that laid down in Table I.

In cases where it is not possible to obtain a CT sample, the factor of increasing levels of dynamic loading (KId) may be determined instead of the KIC value.

The test must be conducted on ductility samples with a groove in the form of a 'Charpy V', with dimensions as indicated at the end of this annexe (Table VIII).

The results must conform to the reference standards.

4. 试验与检验

钢材必须接受的试验与检验有以下几种：

—— 化学分析

—— 拉力试验

—— 抗击强度试验

—— 抗断强度试验

4.1. 化学分析

样品应有至少50克的质量。用百分比表示的化学成分应符合表二中对相应钢材型号所作的规定。

4.2. 拉力试验

试验应对一个截面为圆形的试样进行，试样尺寸在本附录结尾有所规定，该试样从生成剑身受到的同一循环热处理的材料中提取。

数值应与表一中规定的一致。

4.3. 抗击强度试验

应对一个有V形槽口的试样进行试验，其尺寸在本附录结尾有所规定，该试样从生成剑身受到的同一循环热处理的材料中提取。数值应与表一中规定的一致。

4.4. 抗断强度试验

钢材的KIC值应通过对CT试样的拉力试验来确定，试样的尺寸在本附录结尾有规定。该试样从生成剑身受到的同一循环热处理的材料中提取，并以机械方法切槽，在槽口顶端由于疲劳而先出现裂纹。试验应遵照ASTME399准则中做出的限制性规定来进行。数值与表一中的一致。

在不能获得CT型试样的情况下，可以确定KID动力载荷应力的加强系数值，而不需要确定KIC值。

试验应对带有V形槽口的抗击强度试样进行，其尺寸在本附录结尾有规定。

试验结果应符合参考标准。

5. Characteristics of the finished product

5.1. Shape

The blades, classified according to the type of weapon, must have the shapes indicated in Annexe A and satisfy the conditions established by the FIE Rules.

5.2. Surface defects

The blades must be free of surface faults which could compromise their use (folds in lamination, cracks, splinters, decarbonisation).

5.3. Surface roughness

At the conclusion of their manufacturing process the blades must be subjected to finishing to ensure a surface roughness of <= 0.1 mm. The grinding marks must only extend in the longitudinal direction of the blade.

6. Tests and examinations (finished product)

The tests and examinations to which the steel must be subjected are as follows:

- Chemical analysis
- Traction test
- Ductility test
- Test of fracture toughness, KId
- Hardness test
- Microscopic examination of the structure
- Corrosion test
- Non-destructive control
- Fatigue resistance test

6.1. Chemical analysis

The sample must have a minimum mass of 50 g. The chemical composition in percentage terms must conform to that laid down in Table II for the corresponding type of steel.

6.2. Traction test

The test must be conducted on a sample of circular section, taken from the blade, whose dimensions are indicated at the end of this annexe (Figure A.8).

The values of the tension characteristics must conform to those laid down in Table I.

5. 成品特性

5.1. 形状

根据各剑种分类的剑身的形状应符合附录A中的规定，并满足国际剑联规则中确定的条件。

5.2. 表面缺陷

剑身没有能够影响使用的表面缺陷（轧制引起的褶痕，裂缝，裂片，脱碳）。

5.3. 表面粗糙

剑身在经过最后一道精加工后，其生产过程结论应保证粗糙度≤0.1毫米。粗糙纹路应当顺着剑身纵向展开。

6. 试验

钢材应接受的试验有以下几种：

—— 化学分析

—— 拉力试验

—— 抗击强度试验

—— 抗动力断裂的韧度试验KID（暂定）

—— 硬度试验

—— 显微镜下的结构检验

—— 抗腐蚀试验

—— 非破坏性检验

6.1. 化学分析

样品应有至少50克的质量。以百分比衡量的化学成分应符合表二中对相应钢材型号所作的规定。

6.2. 拉力试验

试验应当对一个截面为圆形的试样进行，试样从剑身中提取，其尺寸在本附录结尾有规定。

数值应符合表1中的规定。

6.3. Tensile test

The test must be conducted on a sample taken from the blade, without notches, whose dimensions are indicated at the end of this annexe (Figure A.8). The value must conform to that laid down in Table I.

6.4. Test of strength at the fracture point, KId

The KId value must be established by testing on the traction test samples with a groove in the form of a 'Charpy V', with dimensions as indicated at the end of this annexe (Table VIII).

The results must conform to the reference standards.

6.5. Hardness test

The hardness of the material, determined on the exterior surface of the finished product, must conform to that laid down in Table I.

6.6. Microscopic examination of the structure

The examination must be carried out at 500 magnifications on a sample taken from the blade.

The structure submitted must be smooth and homogeneous, conforming to grain dimensions of 7–8 microns in accordance with the standard of reference and corresponding to that resulting from the heat treatment specified in Table III for the corresponding type of steel.

6.7. Non-destructive control

Before being put on the market, all blades must be subjected to a non-destructive control, using an electromagnetic apparatus employing Foucault currents, to explore for surface and below-surface faults. This control is compulsory, and must be carried out over the entire surface of the blade.

6.8. Alternate bending test (optional)

In order to examine the behaviour of blades and the effects induced on the material when the blades are deformed in a plastic manner by the method of alternate bending, new blades selected at random and supplied from actual production lots must be subjected to test using the special equipment indicated in the annexe.

The test consists of making a section of the blade bend plastically, in one direction with a radius of inflexion of 60 mm, in the opposite direction with a radius of inflexion of 100 mm, in order to obtain an approximate straightening.

6.3. 抗击强度试验

试验应对一个无槽口的试样进行，该试样从剑身中提取，其尺寸在本附录结尾有规定。数值应符合表一中的规定。

6.4. 抗动力断裂的韧度试验KID

通过对一个有V形槽口的抗击强度进行的试验来确定KID值，试样尺寸在本附录结尾有规定。

试验结果应符合参考标准。

6.5. 硬度试验

由成品外部表面确定的材料硬度应符合表一中的规定。

6.6. 显微镜下的结构检验

应用显微镜对从剑身中提取的样品放大500倍来进行检验。

接受检验的样品结构应纯粹且均质，根据参考标准应符合（GRAIN DE 7–8）的大小规格，并且符合表三中对相应钢材型号规定的热处理所得出的结构。

6.7. 非破坏性检验

所有剑身在进入消费市场前，都应用傅科电流下的电磁仪器进行非破坏性检验，以研究表面及次表面的缺陷，这一检验应在剑身整个表面上进行。

6.8. 交替折叠试验（暂定）

为检查剑身在交替的弯曲应力作用下被压迫变形时的表现及其材料感生效应，应借助于附录中指明的专门设备，对指定的几批产品中随意抽出的新剑身进行试验。

试验将剑身的一截形体弯曲，一边弯曲半径为60毫米，相对部分的另一边弯曲半径为100毫米，以便得到近似的矫直。

The section of blade involved in the test must be approximately 155 mm long, of which 60 mm from the point must not sustain any deformation.

A cycle consists of one bending plus one straightening. The result of the test is represented by the number of cycles completed before the blade breaks.

To check safety conditions during the normal use of blades, the samples tested must be subjected to a series of alternate bendings at a frequency of not more than 1 Hz (1 Hz = 1 cycle per second), verifying that the blade does not break before:

— 400 cycles for foil;

— 150 cycles for épée,

when the cycles have been conducted in accordance with the method described above.

6.9. **Fatigue resistance test of Blades** (by bending, etc)

In order to examine the behaviour of the blades during normal fencing activity, the blades to be tested must undergo a test of their resistance to metal fatigue, with a special apparatus, either mechanical or pneumatic homologated by the FIE SEMI Commission.

The test consists of bending the blade without exceeding the limit of elasticity of the material, i.e. to the point where a bend of approximately 220 mm is reached, corresponding to a shortening of the blade by approximately 250 mm, and then allowing it to straighten.

The test machine must be able to allow the bending and straightening of the blade at a frequency of 1 Hz (1 Hertz = 1 cycle per second).

The test benches are designed to reproduce the stresses to which a blade is subjected in normal fencing activity. The stresses do not go beyond the limits of the elasticity of the blades; a permanent deforming of the blade should not take place. The number of bends to which a blade is subjected before breaking defines its resistance to metal fatigue.

The test benches can be used for bending either without impact (with the end of the blade attached to a revolving support) or with impact (with the end of the blade unattached).

The test should continue until the blade breaks. For the result to be acceptable, it must be ascertained that the blade does not break before:

— 18,000 cycles for foil blades;

— 7,000 cycles for épée blades.

剑身上经过试验的相关一截应有大约155毫米长，其中剑尖的60毫米不得受到变处理。

一次折叠和一次矫直合起来构成一次周期。试验结果以直到剑身完全断裂为止所完成的周期次数来表示。

为检验剑身正常使用中的安全条件，试验样品应接受一系列交替折叠试验，同时保持不高于1赫兹的频率，并核查在以下情况之前：

—— 花剑在 400 次周期；

—— 重剑在 150 次周期；

剑身不会断裂，周期按上述形式完成。

6.9. 抗疲劳测试（通过反复折叠和压弯）

为了检验击剑运动中剑身的情况，用于检测的剑身要进行抗疲劳测试，使用的是一种特殊的仪器，一种是机械型的（Baiocco型号），一种是气动的（Husarek/Sofranel型号），图样可以向器材委员会索要。

测试是使剑身弯曲，但不要超过它的金属弹性极限，就是说直到得到一个大约220mm的弓形，等同与250mm剑身缩短的长度，之后再使其复位。

测试仪器要能够使剑身弯曲和复位的频率达到1赫兹（1赫兹等于每秒一个周期）。

试验台能够实现剑身在运动中击剑运动员使用的正常效果。不能出现超过剑身弹性极限的效果；不能出现持续的剑身变形。剑身在断裂前可以弯折的次数决定了它的抗疲劳程度。

试验台可以用于无冲撞弯折测试（剑头固定在一个旋转的支撑上），或者是冲撞弯折测试（剑头不固定）。

测试不断进行直到剑身折断。为了使结果能被接受，要使折断不出现在以下情况之前：

—— 花剑 18000次；

—— 重剑 7000次。

6.10. Evaluation (in percentage terms) of the surface of the progressive fracture

The surface of the fracture obtained at the moment of breaking in the test in points 6.8 and 6.9 above must be analysed in order to measure the extent of the surface over which the rupture has developed progressively.

The measure must be expressed as a percentage of the surface of the entire section subject to the test.

The acceptability of the mechanical characteristics of the blade is confirmed when the measured percentage value is not lower than 15% for foil and 6% for épée.

7. Results of tests and examinations

For each of the tests and examinations detailed in point 6 the results must comply with the following table.

Table IV. Results of tests and examinations

Point of reference	Examination or test	Results
4.1, 6.1	Chemical analysis	Must conform to Table II
4.2, 6.2	Traction test	Must conform to Table I
4.3, 6.3	Tensile test	Must conform to Table I
4.4, 6.4	Test of fracture resistance	Must conform to Table I
6.5	Hardness test	Must conform to Table I
6.6	Microscopic examination of structure	Must conform to point 6.6
6.7	Non-destructive test	Must conform to point 6.7

8. Marking

The identification mark of the manufacturer and the date of manufacture (year and month) must be applied on each blade by cold-stamping near the entry into the guard, to a maximum depth of 0.5 mm.

Note: All the standards may be modified. It is therefore important that manufacturers of blades are absolutely sure that they are in possession of the latest edition or of the latest update page.

6.10. 渐进断裂表面的百分比评估

应按照第6.8条和第6.9条中描述的测试后产生的断裂时的断裂表面进行分析，以测量逐渐形成的断裂面面积。

测量应当用完全坚固的截面积的百分比来表示。

合格剑身的器械特征只有在不小于下列数值的情况下：花剑15%；重剑6%。

7. 试验与检验的结果

第6条中涉及的试验及检验应该在下表中为其中每一种提供指定的结果：

表4　试验与检验的结果

参考条目	试验或检验	结果
4.1, 6.1	化学分析	符合表2
4.2, 6.2	拉力试验	符合表1
4.3, 6.3	抗击强度试验	符合表1
4.4, 6.4	抗断强度试验	符合表1
6.5	硬度试验	符合表1
6.6	显微镜下的结构检验	符合6.6
6.7	非破坏性检验	符合6.7

8. 加标记

在每只剑身的根部附近，应当用最大深度为0.5毫米的冷模压上制造商的标记以及出厂时间（年，月）。

注释：暂定的准则作为试行条款，可以修改。使用相同准则的人应确保拥有最新版本或公开的版本。

EQUIPMENT

2. STANDARDS FOR THE MANUFACTURE OF FENCING MASKS

2.1. MESH OF FENCING MASKS

STANDARDS FOR THE MATERIALS FOR THE MESH OF FENCING MASKS

1. **Purpose**

These specifications concern the technical quality of the round cold-drawn wire of carbon stainless steel intended for the manufacture of the mesh of fencing masks, the processes of its production, and the controls and tests to carry out in its use.

2. **General conditions of raw material**

The steel intended for the manufacture of the mesh of fencing masks must possess excellent qualities of strength and a high level of elasticity and plastic deformation, as well as a very good resistance against corrosion.

3. **Materials**

3.1. **Chemical composition**

The composition of the machined wire to be used to manufacture the wire complying with the present rules, depending on the type of steel chosen, must include the following, in percentage terms.

Table V. Chemical composition

Element	Type of steel		
	304	304 L	321
C	0.03–0.06	< 0.03	< 0.08
Mn	< 2	< 2	< 2
Si	< 1	< 1	< 1
P	< 0.04	< 0.04	< 0.04
S	< 0.03	< 0.03	< 0.03
Cr	18–20	18–20	17–19
Ni	8–10.5	9–12	9–12
Ti	–	–	5 x Cmin (< 0.8)

For information, some of the most widely used types of steel are shown above; they satisfy more or less the following defined standards:

— EURONORM 88-71 (EEC)
— UNI 6901-71 (Italy)
— AFNOR NF A 35-572 (France)
— DIN 17440 (Germany)

装 备

2. 面罩生产的规格

2.1 金属网

2.1.1 击剑面罩金属网材料规格的测试

1. 目的

本规范涉及奥氏体不锈钢进行冷拉丝制成的圆形钢丝的技术性能，这种钢丝用于生产击剑用面罩的金属网；还涉及生产的程序以及为了能够使用面罩要进行的检验和试验。

2. 供应物的总则

用于制造面罩金属网的钢应在抗断强度和弹性及塑性变形方面具有极好的品质，也应有很好的抗腐蚀能力。

3. 材料

3.1. 化学成分

用于制造符合现行规则金属丝的机器金属丝，应符合以下为选定的钢种规定的百分比成分。

表5 化学成分

化学成分	钢材类型		
	304	304 L	321
C	0.03–0.06	< 0.03	< 0.08
Mn	< 2	< 2	< 2
Si	< 1	< 1	< 1
P	< 0.04	< 0.04	< 0.04
S	< 0.03	< 0.03	< 0.03
Cr	18–20	18–20	17–19
Ni	8–10.5	9–12	9–12
Ti	–	–	5 x Cmin (< 0.8)

以上从指定方式提供使用最普遍的钢种中的某些型号的名称，大致包括以下成分：

—— EURONORM 88–71 （欧共体）
—— UNI6901–71 （意大利）
—— AFNOR NFA 35–572 （法国）
—— DIN 17440 （德国）

— BSI PD 6290 (Great Britain)
— MNC 900 E (Sweden)
— JIS G 4306-1972 (Japan)
— GOST 5632-61 (Russia)

3.2. Processing the steel and manufacturing the wire

The method of processing of the steel is entrusted to the supplier. The hot processing to obtain the machined wire must be such that it can ensure a high level of consistency in the materials and an absence of discontinuity and of faults in the interior and on the surface of these same materials.

The process of cold wire drawing, to reduce the section in order to obtain the desired diameter, must provide for adequate intermediate tempering for the manufacture of the tempered materials. In any case the last step of the wire drawing must be preceded by a chemical solution treatment at 1050–1100°C (stainless steel tempering) for types 304 and 304 L or a stabilisation treatment at 850–900°C for type 321.

The last step of the cold wire drawing must involve a hardening process defined commercially as approximately 1/4 hard (H4), with a corresponding reduction in section of <= 15% and carried out in such a way as to ensure the materials possess the minimum values of the mechanical characteristics indicated in point 3.4.2 of this specification.

3.3. Dimensions of the wire and tolerance

Table VI. Dimensions and tolerance

Diameter (d) (mm)	Tolerance * on d (mm)	Section (mm^2)	Weight per 1000 m (kg)
1.0	± 0.02	0.725	6.28
1.1	± 0.02	0.950	7.50

* The lack of roundness of the wire must not exceed half the tolerance.

Intermediate values of the diameter of the wire are allowed on condition that they conform to the tolerances indicated.

3.4. Conditions of supply

3.4.1. State in which supplied

The wire must be supplied bare with a polished surface: the surface must not show any faults such as scratches, pockmarks or other imperfections.

—— BSI PD 6290　　（英国）
—— MNC 900E　　（瑞典）
—— JISG 4306–1972　　（日本）
—— GOST 5632–61　　（俄罗斯）

3.2. 钢材制造及金属丝生产程序

钢材的制造程序委托供应商完成。钢材的加热转化直到获取机丝的工序，应该保证材料的高均质，且在同一块材料内部及表面没有任何物质上的突变和缺陷。

为获得理想直径而进行的冷拉丝工序，应规定进行适合冷锻材料加工的中间退火。不管怎样，在拉丝最后一道工序之前，对于304及304L型钢种在1050℃至1100℃间增溶溶解处理（奥氏体钢的淬火），或对于321型钢种在85℃至900℃间进行稳定处理。

冷拉丝的最后一步应包括状态硬化过程，以商业角度确定为大约1/4硬，还有截面相应减小（<=15%）的过程，且应确保材料至少达到第3.4.2条中规定的机械特性最小数值。

3.3. 金属丝大小及误差

表6　金属丝大小及误差

直径 (mm)	直径允许误差（*） (mm)	截面 (mm^2)	每千米重量（公斤） (kg)
1.0	± 0.02	0.725	6.28
1.1	± 0.02	0.950	7.50

（*）金属丝的椭圆化不得超过允许误差的一半。

只要符合规定的误差，金属丝直径允许有误差。

3.4. 供应品条件及接受条件

3.4.1. 供应品状态

供应的金属丝应不带附加物，表面光滑：表面不得出现类似刮痕，麻点或其他瑕疵的缺陷。

3.4.2. Mechanical characteristics

The values of the mechanical characteristics of the wire which are established at an ambient temperature by the traction test indicated in point 4.1 must be higher than the minimum values shown in Table VII.

Table VII. Mechanical characteristics

Combined loading of breakage	Combined loading of gapping at a proportionality of < 0.2%	Stretching at breakage
R (N/mm²)	Rp(0.2) (N/mm²)	A_{50} (%)
min 700	min 700	min 18

4. Tests and examinations

4.1. Traction test

This test must be conducted on samples obtained directly from the wire and in accordance with the conditions indicated by the standards of each country.

4.2. 180° bending test

The test consists of bending the wire to 180° on a 2 mm diameter mandrel. After the test the wire must not show any small cracks at the point where the bend occurs.

4.3. Micrographic examination of the structure

The examination is conducted on a cross-section of the wire (encased in sufficient resin) at a magnification of x 200 – x 500 after polishing and etching with 10% oxalic acid in accordance with the ASTM 262-70 standard or equivalent.

In practice you should observe a stainless structure with martensite bands; in any case no chrome carbon precipitates may be present on the grain boundaries (see the acceptable structure, in accordance with the ASTM standard already mentioned: 'steep structure').

5. Documents

For the product corresponding to these rules the following documents must be delivered by the manufacturer:

- certificate of conformity of the chemical composition;
- certificate of control of the mechanical characteristics and the results of the bending test and the micrographic examination.

3.4.2 . 机械特性

金属丝的机械特性数值通过第4.1条中提到的拉力试验在环境温度下确定，应高于表一中规定的最小值。

表7 机械特性

断裂单位负载力	比例性小0.2%的分离单位负载力	断裂时的延伸
R (N/mm^2)	Rp(0.2) (N/mm^2)	A_{50} (%)
最小 700	最小 700	最小 18

4. 试验与检测

4.1. 拉力测试

测试应对直接从金属丝上获取的试样进行，且应遵照每个国家标准指明的限制性规定进行。

4.2. 180度折叠测试

测试系将金属丝在一根直径为2毫米的芯棒上折叠成180度。测试后的金属丝的弯曲部分不得出现裂痕。

4.3. 显微镜下的结构检验

在金属丝的横断面上（用一种适合的树脂包住），根据ASTM262–70或类似的规范在进行抛光和电解为10%草酸的化学反应之后，对其放大200–500倍进行观察。

实际上必须注意到一种马氏体带的奥氏体变形结构;不管怎样，颗粒旁不能出现沉淀的碳化铬（按ASTM规范已提到的可接受的结构为“Steep”结构）。

5 . 文件

对于符合本规章的产品，应由生产商发给以下文件：

—— 化学成分合格证书；

—— 对机械性能与折叠测试和显微镜检查结果的检验证书。

2.1.2. TRANSPARENT MASKS

1. **General**

The FIE in its standard practices has established the possibility for fencers to use either traditional masks made with metal mesh or transparent masks.

The transparent visor, when used, must be a minimum of 3.0 mm in thickness and must also have a separate replaceable outer covering (a "sacrificial" layer) at least 1 mm in thickness. The visor must be made of polycarbonate resin thermoplastic, and each mask and each replacement visor must be accompanied, at the time of purchase, with a statement that guarantees the authenticity and origin of the polycarbonate resin thermoplastic. The visor must correspond to the required norms of materials and manufacture as indicated in 2.1.2. of the annex to chapter 3 (Materials) of the rule book.

These transparent masks can be of two types:

— composite masks, made using traditional masks, of which a part of the front mesh has been replaced by a visor of transparent plastic;

— masks made entirely of plastic, of which the front part must be transparent.

Currently only composite masks have been accepted by the FIE.

The wearing of the transparent mask is **forbidden** at all weapons and in all FIE competitions.

2. **Manufacturing norms for transparent masks**

The norms are, at present, valid only for composite masks.

The starting point is a metal mesh mask; into the front part of the mesh, at eye level, a window is made by cutting the mesh to a width that may reach as far as the lateral part of the mesh and to a height that may not exceed 12 cm.

The window must be rimmed by a frame of stainless steel, made of two superimposed sections, of which the first is to be soldered to the mesh and the second fixed to the first by bolts.

The transparent visor made of polycarbonate (Lexan) will be placed between the two parts of the frame.

Care must be taken that:

— The thickness of the steel gauge of each part of the frame must be between 0.8 mm and 1.0 mm.

— The edges of the frame which holds down the transparent visor must not be sharp (cutting) and must adhere to the mesh, without any perceptible projections.

2.1.2 透明面罩

1. 通则

国际剑联在其章程中规定，剑手可以使用传统金属网面罩，也可以使用透明面罩。

面罩的透明部分，其最薄处的厚度应大于3毫米，且应配有至少1毫米厚的可拆卸更换的外覆盖层（易耗品）。面罩的透明部分须由热塑性聚碳酸酯树脂制成，且每个面罩应有与之配套的可替换透明罩，购买时，厂商应提供原材料为热塑性聚碳酸酯树脂保证说明。面罩透明部分的材质和工艺必须符合规则手册第3章（器材）中附录部分2.1.2的要求。

透明面罩可以有以下两种：

—— 复合面罩，由传统面罩而来，是指一部分前面的金属网由塑料镜面取代；

—— 完全由塑料制成的面罩，整个前面部分都是透明的。

实际上，目前被国际剑联接受的只有复合面罩。

国际剑联的所有3个剑种比赛都禁止佩戴透明面罩。

2. 透明面罩的生产规范

目前，此规范只适用于复合面罩。

将金属网护面的前部，从眼睛部位开启一个窗口直到护面两侧，高度不能超过12厘米。

窗口一周要装有不锈钢金属边框，由两部分叠放组成，第一部分焊接在金属网上，第二部分通过螺钉与第一部分固定。

在边框两部分间安装聚碳酸酯的透明镜片（Lexan）。应当：

—— 边框每一部分的金属包边应当在0.8到1毫米之间；

—— 保护透明镜片的边框不能是锋利的，要能够很好的嵌入至金属网，不能有明显的突起；

— The part of the frame that is soldered must be fixed to the mesh before the window is cut, to ensure that the shape of the mask is not altered when the wires of the mesh are cut.

— The bolts fixing the two parts of the frame must not project beyond the nuts into which they screw.

— The polycarbonate transparent visor (Lexan) must have a minimum thickness of 3.0 mm, and a protective layer against damage to the outside surface is recommended.

— The visor must not have any holes in it, must be shaped when hot, and placed in its location in the frame, under no pressure, when cold and, therefore, without being in any way 'stressed'.

— There must be provision for an anti-condensation system on the inside of the visor, or Lexan treated to this end must be used.

— Because of the damage caused to transparent visors during fencing competitions, it is essential that fencers are able to change the visor of their masks simply and easily.

— The padding of the mask must be reduced as much as possible, using any system which will provide a circulation of air virtually equivalent to that of the traditional mask.

— The total weight of the mask must not exceed 2 kg.

3. Safety standards

All transparent visor masks must provide a high level of safety for fencers. They must therefore comply with very strict standards and in particular:

— The whole structure of the mask must be rigid and not be distorted as a result of violent shocks.

— The metal mesh and the bib must have the same strength characteristics as those of traditional masks.

— Because of ageing of the plastic material, the polycarbonate visor must only be used for two years after its manufacture and, therefore, the date of manufacture, using the format of month (two digits) and year (four digits), e.g. 10-2010, must be indicated on it very clearly.

— To avoid degrading the polycarbonate, all contact with chemical agents that can damage the material must be prevented; in particular, any presence of PVC is unacceptable.

— The mask should be kept in a protective bag and it is desirable to avoid putting the mask in the fencing bag (and hence in the aircraft hold) during airplane journeys, but rather to keep it in hand luggage.

—— 在切割窗口之前就要先安装那部分焊接的边框，以防止在切割金属网丝时改变面罩形状；

—— 固定边框两部分的螺丝不能超过螺帽的深度。

—— 聚碳酸酯镜面（Lexan）要至少有3毫米的厚度，最好有保护层以防止被划伤。

—— 镜面不能有任何缺口，要在热的时候弯折，在常温时不能有任何张力的情况下安装在边框内，总之，不能因为任何情况出现“紧绷”的现象；

—— 在镜面内部要预设有防水汽系统，或者使用经过这样处理的Lexan；

—— 如果在击剑比赛中，镜面出现了损坏，剑手要能够采用简单容易的方式自行更换镜面；

—— 面罩内的垫料要尽可能的少，要采用能够使内部空气循环和传统护面尽可能一样的系统；

—— 符合面罩的重量不可以超过2kg。

3. 安全规范

所有透明面罩都要能够为剑手提供很高的安全保障。所以要能够符合严格的安全要求特别是：

—— 整个面罩的结构都要是坚硬的，即使在遇到猛烈冲撞后仍能够保持不变形；

—— 金属网和护舌的抗力特点要和传统面罩一样；

—— 聚碳酸酯材质的镜面，由于其塑料材料的老化，只能从其出厂起使用两年。所以这种镜面必须要清晰的表明生产日期，标注方式为：月（2个数字），年（4个数字），例如：10–2010。

—— 为了防止聚碳酸酯的损坏，要避免一切与可能破坏器材的化学物质接触，特别是任何PVC材料；

—— 面罩要放在保护袋中，建议在飞行途中不要把面罩放在剑袋里，而是随身携带。

4. Homologation of transparent masks and test methods

Before being put on sale and used, all transparent visor masks must be approved and homologated by the SEMI.

4.1. Homologation

To obtain FIE homologation, the manufacturer must send his masks to one of the following three institutes: In Germany "Denkendorf" ; in France CRITT or IFTH. The institute will conduct penetration resistance tests on the metal mesh and the visor in accordance with the CEN norms (e.g. Norm EN 13567).

If the test results are positive, the constructor must send two examples of the mask to be homologated, together with the Institute's certificate, to the headquarters of the SEMI in Lisbon, for the violent-shock tests.

If this result is also positive, the SEMI will issue the homologation certificate to the manufacturer, and the mask may be put on sale and used at official FIE competitions.

4.2. Violent-shock testing

Transparent visor masks must satisfy either the norms established by the CEN Special Commission (cf. the paragraph on masks) or the additional norms established by SEMI relating to resistance to violent shocks.

Therefore, in addition to the tests for resistance to penetration on several parts of the mask as provided for by CEN norms, there is a need for a further test of the resistance of the entire mask to violent shocks, which might occur as a result of impact with the head or the guard of the opposing fencer.

This test will be carried out in the following manner.

4.2.1. Equipment for the test

The machine to be used must provide for a striker, of variable but known weight, to fall from a height which is also variable, up to a maximum of 2 m.

Fixed to the striker there must be a rod, made of tempered steel, ending in a head in the form of a sphere, with a diameter of 20 mm +/- 0.3 mm.

The rod must be 40–50 mm long and provided with a means of attaching it (normally a thread) to the drop test machine (see Figure A.1)

4. 面罩的认证和测试方法

所有透明护面在其商业化和使用前，都要经过器材委员会的认证。

4.1. 认证

为了获得国际剑联的认证，首先要将面罩寄到以下3个研究机构之一：德国的“Denkendorf”,法国的CRITT或IFTH。这些机构将按照CEN规范（例如：规范EN13567）对面罩金属网和镜面进行抗刺穿能力的测试。

如果测试结果为积极的，制造商要将需要认证的面罩的两个样本及研究机构证明寄到器材委员会在里斯本的总部，以便进行抗冲撞测试。

如果测试结果同样是积极的，器材委员会将给生产商颁发认证证书，面罩就可以商业化，并能在国际剑联的正式比赛中使用。

4.2. 防冲撞测试

透明面罩或者是符合CEN特别委员会（参见面罩篇）的规范要求，或者是符合器材委员会对面罩防冲撞能力的附加规范。

所以，不仅要按照CEN规范对面罩的各部位进行防刺穿能力测试，还要对整个面罩进行防冲撞测试，对面罩的冲撞可能是由头或者是护手盘造成的。

这个测试将按照以下的方式进行：

4.2.1. 测试工具

要使用一种能够使已知却不确定重量的敲打锤从不同高度，最大为2米，跌落的装置。

敲打锤是一根淬过火的钢杆，头部是一个球体，球体直径为20mm ± 0.3mm。

钢杆的长度为40~50mm，要有一个固定部件（通常是螺纹加工），可以把其固定在跌落测试装置上（参见示意图A.1.）。

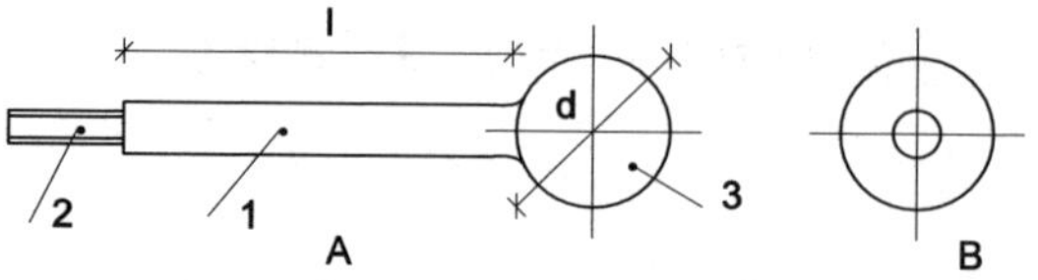

A Side view
B End view
1 Rigid rod
2 Attachment point
3 Sphere

l Length of the rod
d Diameter of the sphere, 20 mm +/Ð 0.3 mm

Figure A.1. Test rod

An appropriate support for the mask must be provided on the base of the test apparatus, to hold the mask firmly during the tests.

On the base of the apparatus, in effect, sliding structures must be in place that can be fixed in an established position, so as to form a sort of rigid box within which the mask is held (see Figure A.2).

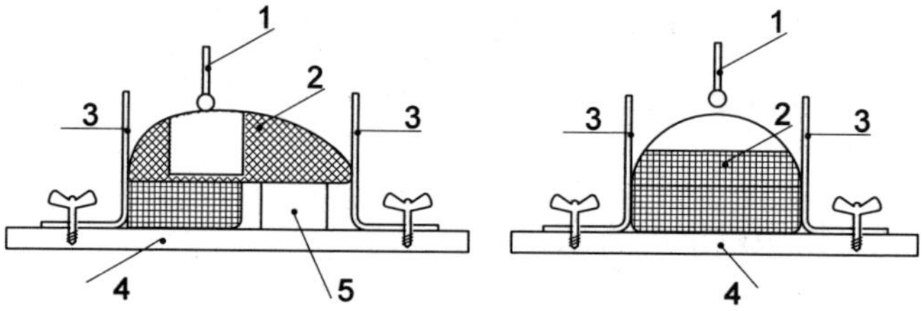

1 Rod and sphere
2 Mask
3 Components to hold mask firmly
4 Solid base of test equipment
5 Support to keep mask level

Figure A.2. Method of affixing the mask

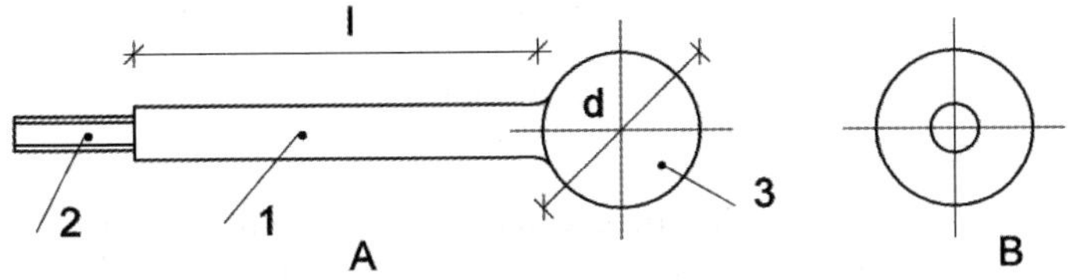

A 侧面图
B 底部图
1 坚硬的钢杆
2 连接点
3 球体
l 钢杆的长度
D 球体的直径
20mm ± 0.3mm

图 A.1.　测试钢杆

要在测试装置的底座上设置一个特别的支撑，以便能够在测试过程中很好的固定面罩，

要在装置的底座上设置滑槽，以便固定位置，形成一个结实的盒子，盒子内部可以固定面罩（参见示意图A.2.）.

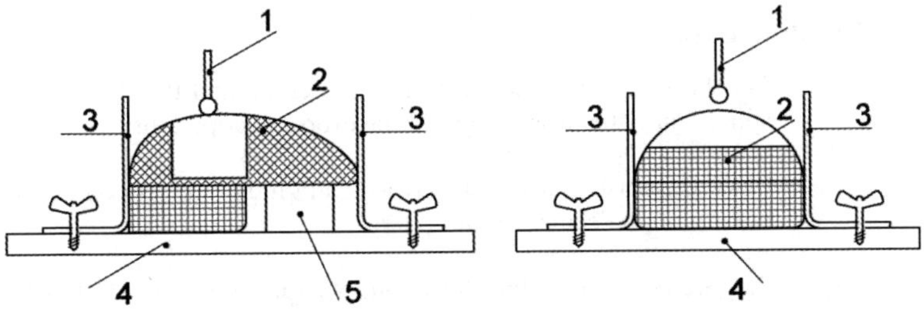

1 钢杆和球体
2 面罩
3 滑槽固定部件
4 测试装置的固定底座
5 固定面罩位置的支撑

图 A.2.　固定面罩的方法

4.2.2. Drop equipment

The equipment to be used must allow a guided mass weighing between 3 kg and 5 kg to drop from variable heights to achieve a maximum speed of

between 5 and 6 m per second at the moment of impact of the striker on the sample to be tested.

A means must be arranged for stopping the drop weight, with the aim that only the rod with the spherical end touches the mask, and not the weight.

The releasing mechanism of the striker must be controlled in such a way as to ensure the same starting conditions, whatever the height of the drop.

The rod, as already specified in 4.2.1, must be fixed to the drop weight.

4.2.3. Sample to be tested

The sample to be tested must be the complete mask, but without the bib and the trimmings.

The mask must be placed on the base of the test apparatus, with the front part turned uppermost.

4.2.4. Successive test cycles

The tests must be conducted in the following order:

1. first test on the visor with the impact point of the sphere on the centre of the mask and on the line crossing the centre of the visor;

2. second test on the same point.

4.2.5. Procedure

1. Fix the mask onto the base of the machine and the rod with the impact sphere onto the drop weight of the drop test apparatus.

2. Place the mask in a such a way as to align the impact point on the mask's visor with the centre of the sphere.

3. Prepare the drop weight for a total weight of 5 kg +/- 0.03 kg, including the rod and the impact sphere.

4. For the first test, raise the drop weight to a height that gives a distance between the sphere and the point of impact on the mask visor of 1600 mm +/- 10 mm, corresponding to a drop energy of 80 joules.

5. Allow the drop weight to fall onto the mask.

6. For the second test, raise the same drop weight to a height of 1800 mm +/- 10 mm, corresponding to a drop energy of 90 joules.

7. Allow the drop weight to fall onto the mask.

4.2.2. 跌落装置

要使用一种可以制造跌落的装置，使一个重量为3到5千克的锤从不同高度落下，以达到敲打锤冲撞样品时产生的速度为5至6米/秒。

要准备一个停止装置，以便跌落捶打时只是钢杆和球体接触面罩，而不是整个敲打锤。

敲打锤的释放装置要能够保证不论从多高的位置跌下都是同样的出发情况。

正如在4.2.1条中提到的，钢杆要固定在敲打锤上。

4.2.3. 检测的样品

进行检测的样品是整个面罩，但不用护舌和填充物。

面罩要放在测试装置上，正面向上。

4.2.4. 测试的连续周期

测试要按照以下顺序进行：

1. 第一次测试是是用球体撞击面罩镜面中央，以及镜面中央横向直线的位置。

2. 第二次测试是在同样的位置上。

4.2.5. 过程

1. 将面罩固定在装置底座上，将钢杆及球体固定在跌落装置的敲打锤上。
2. 放置好面罩，以便使面罩镜面撞击点与球体中心在一条直线上。
3. 准备好包含钢杆及撞击球的完整的敲打锤，总重量在5 ± 0.05kg。
4. 第一次测试，将敲打锤提高到一定高度，使得球体及面罩镜面撞击点的距离为1600mm ± 10mm，以达到80焦耳的撞击能量。
5. 使敲打锤落在面罩上。
6. 第二次测试，将同样的敲打锤升到1800mm ± 10mm的高度，以达到90焦耳的撞击能量。
7. 使敲打锤落在面罩上。

4.2.6. Test result

The result of the test is considered positive if the mask resists the two tests without either deformation or damage to the visor itself, or to the frame fixing the visor to the metal mesh.

Only a small impression on the polycarbonate visor, at the point of impact of the test sphere, is acceptable.

2.1.3. MASKS THAT ARE COLOURED OR DECORATED WITH DRAWINGS

Masks may feature coloured designs, on condition that they are approved by the FIE Executive Committee at least 30 days before being used for the first time in an official FIE competition.

2.2. SHAPE, DIMENSIONS AND METHODS OF PRODUCTION OF THE ELEMENTS OF FENCING MASKS

TECHNICAL SPECIFICATION FOR THE MANUFACTURE OF FENCING MASKS

1. Purpose

These technical specifications concern the shape, the dimensions, the methods of production of the essential constituent elements of protective fencing masks, as well as the technical quality of the materials intended for their manufacture.

2. General conditions

All the materials of which fencing masks are made and the corresponding manufacturing processes must ensure an excellent mechanical resistance, a high degree of visibility and comfort for the fencer and a sufficient resistance to wear and tear and ageing.

3. Shape and dimensions of masks

The shape of masks is indicated schematically in Figure A.3 (viewed from the front, from the side and from above). The dimensions of the frontal grille depend on the dimensions of the mask. Those of the side grille must be as follows: the height corresponding to 3/4 that of the front grille; the width being between 10 and 12 cm.

4. Essential constituent elements

The essential elements of the mask, as shown in Figure A.3, are:

(a) frontal grille protecting the face;

(b) lateral grille protecting the neck and the nape of the neck;

(c) strip for reinforcement and to connect the grilles;

(d) bibs.

4.2.6 .测试结果

如果两次压力后，面罩没有变形，镜面及固定镜面在金属网上的边框没有被损坏，则认为测试结果是积极的。

只是在聚碳酸酯镜面上发现撞击压痕是允许的。

2.1.3 彩色或带有图案的面罩

第一次在国际剑联正式比赛上使用的彩色图案面罩，至少要在开赛前30天通过国际剑联执委会审核批准。

2.2 构成面罩的部件外形、体积及加工方法

生产击剑面罩的技术规格

1. 目的

本技术规格规定了用于击剑的保护面罩基本构成部件的外形、体积大小及加工方法，还包括用于制作面罩的材料的技术品质。

2. 通则

击剑用的面罩包括的所有材料以及相应的制作工艺，应确保面罩具有极好的机械强度，对于运动员有良好的可见度和舒适性能，并且足够耐磨和抗老化。

3. 面罩外形和大小

面罩的外形在图A.3.中以示意图形式作了说明（正面、侧面及俯视图）。正面金属网的大小取决于面罩的大小，侧面金属网大小应当如下：高度相当于正面金属网高度的3/4；宽度在10~12厘米间。

4. 基本组成部件

如图A.3.所示，面罩基本部件如下：

（a） 保护面部的正面金属网；

（b） 保护脖颈的侧面金属网；

（c） 金属网加固与接合带；

（d） 护颈部分。

The other parts, such as the interior protecting facings, padding, elastic bands and the safety retaining devices, whose production is entrusted to the manufacturer, must entirely conform to the conditions required for their use.

In particular, the rear fixing devices must ensure that the mask is located in the correct position on the fencer's head and that it remains in a perfect position, even after blows or shocks.

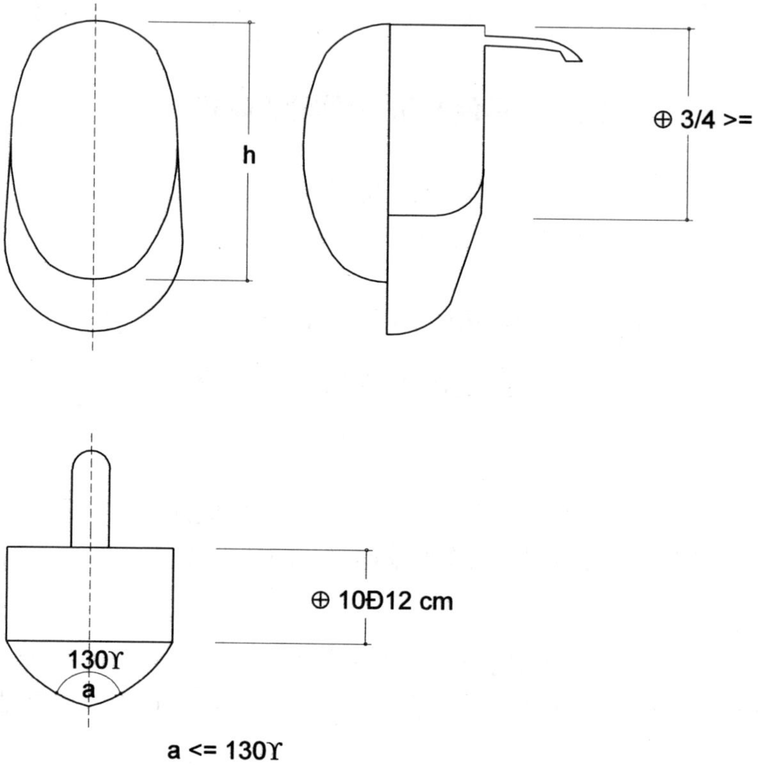

Figure A.3. Design of masks

委托生产商制造完成的其他部分，比如内部保护衬里，垫料，松紧带和紧固装置，无论如何必须符合为其使用而规定的需要的条件。

特别是后部的紧固装置应确保面罩在运动员头上的正确位置，即使在劈刺或撞击之后也应保持在极其平衡的状态。

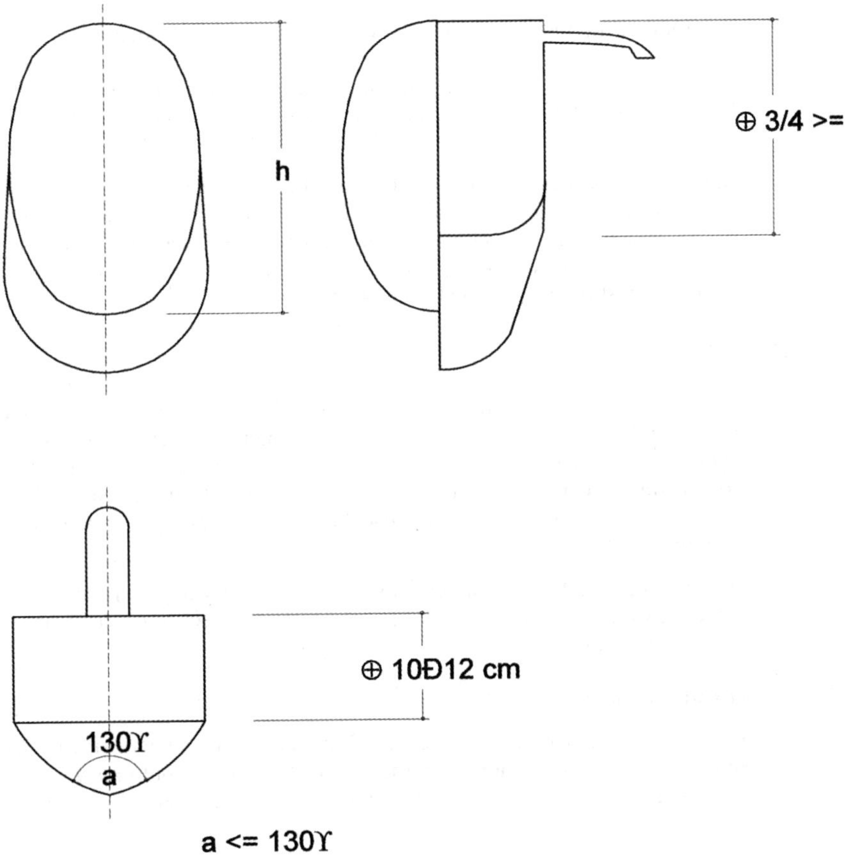

图 A.3.　面罩示意图

4.1. Front and side mesh

The mesh must be made of woven material with a square aperture, with an opening of 1.9 mm, made entirely of round stainless steel wire CrNi 18-10 (the technical quality of the wire for which is addressed in Table V on page 64).

In the curved zone of the grille the presence of mesh with an opening greater in size than that specified is permissible, on condition that it does not exceed 2.1 mm. The frontal grille must form an interior angle of <= 130°, corresponding to the fold of the centre line.

4.2. Junction of the frontal and lateral mesh to the reinforcement band

The joining of the frontal mesh to the lateral one, by the reinforcement band, can be accomplished by a mechanical joining (for example metal wire stitching, use of rivets), or by solder.

In the case of solder, which in any case must be done using the usual techniques for stainless steel, the operation must be completed by a careful mechanical polishing of the soldered area, to eliminate slag and residues. The mesh must be entirely covered in paint with a polymer base. Any heat treatments to harden and stabilise the paint must be carried out at a temperature of <= 400°C.

4.3. Bibs

The bib must be formed from several layers of cloth firmly fixed to each other, of which at least one on the inside must be made of Kevlar fibre or a similar substance; in any case the cloth so formed must ensure a high degree of resistance to penetration equal or greater than 1600 Newtons, to be tested by the methods described in 3.1, below; it must also hinder the forming of stiff creases or the rolling up of the bib itself.

The bib must be fixed to the exterior of the grille starting from the reinforcement band onwards and extending as protection for the neck for a total height of the order of 10–12 cm.

5. Test and certificates

For each model and production series of masks, the manufacturer will send three examples to the SEMI Committee for testing that the mask conforms with the present specifications, as well as photocopies of the certificates delivered by the manufacturer of the mesh.

In the case of a positive result of this test, the manufacturer can place next to the manufacturing mark the following information: 'Conforms with standard … of the FIE' ('conforme à la norme … de la FIE').

4.1. 正面及侧面金属网

金属网应当由开口为1.9毫米的方形网眼构成，完全用铬镍（18~10）不锈钢圆形丝线制作而成（在第5号规格说明书：金属丝的技术品质中提到）。

在金属网弯曲部分，允许出现开口比规定大的网眼，但不得超过2.1毫米。下面金属网在中心线处有折痕，将形成一个<=130度的内角。

4.2. 正面与侧面金属网在加固带处的连接

正面金属网借助加固带与侧面金属网联结，可以用机械接合方式（例如金属丝的刺孔，使用铆钉）或者用焊接方式。

在采取焊接方式的情况下，无论如何应遵照不锈钢的代表性技术进行焊接，为去除熔渣和残余物，必须对焊接缝进行细致的机械磨光工作，将操作补充得更完整。金属网应完全涂满一层聚合物颜料，应在<=400℃温度的下进行可能的颜料成熟与稳定作用的热处理。

4.3. 护颈部分

护颈部分应当由若干层相互连成一体的织物组织，其内部应至少有一层由Kevlar或类似纤维织成；不管怎样，这样构成的织物应当象第号规格说明书（击剑用的制服面料的技术品质）中规定的，确保强度为或高于1600NW的抗穿透力，同样，织物也应当防止抓痕或护颈部分本身缠绕起来。

护颈部分应当自侧面保护带起固定在金属网外部，并且应作为保护颈部的装置以约10~12厘米的总高度延展开。

5. 检验及证书

对于面罩生产的每个型号及系列，生产商将给器材委员会寄去3个样品及和由金属网生产商发给证书的影印件，用以检验面罩是否符合现行规格。

如果检验结果为肯定的，生产商可以在生产商标旁另外贴上以下指示语：“符合国际剑联的……标准”。

3. *CLOTHING*

STANDARDS FOR THE MANUFACTURE OF CLOTHING

For the manufacture of fencing clothing it is obligatory to use material which is able to resist perforation by a force of at least 800 Newtons. This resistance must be verified by the tests defined in the following paragraphs.

3.1. RESISTANCE OF CLOTH AGAINST PERFORATION

STANDARDS FOR TESTING THE RESISTANCE OF CLOTH AGAINST PERFORATION

1. Generalities

The method which is the subject of this standard is intended to determine the resistance against perforation of cloth used to make up fencing uniforms.

The perforation load is defined as the maximum value of impact registered before the sample of cloth is perforated by the test probe: the load is expressed in Newtons or else in kilogrammes of force to one decimal place.

2. Methods of conducting the test

2.1. The test takes place using a high speed dynamometer (as, for example, the INSTROM 1273 apparatus) fitted with a moving test probe with a square section of 3mm, a pyramidal head and an angle at the tip of 120° (see Figure A.4, section A); this probe must be made of high speed or super high speed steel, with a length of 70 mm, of which at least 50 mm juts out from the holding device (see Figure A.4, section B).

2.1.1. The travel of the point must be perpendicular to the surface of the cloth during the course of the test.

2.1.2. The speed of the probe during the test component of its travel must be more than 6 m/s.

2.2. The test must be conducted in a place where the temperature is 20–25°C and with a relative humidity of 50–55%.

2.3. The samples for the test must be taken from a piece of cloth around 50 cm high, free of faults and obtained at random at a distance of at least 2 m from the ends.

The samples must be square in shape with sides of 14–15 cm and they must be fixed on a device with a double vice (see Figure A.5) while leaving a section of 50 mm diameter free for the test.

In the case of fabrics made of several separated layers of cloth, a continuous seam must be sewn along the sides of the square of material which constitutes the sample.

3. 服 装

服装生产规格

所有用于制作服装的面料必须采用最小抗力为800牛顿的面料。面料的测试要根据后面篇章中的描述进行。立即执行。

3.1 织物抗穿孔的能力

为检验织物的抗穿孔力规格的测试

1. 概要

本方法根据现行规范以求确定用于制作击剑服面料的抗穿透力。

在织物样品被穿孔器穿出孔之前所记录的最大值为面料的刺穿负荷：它用牛顿或千克力来表示，只带一位小数。

2. 测试的条件

2.1. 试验使用一台高速测力机（比如INSTROM1273型）进行，测力机配有一个活动穿孔锥，其截面为边长3毫米的正方形，金字塔形的锥面顶端呈120度的角（图A.4.–A）;这个锥子应当由高速钢或超高速钢制成，长70毫米，其中50毫米或以下为固定装置的凸出部分。（参见图A.4.–B）。

2.1.1. 穿孔锥的行程在试验过程中应垂直于织物表面。

2.1.2. 穿孔锥在行程同一部分里的速度应大于6米/秒。

2.2. 试验应在温度介于20℃~25℃间，相对温度为50%~55%的环境下进行。

2.3. 试验用的样品应从一块高50厘米左右没有瑕疵的织物抽取，且应从距织物边缘至少2米处随意获取。

样品应呈正方形，边长14至15厘米，且应固定在一个带双层虎钳的装置（参见图A.5.）上，只留出一个直径50毫米的用于试验的截面。

在面料由若干层分开的织物构成的情况下，试验前必须将方形面料样品的各个边缝合起来，且不能断开。

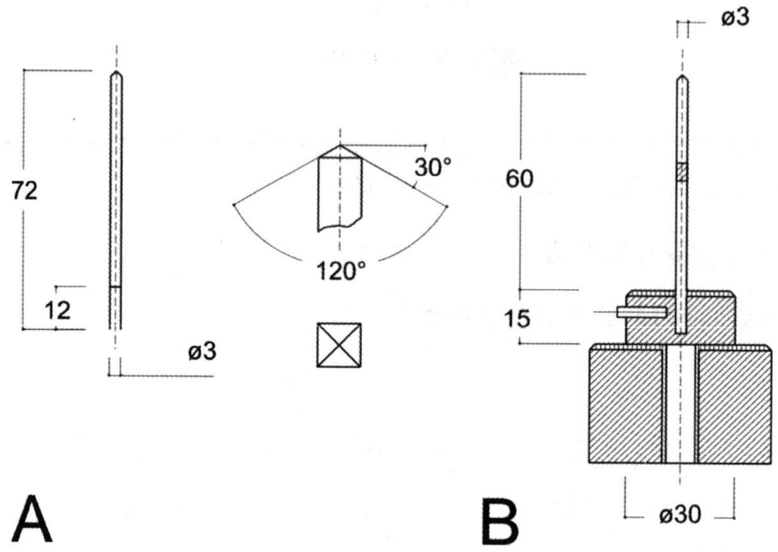

Figure A.4. High speed dynamometer for test of cloth resistance to perforation

2.4. The samples of cloth must be brought to the area where the test will take place at least two hours before the test.

2.5. During the test the force applied by the probe must be registered under the proper conditions of temperature and humidity. The end of the scale for measuring the forces must not be more than 5000 Newtons (with a tolerance of ± 5 Newtons).

2.6. For each cloth, at least three samples must be tested, taken at random from the piece of cloth.

3. Results

The following data must be shown on the certificate confirming that the test has been carried out:

(a) The name of the company applying, type and brand of cloth;

(b) The maximum force at the point of penetration for each sample and their average, and the comparative graphic traces of the test;

(c) The type of dynamometer used, the type and speed of the probe in the test component of its travel, and the conditions of the test (temperature and relative humidity).

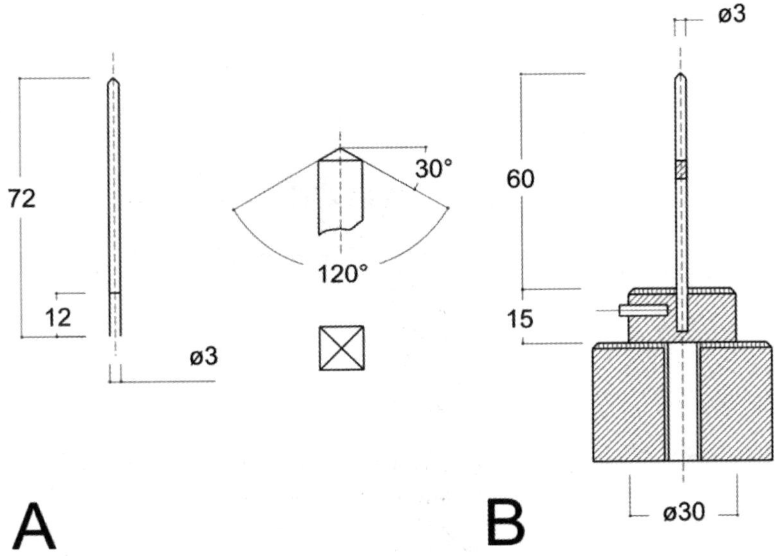

图 A.4.　穿孔锥的结构

2.4.　织物样品应在试验前至少2小时送到试验进行地点。

2.5.　在试验中，应根据时间记录由穿孔锥施加的力。在力的测量中最大等级不得超过5000牛顿（可以误差±5牛顿）。

2.6　对于每一种织物，必须至少测试3片从织物上随意抽取下来的样料。

3. 结果

在确认完成测试的证书上，应注明以下资料：

（a）申请单位名称，织物型号及商标。

（b）每块样料的穿孔负载值及其平均值，相关的测试图表。

（c）测力机型号，穿孔锥的型号及行程中匀质部分的速度，试验的条件（温度和相对湿度）。

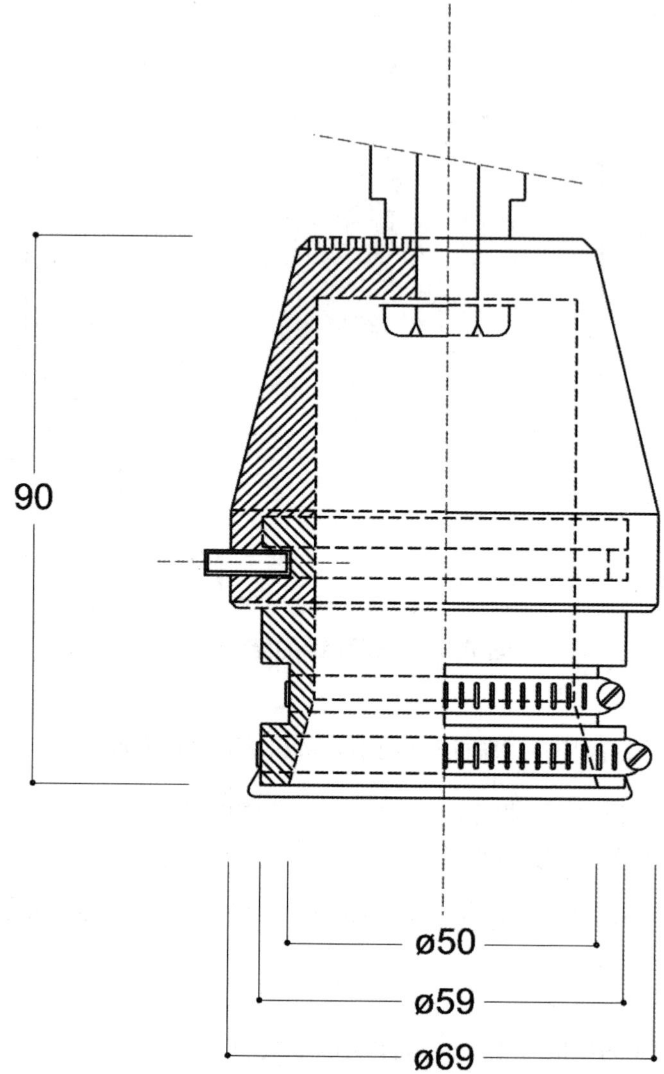

Figure A.5. Fixing device for test of cloth resistance to perforation

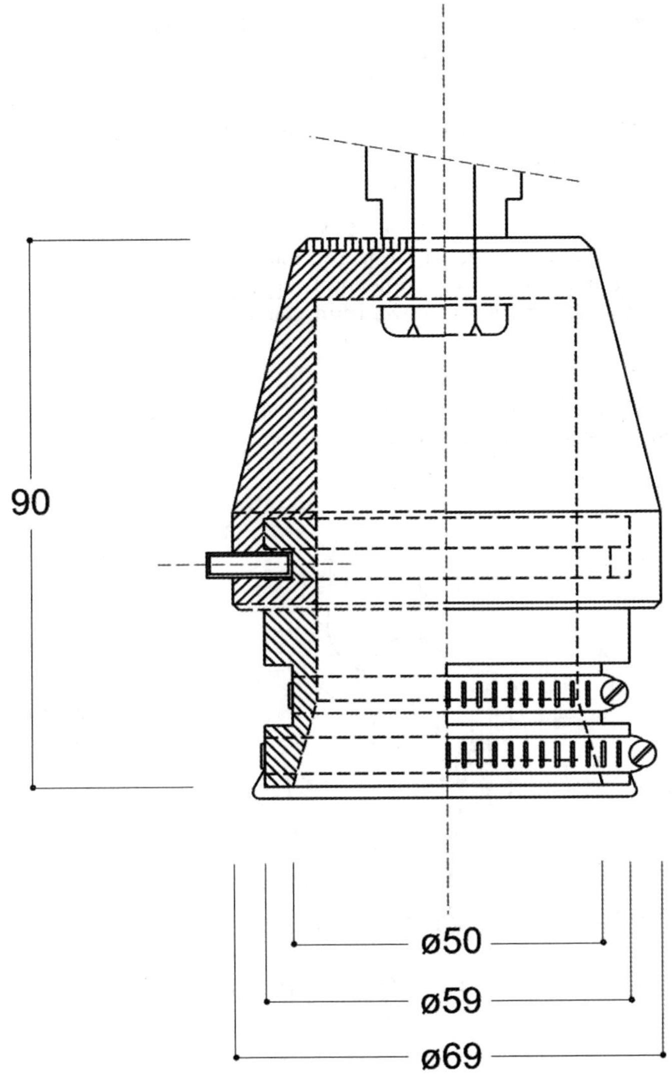

图 A.5. 固定装置

3.2. PARTS OF THE FENCER THAT IT IS VITAL TO PROTECT

Extract from the Minutes of the Medical Committee of the FIE

After discussion the Medical Committee considers that the following ought to be considered as 'parts that it is vital to protect'.

— *Above*

The plastron, which is included in the jacket, must protect the neck under the bib (overlapping with this latter), the two hollows above and below the collar bone, the region surrounding the armpit of the sword arm, and that covering the heart.

— *Below*

Protection included in the trousers must cover the abdomen, the groin and the genital organs (by means of a protective cup).

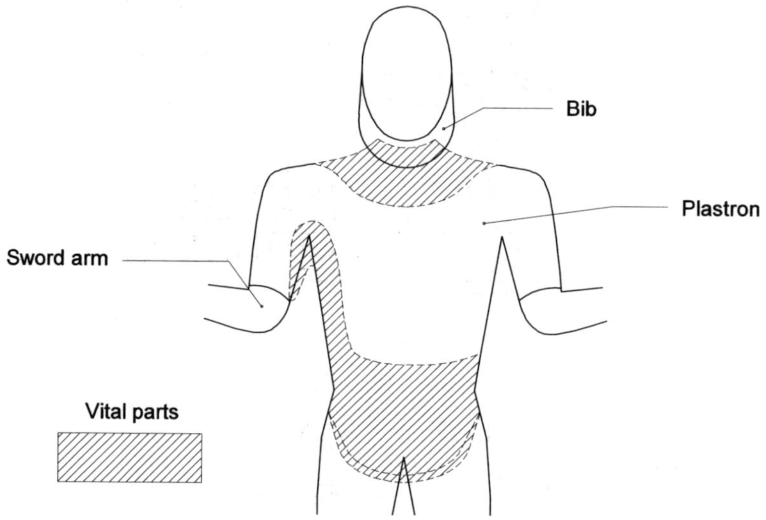

Figure A.6. Vital parts

3.2 运动员需保护的要害部位

国际剑联医务委员会会议记录摘要

在讨论后，医务委员会决定以下应被视作“需保护的要害部位”：

——上半身

穿在上衣内的护胸应通过与护颈的重叠保护护颈以下的颈部，锁骨上下的两个窝，持剑手臂腋部区域及心前区。

——下半身

保护服穿在长裤内：腹部，两条腹股沟区域及性器官（用一个贝壳状的保护装置）。

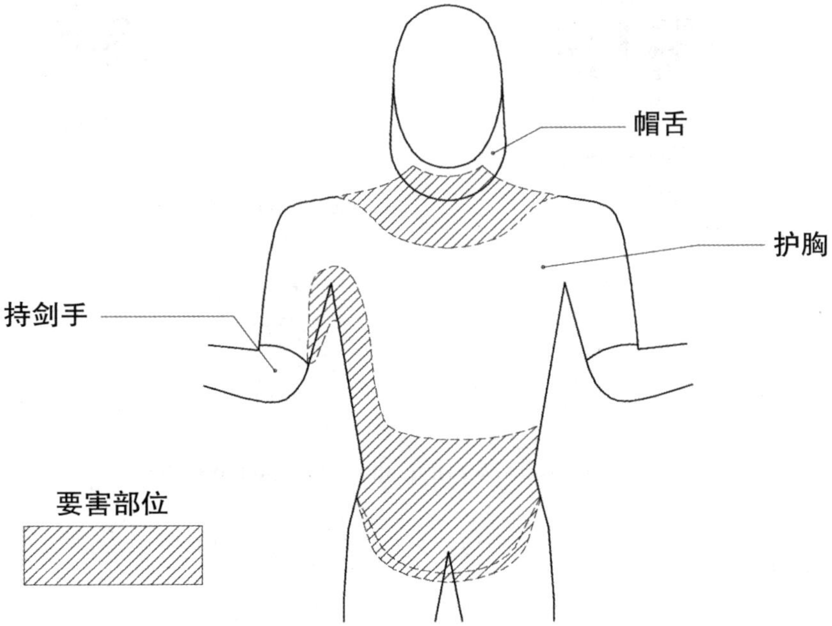

图 A.6. 需要保护的要害部位

4. LABEL OF QUALITY

As far as the quality label is concerned, the Committee has established that it must be indelible, must be circular in shape with a diameter of 25 mm for the mask and 50 mm for the uniform, and must include the following data:

— the emblem of the manufacturer;

— the date (year and month) of manufacture;

— the FIE emblem.

On blades, the label must be 7 mm wide.

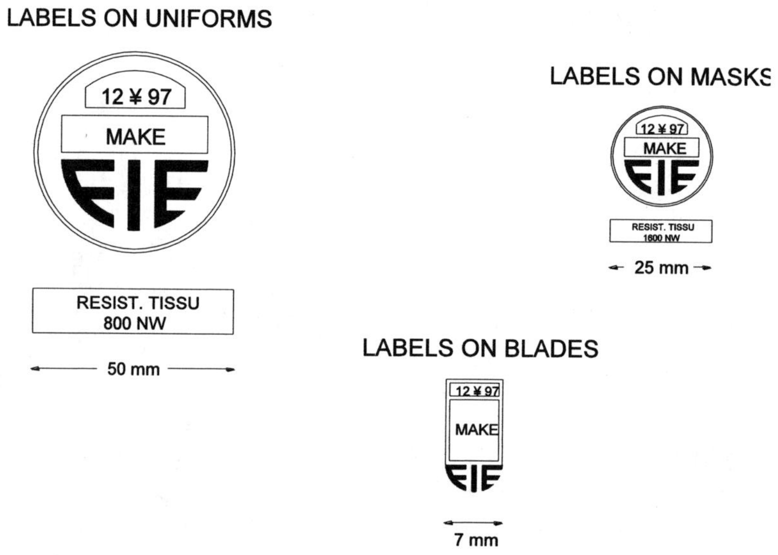

Figure A.7. FIE quality labels (not to scale)

4. 品质标记

尤其关于品质标志的大小，委员会确定该标记应该是擦不掉的，用于面罩上的为直径25毫米的圆形，用于制服的为直径50毫米，并且应包括以下资料：

—— 生产商首字母缩写；
—— 生产日期（年月）；
—— 国际剑联缩写（F.I.E）。

用于剑身的标记宽度应当是7毫米。

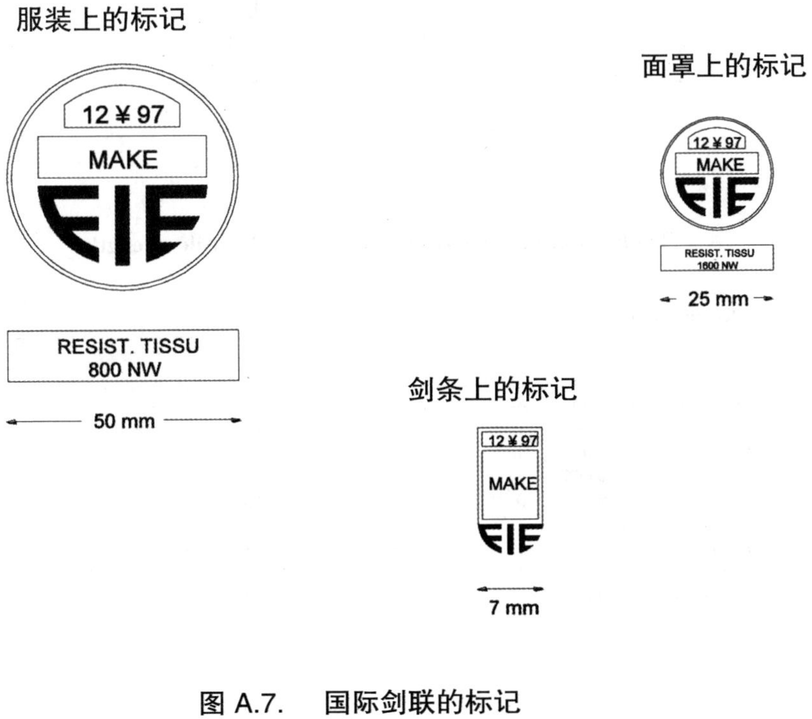

图 A.7.　国际剑联的标记

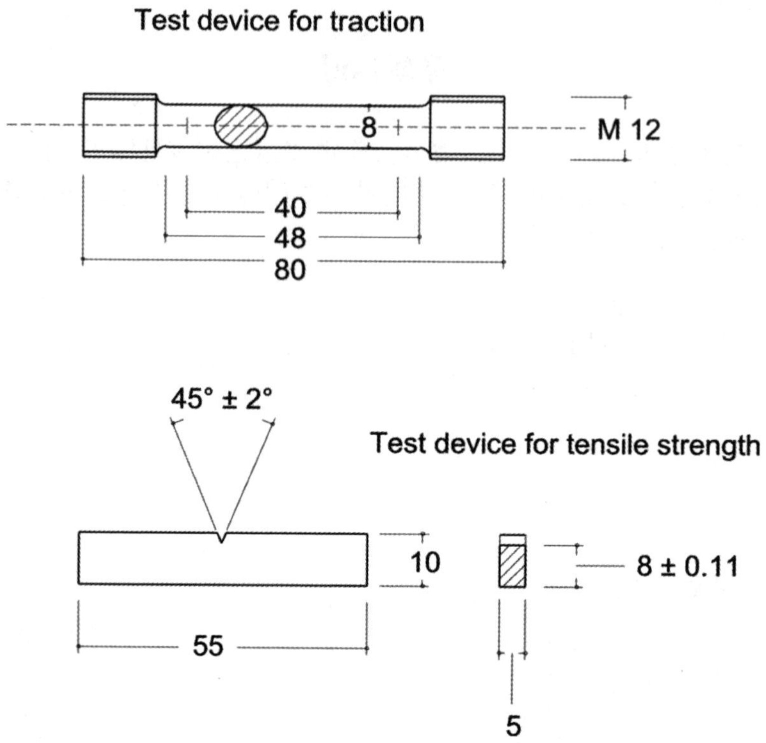

Figure A.8. Test devices for traction and tensile strength

Table VIII. Recommended thicknesses

$Rp_{0.2}$ / E			Thickness recommended B (mm)
From 0.005	0 to 0.005	6	75
From 0.005	7 to 0.006	1	63
From 0.006	2 to 0.006	4	50
From 0.006	5 to 0.006	7	44
From 0.006	8 to 0.007	0	38
From 0.007	1 to 0.007	4	32
From 0.007	5 to 0.007	9	25
From 0.008	0 to 0.008	4	20
From 0.008	5 to 0.009	0	12.5
	0.010	0	6.5

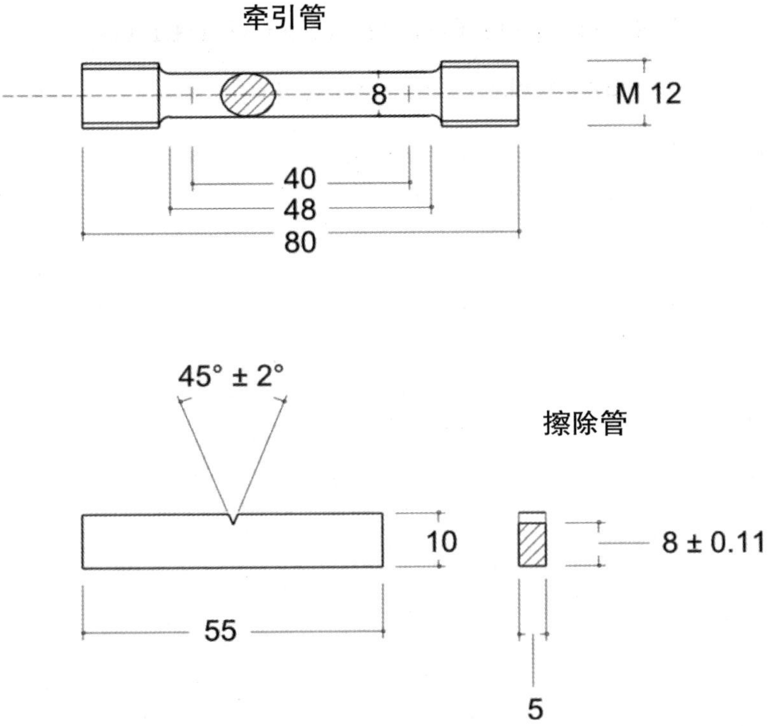

图 A.7. 牵引管和擦除管

表8 推荐厚度

$Rp_{0.2}/E$			厚度要求 B (mm)
From 0.005	0 to 0.005	6	75
From 0.005	7 to 0.006	1	63
From 0.006	2 to 0.006	4	50
From 0.006	5 to 0.006	7	44
From 0.006	8 to 0.007	0	38
From 0.007	1 to 0.007	4	32
From 0.007	5 to 0.007	9	25
From 0.008	0 to 0.008	4	20
From 0.008	5 to 0.009	0	12.5
	0.010	0	6.5

ANNEXE B TO THE MATERIAL RULES

Characteristics of Scoring Apparatus

The installation of a clock and a system for showing the score are both obligatory for the homologation of scoring apparatuses; they must be visible to the spectators.

The clock must always be able to measure the time to a hundredth of second throughout the match and it must transmit the time in hundredths of second to the video refereeing system.

During the last 10 seconds of each period or bout of the match (both individual and teams) it must display the time:

- *to a tenth of second when the judging apparatus is running*
- *to a hundredth of second when the judging apparatus is stopped*

The timer should be equipped with a small remote control, which can be fixed onto two fingers of one hand. The remote control for the referee should be provided with a single start/stop control and a LED light to show that the device is working.

The connection between the remote control and the clock will operate with encrypted radio frequencies: see the specific handbook concerning the radio frequencies. [Application: season 2015/2016 for the World Championships and the Olympic Games only: season 2016/2017 for the World Cup competitions (Junior and Senior), the Grand Prix and the Zonal Championships (Junior and Senior).]

A. FOIL

1. THE CENTRAL JUDGING APPARATUS (cf. m.51)

(a) Principles

1. The apparatus registers when a break occurs in the circuit of the foil, that is to say that the electrical current which is circulating permanently in the foil circuit is broken when a hit is made.

2. The apparatus will show a red signal on one side and a green signal on the other when a hit is registered on target; white signals on either side will indicate hits off the target.

3. The audible signals will consist either of a short ring, or of a continuous note which will be automatically limited to two seconds. Either sort of sound will occur whenever a visual signal appears. The sound signal must be identical for both sides of the apparatus.

附录B　裁判器的特性

计时和比分显示装置的设置是裁判器认证的两个必要条件。这些装置要能够使观众看到。

计时装置必须能够在比赛全程进行百分之一秒精度的计时，并须将所记录的时间传递至录像裁判系统。

比赛最后10秒钟，裁判器上计时装置：
—— 在运行时必须能够显示十分秒
—— 在停止时必须能够显示百分秒。

计时装置应配备小型遥控器，并可固定在一只手的两根手指上。供裁判员使用的遥控器应设有简单的启/停控制开关，以及显示其工作状态的LED指示灯。

遥控器与计时装置之间的连接通过加密无线频率实现：参见关于无线频率的详细手册。（此项规则从2015–2016赛季的世锦赛、奥运会开始执行，从2016–2017赛季开始世界杯、大奖赛、洲际锦标赛也开始执行。）

A. 花剑

1. 中央裁判器（参见第51条）

（a）原则

1. 裁判器通过花剑电路里的电流中断来运转，也就是说当发生击中时，花剑电路里的持续电流便被切断。

2. 对于击中有效部位，裁判器一侧显示红色信号，另一侧显示绿色信号。对于击中无效部位，两侧信号均为白色。

3. 声音信号发出一声短音或是自动限定在2秒钟时限内的长音，两种鸣叫都与可视信号同时发出。两侧声音相同。

4. After registering a hit, whether on target or off target, the apparatus must no longer be able to register a subsequent hit on the same side of the apparatus.

5. No priority must be indicated between a hit registered against one competitor and a hit registered against his opponent.

6. After a period of time of 300 ms (± 25 ms tolerance) after the first hit signalled by the apparatus (this period of time bears no relationship to 'fencing time' which is the basis of judging according to the conventions governing foil fencing), the latter must ignore all signals for subsequent hits.

(b) Sensitivity and regularity

1. Any hit must cause a signal whatever the resistance of the circuits external to the apparatus. The duration of the break of contact which must always ensure that a signal is registered is 14 ms (± 1 ms).

   Depending on the increase in the resistance, the apparatus may register:

   (1) a valid hit only;

   (2) a valid hit and a non-valid hit simultaneously;

   (3) a non-valid hit only.

   The resistance must always be less than 500 ohms for (1) and (2).

2. The registering of a valid hit must be guaranteed when there is a break of contact of 13–15 ms, when the exterior resistance is between 0 and 500 ohms.

3. The contact time is the same for valid and non-valid hits.

   A break of contact of duration of 14 ms (± 1 ms) must always ensure that a signal is registered, when the exterior resistance is between 0 and 200 ohms.

4. The apparatus must be capable of tolerating an increase in the resistance in the closed circuit of the foils of up to 200 ohms, without causing a 'non-valid' signal to register.

5. Even if the resistance of the foil earth circuit is increased up to 100 ohms, none of the following irregular phenomena must occur:

   — that hits are registered on the guard or on the piste;

   — that it is possible to register a hit merely by contact of the blade or the pointe d'arrêt (without depressing it) on the conductive jacket of either competitor.

6. When the blades are in contact, irrespective of the resistance in ohms between them, the apparatus must be capable of registering normally the hits exchanged, valid and non-valid.

7. A specific programme of tests of apparatus under different conditions can be supplied on request by the SEMI Committee of the FIE.

4. 在显示了一次无效或有效的击中信号后，裁判器不得再显示同一侧产生的信号。

5. 裁判器无法显示双方运动员击中的先后。

6. 当裁判器显示第一个击中信号（与花剑的“击剑时间”没有关系）的300毫秒后（可以有±25毫秒的误差），一切后来的击中信号将不再显示。

（b）灵敏度和规律性

1. 不管裁判器外部电路的电阻如何，任何击中都应发出信号，为确保产生信号而中断的电路时间要持续14毫秒（可以有±1毫秒的误差）。随着电阻的增加，裁判器的记录可以显示：
   （1）只有有效击中；
   （2）同时显示有效击中和无效击中；
   （3）只有无效击中。
   对于（1）和（2）两种情况，电阻值始终在500欧姆以下。

2. 当外界电阻为0~500欧姆时，电路中断13~15毫秒，有效击中信号要能够启动。

3. 有效击中和无效击中的接触时间是一样的。当外界电阻为0~200欧姆时，电路中断14毫秒（可以有±1毫秒的误差），无效击中信号要能够启动。

4. 裁判器应能够经受花剑闭合电路里的电阻一直增加到200欧姆，而不起动“无效”击中信号。

5. 即使花剑地线电路的电阻增加到100欧姆，以下不正常现象不应发生：
   —— 击中护手盘或击中场地产生信号；
   —— 花剑扁平部分或剑尖（非凹陷）与任何一方运动员的导电背心接触而记录击中。

6. 当双方剑身接触时，不管它们之间的电阻如何，裁判器应仍然能够正常记录相互的击中，不管有效还是无效。

7. 在器材委员会要求下，可以提供裁判器在变化的条件下进行的程序试验。

8. A specific programme of tests also includes the checking of the functioning of the yellow lamps.

9. The Congress of the FIE has authorised this Committee to modify or add to the above requirements whenever technical improvements allow the construction of apparatus which can ensure the better operation of the electrical foil judging apparatus.

2. ANTI-BLOCKING TYPE CENTRAL JUDGING APPARATUS

This apparatus must conform to the requirements of the rules set out in Articles m.44–m.51 inclusive, as well as paragraphs (a) 'Principles' and (b) 'Sensitivity and regularity' above, with the exception of point 6 of paragraph (b).

Even if a fault in the insulation in a fencer's equipment causes a short between his conductive jacket and his weapon, the apparatus should still be capable of registering both valid and non-valid hits.

Depending on the resistance of the return circuit of the opponent's foil, the apparatus must register a valid hit up to 200 ohms and non-valid hits above this value.

The apparatus must be equipped with two yellow lamps regulated as follows. The yellow lamp on the side of either fencer must automatically light up and remain alight as soon as the resistance between the conductive jacket of that fencer and his weapon is less than 450 ohms. When this resistance is in excess of 475 ohms, the yellow lamp should never light up.

These yellow lamps serve only to indicate insulation faults.

If one or both of the yellow lamps remain lit up, the Referee must stop the bout and call the technical experts on duty to eliminate the fault.

The yellow lamps need not indicate any contact between the fencer's conductive jacket and the conductive piste.

B. EPEE

(a) Principle

The apparatus registers when contact is established between the wires forming the circuit in the épée, thus completing the circuit.

(b) Timing

The apparatus must register only the first hit which is made. If the interval of time between two hits is less than 40 ms (1/25th of a second), the apparatus must register a double hit (both signal lamps must light up simultaneously). When the interval is greater than 50 ms (1/20 of a second) the apparatus must register only one hit (only one signal lamp is lit). The tolerance allowed for timing the apparatus is that between these two limits (1/25th and 1/20th of a second).

8. 程序试验还包括对黄色灯运行的检验。

9. 当技术上的进步使得裁判器的构造可以确保花剑的电动信号更好地运行，国际剑联大会就准许该委员会修改或补充以上规定。

2. “防中断”中央裁判器

这套设备要符合规则44至51条及上述A段和B段的的要求，除了上述B段中的第6条。

即使因为其中一个剑手金属背心和剑接触产生漏电导致绝缘错误，裁判器仍能够记录有效或无效击中。

裁判器能够记录200欧姆以内的因为对手花剑回流电阻产生的有效击中，以及超过200欧姆的无效击中。

裁判器要配有2个黄灯，并调试为以下情况：当剑手金属背心和剑之间产生0~450欧姆的电阻时，设置在此名剑手一边的黄灯要自动且持续亮起；当超过475欧姆时，绝对不可以亮起。

黄灯只是为了显示绝缘错误的。

如果一个或所有的黄灯持续亮起，裁判要中断比赛，要求现场的专家解决这个问题。

黄灯不需要显示运动员金属背心和导电剑道的接触。

B. 重剑

（a）原则

裁判器在重剑电路导线接触形成电流时运行。

（b）调整

裁判器只应记录最先产生的击中。如果两次击中相隔不到40毫秒（即1/25秒），裁判器应显示相互击中信号（两盏灯同时亮）。超过50毫秒（1/20秒），裁判器应显示一次击中信号（仅亮一盏灯）。裁判器的时间校准误差介于这两个时限之间（1/25秒和1/20秒间）。

(c) Sensitivity

When the external resistance is normal, that is 10 ohms, the apparatus must register hits when these are made with a duration of contact of 2–10 ms. With an exceptional external resistance of 100 ohms the apparatus must still register a hit, but without any specific duration of contact.

The apparatus must not register signals of less than 2 ms duration.

(d) Non-registration

The apparatus must not register hits which are made on the earthed material (on the guard or on the conductive piste), even when there is a resistance of 100 ohms in the earth circuit.

(e) Visual signals

1. Visual signals include at least two signal lamps on each side of the apparatus, so designed that if one lamp does not function it does not prevent the other from lighting up nor cause an excessive current through the latter.

2. The signal lamps should give a red signal on one side of the apparatus and a green signal on the other.

3. The apparatus should have a pilot light to show that it is switched on. This light should be dim and not coloured.

4. The apparatus may include lights which indicate short circuits to earth. These should be orange in colour.

5. The light-bulbs which show when hits are registered are usually covered with translucent shades. It must, however, be possible to remove these shades and use naked lights, when the light conditions in the locality make it desirable to do so (strong sunlight or, exceptionally, in the open air).

(f) Audible signals

The apparatus must have a loud sound signal. The apparatus may include a device which allows the sound signal to be stopped before the apparatus is reset.

（c）灵敏度

在外部电阻正常，即10欧姆时，应通过一次2到10毫秒的接触确保信号的起动。对于100欧姆的特殊外部电阻，应仍然确保信号的起动，但对接触时间不作明确规定。

裁判器不应记录短于2毫秒的信号。

（d）相对性

即使地线电路里有100欧姆的电阻，裁判器也不应记录对地线的击中（护手盘或金属剑道）。

（e）灯光信号

1. 灯光信号每侧包括至少两盏灯，其安装方式目的在于：其中一盏出故障时不会妨碍另一盏发光，也不会引起发光的这盏灯超负荷。

2. 信号灯应在一侧显示红色信号，而在另一侧为绿色。

3. 裁判器应配有一盏表明其带有电压的小灯。这盏灯应该无色且发光微弱。

4. 裁判器可以包括表明地线漏电的指示灯。这些灯发橘色光。

5. 击中指示灯通常遮有半透明灯罩。然而如果周围的光线条件需要的话（特别是在阳光照耀的场地或露天时），应该能够取下这些灯罩并使用裸露的灯。

（f）声音信号

裁判器声音应当响亮。裁判器可以包括一个能够在重新装备前中断声间的装置。

C. SABRE

(a) Principles

1. The apparatus works by contact between any uninsulated part of the sabre and the conductive surface of the opposing fencer's jacket, glove and mask.

2. For hits made on these valid conductive surfaces, the apparatus shows a red light on one side and a green light on the other.

If the guard or blade of a fencer's sabre is in contact with the conductive surface of his own equipment (signalled by a yellow light), a valid hit made by that fencer must still register.

3. The audible signal will consist of either one short ring or a continuous note lasting 1–2 seconds, simultaneous with the light signals. The sound will be the same for both sides of the apparatus.

4. Hits made on non-conductive surfaces must not be signalled.

5. The apparatus must be equipped with two yellow lamps, one on each side, which will indicate a contact between the guard or blade of a fencer's sabre and the conductive surface of his own equipment.

6. The apparatus must be equipped with two white lamps, identical to those on a foil apparatus which, if permanently illuminated, accompanied by a sound signal, indicate any abnormal electrical change in circuits B and C of the fencer at fault.

7. The apparatus must not signal a hit made by the blade whipping over to hit the opponent while in contact with his blade or guard.

8. After a hit has been registered, a subsequent hit made by the other fencer will only be registered if it occurs within a maximum of 170 ms (± 10 ms).

9. When the two blades touch, all the other rules should be strictly applied.

10. The SEMI Committee of the FIE reserves the right to change the rules governing the apparatus, either to simplify or to improve its performance.

C. 佩剑

（a）原则

1. 裁判器通过佩剑的地线与对手导电上衣、手套及面罩表面的接触来运行。

2. 当击中有效部位时，裁判器将在一侧显示红灯信号，在另一侧显示绿灯信号。

如果一方剑手的护手盘或剑身接触到其装备的导电部分（黄灯亮），该剑手做出的有效击中应始终被记录下来。

3. 声音信号将在灯光信号发光同时发出短促的声音，或是介于1到2秒间的持续声音。声音对于两侧是相同的。

4 .对不导电部位的劈刺，不显示信号。

5. 裁判器将配备两盏黄灯，每侧一盏，它们将显示一名剑手的护手盘或剑身与其自身装备的导电部分产生了接触。

6. 裁判器将配有与花剑裁判器上相同的两盏白灯，白灯发光并伴有一个声音信号，将显示犯规运动员B和C线路中产生的每一次电路状况的不正常变化。

7. 裁判器不能显示穿过武器或护手盘而击中对手的劈刺。

8. 在一次击中显示信号后，稍后由对方实施的另一次击中只有在170毫秒（±10秒）的时限内发生，才会显示信号并被记录下来。

9. 当两剑身相互接触时，所有其他规则依然应严格执行。

10. 器材委员会保留有关裁判器规则的权利以简化或改善其运行状况。

(b) Sensitivity and regularity

1. The duration of contact during which a signal should be ensured should be 0.1–1 ms. These times may be varied in the light of experience and of laboratory tests carried out by the SEMI Committee.

   An apparatus will be rejected if a hit can be registered with a duration of contact of less than 0.1 ms (time subject to modification).

2. The apparatus should allow an increase in the exterior resistance of the connections up to 100 ohms without any drawbacks.

3. Should a fault in the insulation, down to 0 ohms, cause a leakage of current between a fencer's valid conductive surface and his weapon, the apparatus should still be capable of registering all hits exchanged. The insulation fault will be signalled by the illumination of the yellow lamp on the side of the fencer whose equipment is at fault when the resistance is between 0 and 450 ohms.

   The registering of a valid hit on the guard or blade of the fencer at fault will be allowed provided that the electrical resistance between the guard or the blade and the valid surface is less than 250 ohms.

4. The apparatus should still function when the blades are in contact, or if there is contact between the blades and the guards, or between the two guards.

5. If the contact between the blade and the opponent's target takes place 'through the blade', the apparatus:

   — will register the hit between 0 and 4 ms (+ 1 ms);

   — will prevent the hit being registered between 4 and 15 ms (+ 5 ms), on condition that the contact between the two blades is not interrupted more than a maximum of 10 times in the interval.

6. Should there be a hit made by the whipping over of the blade which has not been signalled, whatever method has been used to prevent the signalling, after 15 ms (± 5 ms) from the contact of the blade with the valid target (the time for the registering of the whip) and unless there has been another hit, the apparatus should allow the normal registering of any subsequent hits.

7. A break in the control circuit (defined as more than 250 ohms) for 3 ms ± 2 ms will be signalled by the illumination of the white lamp on the side of the fencer at fault.

（b）灵敏度和规律性

1. 为确保信号显示的接触时限应在0.1毫秒和最多1毫秒之间变化。这些数值在由委员会进行的实验室试验之后，可以被修改。

   如果接触时间短于0.1毫秒（数值可以修改）时仍有可能记录击中，那么裁判器将被拒用。

2. 裁判器应可以顺利地将联接线路的外部电阻增加到100欧姆。

3. 当绝缘故障（直到电阻为0欧姆），引起一名运动员自上的导电有效部位和武器间漏电，裁判器对介于0到450欧姆间的电阻值，应能够通过犯规运动员一侧黄灯的发光来显示信号。

   只要护手盘或剑身与有效部位间的电阻小于250欧姆，就允许显示对犯规运动员护手盘或剑身有效劈刺的信号。

4. 当双方剑身互相接触，或双方护手盘和剑身之间发生接触，或双方运动员的护手盘相互接触，应确保裁判器的运行。

5. 如果剑身和对手目标之间发生接触，裁判器将对0到4毫秒（+1毫秒误差）之间的击中显示信号，而对4到15毫秒（+5毫秒误差）之间的击中不显示信号，只要在间隙中两只剑身的接触被中断不超过10次（最大值）。

6. 在出现未显示信号劈刺的情况下，不管为妨碍信号显示而使用的方法是什么，从武器接触起15毫秒（±5毫秒）以后（劈刺显示信号时间），只要发生另一次击中，裁判器应可以对随后发生的劈刺做出正常的信号显示。

7. 控制电路（即超过250欧姆）中断3±2毫秒，将通过犯规运动员一侧的白灯来显示信号。

ANNEXE C TO THE MATERIAL RULES

Score-board for Finals

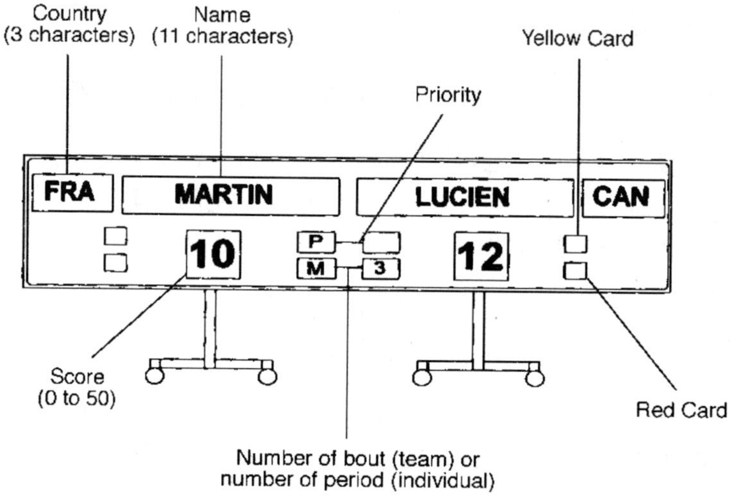

附录C 决赛用计分器板

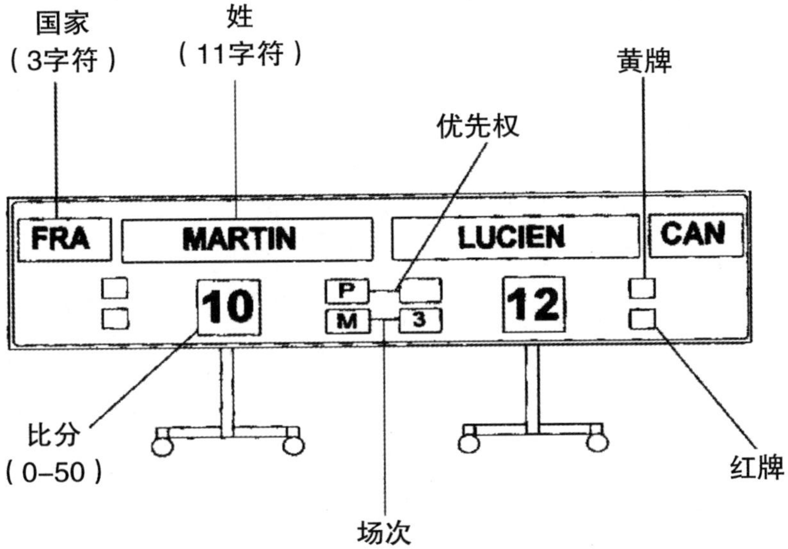

广告规则

APPENDIX — FENCERS' PUBLICITY CODE

FENCERS' PUBLICITY CODE

CHAPTER I. GENERAL PRINCIPLES AND THE RELEVANT TEXTS

p.1. For all **Olympic and pre-Olympic competitions**, only the rules of the Olympic Charter are applicable, particularly Rules 26 and 53 and the texts on how they are to be applied.

p.2. This present code applies, under the terms of the IOC rules, to **all international fencing competitions**, whoever is responsible for the organising of them (FIE, national federation).

p.3. Advertising **in the places where fencing takes place** is the responsibility of the organisers.

It is permitted by the FIE to the extent that, in the opinion of the Directoire Technique, it does not inconvenience the fencers, the judges or the public.

Television requirements must be respected.

CHAPTER II. COLLECTIVE ADVERTISING CONTRACT

p.4. **The parties**

A collective advertising **contract** is agreed between:

1. **The sponsor**, a commercial, industrial or philanthropic concern which proposes to support, under certain conditions, a team, a group of fencers, a club, a regional organisation, a federation or the organiser of a tournament.
2. **A sports organisation** officially recognised according to the norms laid down by the FIE or a national federation.
   - **a)** A contract for the **exploitation of an image** (cf. p.11.1, below) may only be entered into by the FIE, the national Olympic Committee or the national federation of the team concerned (cf. Rule 26 of the IOC).
   - **b)** A contract for **publicity materials** to be worn (cf. p.12, below) may be entered into by the FIE, the national Olympic Committee or the national federation.
   - **c)** An organisation may only enter into a contract within its own competence. **In any case of conflict** between different contracts, the order of priority is the FIE, then the national federation. In the context of the Olympic Games, arrangements made by the International Olympic Committee take priority over those made by a national Olympic committee, the FIE and the national federation.
   - **d)** A sports organisation as organiser of a sporting event may invite any kind of sponsor to support the event, as long as its activity is not in contradiction with the FIE rules and the Olympic Charter.
3. **A fencer may only enter** into an individual advertising contract or receive payment relating to advertising if this is done with the agreement of his national federation, in accordance with the arrangements laid down in Chapter III, below.

第一章 基本规则

p.1. 对于所有奥运会相关比赛，只有奥林匹克宪章中的规则适用，尤其是第26条、53条及如何适用这些条款。

p.2. 根据国际奥委会规则相关条款，本规则适用于所有国际击剑比赛，无论比赛的组织工作由何机构负责（国际剑联、会员协会）。

p.3. 比赛场地的广告由比赛组织者负责。
只要经技术委员会确认，不会对运动员、裁判员或观众造成影响，均可得到国际剑联的允许。
电视转播的要求必须得到尊重。

第二章 集体广告合同

签约各方

p.4. 集体广告合同由以下几方共同签订：

1. 赞助商：在一定条件下支持某击剑队、某击剑者团体、某俱乐部、某地区组织、某击剑协会或某一比赛组织者的工商企业或慈善机构。

2. 符合国际剑联或某一会员协会规范，被正式承认的体育组织。
   a. 形象利用合同（参见下文p.11.1）只能由国际剑联、国家奥委会或相关击剑队所属的国家击剑协会签订（国际奥委会规则第26条）。
   b. 随身广告合同（参见p.12）可由国际剑联、国家奥委会、会员协会签订。
   c. 任一组织只能在其职权范围内签订广告合同。若不同的合同之间出现冲突，优先顺序依次为国际剑联、会员协会。如果是奥运会相关场合，国际奥委会制定的条款将优先于国家奥委会、国际剑联和会员协会。
   d. 任何体育组织，当它作为体育活动组织者时，在不违背国际剑联规则和奥林匹克章程的情况下，可以邀请任何赞助商支持该活动。

3. 根据以下第三章中的条款，运动员只有在取得其所属会员协会同意的情况下，方可签订个人广告合同，领取有关报酬。

p.5. Procedure

1. **The contract** must be drawn up in writing, signed by the parties and accepted by the fencers concerned.
2. **National federations** are responsible to their national Olympic Committees and to the FIE for seeing that contracts entered into by regions and by clubs are within the Rules, and may approve these contracts or lay down procedures for checking them.
3. **In any case of litigation** or breaking of the Rules, the FIE may demand all relevant details from the national federation, including the contract itself with the exception of the economic and financial clauses.

p.6. Position of the fencer

1. No fencer may be made to take part, **against his will**, in an advertising contract, even one in which there is an exclusivity clause.
2. No fencer may be **omitted** from selection or from a sporting activity solely because he does not wish to take part in any advertising activity.
3. A fencer may be **refused a share in a grant** (for travel, maintenance, equipment, etc.) which is financed by an advertising contract to which he does not wish to be party.
4. A fencer who has been selected **may not refuse** to wear and use uniform equipment specified by his Federation for the whole of the national team at any competition.

CHAPTER III. INDIVIDUAL CONTRACT

p.7. Principle

A fencer may **bind himself contractually** to a firm or an institution capable of helping him — including financially — in his preparation, but only with the specific written agreement of his federation.

p.8. Restrictions

The contract may only relate to the use of the **image of a fencer** and it may not contain any provision relating to the method of training of a fencer or to the choice of competitions in which he fences. To be approved by the national federation concerned, the contract must expressly mention that the demands of the federation or of the club **take priority systematically** and in all circumstances over those of the firm or the institution with whom the contract has been signed.

p.5. 程序

1. 合同必须以书面形式订立，须有合同各方的签字，且须得到有关运动员的同意。

2. 各会员协会须就地区或俱乐部所签合同的合法性对本国奥委会和国际剑联负责，各会员协会可对合同进行审批或制定审核程序。

3. 在出现争议或违反规则的情况下，国际剑联可要求会员协会提供所有相关细节，包括合同本身，合同中的经济、财务部分内容除外。

p.6. 运动员权利

1. 不得违背运动员意愿签订广告合同，即使合同中有排他性条款。

2. 不得仅仅因为运动员拒绝参与一项广告活动而取消其被选拔或参加某项体育活动的资格。

3. 运动员将被拒绝享受其不愿参与的广告合同出资的赞助（旅行、食宿、器材等）。

4. 比赛期间，入选运动员不得拒绝佩戴和使用其所属会员协会为其击剑队全体队员统一确定的装备。

第三章　个人合同

p.7. 原则

运动员在得到其所属会员协会明确的书面允许的情况下，可与某企业或机构签订合同，该企业或机构有能力为运动员提供包括财务上的帮助。

p.8. 限制条件

合同只可涉及运动员形象的使用。合同中不得包含任何与运动员的训练方式以及参赛选择有关的条款。为取得相关会员协会的同意，合同中必须明确说明协会或俱乐部的要求在总体上优先于与运动员签约的企业或机构的要求。

CHAPTER IV. SPECIFIC REGULATIONS

Marks

p.9. **Definition**

The mark is the name or badge which identifies the origin, the manufacturer or the seller of a particular piece of the fencer's equipment.

As soon as the mark exceeds the normal or authorised dimensions, it becomes **an advertisement** and comes under the jurisdiction of the regulation below (cf. p.12).

p.10. **Position and sizes**

1. The articles of the fencers' **equipment** may carry the following visible marks:

a) **Mask**	One mark, maximum size 12.5 cm^2, on the rear of the spring
b) **Jacket**	One mark at the bottom of the jacket on the hip on the side of the non-sword arm, maximum size 30 cm^2
c) Trousers	One mark at the bottom of the trouser leg, on one side only, maximum size 30 cm^2
d) Socks	One mark on each sock, maximum size 10 cm^2
e) **Shoes**	The name of the brand on each shoe, maximum 10 cm^2, or the normal badge or insignia (e.g. bands)
f) **Glove**	One mark: maximum size: 10 cm2. If the mark is fixed on the glove as a label (glued or sewn), it must be on the cuff.
g) **Weapon**	Maximum size: 2.5 cm^2
h) Electric Jacket	One mark at the bottom of the jacket on the hip of the non-sword arm side. Maximum size: 30 cm^2.

2. The article of equipment may not have any distinctive **mark** (band, design, border, etc.) other than those authorised above.
3. **Ancillary equipment** may carry the following manufacturer's marks:

a) **Tracksuit**	The normal mark as it appears on all articles by the same manufacturer (e.g. bands for Adidas) and one badge, maximum size 10 cm x 10 cm, on the left-hand side of the chest or the name, maximum size 10 cm x 4 cm, on the left-hand side of the chest
b) **Fencing bag**	No limitation
c) **Sports bag**	No limitation

第四章　具体规定

商标

p.9.　定义

商标是用于识别运动员所用器材装备的原产地、制造商或销售商的名称或标志。

商标一旦超出通常的或规定的大小，将成为广告，则须符合下文规定（参见p.12）。

p.10.　位置及尺寸

1. 运动员的所有装备可带有以下各项可见商标：
   a. 面罩：后部安全固定板上可以有一个商标，大小不超过12.5平方厘米；
   b. 保护服上衣：非持剑手一侧的底部臀部处可以有一个商标，大小不超过30平方厘米；
   c. 保护服裤子：裤子底部仅其中一侧可以有一个商标，大小不超过30平方厘米；
   d. 保护袜：每只袜子上可以有一个商标，大小不超过10平方厘米；
   e. 运动鞋：每只鞋子上可以有一个品牌商标，大小不超过10平方厘米或为常规标志（如：带状图案）；
   f. 手套：可以有一个商标，大小不超过10平方厘米；如果此商标是通过标签粘贴或缝制在手套上，则其位置须位于袖口上；
   g. 武器：大小不超过2.5平方厘米；
   h. 金属衣：非持剑手一侧的底部臀部处可以有一个商标，大小不超过30平方厘米。

2. 除了以上被允许的商标，器材装备不可带有任何可识别的标识（条纹、图案、镶边等）。

3. 附属器材可带有下列商标：
   a. 运动套装：常规的用于同一制造商所有产品的商标（如：Adidas条纹图案）；以及位于左侧胸部尺寸不超过10×10厘米的标志或尺寸不超过10×4厘米的名称。
   b. 剑袋：无限制。
   c. 运动背包：无限制。

p.11. Exploitation of the fencer's image

1. Definition

This heading concerns advertising contracts which propose:

a) exploitation of the **presence** of a fencer;

b) exploitation of the **name** of a fencer;

c) exploitation of the **picture** of a fencer;

d) exploitation of **things said** by a fencer;

e) exploitation of a fencer's **performance**;

f) any other exploitation of the **image** or **fame** of a fencer for publicity purposes.

2. Regulations

The measures outlined above (cf. p.4, p.5, p.6) are **alone** applicable, as are Article 8.1.1 of the FIE Statutes and Rule 26 of the IOC.

p.12. Advertising which is worn or carried

1. Definition

a) Advertising worn or carried refers to any name or badge other than the mark of the manufacturer or seller of the equipment in question (cf. p.9) which appears on a fencer's main or ancillary equipment.

b) A mark which is larger than the sizes which are usual or laid down above (cf. p.10) constitutes **advertising**.

c) All advertisements **contrary to the law** of the country in which the competition is taking place are forbidden.

2. Fencing clothing and equipment

a) If a federation and/or a fencer have signed a **sponsorship contract** with a commercial or other company, the logo of that sponsorship partner, maximum 125 cm^2 in size, may be fixed at the top of the sleeve of the non-sword arm of the fencing jacket, on the side of the breeches (left or right) or on the socks. At sabre a logo may not be worn on the sleeve.

The sponsor's logo may be displayed on each side of the mask. Maximum size: 100 cm^2 on each side of the mask.

b) A fencer may not display more than five such logos. The **total surface area** of all these logos added together must not exceed 500 cm^2.

3. Tracksuits and clothing

a) On national federation tracksuits one advertisement is allowed, on the back between the shoulders:

i. either **one line**, not exceeding 10 cm in height;

ii. or **one badge**, not exceeding 15 cm x 15 cm.

p.11. 运动员形象利用

1. 定义

此类广告合同涉及以下各项：

a. 利用运动员的出场；
b. 利用运动员的姓名；
c. 利用运动员的肖像；
d. 利用运动员的话语；
e. 利用运动员的成绩；
f. 以广告为目的的其他任何对运动员形象或声誉的利用。

2. 规定

上述条款（参见p.4、p.5、p.6）独立适用，国际剑联章程第8.1.1条及国际奥委会规则第26条也同样如此。

p.12. 随身广告

1. 定义

a. 随身广告是指除了制造商及经销商的商标外（参见p.9），所有出现在运动员的装备、器材或附属器材上的名称或标志。

b. 超出通常或规定大小的商标（参见上文p.10）即构成广告。
c. 禁止所有与比赛当地法律相违背的广告。

2. 击剑服及器材

a. 如果运动员和/或其所属会员协会与某商业机构或公司签订了赞助合同，则该赞助商的标识可粘贴在非持剑手一侧的衣袖顶部，或裤子一侧（左侧或右侧），或袜子上，大小不超过125平方厘米。佩剑衣袖上不可以粘贴任何标识。

赞助商标识可出现在面罩的两侧，每侧标识的大小不超过100平方厘米。

b. 赞助商标识的总数量不超过5个，所有标识的总面积不超过500平方厘米。

3. 运动套装及运动服

a. 会员协会运动套装上允许有一处广告，位于背后，两肩之间：

i. 或为高度不超过10厘米的一行文字；
ii. 或为大小不超过15×15厘米的一个标志。

b) The **logo of the sponsorship partner** of the federation or chosen for the weapon concerned may furthermore be affixed horizontally on the front right-hand side of the tracksuit. The surface area of this logo may not exceed 50 cm^2.

c) In addition, if a fencer has signed a sponsorship contract with a commercial or other company, the official tracksuit may display the **same logos** as the fencing clothing.

d) At the World Championships, only **national federation tracksuits** may be worn (cf. p.12.3 a)).

e) At **other competitions** (except on the podium at World Cup competitions), advertising on tracksuits, bath robes and any other clothing **is unrestricted** and is only limited by the consent of the national federation to which the fencer belongs.

4. Ancillary equipment

Advertising on fencing bags and sports bags is **allowed** without limitation.

5. Television

a) When a competition is being **televised**, the requirements of the television company are paramount, within the limits of the regulations described above.

CHAPTER V. PENALTIES

p.14. Individual contract (cf. p.7, p.8)

In the case of **failure to observe** the rules relating to an individual contract the penalty is the suspension of the fencer concerned. Should the fencer, at the end of the period of suspension, again break these rules, he loses his amateur status and his licence is withdrawn. See the Disciplinary Code of the FIE (Chapter VII of the FIE Statutes).

p.15. Mark not conforming to the regulations (cf. p.10.1.a)–g))

Obligation to **change** immediately the article of equipment and **warning**, then **application of penalties** as provided for in Articles t.114, t.118, t.120/third group.

p.16. Advertising on clothing (cf. p.12.2.a)–b))

Obligation to **change** immediately the article of equipment; and **application of penalties** as provided for in Articles t.114, t.118, t.120/third group or t.108.

b. 会员协会或某个剑种的赞助商标志还可横向粘贴在运动套装正面右侧。此标志大小不得超过50平方厘米。

c. 此外，若运动员已与某一商业企业签订赞助合同，则运动套装上可带有与击剑服上相同的标志。

d. 在世锦赛上，只能穿着会员协会统一的运动套装（参见p.12.3a）。

e. 在其他比赛中（世界杯赛领奖台上除外），对运动套装、浴巾及其他任何衣服上的广告不做限制，只需取得运动员所属会员协会的同意即可。

4. 附属器材

剑袋和运动包上的广告不受限制。

5. 电视

a. 当比赛进行电视转播时，电视转播机构的要求在遵守以上规则的前提下具有最高优先权。

p.13. （组委会提供的广告，略）

第五章　处罚

p.14. 个人合同（参见p.7、p.8）

对于违反个人合同相关规定的情况，将给予运动员停赛处罚。若停赛期满后，运动员再次违反规定，则该运动员将失去业余运动员资格，其参赛许可证也将被吊销。参见国际剑联纪律规则（国际剑联章程第七章）

p.15. 不符合规定的商标（参见p.10.1.a–g）

必须立即更换违规器材装备，给予警告，并根据技术规则t.114、t.118及t.120/第三组处罚办法给予处罚。

p.16. 击剑服上的广告（参见p.12.2.a–b）

必须立即更换违规器材装备，并根据技术规则 t.114、t.118及t.120/第三组处罚办法或 t.108给予处罚。。

p.17. Advertising not conforming to the Rules or not authorised (cf. p.12.3.a)–e))

1. Obligation to **remove** the offending article from view, and a **warning**.
2. In the case of a **repetition** of the offence during the competition, **application of penalties** as provided for in Articles t.114, t.118, t.120, third group.

p.18. Leg-bands and self-adhesive badges (cf. p.13.1, p.13.2)

1. A fencer who **refuses to wear** the leg-band or badge, when its wearing has been duly announced beforehand, will be excluded from the competition and will not appear in the overall classification of the event.
2. If the leg-bands or badges do not **conform with the rules**, the organisers must withdraw them; if they fail to do so, they are liable to a fine of $500, payable to the national federation.
3. If it is a competition which counts towards the **World Cup** (Category A), the fine is US $1500 to the FIE and the competition automatically loses its Category A status for the following year.
4. In the case of a **repetition** of the offence within the following five years, the fine is doubled and the competition will not appear on the International Calendar for three years.

p.19. Image advertising (cf. p.11)

Penalties

1. The **first offence** concerning exploitation of the fencer's image other than by a properly drawn up contract is penalised by a warning from the national federation or the FIE.
2. The **first repetition** is penalised by a suspension of six months.
3. The **second repetition** is penalised by a suspension of one year.
4. Any **subsequent repetitions** are penalised by a suspension of two years for each offence.

p.20. Offence

1. The fencer concerned is assumed to be at fault.
2. If the fencer **denies his responsibility** for the offence, he must give the FIE every authority to proceed with the necessary investigations and must cede to the FIE his rights to act against the party guilty of misuse of his image. If he does not, point 1 above automatically applies.

p.21. Competence and procedure

1. The Disciplinary Commission of the FIE is the body of the FIE competent to deal with these matters — see the Disciplinary Code of the FIE (Chapter VII of the FIE Statutes).
2. The FIE will notify the national federations of all penalties that have become definitive.

p.17. 不符合规定或未经允许的广告（参见p.12.3.a–e）

1. 必须移除违规物品并给予警告。
2. 在比赛期间若再次违规，则根据技术规则t.114、t.118及t.120/第三组处罚办法给予处罚。

p.18. （组委会提供的广告，略）

p.19. 形象利用广告（参见p.11）

处罚

1. 第一次涉及形象利用广告的违规行为，将受到会员协会或国际剑联的警告处罚。
2. 第一次重犯将被停赛 6 个月。
3. 第二次重犯将被停赛 1 年。
4. 以后每重犯一次被停赛 2 年。

p.20. 违规

1. 相关运动员被认定为犯有过失。
2. 若运动员对其在违规行为中所负责任存在异议，他必须全面授权国际剑联以便开展必要的调查，并授权国际剑联对违规使用其形象者采取行动。否则，上述第1点即成立。

p.21. 职能及程序

1. 国际剑联处理此类事务的职能机构为纪律委员会——参见国际剑联纪律规则（国际剑联章程第七章）。
2. 国际剑联将最终处罚决定通知会员协会。